Owners of the Map

Owners of the Map

MOTORCYCLE TAXI DRIVERS, MOBILITY,
AND POLITICS IN BANGKOK

Claudio Sopranzetti

UNIVERSITY OF CALIFORNIA PRESS

University of California Press, one of the most distinguished university presses in the United States, enriches lives around the world by advancing scholarship in the humanities, social sciences, and natural sciences. Its activities are supported by the UC Press Foundation and by philanthropic contributions from individuals and institutions. For more information, visit www.ucpress.edu.

University of California Press
Oakland, California

Library of Congress Cataloging-in-Publication Data

Names: Sopranzetti, Claudio, author.
Title: Owners of the map : motorcycle taxi drivers, mobility, and politics in Bangkok / Claudio Sopranzetti.
Description: Oakland, California : University of California Press, [2017] | Includes bibliographical references and index.
Identifiers: LCCN 2017020435 (print) | LCCN 2017022860 (ebook) | ISBN 9780520963399 () | ISBN 9780520288492 (cloth : alk. paper) | ISBN 9780520288508 (pbk : alk. paper)
Subjects: LCSH: Motorcyclists—Thailand—Bangkok. | Taxicab drivers—Thailand—Bangkok. | Thailand—Politics and government—1988- | Thailand—Economic conditions—21st century. | Demonstrations—Thailand—History—21st century. | Political violence—Thailand—Bangkok.
Classification: LCC HD8039.T162 (ebook) | LCC HD8039.T162 T57 2017 (print) | DDC 388.3/47509593—dc23
LC record available at https://lccn.loc.gov/2017020435

Manufactured in the United States of America

25 24 23 22 21 20 19 18
10 9 8 7 6 5 4 3 2 1

In loving memory of Lek
December 15, 1964–September 12, 2016

CONTENTS

ILLUSTRATIONS

FIGURES

MAPS

ACKNOWLEDGMENTS

The debt of gratitude that I owe is too large to fit within a few pages and the people who deserve it the will most likely never read this text. My first and deepest thanks go to the motorcycle taxi drivers who accepted my presence and endured my insistence since the very first day of my fieldwork: to Hong and Adun, Boon and Wud, Yai and Lek, Lerm and Oboto, Pin and Sun, Id and Samart, as well as the hundreds of others who gave me a home while in Bangkok, shared with me endless hours on the side of the road, and welcomed me into their homes and lives, always ready to be my Virgils into the underworld of Bangkok. Without their quiet guidance, caring presence, and desecrating political ardor this book would not exist.

In Thailand a number of scholars, journalists, and researchers have been an endless source of inspiration both for their dedication to academic analysis and for their vocal pursuit of social, economic, and political justice in the country. In particular Pitch Pongsawat, Pavin Chachavalpongpun, David Streckfuss, Paul Chambers, Christine Gray, Charnvit Kasertiri, Duncan McCargo, Yukti Mukdawijitra, Viengrat Nethipo, Tyrell Haberkorn, Jakkrit Sangkhamanee, Chris Baker, Pasuk Phongpaichit, Niti Pawakapan, Andrew McGregor Marshall, Craig Reynolds, Federico Ferrara, Serhat Ünaldi, Eugenie Merieau, Andrew Johnson, Kevin Hewison, Charles Keyes, and Nick Nostitz have been invaluable models and companions. To them goes my deepest respect and gratitude. In Bangkok, Wittawat Tucharungrot, Carla Betancourt, Marc Stuart, Pablo Andreolotti, Nico Dali, Agnes Dherbeys, Daniel Feary, Sun Thapphawut, Dane Wetschler, Parn and Parut Penpayap, Aphiwat Saengpatthasima, Stefano di Gregorio, Edoardo Fanti, Margherita Colarullo, Todd Ruiz, and Alice Dubot accompanied and supported me throughout my fieldwork and shared their ideas, observations, and comments, as well as countless meals, beers, and relaxing hours. A particular thanks goes to Chanutcha Pongcheen, who worked as my research assistant for a portion of my fieldwork, Chutimas Suksai who over the course of last ten years helped me in countless occasions, and to the staff of the Sumaa Culture and Language Institute, who provided invaluable support and help with the intricacies of the Thai language.

The Wenner Gren Foundation Dissertation Fellowship, the Social Science Research Council International Dissertation Research Fellowship, the Harvard Sheldon Traveling Fellowship, the Harvard Asia Center, the Harvard Geographical Analysis Center, the Chulalongkorn ENITS Fellowship, the Cora-Dubois Writing Fellowship, the Kyoto CSEAS Visiting Fellowship and Oxford All Souls College supported the research that went into this book and kept me fed while I was conducting it. To all of these organizations go my utmost appreciation for their invaluable work in support of the social sciences.

Enormous debt goes to the members of my dissertation committee, who provided inspiration and encouragement throughout my long years in graduate school: to Ajantha Subramanian for helping me to get my work closer to where it wanted to go and, word after word, allowing my ideas to develop—anybody would be fortunate to have a mentor like her; to Mary Steedly for providing punctual and thoughtful guidance when I needed it the most, while reminding me to take advantage of the present—both in academia and beyond it—without ever preaching her views; to Michael Herzfeld for many more reasons than my words will ever be able to explain, I am honored to call him not only my advisor but also my friend. Other scholars have been pivotal to the development of my thinking and helped set the horizons of my work, in particular Engseng Ho, Steven Caton, James Watson, Ted Bestor, Maria Minicuci, Piero Vereni, Mary-Jo Good, Byron Good, Michael Fisher, Neil Brenner, Lilith Mahmud, Maple Razsa, Thomas Malaby, Thongchai Winichakul, Brian McGrath, Margaret Crawford, Marco Cenzatti, Peter Rowe, Erik Harms, Setha Low, Julia Elyachar, Farha Ghannam, Andrea Muehlebach, Dimitri Dalakoglou, AbdouMaliq Simone, Michael Keith, Laura Bear, Avner Offer, Stephen Smith, Judith Scheele, and David Gellner. A special thanks goes also to the staff of the department of anthropology at Harvard University—Cris Paul, Marianne Fritz, Marilyn Goodrich, Sue Hilditch, Susan Farley, Penny Rew, and Karen Santospago—and at the University of Oxford—Kate Atherton, Vicky Dean, Mark Gunther, Gil Middleton, and Stacey Richardson—who always found ways to put a patch on my excruciating lack of organization.

Nobody has influenced and directed my work and my life more than the extraordinary group of graduate students and friends whom I had the honor and pleasure to meet during my Ph.D. and postdoctoral work: Anand Vaidya for his thoughtful questions, warm friendship, and unmatched dancing skills that left me enriched after every moment we spent together; Arafat Muhammad for his moral compass and calm energy, for allowing me to be part of his wonderful family, and for endless evenings with chicken curry and shisha, whether in Boston, Bangkok, or Singapore; Alex Fattal for being my first guide to American life, for hours and hours of brainstorming, controlled craziness, and fierce conversation, as well as for telling me, on a regular basis, to shut up; Chiaki Nishijima for her support and reality checks; Dilan Yildirim for both her rigid critiques and our gentle discussions after sundown; Emrah Yildiz for never letting anything slide, both intellectually and emotionally, and for holding me accountable and sharp; Federico Perez for his quiet depth and intelligence and Ivette Salom for her interminable depth and explosive energy; Hassan Al-Damluji for his ability to always see the larger picture and bring out a smile in everybody around him; Naor Ben-Yehoyada for constantly urging me to think twice, to reconsider every thought, while also being around when it was time to stop thinking and drink a Campari; Juana Davila for giving humanity to intellectual digressions and Felipe Gomez Ossa for bringing funk back into my life; Julie Kleinman for being an intellectual and emotional sister throughout this process; Scott Stonington for his intellectual support and playfulness and for welcoming me into his home; Tara Dankel for making me feel that the U.S. could actually become a home and for leaving cheesecake outside my window; Andonis Marden for the most honest and unexpected conversations, the many laughs in the middle of the night, and accepting the ungrateful task of reading every line of this book; Arthur Asseraf for mixing his relentless intellect with emotional intelligence; Brian Kwoba for providing a living model of decolonized scholarship and emotional life, when the cloudy skies and the ivory spires of Oxford seemed to deny the very possibility of its existence. Davide Ugolini for bringing back a dedication to radical politics and a critique of dominant economic theories; Giulia Gonzales for sharing with me many long afternoons of work and always providing a fresh perspective; Luul Balestra for questioning my simple-mindedness and showing me, often the hard way, that apparently contradictory thoughts can live side by side; Max Harris for teaching me every day how to be a more gentle human and a more forceful thinker; Michael Kebede for proving to me that two people born thousands of kilometers away can be more similar than we care to admit and for pushing me to never forget the debt we owe to social theorists. Particular thanks go to Felicity Aulino and Kevin Moore. This wonderful couple and their children Ren and Eamonn have, over the last ten years, provided the most incredible demonstration of how intellectual rigor and sharpness, emotional generosity and depth, political enthusiasm, and commitment can and do live together in amazing, unstable equilibrium.

A particular appreciation is reserved for the long list of research seminars, writing groups, and individuals who commented on and edited my work. In particular the SSRC Anthropology writing group composed of Julie Kleinman, Louisa Lombard, Jonathan Echeverri Zuluaga, and Rebecca Woods; the Thai Studies writing group, composed of Felicity Aulino, Eli Elinoff, Ben Taussig, and Malavika Reddy; and the Southeast East Asian Writing Group in Oxford made up of Kevin Fogg, Khin Mar Mar Kyi, Petra Mahy, and Matthew Walton. They worked on and polished every page of this book but, most importantly, provided a group of outstanding thinkers and an example of the collective engagement and intellectual generosity that keeps me in academia. Toward the end of the process, Jyothi Natarajan, Lizzie Presser, Jayati Vora, and Jennifer Munger offered the best editorial team an academic writer could ever dream of while Daniel Feary helped with the cover design and Carla Betancourt with the maps. Finally, the production team at University of California Press, in particular Reed Malcolm, accompanied me each step of the way, gently pushed me to polish the manuscript into its present form, and kept my indecisiveness on a leash. To them all goes my heartfelt gratitude.

I want to conclude by thanking my family, both the given and the chosen. Without them the process of writing this book, and that of being alive, would be unthinkable and unbearable. To my father and mother who, with their earthy wisdom, have warned me along the way that intellectual pursuit without human and political engagement would be a waste of time and energy. To my brother Paolo, two sisters Silvia and Laura, brother-in-law Tony, and nieces Elena and Greta, who remind me every day that life is to be lived and shared. To my larger family Andrea, Angelo, Balea', Batto', Carlo, Caterina, Cecilia, le Chiare, Coccia, Coppa', Danie', Davide, Emilia, Fran, Greg, Guido, Ianna, Leo, Marco, Michela, Pallutti', Stefania, Stefano: you simply keep me alive. I love you all beyond what words could ever express. Thank you from the bottom of my heart.

Introduction

ON MAY 19, 2010, the Royal Thai Army deployed tanks, snipers, and war weapons to disperse thousands of protesters who had taken over the commercial center of Bangkok. Two months before, following four years of political unrest, these protesters, known as the Red Shirts, had taken over the Ratchaprasong intersection, the main space of elite consumption in the city and a nexus of transportation and trade in the city. The protesters demanded the dissolution of the government headed by Abhisit Vejjajiva, new democratic elections, and an end to the political and economic inequalities and double standards they experience every day. Key to the mobilization were motorcycle taxi drivers who slowed down, filtered, and arrested the movement of people, commodities, and information in the area. The drivers had proven to be an uncontrollable force, capable of playing cat-and-mouse with security forces, evading military checkpoints, and rescuing protesters and their leaders once the army attacked them. People who normally operated unnoticed as part of Bangkok's transportation infrastructure had taken over the city, challenged state forces' ability to control their capital city and revealed the fragility of their power. On May 20, when the army's attack against the Red Shirts came to an end, the motorcycle taxi drivers were nowhere to be seen. After weeks of occupying the streets and providing the only form of transportation through it, they had left the area, taking advantage of their mobility and profound knowledge of the city's shortcuts and backdoors to slip away before the military's fist clenched around the protesters. The military dispersal left behind ninety-two dead and more than two thousand injured. 7-Eleven shops, bank branches, the Stock Exchange of Thailand, as well as Central World, the biggest shopping mall in the country, had been set on fire (see fig. 1).

FIGURE 1. The burning ashes of Central World shopping complex after the army dispersal. Photo by Nick Nostitz.

The morning after, the Ratchaprasong intersection, site of the protest camp and the theater of the military violence, was eerily quiet, populated only by abandoned chairs and sleeping mats, empty stalls and a bare stage. The pungent smell of burned plastic and putrid puddles of water filled the area as burned-out shells of buildings stood watch over the deserted square. A few hundred meters away, a crowd of detained Red Shirts sat in silence inside the National Police Headquarters, fearfully awaiting their fate. As the sun started to recede, police officers began escorting them to charter busses and trains bound for the rural villages many of them came in from. I boarded one of these trains. Sitting in a car filled by demoralized protesters, I wondered, like many others around me, how I had ended up in this situation.[1] I had come to Thailand to study urban mobility and its role in producing and reproducing Bangkok. More than a year later, I found myself on a carriage heading hundreds of miles away from the city, witnessing the apparent defeat of the largest social movement in Thai history, a movement that for months had taken control and blocked the very urban mobility I wanted to explore. As I thought about how this journey started, my mind went back to my childhood.

1. For a more detailed narrative of the train ride see Sopranzetti 2012b.

When I was a kid I used to cheer every time a mercury thermometer broke in my house. Away from the eyes of my parents I would put the spilled quicksilver on a table and kneel down, eyes close to the surface. I moved the mercury through small objects watching the stream cluster, cleave, and reunite as it filled the tiny spaces between them. The first time I crossed a four-lane road in Bangkok I stopped midway through the overpass to watch the flow of thousands of motorcycles twisting and squeezing through the static lanes of cars at a traffic light, feeling like a child again, entranced and exposed to toxic material. After that, almost every day I climbed up one of the thousand pedestrian overpasses that were built in the 1970s and 1980s to minimize interruptions to the flow of traffic and business. From there I watched the dance of thousands of motorcycles, finding routes and inventing passages where automobiles and buses waited, frozen. The bikes arrived from behind and made their way to the front of the line to cluster in a dense cloud a few meters away from the first cars. From above I stared, waiting for the traffic light to turn green and motorbikes to speed into the empty road until the next red light.

Mobility and traffic, street life and elevation, were my introduction to Bangkok. As I spent more time in the Thai capital it became clear that most residents lived their lives continuously using and discussing their knowledge of moving through the city, detecting the best way to proceed from point A to point B depending on time of the day, their economic means, urgency, and willingness to be exposed to heat, foul smells, potential accidents, or toxic fumes. In a megalopolis of 15 million people, infamous for traffic gridlock, limited public infrastructure, and environmental hazards, sensing when to switch modes of transportation could make the difference between being on time or stuck for hours in the tropical heat. Buses, taxis, cars, *tuk-tuk,* Skytrain, subway, canal boats, river boats, vans, *sǫng thǣo,*[2] bikes, motorbikes, motorcycle taxis—all of these possibilities present themselves to denizens on the move, according to location and income. The two most recent entries into this transportation puzzle, Skytrain and subway, offer predictable and regular schedules—malfunctions permitting—but only cover a minimal portion of the city. For the rest, moving smoothly through Bangkok requires a high degree of expertise.

New residents, whether foreign anthropologists or the million migrants who populate the city, start building this knowledge quickly, out of experiences

2. Open-rear vans in which passengers sit on two rows of benches.

with nerve-wracking failures, and innumerable hours spent moving through and getting stuck in the city. They learn that the affordable buses are slow-moving from eight to nine in the morning, from and from noon to one-thirty, and again after four-thirty in the afternoon, and, as in the United States, are almost exclusively used by the urban poor; that taxis are never worth their price during peak hours, when a short ride may add up to a day's income, but can be otherwise counted on for a long detour and interesting conversations with drivers; and that water transportation never undergoes gridlock and in its predictable slowness can save the day if you are willing to take a smelly ride on the polluted waterways.

In time, the newcomers learn that moving around in Bangkok is a matter of navigating the city, its landmarks and rhythms with prompt reactions and creativity. During traffic hours, they discover, mixing and switching is the way to go: a section on a bus and then be ready to get off once it gets stuck in traffic, a short ride to the canal, another tract on a boat, and a final ride in a cab after you get out of the congested area. Nonetheless, when the traffic grinds to a halt, the subway and Skytrain are too far away, boats are not available, and buses are stuck, hopping on one of the two hundred thousand motorbikes operating as taxis is the only way to get anywhere fast. At more than five thousand stations across the city, small groups of migrants from the countryside in colorful vests wait for clients to jump on their scooters' backseat and take them to their destination, zigzagging through the congested city (see fig. 2).[3]

My fascination for motorcycle taxi drivers may have stemmed from my childhood games and my adolescence meddling with scooters, but my research interest in urban mobility has been grounded in a disjuncture between urban theory and urban ethnographies. For centuries, urban plan-

---

3. The vast majority of drivers are males between the age of twenty and forty, mostly with primary and, in few cases, secondary education. About 90 percent of them were are not born in Bangkok, with Isan (Thailand's northeast) being by far the most common region of provenience (Jetsada 2004). Even though men represent about 95 percent of the drivers, the number of women has been slightly increasing since the 1997 economic crisis, in which women were particularly hit by the lay-offs that pushed many workers toward this informal market (Mills 1999b). The drivers ride a variety of motorcycles and scooters, with the latter dominating the business given their manageability in traffic. The majority of them are Japanese brands, mostly Honda, Yamaha, and Suzuki. Given the large national production of bikes, their costs remain relatively affordable. A driver's monthly income—normally between 12,000 baht ($400) and 30,000 baht ($1,000) depending on location—buys a second-hand bike in decent condition.

FIGURE 2. A motorcycle taxi driver leaving his station with a passenger. Photo by Agnes Dherbeys.

ners, mayors, and social theorists have acknowledged the centrality of circulation to the birth, growth, and functioning of the metropolis. Nonetheless, when ethnographers started to explore cities, they did not bring into their purview the infrastructures that allow for urban circulation, the lives of the people who manage and operate the means of public transportation, or the effects of circulation on urban experience.[4] In the late 1990s anthropological studies, faced with the accusation of being more interested in stable roots

4. Since the beginning of my research in 2008, however, a number of ethnographies that focus on urban circulation have come out. In particular Elyachar 2010; Ghannam 2011; Harvey and Knox 2015; Luque-Ayala and Marvin 2015; Monroe 2016; Shortell and Brown 2016; Simone 2005; Truitt 2008.

than in ever-changing routes,[5] began to emphasize "interrelations and linkages between local settings and larger regional or global structures and processes."[6] In cities this meant continuing to explore traditional objects of urban anthropology—neighborhoods, marketplaces, enclaves, ethnic groups, and urban deviants[7]—but also stressing their relations with the larger circulation of people, commodities, ideas, and modes of governance rather than their boundedness. The resulting studies unraveled the complexities of localized worlds and their interactions with larger-scale realities, yet mostly ignored the city as an entity beyond the sum of its neighborhoods and communities. In order to describe urban life most of these works adopted one of the oldest tricks in the anthropological book: they assumed a metonymical relation between the scale of local fieldworks and that of the city as a whole. By studying the first, they made claims about the second. In so doing, they implicitly postulated that dynamics visible at one scale must be present and parallel at the other, without questioning how those scales are produced, connected, and reworked in everyday life.

While scholars—particularly proponents of political-economic approaches, the mobility turn, and actor-network-theory[8]—have debated at length these shortcomings, I set out to approach them ethnographically rather than at the theoretical level.[9] My idea was to explore the work needed to knit the city together and keep it connected, the people and infrastructures that perform it, and their roles in making and remaking the urban scale.[10] Studying a city like Bangkok, where that work is painstakingly real and quotidian, but neglecting these dynamics meant missing an essential

5. Clifford 1997.

6. Gupta and Ferguson 1997, 7.

7. Bestor 1989, 2004; Bourgois 1995; Bourgois and Schonberg 2009; Herzfeld 2009; Levitt 2001; Low 2003; Mathews 2011; L. Ralph 2014; Stoller 2002.

8. Latour 2005; Latour, Hermant, and Shannon 1998; N. Smith 1992; Urry 2000, 2007.

9. How to deal with different scales ethnographically, I believe, remains one of the most poignant questions for contemporary anthropology. As Jane and John Comaroff have argued, the key problem of doing ethnography "is ultimately a question of scale [not] easily captured by the ethnographer's lens. Should each of them nonetheless be interrogated purely in their own particularity, their own locality? Or should we try to recognize where, in the particularity of the local, lurk social forces of larger scale, forces whose sociology demands attention if we are to make sense of the worlds we study without parochializing and, worse yet, exoticizing them" (Comaroff and Comaroff 2003, 151).

10. For a more detailed analysis of the relation between mobility and the birth of urban anthropology see Sopranzetti 2018 (forthcoming).

aspect of how the city is lived and preserved and how commodities, people, rumors, aspirations, and power circulate through its veins.

Attracted by these questions, I began to develop an interest in the only people who can keep the city moving when everybody else is stuck in traffic: the drivers who carry passengers on their scooters' backseats. When I asked people in Bangkok about them, stories came pouring out—to my surprise often preceded by laughter at the thought of a researcher coming halfway across the world to study the infamous and mundane *mǭtǣsai rap čhāng* (motorcycles for hire). Laughter, Mary Douglas would say, is the result of bringing together disparate elements and arranging them in a way that challenges accepted relations.[11] A student at a prestigious university hanging out with people considered dangerous and lazy by Bangkok urbanites and popular media fit that description. "Motorcycle taxi driver? This is what my son will become, if he doesn't work hard," a young mother who worked in a small office in central Bangkok told me half-joking and half-concerned as we chatted at a subway stop. When she was young, tending water buffaloes was the bogeyman fate reserved for disobedient and lazy youngsters. Now that the country is urbanized and buffaloes sparse, becoming a motorcycle taxi driver has taken its place as the epitome of the undesirable job for the urban middle classes. "Why would you want spend years talking to them?" she continued, referring to the drivers. "You study culture, you should focus on Buddhism."

More interested in street life than in the quiet of monks' quarters, I continued to ask people about those alleged good-for-nothings who allow the city to function and its movements to continue. As the laughter faded away and my interlocutor realized I was not joking, stories replaced puzzlement. Everybody seemed to have an anecdote to recount, a driver they knew, a tale to tell. The first story was generally the recounting of an insane ride, knees hitting stationary cars while zipping through clogged traffic, or a deadly accident they saw happening. These were followed by stories of thefts and drug deals. These tales, however common to the actual experiences of riding motortaxis, often had the rhetorical marks of urban legends. They happened to a friend of a friend, somebody they knew, a slightly too removed acquaintance. Rather than presenting first-hand experiences, they strengthened the diffuse perceptions of the drivers as unsafe, unreliable, and lazy citizens.

"So you don't use them?" I would ask, waiting for the smile that often opened up on the person's face. Another flood of stories would gush forth, this

11. Douglas 1975, 96.

time not about *the* stereotypical driver but about *a* particular driver, a specific person they used daily: some to go to work, others to ferry their kids back and forth from school; some to pick up food and fix a broken pipe in their house, others to get their regular stash of drugs. Everybody I met seemed to be connected to and through a motorcycle taxi driver. Municipal and post offices in Bangkok are filled with drivers waiting to pay bills, deliver packages, or turn in documents. Banks are enlivened by their colorful vests, standing in line to deposit checks or collect stipends for regular clients. Offices rely on them for deliveries. At late-night parties, when the alcohol starts to run low or the ice has melted away, a phone number of a night driver will pop up and the party will be extended after a fast delivery. Even e-commerce businesses offer expedited one-hour motorcycle taxi delivery services, for an extra fee.

The longer I lived in Bangkok the more I grew captivated by the drivers—for the most part men from the interior of the country—who sat in small stations at almost every corner in the city. Riding to and from those stations, they connected houses, offices, factories, shops, and other transportation networks but were ignored in transportation and academic studies, beneath government recognition, and occasionally disdained by popular press and culture. How did these migrants become so central to the daily operations of the city? What motivated them to take up this occupation? What techniques did they deploy to navigate the physical, social, and legal landscapes of Bangkok? How did their lives on the move affect their relations with the city and the villages they migrated from? How were conflicting conceptions of the city, formal and informal economies as well as public and private spaces, sustained, adopted, or challenged by their different forms of mobility? With these questions in mind, I began my investigation of mobility in Bangkok, ready to move with the flow or getting stuck within it.

Like the quicksilver that fascinated me as a child, the system of motorcycle taxi drivers proved hard to confine and difficult to grasp, especially with the tools of traditional anthropological research, developed to study relatively stable and static social groups. Motorcycle taxi drivers were nothing like that. They hardly thought of themselves as a unified group; each station was completely autonomous and operated with almost no coordination with the others, and even within a station, drivers often came together only during working hours, after which they dispersed back into the city. Time and again during my research, these features became a source of frustration. Yet, when I was in a good mood it also provided some of the most useful methodological challenges and intellectual stimulus. These difficulties, I realized, were the result of a certain degree of disciplinary orthodoxy and methodological conservatism in anthropology which "tended to bring the anthropologist to the ethnic enclaves, the ghetto, which had cultural and organizational characteristics with which he [sic] could—in his own curious way—feel comfortable."[12]

As my fieldwork progressed, I regularly found this methodological predisposition pushing me toward a street corner, a group of drivers, or a neighborhood as the preferred scales of analysis. My research, therefore, became a continuous struggle to resist this comforting dimension. If I did not want to reproduce the disjuncture between traditional urban anthropology and urban theory, I had to adopt a flexible and mobile methodology, one that actively strove to "move along with people, images, or objects that are moving and being studied."[13] If I spent a few months with a group of drivers in their neighborhood, I would then shift to conducting research with state officers or labor unionists who think about the roles of motorcycle taxi drivers across the city and the effects of transformation in labor practices on their lives. If the recent economic history of Thailand became the focus of my work, I would then go back to the drivers' villages or visit their families to see how the city and the drivers' lives were perceived from there. If the migration attracted my attention, I redirected it toward the drivers' bodies and explored what the constant movement was doing to them. In this sense, my research aimed at following the motorcycle taxis' meandering mobility by shifting constantly between different scales and disciplinary methods—from spatial analysis to participant observation, from archival research to mapping, from social history to visual analysis. Circulation not only became the object of my analysis, it also structured its methodology.

Once I took this approach and stopped slicing the drivers' experience into one specific scale or area of the city, the full extent of their roles in weaving Bangkok together and performing the work necessary to keep it alive begun to emerge. Ferrying customers across the urban landscape to their homes, schools, and jobs, moving commodities, stories, and aspirations both within the city and out in villages, the drivers made and remade Bangkok, day after day, one trip at a time. Following them, the geography of the city—with its landmarks, rhythms, flows, and blockages—started to become familiar. Yet, this concrete space was just one of the landscapes that the drivers traversed and operated in. As my research progressed, a complex geography of organizational structures,

12. Hannerz 1980, 3.
13. Urry 2007, 6.

illegal economies, self-representation, historical events, and political figures came into relief. In time, it became clear that their everyday life in the city was reorganized by the economic transformations that took place after the 1997 financial crisis and pushed many of them out of the factory floor and onto the street, where they operated as service providers and entrepreneurs of urban mobility. The change both affected and was effected by new forms of body discipline that the drivers experienced on the move. Similarly, it reshaped their perceptions of themselves, the city around them, and the country as a whole. This, it seemed, created new expectations and desires both for them and for their families back home. From those desires, something else was emerging: a series of collective demands and a growing dissatisfaction with the country's political and economic situation.

These processes showed the complex entanglements between new forms of capitalism in Thailand, the drivers' bodies, discourses, and actions, and their political mobilizations. Yet, whenever I tried to talk to them about the relation between these aspects, I found that the drivers did not think of them as cause and effect but rather as moving landmarks through which they oriented and adjusted their trajectories. Their approach urged me to bring the same refusal to adopt a single entry point that directed my methods to inform my theoretical framework. This became the main theoretical challenge and contribution that runs through this book.

While inquiries into political economy, everyday life, and political action have dominated social sciences in recent decades, they have often remained separate and generated conflicting theoretical reflections. Marxism, phenomenology, and post-structuralism all have struggled with reconciling these three elements but often overemphasized their separateness and relative hierarchy. Orthodox Marxism tends to reduce everyday life and political relations to the logic of capital and its contradictions. Phenomenology, on the contrary, elevates everyday life and perception to the realm of an irreducible universal, frequently underestimating both their relation to capitalism and to political configurations. Finally, post-structuralism focuses on the discursive component of power relations so strongly as to leave little space for an analysis of material relations and everyday acts of subversion. Many scholars have attempted, and managed, to work in between these three schools. Such productive engagements, however, have been largely pursued by dodging or resolving the contradictions between the three schools and factors.

The drivers were bringing me down a different road. Their actions and reflections pushed me to analyze the concrete entanglements among economic restructurings, everyday life, and political actions without emphasizing any of the factors as primary. It was the unresolved tensions between the three elements that defined and propelled the drivers' lives, not a cause-and-effect relation between them. This realization put me on the road laid down by Henri Lefebvre in *Critique of Everyday Life,* a road that remained widely unexplored because it departed from that of orthodox political-economic analysis and crossed the paths of phenomenology and post-structuralism. Lefebvre's approach, like the one the drivers were inviting me to follow, started from an analysis and critique of the everyday as the territory where structures, processes, and practices meet and question each other.

The necessity of such an approach became evident when the drivers' political demands started to gain momentum. For the first year of my research, their critical voices populated half-drunken conversations at the end of long days at work and occasional nights at a karaoke bar. Then they began to coalesce around small protests that called for the resignation of the ruling government in 2009. At the beginning of 2010, however, those sparse protests coalesced into a mass social movement: the Red Shirts. That March, Red Shirts protesters took hold of Bangkok and blocked its main centers with the help and support of large portions of the city's motorcycle taxi drivers. In the weeks that followed, I found myself in the midst of the biggest political mobilization in modern Thai history, with a unique set of connections in place to make sense of the rapidly evolving events. As a result, my research was radically transformed.

What had started as an investigation into urban circulation turned into something much larger. I was, unexpectedly, witnessing collective action emerging among precarious workers. Over the previous decade, in fact, the drivers had come to think of themselves as individual entrepreneurs in competition with one another. Yet they were now acting as a collective and adopting circulation, and the ability to take control of it, as a technique of political mobilization. The uprising and the central roles of the drivers demonstrated that operators of mobility had the potential to take control and sever the very connections they had helped create. During the protest this potential was realized and the drivers brought the mobility of central Bangkok to a halt.

Their influence should not come as a surprise. Both in academic and larger public debates, the rhetoric of mobility has taken an increasingly central stage since the end of the twentieth century. Studies of migration, transnationalism, media, and globalization have put mobility at the center of academic discussion as well as daily conversation. In particular, analyses of contemporary capitalism have noticed the decreasing importance of factory-line modes of production in favor of more flexible economic practices, centered on mobile financial capital and floating labor.[14] Financial markets, communication technology, global trade and migration—just to mention a few phenomena—have forced us to rethink the way we look at space, time, economy, society, politics, and human relations. Nonetheless, the people who allow the channels of economic, social, and conceptual exchange to remain open are seldom named and reflected on. The events in front of my eyes showed that these people could also take control of flows and reclaim their centrality by adopting mobility as a tool of political mobilization, not just as a form of labor or a locus of capitalist accumulation.

I remembered underlining, fervently with a sharp pencil, Anna Tsing's observation that "mobility means nothing without mobilization."[15] This lesson was now delivered in a very concrete way by Bangkok's motorcycle taxi drivers. While my first year of fieldwork dealt with the drivers' role in making the city, my second year focused on the increasing importance of circulation in contemporary Thailand, its transformation into a toll of political mobilization, and the unmaking of urban connections. How and why did the drivers emerge from their invisibility as an urban infrastructure to take on such a critical political role? What made them into such effective political actors in protest? What did this reveal about the role of circulation in Thailand after the 1997 economic crisis and about state forces' struggle to control their own territory?

Trying to remain faithful to the entanglement between mobility and mobilization among the drivers, this book is composed of two interlocking trajectories, organized around eight chapters divided into two even parts. Part 1 looks at the drivers' everyday lives and how their circulation brings the city into being as they carve channels through it. In it, I analyze how histories, relations of exploitation, everyday practices, and legal arrangements are inscribed onto the drivers' bodies, trajectories, and aspirations, both in the city and in their villages, and have come to orient and shape their consciousness as residents, migrants, and political actors. In chapter 1, I reconstruct the conditions of possibility—material, technological, economic, and social—for the emergence of the motorcycle taxi in the early 1980s as an unintended

14. Amin 2013; Bryan and Rafferty 2006; Harvey 2012; Lazzarato and Jordan 2010; Mezzadra and Neilson 2015; Mezzadra et al. 2013; Roberts 2010.
15. Tsing 2005, 215.

consequence of the conflicting orders configured by processes of urbanization, privatized land development, industrial expansion, and new informal economies. In chapter 2, I explore the drivers' everyday lives as urban connectors, mediating between urban spaces and classes. I analyze the ways in which driving a motorbike shapes perceptions and practices of urban space and configures the drivers' meandering and path-seeking presence in the city. Chapter 3 branches out from the city into a larger rural geography. Here I analyze how the drivers' mediation of desires and lifestyles configures a hierarchical relation between the city and the villages and generates expectations that their circular migration often fails to fulfill. Finally, in chapter 4 I position this gap between expectations and reality in the post-1997 capitalist restructuring in Thailand and the paradoxes of the driver's reorganization as free entrepreneurs which emancipated them from the discipline of the factory floor while inscribing them in a new system of precariousness.

While part 1 focuses on the drivers' everyday mobility, part 2 of the book examines how that mobility morphed into and shaped their political mobilization. In it, I reveal how circulation emerged both as a characteristic and a strength of contemporary capitalism but also a weak spot, always open to challenges from the people who operate economic, social, and conceptual exchange yet are excluded from its effects. Chapter 5 follows the government's realization of the drivers' strength in the city in 2003. I explore the resulting attempt to formalize and control the drivers' operations as part of a larger struggle over the Thai state, a struggle that cost Prime Minister Thaksin Shinawatra his position in a military coup in 2006. In chapter 6, I analyze how the drivers' position in urban circuits generated new desires among them, and how after the 2006 coup, the government repressed those desires and saw them transforming into collective demands. In chapter 7, I explore how those demands resulted in the Red Shirts' protests in 2010. During this time, the drivers' mobility, their knowledge of the urban terrain, and their invisibility to state forces not only defined their political subjectivities but also their actions in the mobilization. Finally, in chapter 8, I examine the forms of organization that the drivers adopted, under conflicting leadership and conceptions of power, during and after the Red Shirts' uprisings of 2009 and 2010.

Overall, this book explores the work performed by motorcycle taxi drivers in their constant making and unmaking of Bangkok, not by focusing on the sturdiness of material forms, established hierarchy, and political hegemony or on the ubiquity of everyday resistance and unbounded ingenuity. Rather,

I center on contradictions, tensions, and fragilities as unyielding features of social life in Bangkok, on the drivers' all-too-human need for resolution that can never be fulfilled, and on the doomed attempts by state forces to impose order over the kaleidoscopic realities of contemporary Bangkok—its rhythms, apertures, blockages, pretenses, and dirty business. In each chapter, I explore the productive nature of these predicaments: those that created Bangkok; the contradictions and contingencies that animated the drivers daily mobilities and their risks; those engrained in their role as mediators between the city and the countryside; those present in the freedom that motivates them to take up their line of work; the contradictions that the drivers experience in their expectations, dreams, and desires that in turn build their political consciousness; and finally those inherent to power in contemporary Thailand and the multiple ways of understanding it.

Behind this narrative, however, stands a deception: that of claiming to say something about the city as a whole. Bangkok, like any other city, contains infinite cities, each composed of invisible threads, each distinct but never complete. Each of its residents, observers, and planners has created a mental image and an imagined totality which they see as *the city*. They have locations, foods, smells, styles, buildings that come to define their city. Yet, each of them sees different shapes, different layers, and maps unique in their partiality yet common in their pretense to be Bangkok. Cities are, after all, a glass shop full of kaleidoscopes pretending to be monocles. The same goes for social movements, protests, and other forms of collective organization, including the nation-state. Behind their pretense of coherence and unity stands the multiplicity of masses of people, all with their own personal stories, demands, desires, hopes, and frustrations. Behind the imagined communities, the political ideologies, the networks, the factions, and the orchestrated strategies, lies the unbounded messiness and tragic beauty of human nature.

This book, like any other rendition of a city or a protest, hides that deception, a laughable pretense of unity if not of plenitude. Its blind spots and unexplored routes are too numerous to list. However, a few are worth pointing out. First, my engagement with the city has been dominated by masculine gazes, both mine and those of the drivers, who for the most part are men. Even the few women who work in the system do so by accepting and endorsing forms of masculinity. Second, my navigation of the protests was, as any trajectory inside any social movement, occasional and personal. The people I met, the conversations I listened to and participated in, as well as the demands they voiced were a tiny fraction of a movement that was defined and strengthened by its heterogeneity and multiplicity of forces it included. These blind spots, along with many other omissions and partial views, make any attempt on my part to come to a unifying conclusion little more than a fated endeavor, as doomed as any other in this story, to find a resolution. The reader, aware of the limits, might decide to ignore them. The author, aware of his ignorance, decides to pretend, hoping that this deception will allow glimpses of clarity rather than obscurity. Alan Moore, the author of *V for Vendetta,* said that artists use lie to tell the truth, while politicians use them to cover the truth up.[16] In this text, I tried my best to follow the first model, aware of the risk of reproducing the second. As I write the last revisions of this book, the tension between my attempt to describe and understand something about Bangkok and the Red Shirts movement and the absurdity of such an enterprise—especially as a military dictatorship is once again ruling Thailand and a new king in power—remains very much unresolved, looming over this whole project. The only solution I could find was learning from the motorcycle taxi drivers and, rather than reconciling this tension, leaving it unresolved and allowing it to become a productive force, an engine propelling the book. As is the case for the drivers, once I took this path the road ahead was uncertain. Sometimes it led to successful navigations, other times to terrible accidents. Which of these this book is, it is not for me to say.

16. Moore 1988.

Prologue

APRIL 26, 2010. IT IS A QUIET afternoon in Bangkok. At the entrance of an alley off Sathorn Road—a major artery in the city's financial center—a group of twenty young migrants in colorful vests lounge in the heat of the day. A few of them sit on their motorbikes, looking for passengers. Others fight the boredom of the off-peak hours, tucked between a four-story shopping center, the parking lot of an upscale spa, and the heavy concrete shafts of Bangkok's elevated train. The occasional car drives past the group, filling the empty six-lane street with its roar. Above them, the Skytrain darts through, indifferent to the ups and downs of the urban rhythms below, before slowing down a few hundred meters away into the nearby Chong Nonsi Station. A sleepy dog roams among the drivers before lying down on the stairs of the shopping center. Once in a while, a customer passes through the automated doors of the shop, releasing a momentary blast of freezing air and a few notes of mellow music that dissipate as they glide down the concrete stairs in front of the drivers' angle-parked motorbikes. A few steps away, the humidity and enervating echo of the sparse traffic remain untouched by the blast, revealing the group's ingenuity in choosing its location.

A young driver sits on his bike, staring into the rear mirrors as he plucks rare facial hairs by pinching five-baht coins together as tweezers. Next to him another driver lies on his bike, arms crossed behind his head. Years of practice have taught his body to conform to the machine. The seat transforms into a mat for the driver's back. The two rear mirrors are bent inside-out on top of the handlebar to hold the back of his head as earplugs channel music from his cell phone. One leg hangs from the bike tail, a few inches away from the burning exhaust pipe. The other leg is crossed, foot against the opposite knee over the taillight. A couple of drivers squat on the sidewalk, immersed in sports sections of multiple newspapers spread out around them. Smoking avidly, they fill in illegal soccer betting slips that a man will later come to pick up and deliver to the local bookie. One of them stands up, folds his slips and hides them away from the eyes of local police inside the metal frame of a public phone booth that the group has transformed into their storage room. The heat inside the booth is unbearable. Colorful helmets dangle from a wire that used to connect the phone to the electricity post. On top of the old phone, jackets emblazoned with the logos of companies where some of the drivers work as part-time messengers pile up. Other wires have been unplugged from the phone and bent into metallic hooks for hanging the drivers' bags, to which I add mine.

I have come to see Hong, a thirty-year-old driver with long hair and a widening bald spot that he hides beneath a hat. Hong was born in a small village in the northeastern province of Nong Bua Lamphu and moved to Bangkok attracted like most of his colleagues by the prospect of better job opportunities and a vague idea of a more exciting life. Following his dreams, Hong attend high school in the city where he joined his two older sisters who worked in a garment factory and a brother who had risen in the rural monastic ranks and was sent to Bangkok to study further. After finishing school, unable to afford university training, Hong ventured into the tortuous spiral of low-paid occupations and exploitative bosses experienced by many drivers in the formal economy of the city. Adapting to the discipline of labor on the factory floor and to the urban bias against northeastern migrants proved difficult. In 2001 he began to work at a Korean company a few blocks away from where he now operates as a driver. "Two years in there were long enough to decide I would not work in a factory ever again," he tells me, remembering with bitterness his belligerent boss. Fed up with being insulted all the time and considered a stupid water buffalo from the countryside, Hong invested all he had saved in his two years in Bangkok—25,000 baht ($830 USD at the time)—in the purchase of a motorcycle taxi vest. It was March 2006, three years after motorcycle taxis were formalized and registered by the government of Thaksin Shinawatra and a few months before a military coup removed him from office. Hong was now a motorcycle taxi driver.

Hong has been working at a motorcycle taxi station in the same street corner ever since, delivering newspapers in the early morning before shifting to passengers, goods, and documents for the rest of the day. Every day he moves confidently through a concrete landscape he has come to know "even better than my own village," he smiles. His village, however, never faded from his mind, both as an imagined place of nostalgia and as a home to go back to as a prize for his sacrifices. In the city, Hong claims, he is just saving money to build a house back in the village, where he hopes someday to return with the economic and social capital to marry and set up a home-stay hostel. If daily wages, much higher than those of other unskilled jobs available to the drivers in Bangkok, brought Hong to this profession in the first place, ʻitsaraphāp (freedom) keeps him in this hectic, stressful, and health-threatening job.

Taking advantage of this freedom, Hong sits next to a phone booth with six other drivers on makeshift wooden benches. He shakes dominoes inside a reused plastic detergent bottle before starting a new game, with the usual five-baht stake. "Are you playing?" He drops seven pieces in my hand, without waiting for an answer. A few steps away, one of the drivers helps an older woman to tidy up the pile of dirty plastic bowls that have accumulated on the tables around her noodle cart during the recent lunch rush. At the street corner Adun—another driver—sits alone, immersed in a newspaper's political section plastered with images of a massive street protest that has been taking place just a few miles away. To his side, hanging from one of the trees that shade the motorcycle taxis' station, a plastic board with a local business advertisement helps the drivers keep track of who is next in line. The board is covered with numbered tiles corresponding to the number each driver has on his vest. Down the road a young woman waves at the group. Adun raises his eyes to the board. "Twelve!" he shouts at the colleagues playing dominoes. Hong, whose vest bears that number, drops his pieces, jumps on a bike, puts on his helmet without bringing a second one for his passenger, and kick-starts the engine, speeding down the small alley. Hong's tile is moved to the end of the board and Adun distractedly takes his place next to me at the domino table.

A few minutes later Hong is back to the typically slow rhythm of the early afternoons: sporadic passengers, an occasional delivery of documents to faraway offices, a cigarette, some money won and lost at dominoes, and an endless search for distractions. It is during this apparently dead time that many of the driver's social relations are forged and sustained. As the life of the street unfolds in front of them, the drivers chat, joke, and interact with street vendors, office workers, and urban dwellers. While during peak hours the drivers speed through traffic muttering few words to their clients, in these extended waiting periods they engage directly in the social life of the neighborhood: a casual remark to a woman who works nearby; a short chat with the older man who stops every time he comes home from his afternoon walk; a helping hand to a vendor pushing a cart along the road. Through these mundane interactions the drivers fight the boredom of off-peak hours but also solidify their presence in the city and knit together the physical, social, and economic fabric of the neighborhood around them. They do so, not just by moving people and commodities, but by controlling movement in and out of the area and offering readily available help for neighbors, whether by keeping an eye on their houses, moving their furniture, or paying their bills, as they wait for traffic to pick up again. Through physical presence and boredom, not just speed and movement, the drivers become important characters in the theater of life at a street corner: side characters by all means, yet always onstage.

Around five in the afternoon, when rush hour usually starts, Hong and his colleagues tuck the dominos away and jump on their bikes, ready to ferry clients to the Skytrain or bus stops or, if the traffic gets really bad, all the way to their homes. Around them, sleepy vendors wake up and move their carts to cater to the after-work flood of clients. Tables are replenished with goods and noodles are prepared. Then, as if responding to an unspoken call, the streets revive, dense with the physical and economic circulation released by offices and schools. Children run around looking for after-school snacks. Office workers hurry out to avoid the worst traffic. Young workers stand in small groups deciding what to do next. Mothers pick up food, neatly packed in plastic bags, and head home. All around, smoke engulfs food carts. A thick paste of chili and garlic sizzles inside charred woks. Slowly marinated meat hits the grill. Stuffed fish rests on charcoal. Individual portions of rice are spooned out of enormous steaming pots. In this mixture of fumes, vegetables are pan-fried, stir-fried, deep-fried. Seafood mixes with vegetables, with egg, with noodles, with curry, with soup. Other ingredients are added in and rapidly stirred. Woks are emptied into rice boxes. Water washes the pan and then is rapidly discarded into a big plastic bucket. Again chili and garlic paste are added: a new cycle begins.

Hong looks over the scene from atop his bike, one hand in the air to attract clients, peering at potential customers, scrutinizing their faces for a movement of eyebrows, an elevation of chin, or the hint of a hand signal to indicate interest in his service. Beside him, the streets are specked with cars, pick-up trucks, vans, and buses. For a while the traffic gets denser, without affecting the speed of motion. Then, slowly, the rhythm of the traffic lights ripples along the road, all the way to the entrance of the alley, often hundreds of meters away from the intersections. Green light: slow but steady movement of vehicles, people accumulating on the sidewalks, chatting and buying from vendors. Yellow light: the pace of cars gets faster, more nervous. People on the sidewalk walk away from the vendors and concentrate at the pedestrian crossing. Red light: again the winding line of vehicles stretch past the motorcycle taxi group while people cross the street. This cyclical routine repeats with minor variations for about an hour. Then, at around six-thirty, the traffic comes to a complete halt.

Now the traffic lights change color but no perceptible movement results. Cars and buses rest, engines on, in the middle of intersections, attempting in vain to move a few feet while pedestrians cross the street through the halted vehicles. As the city experiences its infamous traffic jams, motorcycles become the only way to move. At peak hours, housewives, businessmen, schoolchildren, office workers, and vendors—regardless of class, age, and gender—all sit on motorbike backseats, driven most likely by a young man from the provinces. In the uncommon physical proximity of the bike, the passengers tuck in their knees to avoid hitting cars and dive into Bangkok's intricate traffic, carried through the jigsaw puzzle of cars, taxis, *tuk tuk* (auto rickshaws), trucks, buses, and pick-ups by drivers in bright vests ready to see any small opening in between the metal maze. In these slow-moving, smoke-smelling, nerve-wracking gridlocks the weaving progression of motorbikes conquers the city, occupying and finding paths in the empty gaps between vehicles. Seen from a car or bus, the street looks blocked; from atop a motorbike, small highways emerge. As cars try unsuccessfully to shift to other lanes, these paths rapidly open and close framed by rearview mirrors and tail lights. In these spaces motorcycle taxis find their ideal habitat, pathways invisible and impervious to any other mechanical means of transportation.

Eyes glued to the street, Hong reads these emerging roads, constantly looking for a path that will open up and trying to predict which one will close next. In this situation all his driving skills are summoned. Getting to his destination rapidly means returning to his station faster and getting another client sooner. Speed and money, in traffic, become synonyms for drivers like Hong, in ways they do not for cabs. When facing a yellow traffic light, the cab driver breaks, happily leaving the meter running. Hong, on the contrary, rushes through at full speed: right hand on the accelerator, twisting it all the way, zipping in between two rows of slowing cars, swinging just enough to dodge their mirrors. As cars move to one side, attempting to change lanes, his right hand pulls the front break lever. Simultaneously the right foot pushes the pedal down, applying the rear break. Left heel pushes on the gear selector to lower the gear. Knees move in. Left arm extends. Sharp turn between two cars to find another space that opened in the right lane: a new sliver of street pavement. Left foot presses down, gear up. Right hand twists the grip, accelerates. Hong's whole body adjusts to the rhythm of the mercurial traffic. Eyes, hands, feet, knees, he reads and reacts to the pace of moving traffic, deploying complex skills embodied to the point of becoming automatisms.

As Hong's wallet fills up, fatigue and pain gradually conquer his body. It starts with his hands, stiff from gripping the handlebars. As his knuckles begin to hurt, the pain spreads up his arms, tense from a long day of zigzagging with the weight of a passenger in the back seat. His calves are next, cramped by the continuous braking and changing of gears. Finally, the tension moves from his neck creeps down his back, curved from hunching over the bike. By the end of the day, when the traffic dies out, his whole body is unbalanced from the stress of regular accelerations and braking.

At this point Hong and the other drivers in his group would normally buy northeastern food from a nearby street vendor along with a few beers or a bottle of cheap whisky, if it had been a good day of business. They would eat under a lamp pole at their station, letting their cellphones blast music and occasionally leaving to carry a few late passengers. Lately, however, after finishing their day's work some of the drivers jump on their bikes and head to the Ratchaprasong intersection, the commercial core of Bangkok, where thousands of workers and citizens from all around the country are gathered in protest since the previous month. I jump on my bike and join them.

As we ride in that direction, the sun rapidly disappears behind skyscrapers, casting a lingering light that gives depth to the layers and layers of buildings that compose this part of Bangkok. We could be riding through the roads of any global capital, skyscrapers overlooking a giant park where office workers normally go to eat their quick lunches or jog after work. Then, as we take the last turn, a tall wall of bamboo sticks and car tires, tied together with red ribbons, blocks the street, reminding us where we are. Four days before, a grenade exploded in the middle of Bangkok financial center around Silom Road, killing one person and injuring a group of citizens who were protesting against the Red Shirts' prolonged shutdown of this part of the city. Fearing military reprisals, the Red Shirts erected the barricades, shutting off the area (see fig. 3). On top of them a lonely red board says in English: "Stop Corruption. Dissolve Parliament."

FIGURE 3. Red Shirts' barricades at the end of Silom Road, built to protect the protesters from a potential attack by the army. Photo by the author.

We park our bikes nearby and walk to the barricades. "Do you smell it?" Hong asks me. "It's petrol, they poured it on the tires so that if the military attacks they will have a problem passing." The Red Shirts have tightened their security and we are required to show our bags before walking in. Behind the barricades, crowds of people armed with sharpened sticks roam aimlessly or sit on the ground, half-vigilant and half-bored. The ground is covered with small piles of stones, common ammunition of protesters around the world. The atmosphere at the barricades is tense and rumors run wild, predicting an impending military attack, "most probably within forty-eight hours," one of the guards tells Hong. A few hundred meters behind, the tension quickly dissipates. From here on, the protest resembles a carnival or a temple fair more than a stand-off with a heavily armed military force historically prone to violence against its own population. The sound of huge speakers pervades the four-lane street that connects the barricades to the central stage, reaching our ears as we move through the crowd. "Brothers and sisters, it is time for this government to step down. For too long Thailand has been controlled by an aristocracy ['ammāt]. Now it is time to give power back to the people, to the serfs [phrai]." The crackling sounds from the speakers mix with folk music and loud voices coming from portable kitchens. "The time for democracy has arrived."

Around us the the crowd is swelling as more protesters join in after their working hours. It now takes half an hour to reach the center of the protest, stretching the usual travel time tenfold. While street vendors are normally present in this area, settling into the small spaces between retail shops and transportation routes, now they conquer the street and spill over the road pavement, becoming its center instead of occupying its leftover niches. In front of us, three lines of motorcycle taxi drivers have also invaded the street. They wait for passengers, fingers in the air, ready to utter their usual first sentence: *Pai nai?* Where to? The first line of drivers, further away from us and closer to the core of the protest, sit astride their bikes, with their vehicles slightly tilted and one foot on the ground, ready for passengers. The second line, less interested in clients, sit with both feet up on the pegs, or stand with one knee bent on the seat. In the third row, right in front of us, drivers chat distractedly, sitting on their bikes or standing, backs to us. All of them wear the orange sleeveless vest distributed by Thaksin's government in 2003, stamped with a number and the insignia of Bangkok—the god Indra riding a white elephant. A few hundred meters away, the crowd of protesters starts to thicken. Only motorcycle taxis can navigate through this sea of protesters, finding routes where all other modes of transportation see an impenetrable wall. Once in a while one of them emerges from the crowd and drives to the back of the pack, parking at the end of the third row, as everybody moves a position up. "*Pai nai?*" repeat the drivers in the front row.

Hong greets Ta, one of these drivers who normally works not far away from his station and comes here after hours to make a few more baht and take part in the protest, mixing economic profit and political participation. They chat for a while, filling each other in on the military movements around the protest area and the negotiations between the protest's leaders and the government which initiated a few weeks before. "Jump on the bike," Ta tells both of us. "Let's go eat something." We squeeze onto his backseat. The bike proceeds slowly around the periphery of the rally, zigzagging though protesters, parked cars, and scattered vendors selling Red Shirts' paraphernalia: T-shirts and jackets, books and posters, wristbands and armbands, clappers and music. As we get closer to the crowds, food and drinks stalls take over. Money changes hands, fueling the economy of the protest and providing an addition motivation to street vendors to join the movement.

Thousands of people dressed in red sit on the street pavement, while the sidewalks are taken over by large tents. Most of the tents have banners on top with the names of their occupants' provinces. Some function as mobile hospitals or registrations booths for the UDD (United Front for Democracy against Dictatorship), the most structured section of the Red Shirts; others as massage parlors, resting areas for monks, or small radio and TV stations. Protesters move from tent to tent, chat, buy something to eat, and make their way to the central stage. A few hundred meters away, the ground is covered in plastic tarpaulins and portable chairs. Seated on the asphalt, the crowd becomes impossible to penetrate, even by a motorcycle taxi driver. We stop, park the bike, and continue on foot.

In a few minutes we arrive at the Ratchaprasong intersection, a central transportation node and an iconic space of glamorous middle-class consumption in Bangkok. Towering over the intersection are the biggest shopping malls in the country, upscale hotels, the largest clothing wholesale market in the city, and a prime open-air shopping and entertainment plaza—all of which were shut down by the protest. Above us is Siam Square Station, where the two lines of the Skytrain meet. The station usually serves between forty thousand and fifty thousand passengers per day. Today, however, it is completely empty, closed down following the protesters' threat to occupy it. A disorienting stillness occupies the space where continuous flow is the norm. In the middle of the blocked intersection sits a huge stage. On top of the stage a large banner declares, in English, "Protesters Not Terrorists." Underneath, a larger banner shows a fighter with open hands, similar to Zapatista stencil art, topped by a white inscription, *phrai* (commoners or serfs). On the grounds in front of Central World, the largest shopping mall in the country, the crowd is more dispersed. Some people sit on the pavement listening to the speeches on stage. Others move around, searching for a space to sleep for the night. Some walk with chairs, some lay down mats and renegotiate the use of space with protesters who have been here all day.

A few meters away from us, damp laundry dries on the handrails of the Skytrain stairs, facing a small plastic shack adorned by beef jerky hanging from a rope tied between an advertisement board and a street light. On the other side of the street, three young models overlook the crowd from huge advertisement boards displaying the names Gucci, Louis Vuitton, and Versace. In the middle, a large screen broadcasts a recorded video of Thaksin Shinawatra. From his studio in Dubai, the prime minister who was ousted by a military coup in 2006 fires up the crowd, criticizing the injustice of the present government and its refusal to give people access to opportunities. Some protesters stare enchanted at their exiled hero. Others walk around distractedly, uninterested by the words of somebody they see as tangential to their struggle, a useful ally but one who risks hijacking a fight larger than him. Hong belongs to the latter group; Ta, it seems from his focus on the screen, to the former. Hong and I leave him to listen to Thaksin and keep walking down the avenue.

Whatever their opinion of the former prime minister's role in the movement, thousands of motorcycle taxi drivers have peppered the crowd since the Red Shirts descended on Bangkok a few weeks earlier. Many of them—like Ta—are part of the protest's infrastructure as transportation providers, political mobilizers, leaders' personal guards, spies, or guides for other protesters. Others, like Hong, are simply supporters, coming in every night to swell the Red Shirts' ranks, eat some food, and meet with people from their villages who have come to the city to support the movement. As we arrive at the tent of Hong's province, he smiles at Parn, a young woman he has been spending more and more time with during the protests. I understand that this is my clue to leave him alone. I say bye to them and walk into the crowd, hoping to reach the leaders' backstage area to find Oboto, a driver who rose to prominence as an organizer during Thaksin's premiership and who now acts as a go-between for the drivers and the protest's leaders.

A charming man in his forties, Oboto was born in a village outside Ubon Ratchathani, in northeastern Thailand. As a teenager, he moved to Bangkok and became a political organizer in the slum of Klong Toey, where he still lives and works. After the economic crisis that hit Thailand in 1997, Oboto was laid off from his job as a hospital porter and started working as a motorcycle taxi driver. By 2003, when Thaksin's government began to register motorcycle taxis in Bangkok, Oboto had already become a prominent leader among Klong Toey's drivers. As the registration brought disgruntled drivers together, he met other drivers who had been fighting across the city against meddling by people of influence—mostly government officials—in their activities. Motivated by the sudden attention to their suffering, these drivers became increasingly visible in the Thai public sphere, and allied with Thaksin. Even after the prime minister was removed by a military coup in 2006, this alliance was not broken. A month before the beginning of the Red Shirts' protest in March 2010 Oboto and the other leaders decided to formalize their collective organization and established the Association of Motorcycle Taxis of Thailand (AMTT), an informal trade union with the dual purpose of protecting drivers from racketeering and of increasing their visibility and negotiating power.

When the mobilization began, the AMTT immediately entered the orbit of the Red Shirts. Their collaboration, however, was not without its risks and difficulties. On a personal level, the drivers' support for an antigovernment movement put their livelihoods in danger as the new prime minister made repeated threats to revoke their licenses if they took part in the protest. On a collective level, becoming closely affiliated with one side of the struggle could potentially jeopardize their ability to negotiate with opposing governments, both present and future, on issues of social welfare and job security. While most of the other leaders of the association supported the Red Shirts personally but saw their association's participation in the protest as a way to bargain with the government and the army, Oboto and a few others in the AMTT refused to see the protest just as the means to the drivers' ends. For them the political struggle carried out by the social movement was an end in itself and trumped all other forms of labor organizing. As a result, Oboto slowly drifted away from the association and became the main liaison for the Red Shirts among the drivers.

When I met Oboto for the first time, on March 15, 2010, three days after the beginning of the march that brought thousands of protesters into Bangkok and initiated the Red Shirts' mobilization, the conflict between the drivers' leaders had not yet emerged but Oboto had already risen to a prominent position in the movement. The Ratchaprasong intersection had yet to be occupied. Instead, convoys of protesters were roaming the city, challenging police and military forces to stop them and inviting people to the streets to show their support with the urban lower classes. Oboto had a central place in these caravans. With tidy black hair, a medical mask on his face, and aviator sunglasses, Oboto perfectly embodied the stereotype of a masculine and distant leader. His eyes moved frantically, following the movements of half a dozen motorcycle taxi drivers who were organizing and directing other bikers into long rows. People around him guided the staging, shouting and honking and gesticulating to direct the crowd's movement. Half-hidden by the fumes of motorcycles and cars, Oboto silently watched. Behind, his red motorbike glimmered in the sun, enfolded by a giant Thai flag flapping in the wind, attached to his bike with rolls of brown tape. Further behind, monks, street vendors, youths, older women, middle-aged men, and small families dressed in red sat on thousands of bikes, waiting for a sign by Oboto to start moving.

Around us, the rumble of engines was building: the loud roar of knock-off Harley-Davidsons, the baritone screams of used-up sport Yamahas; the popping dialogue of the few Vespas mixed with the larger chorus of the new Japanese scooters, dominated by the mechanical regularity of the Hondas and Yamahas but peppered with the high-pitched sounds of the Kawasakis and Suzukis. A few hundred meters behind us, protesters' cars, pick-ups trucks, vans, auto-rickshaws, trucks, and taxis blasted Thai country music. The odd procession of Red Shirts protesters crowded around a big truck, its deck opened and filled by huge speakers through which a young woman's voice harangued the protesters. On the right side of the street, a couple of motorcycle taxi drivers in their vests rode up and down the rows of vehicles bringing orders back and forth between the protest's main stage and Oboto. "Call me later," he told me hastily as I tried to engage him in conversation, jotting down his phone number on a piece of paper. Suddenly, all the motorcycle taxi drivers' under Oboto's control removed their vests, carefully folded them, and covered their license plates with boards or plastic bags. "This way they will not know who is who," Oboto told me without taking off his vest, conscious of the prime minister's threat to take the licenses away from drivers who were recognized in the protest. Then, as if in a carefully rehearsed choreography, Oboto jumped on his bike and the huge caravan started moving through the streets of Bangkok. The procession brought traffic to a standstill, redefined streets and spaces of transit as political arenas, and challenged the state forces to control the mobile protest. In the confusion, I somehow managed to lose Oboto's phone number. Later, I searched for it in every jacket, bag, and pair of slacks I owned but to no avail. In mid-April, the Red Shirts stopped using caravans as a strategy and, as a result, I had lost sight of Oboto.

Now, on April 26, I was told that a representative of the motorcycle taxi drivers would be speaking on stage. I hoped he would be Oboto. As I walked toward the stage leaving Hong and Parn to their flirting, I saw his face broadcast through the half-dozen big screens scattered around the newly formed plaza. "The two hundred thousand motorcycle taxi drivers in Bangkok are here to help and support the Red Shirts," he reassured the crowd, standing straight in the middle of the stage. I walked backstage and saw him stepping down a small iron staircase after finishing his speech. Oboto was wearing his usual vest, but no sunglasses or mask this time. As he juggled conversations with a protest leader and two other drivers, Oboto caught sight of me. "You disappeared," he said, smiling. "People keep telling me about you. Are you sure you don't work for the government?" He joked as he introduced me to the other drivers with him. "They work as personal guards to the Red Shirts' leaders." He continued. "If you want to get out fast, motorcycle taxi drivers are your best choice. Everybody wants us on their side. We know how to move, how to get out. Nobody knows the city as well as us. We are the owners of the map." He laughed, raising his eyebrows defiantly.

PART ONE

Mobility

ONE

The Unsettled Layers of Bangkok

> A genealogy ... will never confuse itself with a quest for their "origins," will never neglect as inaccessible the vicissitudes of history. On the contrary, it will cultivate the details and accidents that accompany every beginning; it will be scrupulously attentive to their petty malice; it will await their emergence.
>
> MICHEL FOUCAULT, *Nietzsche, Genealogy, History*

ON OCTOBER 3, 1983, *THAILAND BUSINESS,* a bilingual magazine, published a five-page article entitled "Soi Bikes." "Living in Bangkok nowadays," the article began, "you must have seen many different groups of motorcyclists ... operating a new kind of business by picking up passengers and taking them to their destination."[1] Harnessing widespread curiosity about the new service and its operators, the magazine set out to investigate "who they are, when it first started, where the idea come from, how they operate the business, and whether it is illegal or not to earn money by using motorcycles for public hire."[2] The article traced the growth of the system out of a Navy housing complex in *soi* Ngam Duphli, a few roads away from Bangkok financial center. It investigated the drivers' daily lives, their organization in informal groups clustering around a station, the rules of their queuing system, as well as the cost of renting the vests which all the drivers wore to be identified.[3] While motorcycle taxi groups had been developing an internal organization, the magazine revealed, they operated in a legal gray area in which local police officers extorted money from them, acquired control over the groups' operations, and used the drivers as assistants in patrolling their neighborhoods. Even with the police involvement, the author concluded, the rapidly diffusing system offered potential economic rewards to local businesspeople willing to invest in it.

1. *Thailand Business* 1983.
2. Ibid.
3. During this phase vests were distributed by local people of influence who collect money from the driver to allow them to operate uninhibited. See chapter 5 for more details.

While the promises of economic return enticed the business community, legal diatribes regarding the new enterprise animated state bureaucracy. Inside their offices a debate over the safety and legality of using motorbikes for public transportation took place in much drier language. The Ministry of Land Transportation, which had banned three-wheeled rickshaws from Bangkok in 1960 because of their outdated slowness,[4] found the new system of transportation dangerous, undeveloped, and unfit for their dreams of Bangkok as a modern metropolis. Resolved to outlaw the proliferating motortaxis on the grounds of safety, throughout the 1980s the ministry produced a wealth of statistical data on motorcycle accidents. At the same time, across town, another ministry found itself preoccupied with the new transportation system. In June 1983, a committee headed by the interior minister and the director of the Office of Policy and Planning began considering the legality of motorcycles for hire.[5] According to Thai law at the time, vehicles registered for public use, marked by a yellow plate rather than the white one reserved for private use, had to be either three- or four-wheeled, such as buses, taxis, tuk-tuks, and the recently banned rickshaws. Motorcycles, one wheel short, would not qualify. Experts in the ministry debated: Should the limits of the law be expanded to incorporate this new mode of transportation? Should police officers, at least for the time being, arrest motortaxi drivers? What about their supervisors and group leaders?

As the ministerial bureaucracy discussed the legal minutiae of the driving code, the number of wheels allowed to a vehicle for public use, and the kinds of urban flows it wanted to sustain or eliminate, thousands of young rural migrants continued to buy motorcycles and transform them into sources of income. Motorcycle taxis responded to the needs of a rapidly expanding metropolis and thrived in this niche, spreading faster than legislators' decision making. Bangkokians grew accustomed to the sight of migrant men in colorful vests, perched atop their bikes, waiting to pick up clients. Their back seats became familiar to city dwellers and carried children, office workers, and local dwellers through smoky traffic during peak hours and poorly lit alleys late at night. Whether legal or illegal, this system had become part of

4. Robert Textor explored the lives of rickshaw drivers in Bangkok in the 1960s. Like motorcycle taxi drivers, they were for the most part male migrants from the northeastern provinces who struggled to participate in both the urban and rural life of the country (Textor 1961).

5. Mōtǣsai rap čhāng, literally motorcycles for hire, is still today the Thai name for motorcycle taxis.

their everyday life. In this legal uncertainty, police officers and army officials thrived. Realizing the potential of the new business, they took the lead in operating new motorcyclists' groups, rented out handmade vests that operated as drivers' informal licenses, or simply demanded money from existing groups in exchange for directing their gaze elsewhere.

Lieutenant Somboon Boonsuckdi, a navy officer who assumed the role of administrator of the Ngam Duphli motorcycle transport service—often referred to as the first motortaxi group in Bangkok—was the first to seize this opportunity. He told the *Thailand Business*'s reporter that although the police refused him permission to open a station, he went ahead anyway and nothing happened to him, probably because he himself was a government official. His case was not unique. All across Bangkok, state officials like Somboon were expanding their hold over the new business, supplementing their meager official income with less transparent enterprises, as they had done and continue to do with prostitution, illegal casinos, and drug trade. In a dynamic known to Thai scholars as "using power/authority as influence,"[6] these officials were transforming formal authority (*amnāt*) derived from their role in the state apparatus into influence (*itthiphon*), a form of control over the operations of the urban gray economy based on fear and indebtedness.[7]

The diffusion of motorcycle taxis, therefore, raised questions well beyond transportation policy and road safety. Their presence engendered questions about who legitimately controls urban space; about freedom, desire, labor, and migration; about legal structures and economic relations; and ultimately about existing power structures, their brokers, and internal struggles. The new transportation infrastructure for Bangkok was much more than a solution for a traffic-ridden metropolis. It emerged as the result of political-economic, legal, administrative, technological, spatial, and epistemological transformations in the city. Yet, through its operations, it ended up solidifying, developing, and at times pushing back against those transformations.

In particular, four conditions of possibility, which came together in the 1980s, allowed the motorcycle taxis to appear. The first was a mode of administration: a set of formalized, yet often informal, interactions between state officials, citizens, and territory—the dynamic of transforming authority into influence—which emerged at the turn of the twentieth century and continued to organize street life in Bangkok. The second revolved around a group

6. Nithi 2010 [Buddhist year 2553]; Sangsit 2005 [Buddhist year 2548].
7. Persons 2016, 156.

of actors: millions of young and relatively unspecialized migrants from rural Thailand who, from the late 1950s, provided the city with cheap labor. The third condition was technological: affordable motorcycles which flooded Thailand in the 1960s. Finally, a physical setting: the maze of long and narrow alleys, known as *soi*, which solidified in the 1970s and rendered extensive mass public transportation in Bangkok virtually impossible.

None of these elements emerged with motorcycle taxis in mind. They were not part of a unified strategy directed by state forces, government officials, local business people, or drivers. Rather they were the unexpected and unpredictable outcomes of a century-old struggle between aspirations to impose order on the city and the unbounded messiness of its everyday practices. The city in which the drivers started to operate in the 1980s was itself the product of this struggle, a material canvas on which state forces constantly attempted to superimpose new ordered layers but remained unable to erase or scrape away the stubborn persistence of existing practices.[8]

The history of humankind is dotted by such canvasses, outcomes of the tension between scarce resources and the all-too-human pretense to leave traces and rewrite history. These objects are known as palimpsest. In antiquity, parchment was a rare and valuable commodity. As a consequence, the same piece of animal skin was reused, often multiple times, by erasing the previous layer and adding a new one. The results were called palimpsests, documents in which faint traces of the former writings remained visible between the lines. Over the centuries, these traces would resurface, enough to be readable, from the oblivion of history. Cities are like these documents. Favorable geographic position and easy access to resources, much like parchment in antiquity, have always been scarce. As a result, new urban conglomerates grow atop older ones, giant palimpsests onto which new configurations are constantly scripted. Walking around a city, any city, we are constantly faced by the traces of overlaying: warehouses that reveal the neighborhood's

8. This dynamic has often been analyzed through the lens of Michele de Certau's contrast between strategies and tactics (de Certeau 1984, xiii–xiv). The first—the French philosopher argues—are calculations made by a subject that has control over a space that it can call as its own; the second by an entity that always operates in a space that belongs to another. As a consequence, he shows, when the first one succeeds it restructures space. On the contrary, when the second one does so, the victory is only temporary and, "whatever it wins it does not keep" (de Certeau 1984, xix). This distinction hardly fit what I saw in my fieldwork. Here no one—whether state forces, planners, city dwellers, or motorcycle taxis—had control over any space. Rather the territory of the city—and the state itself, as I show in the following chapters—were fields over which different groups, state factions, and people battled.

industrial past converted into yuppies' apartments; grooved cobblestone roads that remind us of a time when people moved on carriages made into walking streets; spaces underneath urban highways turned into small parks. Those traces are ghosts haunting contemporary cities and showing us the doorsteps of their past while drawing the contours of their future. Especially in cities like Bangkok, where informality and extemporaneous responses have undermined any attempt to plan, regulate, and control urban life, those traces are concrete reminders that everyday practices always spill out of the tidy paths that urban institutions, planners, and builders try to draft for them.[9] Those paths always present themselves as "a truly radical break with history and tradition,"[10] and claim a clean departure from an imagined tabula rasa. Yet, they often fall short from these aspirations and show the signs of struggle between past and present, between the neat logic of blueprints and the concrete messiness of reality.[11] The result is a different type of order, one

9. Simone 2010, 3.

10. Scott 1998, 93

11. These tensions remains always unresolved, always the fleeting product of failed antici-pations, unsuccessful attempts, and pragmatic engagements. Reconstructing a history of these unresolved struggles, as Rabinow and Bennet have argued, "provide[s] a means of showing the contingency of the present and thereby contribute[s] to making a more open future" (Rabinow and Bennett 2010). This chapter aims at exactly this objective: revealing some of the cracks, a word dear to both Foucault and Gramsci (Foucault 1970, 1972; Gramsci 1988), into the mate-rial sturdiness of the present in the Thai capital. In this sense, I follow the methodological proposal developed by Michel Foucault in order to build a history of the present which "is not that of its growing perfection, but rather that of its conditions of possibility" (Foucault 1970, xi). However methodologically similar to his explorations, this chapter operates out-side the limits of the "particular fields [of] the history of ideas, or of thought, or of science, or of knowledge" (ibid.) to which the French theorist constrained his project. In so doing it differs both from Foucault's project and from Kant's quest for conditions of possibility to which Foucaltian analysis was a reaction. My investigation, in fact, does not rest either on the idealistic dimension of Kantian anthropology—a research of the conditions for the "regulative principle that can lead us from an initial condition of 'a folly and childish vanity' to 'our destiny' as a cosmopolitan society" (Harvey 2007, 44)—nor on the discursive analysis that animates Foucaultian archeology of knowledge—an illumination of the "epistemological field, the episteme in which knowledge . . . grounds its positivity" (Foucault 1972, xxii). Rather, I focus on the material, social, and political-economic fields in order to explore the conditions of possibility in which a specific technology of mobility grounds its existence and continuous expansion. In this sense, I follow a deeply Gramscian approach, one in which tracing shifts in discourse, what Foucault called the "historical a priori" (Foucault 1970, 10), becomes part of the process as a way to identify and delineate the hegemonic power that sustained material, social, and political-economic transformations. Not the privileged locus for such a history, discursive shifts represent part of the fields in which reconfiguration of relations of produc-tion, center-periphery interactions, and (inter)national markets take place.

generated though repetition, uncontrolled flows, and eruptions, rather than top-down plans. This order itself is constantly challenged, exceeded, and reshaped, in an infinite cycle of thwarted plans, resilient practices, and contingent responses that make up the apparently stable—yet ever shifting—entity that people understand as Bangkok.

Motorcycle taxis were one of those responses. Started timidly in a small road, the system eventually came to be central for allowing the city to function regardless of its traffic jams yet remains a thorn in the side of city planners and their dreams of control. To explore the conditions of possibility for emergence of motorcycle taxis—whether in terms of physical forms, technological tolls, migrant bodies, or administrative relations—means therefore necessarily to excavate those Icarian dreams, their doomed attempts to control flows and impose order, the multiple layers they generated, and the struggles they underwent at each level. It means, in other words, conducting an archeology of the fragile history of urban layers, orderings, and practices that gave birth to motorcycle taxis in the 1980s but started with the founding of Bangkok.

THE BIRTH OF THE AQUATIC CITY

Bangkok began as a floating shop, moored near the mouth of the Chao Praya River, downstream from Ayutthaya, the capital city of the eponymous kingdom.[12] The small trading and customs outpost of Bang Kok developed in the late fifteenth century as a Chinese-dominated node in the lucrative trade network that connected the Gulf of Siam to the Indian Ocean and Southern Chinese Sea. Its position guaranteed the town commercial success and strategic importance, especially after the Burmese attacked and sacked Ayutthaya in 1767. The following year, King Taksin (r. 1767–82), a warrior who had managed to push back the Burmese offensive, relocated the capital of Siam to Thonburi, an easily defendable area near the outpost, on the western bank of the river. Fifteen years later, Buddha Yodfa Chulaloke, later known as Rama I, staged a revolt against Taksin, ordered his beheading, and established the still-reigning Chakri dynasty. A new capital was founded on the

---

12. The etymology of the name *Bangkok* remains unclear. *Bang* is used to refer to a town situated on a riverbank, while the origins of the second part of the name remains debated. Some people think that it comes from *Ko* (island), as a reference to the landscape of the area. Another theory speculates that it is shortened *Makok,* the name for an autochthonous olive tree.

opposite bank of the river, by displacing a few miles south the Chinese traders who occupied the outpost. It was 1782, a year that was memorialized as the birth of Bangkok.

Relocating the capital across the river, however, was not enough to guarantee the legitimacy of the new dynasty. The new king needed to claim a direct connection with the previous sovereigns of Ayutthaya. With this in mind, the new capital was named Krung Rattanakosin Ayutthaya, which still remains as the name of Bangkok's historical district.[13] The connection between the new capital and the older royal city of Ayutthaya, however, was not just a matter of toponyms. While royal historiography was set in motion to link the new monarchs with the former rulers,[14] the new city underwent radical topographic and architectonic interventions to mimic the previous capital. Ayutthaya was on an island, located at the confluence of two rivers, from which departed a maze of canals, connecting it to its hinterland. Major engineering was needed to carve an island into the river bend where Krung Rattanakosin was to flourish. In 1783, Rama I ordered the digging of a canal by Chinese workers, whom he rewarded with access to land along the waterway and south of the newly created island, in an area that would become the economic core of the city. From this first canal more and more branches were added during the first four reigns of the Chakri dynasty (1782–1868), coextensive with the expansion of the monarchs' sphere of influence.

Once the terrain of Bangkok looked similar to that of Ayutthaya, its buildings followed suit. The spatial and symbolic layout of the former capital followed Hindu and Buddhist cosmology.[15] Urban structure, organized to mirror their shared cosmology, revolved around a walled palace that housed the main religious sites, the royal court, as well as most of the population. Each of the main buildings was oriented according to astrological considerations, which the sovereigns of Ayutthaya had imported from Khmer Brahmins, together with royal rituals. The urban structure, cosmological tradition, and court rituals that had traveled westward from the Khmer

---

13. During the reign of Rama III, the city name was changed again to the present-day name. Nonetheless, the name of the previous trading post—Bang Kok—remained how the Siamese capital was known internationally. In this text I decided to refer to the city as Bangkok in order to accommodate an international standard. It is worth noticing, however, that none of my local interlocutors ever referred to the city as "Bangkok" but only as Krung Thep.

14. Charnvit 2015, 219–52.

15. A. A. Johnson 2014.

empire now traveled downstream to Krung Rattanakosin. Along with them, bricks from Ayutthaya's most notable buildings were shipped and used in the new city. What the Burmese pillage had left standing, the Chakri dynasty disassembled and reconstructed in the new capital as a way to save money and as material evidence of Rama I's self-professed role as the restorer of the Ayutthaya Kingdom.[16]

In the new city, as it had been in Ayutthaya, canals became the main channels for the mobility. Even if the early life of the new capital took place mostly inside the walls, its connections to the outside world were mediated by water. Commerce, ceremonies, transportation, war, political and cultural influence traveled , for most of the first five reigns of the Chakri dynasty, on water and made the city famous among European travelers as the Venice of the East. While rivers and canals guaranteed the functioning of the Siamese Kingdom, salty water carried a major challenge to its survival. In 1818, the British Crown—guided by the maritime expansion of the East India Company—acquired Singapore. By 1824, the whole of Malacca was under British control and two years after significant parts of what came to be known as Burma fell to the colonial expansion. In 1859, French forces conquered Saigon and by 1863 the Kingdom of Cambodia had become a French protectorate.

The kings of Bangkok found themselves surrounded by colonial powers that were slowly eating away the semiautonomous tributary reigns and sultanates around them. They responded by emulating colonial powers. This meant raising capital, purchasing military hardware, and constructing a transportation infrastructure necessary to establish and consolidate their control over areas and kingdoms they never previously cared to subjugate.[17] The adoption of these colonial techniques would, inadvertently, set in motion three of the conditions of possibility for the emergence, a century after, of motorcycle taxi drivers in Bangkok. First, they would grant local officials the immunity from legal scrutiny and repercussions that became the first condition of possibility for the drivers' operations in a gray legal area. Second, they created the conditions of uneven development that fostered mass internal migration from the outer provinces to Bangkok. And third, they generated a network of roads, with a specific shape they retained from their previous lives as canals, which provided the terrain for the motorcycle taxis' diffusion in the city.

16. Peleggi 2007, 31.
17. Vandergeest 1993.

THE AMPHIBIOUS ERA: *SIWILAI*, NATION BUILDING, AND URBAN CENTRALIZATION (1860–1910)

In 1861, a group of foreign consuls wrote a courteous yet resolute letter to King Mongkut. Complaining of ill health due to the lack of leisure activities in Bangkok, they requested the construction of a proper road on which to drive their horse-drawn coaches, impossible to do on the existing murky paths around the palace. The king, resolute in his intention of giving an international image of civility to his reign, immediately ordered the construction of the first paved street in Bangkok. In 1863, Charoen Krung—literally "progress of the city"—was opened to traffic.[18] The new road connected the royal palace to the southern section of the city and extended through Samphaeng, the area where the economically dominant Chinese population had been previously relocated. Charoen Krung quickly became the city's main commercial thoroughfare. Soon after, several other streets were built around the palace. This marked the beginning of a slow shift in the orientation of the city away from water.

During the rest of Mongkut's reign (1851–68) and that of his son Chulalongkorn (1868–1910), Bangkok led an amphibious life. The urban landscape was still crisscrossed by boats and swarmed with floating houses, yet Bangkok increasingly oriented itself toward land. The names of the new streets revealed this trajectory. The three main roadways—Charoen Krung (progress of the capital), Fuang Nakhorn (diffusion of the city), Bumrung Muang (nourishment of the urban)—epitomized how progress and expansion were now discursively and spatially tied to roads and land rather than canals and water. Bangkok was shifting from what came to be seen as the unruly flow of waterways toward a civilized land-based city, one in which fluxes were ordered into established and fixed paths. As these paths expanded into a road network, new modes of transportation emerged. In 1872, Praya Choduek, a wealthy nobleman, imported the first rickshaws from Japan.[19] They proved a success and spread rapidly across Bangkok, now a city of about 170,000 people.[20] Pedaling them around were Chinese coolies, who constituted the majority of the urban labor force. Under their bodies, the

---

18. On the shifting significance of *charoen* as a form of moral growth and expansion in relation to material development (*phatthanā*) see A. A. Johnson 2014; Thongchai 2000, 526.

19. Radom 1960 [Buddhist year 2503], 128.

20. Sternstein 1982.

number of rickshaws grew so significant that, to regulate their numbers, their use of street pavement and sidewalks, and their behavior in the street, the newly formed Ministry of Interior introduced the first traffic legislation in the country—the Rickshaw Act of 1903.

The kingdom's reorientation toward land not only produced new roads, transportation methods, and legal deliberations, it also changed its ideological, economic, and political structures. The establishment of land as the dominant space for capital accumulation and the privileged channel for trade and political control was part of a larger attempt to centralize power. This plan posed a variety of logistical and political challenges, including that of framing it as a legitimate enterprise. For this purpose, royal elites produced and diffused a new discourse of *siwilai* (civilization), which presented the country as part of a world system in which European cities sat at the top of the pyramid followed by Bangkok, regional centers, rural villages, all the way to remote forests and their inhabitants resting at the very bottom. As a result, regional towns and villages were cast as urban backwaters, loci of uncivilized—both beastly and pristine—ways of life.[21]

The new spatial and moral hierarchy reorganized the city and its relation to tributary statelets and, mirroring the French *mission civilizatrice* and the British white man burden, justified the expansion of Bangkok's control over them as a civilizing mission.[22] This narrative, which survived well beyond this period and still colors the relations between Bangkok and the rest of the country, allowed the monarch to reframe what had been semiautonomous states as Siamese provinces and expand his control over them. Paraphrasing Thongchai Winichakul, the monarch drafted the nation's modern geo-body, a technology of territoriality that created Siam spatially by marking its borders and plotting its internal divisions. This process, however, also included a new temporal organization, one that discursively sunk regional capitals and villages into the past while it presented Bangkok as the location of Siam's *siwilai* future.[23]

The challenge was how to control and administer those formerly semiautonomous tributary principalities. At first this meant creating a new transportation infrastructure to expand military, administrative, and economic control over them as well as to extract taxes and resources, both agricultural and

21. Dayley 2011.
22. Thongchai 2000.
23. Thongchai 1994, 16.

human. While previous Chakri's monarchs opted for canals and water transportation as their main infrastructural investments, King Chulalongkorn, responding to the amphibious shift in the capital and the strategies of colonial powers in the region, decided that railways would become the new nation's circulatory system. Faster than canals and more easily subjected to centralized control than roads, the first railroads developed at the turn of the century. In 1893, the first line connected Bangkok to Pak Nam (water's mouth), a commercial and military harbor thirty miles south of the city, on the delta of the Chao Praya River. In the following decade, the king ordered the construction of another two lines: one connecting the capital to the northern region, where British forces were starting to show their presence, the other from Bangkok to the northeastern region, at that moment ridden by local insurgencies and potentially the next frontier for French colonial expansion in Indochina after the invasion of Vietnam in 1887 and the blockade of Bangkok's harbor in 1893.[24] Over these years, not only were states waging wars in the area, but wars, or in this case the threat of colonial occupation, were making local states.[25]

The new railways had a central role in the creation of the Siamese state: they brought the formerly semiautonomous territories closer to Bangkok and allowed the penetration of its forces in these areas while also making the circulation of rice and, to a lesser degree, other forest and agricultural commodities faster and cheaper.[26] Siamese products started to flood global markets, swelling the king's pockets. Agricultural land became, for the first time

24. "A few years before, in fact, the threat of French expansion had materialized in Bangkok. Following a dispute over the control of the territory of the Laotian Kingdom, on July 13th 1893, two French gunboats blockaded Bangkok's harbor, forcing the Siamese government to accept a new territorial order. Even if the French retracted after signing a treaty, it became clear that Siam ran the risk of falling under colonial domination (Thongchai 1994). The Siamese response was twofold. On one hand, Siam played a delicate international game of equilibrium between England and France, which culminated in the 1896 Franco-British agreement to keep Siam as a buffer zone. On the other hand, the Siamese monarchs adopted forms of governance from colonial powers and applied them to the Siamese provinces. Among them, railways figured prominently, as was the case in colonial India (Prakash 1999) and Egypt (Mitchell 1988), "envisioned as both a technology of governance and social improvement" (Elinoff 2013, 92).

25. Tilly 1990.

26. "If in 1890 it took 11 days to travel from Bangkok to the northeastern city of Khon Kaen, by 1932 the journey was cut down to two days. The same was true for the northern city of Chiang Mai, now reachable in one day and a half, as opposed to forty two in 1900" (Kakizaki 2005, 156).

in Siamese history, a desirable asset and a source of wealth.[27] With the countryside turning into a space of production, land prices increased and Bangkok's elites started to look at outlying territories as an opportunity for investment and extraction of resources. The largest among them was the monarch himself, who financed its military expansion with capital coming from these enterprises.

The shift from water to land was not just a change in ecology but a shift in the loci of economic accumulation that went hand in hand with the emergence of a territorial, and increasingly national, organization of power. In 1892, King Chulalongkorn initiated a restructuring of the Siamese administrative apparatus. Semiautonomous territories were organized into provinces, districts, and villages. While railways reorganized the flow of people and commodities toward Bangkok, a new class of administrators loyal to the centralized state, known as servants of the monarch (*khā rātchakān*), were needed to govern its territory. A new educational system was rolled out to create this new class and soon the emerging bureaucrats were sent out to administer the outer territories.

Chulalongkorn's administrative reform was an attempt to impose centralized order and control the flows of people, commodities, and taxes around the newly unified country. Before the reform, local powerful people were left free to administer their territories, introduce taxes, and extract resources from the area under their control as long as their interest did not conflict with those of the monarch and they sent tributes and soldiers to Bangkok, when needed.[28] While this configuration ran the risk of disenfranchising local residents and leaving too much power to local administrators, it saved the monarch some money and guaranteed him man power, more important to the king in Bangkok than direct territorial control. With the expansion of colonial powers into the region, Chulalongkorn understood that this arrangement could not be sustained. The king needed to control the degree to which local lords were allowed to extract wealth from their subjects and to

27. In contrast to European feudalism, the *sakdina* system, which preceded the administrative reform in Siam, was predicated on controlling not territory but rather human power. In Siam, land was not considered a scarce resource, labor was. As a result land was hardly desirable and rarely part of economic transactions (Peleggi 2007). In 1892 a new property law was introduced and the concept of private ownership of land was formalized, to adapt to the growing value that agricultural land was acquiring as an effect of intensive cultivation (Askew 1993).

28. Siffin 1966.

formalize their relation to Bangkok by making them politically and economically dependent on the capital, rather than on their ability to mobilize local resources.

Convincing them to agree and guaranteeing their loyalty proved a messy endeavor riddled with more difficulties and resistance than classic Siamese historiography has acknowledged. In the period between 1898 and 1905, a number of revolts exploded in provincial towns both in the northern and the northeastern regions of Siam.[29] These revolts, especially in the northern capital of Chiang Mai, were often instigated by the same local powerful men who were to become the backbone of the new Siamese state but opposed its expansion. Although local resistance was choked on their own blood and the reform largely succeeded in unifying and centralizing the nation, control over bureaucrats remained partial and often rife with tension because of their relatively low pay and their strong local authority. As a consequence, new state officials retained broad room to maneuver, finding ways to establish themselves as local patrons. Familiar with local forms of patronage, the new administrative class ended up simply positioning themselves as local patrons. Patron-client relations were reorganized around access to state posts, which became the single most socially acceptable source of wealth and power. In this system, official authority (*amnāt*) went hand in hand with personal political, economic, and social influence (*itthiphon*) over local subjects. If this influence had previously been located outside the state, depending on personal ability to distribute resources, instill fear, and mobilize local manpower, now its source relocated in the state itself: official authority guaranteed control over locals. This new relationship between bureaucrats, their posts, and local citizens outlived the period, and provided state officials with the opportunity to transform their authority into influence over their subjects.[30] A century later, as *Thailand Business*'s article reported, this opportunity guaranteed the first condition of

29. Ji 2003.

30. As Siffin argues: "The new and the old had more in common than appearances would suggest: the bureaucracy continued to serve as the chief source of status, security, and identity for Thais above the level of villages" (Siffin 1966, 148). Even with the 1932 coup that ended the absolute monarchy, "control of the government passed to a shifting succession of cliques, nominally operating within a constitutional framework but in reality depending upon control of military forces. The bureaucracy continued" (ibid.). It was in fact after the 1932 revolution that the bureaucracy became the main power broker in Thailand. The concept of "bureaucratic polity" (Riggs 1966) was developed to describe this configuration in which most political leaders until the 1990s emerged from the ranks of state bureaucracy rather than through elections.

possibility for the emergence of motorcycle taxis in Bangkok and granted local officials immunity from legal scrutiny and repercussions, allowing them to operate motorcycle taxi groups in a legal gray area.

At the same time that the nation's outer territories were reorganized through commodification of land, new modes of transportation, and centralized administration, its capital city underwent a reconfiguration along similar lines.[31] In 1890 the king created the Privy Purse Bureau (PPB)—renamed Crown Property Bureau (CPB) after the abolition of absolute monarchy in 1932—to administer the monarchy's private possessions and direct investments, which mostly revolved around land development; two years later, he established the Ministry of the Capital to administer Bangkok. These two organizations composed a new governance apparatus that oversaw the city's refashioning as a *siwilai* metropolis. In particular, they financed and built the web of new roads which, following European cities, reoriented Bangkok away from water.[32]

In 1899, King Chulalongkorn ordered the construction of Ratchadamnoen Avenue, literally "royal procession," a name inspired by Kingsway in London. If its name was a British inspiration, the avenue itself was part of an urban transformation modeled on Baron Haussmann's remaking of the French capital and came to be known as the Champs-Élysées of Asia. The linear expansion of Ratchadamnoen broke down the previous structure of the city inspired by Ayutthaya.[33] The new avenue physically directed the city away from the riverfront toward the European-influenced grid of the Dusit district, where Italian architects designed the new throne hall and royal palace.[34] A new layer was added over the urban palimpsest in an attempt to impose a European, and therefore *siwilai*, urban structure over the aquatic city. This

31. Askew 1994; Povatong 2011.

32. Along these roads, the two institutions diffused a new architectural form, known as the shop-house. King Chulalongkorn had taken note of shop-houses—two-story structures with a commercial ground floor and a residential upper floor—during a visit to Singapore in 1870 and decided thereafter to import them to Siam. In the kingdom this structure was pushed by the Siamese monarchs, who became the main builders and renters in Bangkok. In a few years, shop-houses became the dominant architectural form in Bangkok and the monarchs accumulated immense wealth from their construction. While the architecture of the city obtained a more *siwilai* look, modeled on Southeast Asian colonial cities, its urban structure was reorganized following the European metropolis.

33. For a treatment of this break and its relation to previous mandalic urban structures see Herzfeld 2016b, 80–85.

34. Filippi 2008.

layer required new ways of circulating through the city. By the end of the nineteenth century the first cars, which would become the dominant mode of transportation in post-1960s Bangkok, traveled the capital's newly created road network. In 1907, internal combustion engine buses were introduced in the Siamese capital, only thirteen years after Karl Benz—the founder of Mercedes Benz—had built the world's first prototype. Land-based transportation, in the early life of the capital, closely followed new developments occurring in European cities and projected Bangkok into the splendor of a colonial metropolis. Nothing materialized this progress and Bangkok's dreams of *siwilai* more than the tram, a new mode of transportation that was conquering European cities from Paris to London. The first electrified systems of transportation in Asia appeared in Bangkok in 1893—only thirteen years after the first tramline in the world was established in Saint Petersburg—and, in the elite imaginary, ferried Siam into the age of civilization.

By 1910, when Chulalongkorn died, Bangkok had changed its appearance and initiated an expansion away from water that would continue well after this period. Between 1890 and 1910, under the new system of local administration, more than 120 roads and 30 bridges were built; new patterns of land development, rent, and speculation had emerged; and new transportation technologies (trains, trams, buses, and cars) were conquering the city and the nation. All of these changes solidified the image of Bangkok as a modern capital firmly based on land, kept in rhythm by the mechanical time of buses and trams and embellished, as a British journalist reported upon visiting Bangkok in 1904, by the "broad and well-kept roads, the row of new-built houses and rapidly spreading shops, with the stuccoed walls of palaces and prisons, of barracks and offices, displaying the Haussmann-like changes that King Chulalongkorn I (Rama V) has effected in the outward appearance of his capital."[35]

ENVISIONING THE FUTURE CITY: LABOR MOBILIZATIONS (1923–32)

If the outward appearance of Bangkok reminded the visitor of the grandeur of European capitals, Chulalongkorn's *siwilai* city was much less magnificent when seen from street level. The everyday experience of the city hardly fitted the depiction of an epoch-changing rupture that contemporary writers and later Thai

35. Norman 1904, 124.

historians magniloquently presented. Chulalongkorn's dream of *siwilai* remained largely an aspiration, an incomplete project haunted by the previous layers of the city, partial implementation, and unruly everyday practices. These realities would give Bangkok the fractured road network that provided, a century after, the background for the diffusion of motorcycle taxi drivers.

The trams, flagships of the new era, epitomized the contingency of this urban transformation and the contradictions that besieged it. When, in 1893, the Siam Electricity Company (founded by two Danish businessmen) acquired and electrified the failing horse-drawn tram, citizens responded less than enthusiastically. Initially, the marvel and terror of electricity nearly brought the tram's operations to bankruptcy. Faced with diffused fear of electrocution,[36] strengthened by two such accidents within the first days of operation, Siam Electricity decided to offer tram rides free of charge for the first four months to attract customers and get them accustomed to the new system. The strategy was successful, and after a few months the company started ferrying more and more paying customers. Bangkokians, however, remained wary of the *siwilai* nature of the trams, and nicknamed the new cars after one of their not-so-civilized characteristics. Formally named "cars on rail" (*rot rang*), the tram became known in the streets as "smelly cars" (*rot ai*), a moniker of the experience, introduced by mass transportation, of being packed with strangers inside a steamy box in the tropical heat. Aside from its odors, the tram regularly faced setbacks, electricity shortages, and accidents that forced riders back to the canals and water-based transportation in order to move through Bangkok. Not all of the tram stoppages, however, were due to infrastructural failures or accidents. Occasionally they were the result of political mobilizations that, rather than sending passengers back to Bangkok's past as an aquatic city, envisioned a new future for the Thai capital, one in which internal migrants manned its labor force. A prolonged strike of tram workers in 1923—the first labor mobilization in the history of Siam—offered one such occurrence and a glimpse into the emergence of a politicized Thai urban working class, a class that would come to dominate informal economies of Bangkok and, sixty years later, drive motorcycle taxis.

The 1923 strike was the result of mounting tensions among the trams' European administration, its Chinese middlemen, and Thai low-level workers. In mid-December 1922, Hui, a Chinese foreman, sacked a Thai tram worker. His fellow Thai employees appealed to the Danish owners of Siam

36. Brian Larkin has called this relation "the colonial sublime" (Larkin 2008).

Electricity, arguing that the worker had been fired without reasonable cause. When the owners backed Hui's decision, Thai newspapers reported the Chinese executive saying to his Danish superior: "Sir, you should not take care of Thai workers since they are just like a bunch of dogs, running back to our company after hearing the knocking of coconut shells with dog food."[37] These words, whether really uttered or not, sparked the largest workers' mobilization in Siam and escalated the already palpable tension between Thai and Chinese workers.

Anti-Chinese sentiments had been mounting in the country since the early twentieth century and had been most famously voiced in 1914 by King Vajiravudh (Rama VI) in one of the many editorials he published in the thriving popular press of early twentieth-century Siam titled the "The Jews of the Orient." In this article the king—under the pseudonym of Asavabahu—responded to the mounting European and North American discourse of the "Yellow Peril,"[38] stressing the difference between Siamese and Chinese. He referred to all Chinese people, regardless of how long they had lived in Siam, as "aliens by birth, by nature, by sympathy, by language, and finally by choice, ... utterly without morals, conscience, mercy, pity. [A population that] where money is concerned, ... like chameleon, change their color to suit their surroundings."[39] Adopting an anti-Semitic repertoire familiar to European publics, the king cast the Chinese population as untrustworthy and devoid of any national loyalty—in short, a potential threat to the Siamese nation that should be monitored and kept under control. When 122 Thai tram-workers went on strike on December 31, 1922, they adopted xenophobic language to oppose the Chinese domination of the city's labor market.

The workers gathered in front of Siam Electricity offices to demand fair wages, a clear set of rules to govern their working activities, as well as the removal of Hui, his assistant Phin, and Ericson, the Danish traffic manager, for cruel and exploitative practices. Faced with the company's refusal to accept their conditions, they brought their demands to the minister of the

37. Brown and Hewison 2004, 23. On the use of animal epithets in Thailand see Tambiah 1973.

38. The discourse of the Yellow Peril originated in the late nineteenth century with the migration of Chinese population to Europe and the United States. The term was used to express the fear that the mass immigration of Asians threatened white wages and standards of living and that they would eventually take over and destroy western civilization, their ways of life and values.

39. Vajiravudh 1914.

interior, hoping that a fellow Thai would listen to their complaints. The minister agreed to negotiate with Siam Electricity and the workers went back to the company. To their disappointment none of the demands were met. On January 13, 1923, the workers went back on strike, for the third time in a month. This time three hundred workers, about 90 percent of the company's employees, joined the protest. The minister, worried about his popularity, attempted once again to calm them by adopting the same nationalist discourse that the strikers had used. One of his aids, Phraya Phetphani, addressed the strikers, declaring that "the Minister wishes it to be known that he is a real Thai, as are [you] workers. Therefore the Minister fully intends to help you to the best of his ability and he will not show any favoritism to foreigners."[40] Unimpressed by the minister's empty message, the tram workers refused to return to work.

In the following days, the struggle turned violent. Groups of hooligans and boxers were recruited by the Danish owners to break the strike. On the other side of the picket line, the workers who did not strike faced violent attacks and accusations of being anti-Siamese and supporting Chinese domination. As Siam Electricity continued to ignore the workers' demands and hire scabs, the attacks on trams intensified. Beatings and bombings replaced bad odors and electrocutions as concrete risks of a tram ride. By the end of January 1923, local newspapers reported that tram service was interrupted by bomb attacks that had damaged multiple tracks, shootings of passengers, and appearances of barricades across the tramlines. Although disruption of service and protests continued until the end of February 1923, the struggle died out by the beginning of March and most of its participants were replaced by new workers.

Aside from the historical importance of this strike for workers' politics in Siam, the language of national belonging, ethnic inequality, and xenophobia revealed a mounting tension around the ethnic composition of Bangkok's labor force in the first decades of the twentieth century, a tension that would eventually push the Siamese government to limit the number of Chinese migrants and foster internal migration from the outer provinces. The strike not only showed the fragility of Bangkok's dreams of *siwilai,* condensed in the tram, but also foreshadowed a different urban future—one populated by a labor force largely composed by Thai internal migrants who would replace the Chinese in the underbelly of the city. The restructuring of the urban

40. Brown 2004, 36.

labor markets, fueled by a nationalist turn in the country's administration, would take three decades to complete. The process would eventually curtail international labor immigration and attract millions of migrants from the Thai hinterland into Bangkok. Their arrival provided the second condition of possibility for the emergence of motorcycle taxis in Bangkok: the availability of a cheap labor force made up of internal migrants for the northern and northeastern provinces.

THAILAND TO THAIS: *CHĀTNIYOM* (NATIONALISM) AND URBAN LABOR FORCE (1932–57)

On June 24, 1939, the Siamese National Assembly, instituted after the deposition of the absolute monarchy in 1932, changed the country's name from Siam to Thailand. This decision was pushed vehemently by then Prime Minister Plaek Phibun Songkhram and his propaganda mastermind Luang Wichit Watthakan. The change was part of a larger Thai-fication of Siam that had been taking place since the 1920s and that accelerated with the fall of the absolute monarchy. Exactly seven years before, on June 24, 1932, a group of civil servants—of which both Phibun and Wichit were prominent members[41]—had staged a bloodless coup that forced King Rama VII to accept a constitution and an elected government. With the formal abolition of absolute monarchy, the country required—as it did four decades earlier with Chulalongkorn's reforms—a new hegemonic discourse to substitute the royal paradigm and its obsession with *siwilai*. Nationalism *(chātniyom)* filled the gap.

Even if nationalist rhetoric had emerged inside royal circles, most notably through the writings of King Vajiravudh,[42] it was not until the demise of absolute monarchy that it became the driving force behind the state's economic and social policies, first under government of Phahon Phonphayuhasena

41. Descendants of Chinese immigrants, the two men had met in Paris, where Luang Wichit was working in the Royal Siamese delegation as well as studying law and political science. Phibun, a young military officer, was also studying in France and was part of group of young Siamese who were later to become the main actors behind the 1932 deposition of the absolute monarchy. Among them, another Chinese descendant figured prominently: a law student named Pridi Banomyong, whose collaboration with, and later opposition to, Phibun would come to dominate Thai politics for the following three decades.

42. In particular, King Vajiravudh had employed a nationalistic discourse against the first attempt to remove him from power in 1912, suggesting that those "rebels" had been directed by the Chinese.

(1933–38) and later, more fully, with the election of Phibun as prime minister in 1938. Soon after becoming prime minister, Phibun instituted a four-person committee headed by Luang Wichit which would promulgate cultural mandates to remove what they saw as "flaws of Siamese society" that hampered the country's progress. Central to this enterprise was a representation of Siam as an ethnically homogenous nation. With this in mind, the first cultural mandate suggested renaming the country Thailand.

The decision to connect the nation to a specific ethnic group—namely the Tai[43]—claimed a direct correspondence between the dominant, but by no means sole, population in Siam and the citizens of the Thai nation. The committee's declared goals were to promote cultural homogenization and to expel perceived outsiders from the national body, united under the slogan "Thailand to the Thais." Highland tribes, southern Malays, and other ethnic minorities were to adapt and adopt Thainess (*khwām pen thai*). Foremost among these were the economically dominant Chinese. Xenophobia and distrust of Thai-Chinese's loyalties, which had colored the 1923 tram strike, reemerged under the government of Phibun and were magnified by an unfortunate international configuration. At a time when Thailand was knitting closer relations with Japan, China was at war with the emerging Asian power. In 1937, following the Japanese invasion of Manchuria, the second Sino-Japanese War broke out. Japanese forces blockaded the main southern Chinese ports in 1938 and Chinese merchants throughout Southeast Asia launched a boycott of Japanese goods. This put the Thai-Chinese population in a tight spot: while as Thai they were allied with Japan, as Chinese descendants they were presumed to be collecting money to finance the war effort and participating in the boycott. In a period of nationalist zeal, their double loyal-

43. As Thongchai Winichakul has argued, "in contemporary Thai, the word that connotes the Tai/Thai ethnicity is spelled in two ways. With exactly the same pronunciation—'thai'—one is spelled with a y at the end and the other without, respectively as 'thaiy' and 'thai'. When spelled 'thaiy' the word denotes the modern nation-state and its citizens, although in its Romanisation as 'Thai(land)', the letter 'y' is dispensed with. When spelled without the y ending, it is a looser term denoting the ethnic peoples whose languages belong to the same Tai/Thai linguistic family. This 'Thai' (without a y ending) includes the Shan of Burma, the Lao people on both sides of the Mekong, and people speaking various Tai/Thai dialects in Thailand today, including the Muang people of former Lanna (Chiang Mai), the Tai Lue, the Tai Maung, the Tai Khoen in the border areas between China, Burma and Laos, the Black and White Tai in Vietnam, and others" (Thongchai 2008a, 576). In the writing of Luang Wichit the two terms were conflated, overlapping ethnicity and citizenship.

ties were considered unacceptable, bordering on treason.[44] Non-Thai ethnic dress and surnames were forbidden, education in languages other than Central Thai prohibited, and the population was encouraged to support Thai products and restrain from buying foreign goods. All of these measures had a direct effect on the Chinese communities that controlled both commerce and labor markets in the capital. Thai-fication of the national economy, and in particular its manual labor, became a central objective of the Thai government. Distinct from other cultural mandates, this objective was supported both by the nationalist prime minister and his socialist alter-ego, Minister of Finance Pridi Banomyong. This unprecedented consensus initiated an enormous shift in the composition of Bangkok's labor markets, away from the hands of Chinese coolies toward Thai bodies.

By the late 1930s, Phibun created national companies and restricted the access of non-Thais to the production and distribution of commodities deemed of national interest, such as petroleum, tobacco, salt, and livestock. Remarkably, among the markets reserved to Thai nationals were taxis and rickshaws, which were rapidly spreading across the city. Until that moment, transportation in Bangkok had been borne by the hands, feet, and shoulders of Chinese coolies. Now the government was resolute in giving control to Thai nationals, where it remains to this day. The proponents of these legislations knew that without changing the attitudes among Thais—who were seen as looking down on manual labor—their interventions would remain only on paper. Again, Luang Wichit stepped in. In a lecture at the Ministry of Defense on November 16, 1939, he credited the widespread disdain of manual labor to a royalist elitism that was a product of Khmer influences and not Thai culture. Luang Wichit called for a human revolution aimed at recognizing work as a source of joy, life, and honor, in an attempt to manufacture the compulsion to work among Thai workers.

Even if this shift in attitudes and policies were sidetracked by the Second World War—in which Thailand first allied with the Axis but was then invaded by the Japanese in December 1941—the idea that Chinese prominence over the Thai economy needed to be limited and their migratory flows

44. Once again, Luang Wichit played a central role in voicing these concerns. In July 1938, during a public lecture at Chulalongkorn University on the Nazi annexation of Austria, Wichit resuscitated the language of Vajiravudh and aligned it to the growing tide of German National Socialism. In his words, the Chinese were worse than the Jews and he suggested that time had arrived for Siam to deal with its own Jews, following the model of German racial campaigns.

controlled, survived the disastrous world conflict. In 1947, during the few months he remained prime minister, Thamrong Navaswadhi took a major policy decision, one too often overlooked in Thai historiography. On May 1, the prime minister signed a decree that established a yearly quota of ten thousand Chinese immigrants. In 1949 the quota was reduced to two hundred people, after decades of Chinese migration to Thailand on the order of millions. The numbers of Chinese migrants to Thailand dropped rapidly, both as a result of the new policy and of Mao's rise to power, which blocked emigration from China. The importance of this change cannot be overstated. In the five decades before 1949, Bangkok had grown from around two hundred thousand people to more than six hundred thousand. Most of this growth was driven by Chinese immigration, which had peaked in the 1920s when 408,100 Chinese citizens had moved to Thailand.[45] The city's roads, shops, and factories were dominated by them. If you were to interact with urban workers in construction, commerce, industry, services, as well as transportation, you would be dealing, in all probability, with first-generation Chinese migrants. In Siam, rural wages had historically been higher than urban wages, making migration from the provinces unattractive for all but members of the regional elite looking for a way into the expanding state bureaucracy.[46] Once Chinese migration was curtailed, businesses in Bangkok started to look for labor inside the national territory. Rural workers, however, had no incentives, necessities, or desires to move to the city. Phibun, who had orchestrated a military coup against his own government on March 1, 1948, set out to solve this problem.

In 1955, the military dictator introduced a new tax that would revolutionize the structure of the Thai economy and its labor markets. The rice premium, a levy on rice exports, was supposed to regulate the internal prices of the main food staple in the country and produce more revenue. Its effects, however, were much deeper and enduring. More than any other measure, this policy reorganized the relation between Bangkok and the Thai countryside. First, rural production was undervalued, forcing many farmers, impoverished by the burden of taxation on their main agricultural product, to move to the city in search of more remunerative occupations. If Luang Wichit's human revolution tried to generate the compulsion to work, the rice premium forced workers into a compulsion to migrate. Once in the city, many of them found urban wages lower than they expected. Wages were calculated in relation to

45. Skinner 1957, 177.
46. Porphant 1998, 98.

the price of reproduction of labor—the cost of surviving in the city in a way that allowed the workers to keep working.. By discouraging exports, the tax de facto cut the price of rice and consequently provided the Thai industrial sector with a cheap work force. At the same time, the money taken from taxing agricultural production was invested in fueling the industrial growth of Bangkok, rather than reinvested in the agricultural areas from where they were collected.[47] The transfer of resources was immense and Thai villages were impoverished to develop Bangkok. An unprecedented quantity of human, agricultural, and economic resources were extracted from rural Thailand and used to finance Bangkok's development. It was this dispossession that kick-started the country's urban boom and forced millions of agricultural workers, who could not cope with the rapidly decreasing economic margins of agricultural activities, to join its labor force.

For the first few decades after the tax was put into effect, most of the migrants arriving in Bangkok were farmers from the central region. That would soon change.[48] Within twenty years, the city was flooded with migrants from the northeastern provinces, traveling down a newly built road network.[49] Their arrival radically shifted the composition of Bangkok's labor force and restructured the social and economic geography of the Thai nation around the capital, transforming the northeastern provinces into a labor reserve for Bangkok. In the decade between the introduction of a quota on Chinese immigration in 1947 and the end of Phibun's dictatorship in 1957, Bangkok's population doubled, from 604,530 to 1,204,894, and the city established its economic primacy over the country. Most of its growth was led by young internal migrants who would

47. Feeny 2003; Parnwell 1996.

48. In 1960, 61 percent of migrants in Bangkok were coming from the central region and only 20 percent from the Northeast. By 1980 northeastern migrants composed more than 50 percent of Bangkok's labor force (Sternstein 1971).

49. These roads, however, were not built with the aim of assisting the transfer of resources, natural and human, from the outer provinces to the city; rather they were put in place with the opposite trajectory in mind. Starting with the Korean War (1950–53), Thailand emerged as the United States' primary ally in a region seen as at the forefront of communist expansion. After the French withdrawal from Indochina in 1954, and the beginning of the Vietnam War, the American presence grew exponentially. Concern over the potential expansion of communist forces into Thailand drove U.S. funds into the country. This economic support materialized, among other things, through a capillary system of roads built to guarantee easy access to areas of potential risk, particularly in the northeastern region. The Friendship Highway, built in 1955 to connect Bangkok to the northeastern city of Korat, was the main infrastructural intervention in the area.

eventually start driving motorcycle taxis. At this time, however, they joined the available, underpaid, and often unspecialized labor force that sustained the booming Thai industrial economy. It was this boom that provided the third condition of possibility for the emergence of motortaxis in Bangkok: affordable motorcycles.

INDUSTRIAL BANGKOK: *PHATTHANĀ* (DEVELOPMENT) AND PRIVATE TRANSPORTATION (1958–80)

On October 20, 1958, Field Marshal Sarit Thanarat led a coup d'état against a military government that he himself had installed just a year before. Sarit, a charming officer born in Bangkok and raised in the northeastern town of Khon Kaen, presented his seizure of power as a revolution. While the previous revolution in 1932 had removed the Siamese absolute monarchy and propelled the country toward what its leaders saw as the modern world of constitutional monarchies, Sarit's revolution was faithful to the astronomical origins of the word and plotted a return to a political system that he saw as more Thai, one in which the monarchy regained its centrality.[50] As Sarit looked to reverse the democratic turn of the 1930s, his revolution faced the same challenges encountered by its predecessors. A new hegemonic discourse was needed to support the emerging political-economic system and make its radical changes acceptable. *Phatthanā,* or development, was the answer. "Our important task in this revolutionary era," Sarit declared in a brief piece he penned in 1960, "is development which includes economic development, educational development, and administrative development."[51] For Sarit, *phatthanā* relied on three principles: economic progress, order, and political obedience. His ideology focused on social and economic progress and dismissed democratization as a foreign influence, inapplicable to Thailand. Nonetheless, much of his economic policies were inspired by international developmentalist states. In particular, the first World Bank economic report on Thailand, which was carried out in 1957, became the blueprint for Sarit's boost to industrial development through private investments, rather than through state investment as it had been the case under Phibun.

50. Thak 2007, 92.
51. Ibid., 151.

Under the newly created NEBD (National Economic Development Board), later renamed NESDB (National Economic and Social Development Board), the first national plan came into action in 1961, supported by money and expertise from the United States as part of their increased imperialist and anticommunist interventions in the region.[52] The objectives of the plan were double: upgrading national infrastructure—roads, water, and electricity—and promoting private industrial development. Sarit's government, following the advice of the World Bank, focused state investments on infrastructural development while leaving manufacturing to private capital, domestic or foreign.[53] In order to attract such capital, new economic incentives were introduced to subsidize industries considered essential for the national economy—including the automotive sector—and labor markets were deregulated. Four decades of labor organizing, which had started with a tram workers' strike in January 1923, were erased overnight.

The new direction introduced by Sarit continued to dominate Thailand well after his death in 1963. Between 1960 and 1972, foreign investment in industry amounted to 32 percent of the total registered capital. Among them Japan was the largest investor, accounting for 38 percent of the total, followed by Taiwan (16 percent) and the United States (14 percent).[54] The emerging local automotive industry attracted a significant percentage of these direct investments, particularly from Japan. In the years following the first national plan, the major international automobile manufacturers began opening production lines in Thailand. Nissan Motors paved the way in 1962, followed by Toyota Motors (1963), Honda Motors (1964), Ford Motor Company (1970), and General Motors (1972). Together, they slowly transformed the industrial outskirts of Bangkok into what came to be known as the Detroit of Asia. Inside the automotive industry, motorcycles played a central role. In 1966, the first motorcycle assembled in Thailand came out of the newly opened Siam Yamaha factory. Two years later, Honda—which soon came to dominate the Thai market—opened its first out-of-Japan motorcycle production line in the

---

52. In the period between 1962 and 1970, under the umbrella of USOM (United States Operation Mission), American funds to Thailand averaged 14.2 billion baht a year, roughly 12 percent of the total national earning from exports. Not only money, however, was offered to Thailand. Engineers, security experts, military personnel, agricultural and irrigation experts, urban planners: a whole transfer of expertise supported the alliance between the two nations.

53. Suehiro 1989.

54. Ibid., 187.

outskirts of Bangkok, in one of the many industrial developments funded with tax revenues from the rice premium. The two other main Japanese motorcycle producers, Suzuki and Kawasaki, followed the lead and opened factories in 1968 and 1976.

Over this decade, cheap locally assembled motorcycles spread rapidly. The opening up of village economies, out-migration, and the growth of disposable income contributed to the diffusion of motorcycles. In particular, when the 1973 economic crisis drove up the global price of oil and Thailand's inflation, motorcycles, with good fuel economy and affordable purchase prices, became an attractive option for the country's mobility needs. The industry grew by a steady 30 percent a year in the mid-1970s and motorbikes became the preferred mode of transportation and status symbol for a new class of seasonal rural migrants who complemented their agricultural income with migration to the city. When Sarit first seized power in 1957, Thailand had 1,617 motorcycles—owned by elite families and imported mostly from the United Kingdom. By 1981, the number of motorcycles had skyrocketed to 307,168, of which 99 percent were produced domestically. The great majority of these motorbikes were not in Bangkok but rather in the Thai countryside, where unpaved streets and limited income made them the only viable means of transportation. It was on those muddy roads that many of the migrants who would become drivers learned to ride a bike.

If in regional centers and villages the era of *phatthanā* was experienced atop a bike, cars driven by the growing urban middle classes crowded the streets of Bangkok, under the pressure of a new urban model that had traveled from the United States, together with funds, expertise, and urban planning techniques. In 1958, the USOM (United States Operation Mission) had sent a group of urban planners from MIT to Thailand to devise the first master plan for its rapidly expanding capital. After an extensive study of Bangkok's urban infrastructure, economy, and everyday life, in 1960 the group presented to the Thai government a final document—the Greater Bangkok Plan 1990. The plan, even though never officially ratified, provided a framework for the development of Bangkok over the next three decades. Its main contribution was the transformation of the Thai capital into a car-based city, a model most famously realized in Los Angeles. Two main proposals, consistent with dominant principles of modernist urban planning,[55] emerged from this document: building new highways to connect the central business dis-

55. Holston 1989.

trict directly to outer ring roads and introducing zoning practices to allocate different areas of the city to different functions—commercial, industrial, and residential. Both proposals demanded a departure from the urban structures and practices that had dominated Bangkok since the reign of Chulalongkorn. Once again, this new vision presented itself as a rupture which would erase the previous layers of the city to make space for itself.

Bangkok became a laboratory for the implementation of state hegemony. While Parisian boulevards and European-style public transportation—such as buses and trams—had shaped *siwilai* Bangkok between the 1890s and 1960s, the new *phatthanā* city was to be dominated by American-style high-speed highways and private transportation. Canals, which had played a secondary yet important role in the previous amphibious urbanism, were filled in to make space for new roads. The unruly urban flows were once again to be concentrated and controlled, this time into individualized vehicles. Similarly, the landscapes through which these flows occurred were to be divided and reorganized to make space for a new, top-down order. Residential, commercial, and industrial spaces, which had previously mixed, would be disentangled. In the plan, commercial areas would remain in the city center, residential districts would move beyond them, and industrial production would be segregated to the urban periphery.

As had happened with Chulalongkorn's *siwilai* city, the grand plans, if coherent and definitive on paper, crashed against the messiness of everyday life and the fragmented state apparatus that was supposed to implement them. The dream of rewriting the city looked, in practice, more like a confused entanglement of scribbles than a tidy overlay. Flows remained fractured and unruly, landscapes entangled and mixed. The master plan was only partially adopted and large portions of its implementation were left to private developers who only followed through on selected measures and left other aspects untouched.[56]

56. An example of this piecemeal implementation was the construction of shop-houses, which had dominated Bangkok in the previous century and represented the epitome of mixed use. These structures became less omnipresent in the city and were often replaced by concrete residential buildings, increasingly taller and spread out. Yet they did not entirely disappear. New shop-houses continued, and continue today, to be built in the center of the city and in its newly formed suburbs, displacing the suburban dreams and zoning principles that American planners had introduced to Bangkok in the 1960s. Similarly, the dream of moving the city through private means remained unfulfilled. As Bangkok sprawled, investment in buses was cut to the bone. For two decades, no new routes were added, and in that same period, other forms of public transportation were eliminated—rickshaws were banned in 1960, tramways in 1968. However, their presence—or rather their absence—remained

In particular, where the master plan had imagined large investments to create a grid-like road network, private investors mostly developed secondary roads by filling in existing canals. The very name of the new roads—*soi*—had been previously used to refer to small waterways. If the names of the new roads hinted at Bangkok's aquatic past, natural forces cyclically threw the city back into it. Floods, in particular, marked the history of the Thai capital and provided, and still provide today, a reminder of Bangkok's complex relation with its previous life as an aquatic city, submerging the streets of the Thai capital and inundating decades of land-based development. As a result, the traces of Bangkok's past aquatic life shaped, challenged, and often impinged upon the dream of *phatthanā* Bangkok. Those traces shaped the final conditions of possibility for the emergence of motorcycle taxis in Bangkok: a maze of disconnected and narrow *soi* that made motorcycle taxis indispensable for public transportation in the city.

The *soi* urban structure was the result of leaving urban development in the hands of private investors without regulating their activities. Land development, which had been directed by the Crown Property Bureau (CPB) and the Ministry of Public Works, emerged in the mid-1960s as a viable opportunity for private enterprises to turn a profit. Developers started to buy large portions of land, mostly on the outskirts of the city, and to transform them into residential plots. This urbanization of rural land proceeded according to a familiar script. First, the developers acquired the plot either from private landowners or from the public administration and carried out essential land and drainage improvements. Second, basic infrastructure such as roads, water lines, electricity, and sewage systems were put in place, at their expense. Finally, the land developers divided the area into smaller plots to be sold to housing developers or directly contracted to house builders. Once the construction was completed, the houses would be sold to individual buyers.[57]

While the reliance on private investors saved the Thai government heavy investments in road and land improvement, it also left developers free to

---

engrained both in the collective memory and in the material features of the city. Not only did the nostalgic remembrances of the trams' quiet pace and whistling sounds survive, but the very tracks on which the carriages ran remained—and still remain today—mounted on the road surface, reminders of a previous layer of the urban palimpsest. As every driver in Bangkok knows, these tracks still groove the road pavement and disrupt the smooth flow of new private means of transportation, causing drivers to slightly swerve their cars and motorcyclists to incur more serious accidents, reminders of the previous layers.

57. Durand-Lasserve 1980, 2.

maximize the amount of land transformed into housing, which they could sell, and minimize the amount of space and money allocated to infrastructure. As a result, the city grew and to this day it remains without any centralized service: no citywide sewage system, no gas grid, and no functional street network. Road surfaces in particular suffered greatly from this mode of financing. They, as the only portion of land that developers could not sell, were kept to a minimum and often obtained by filling preexisting small canals. These long, narrow, and often dead-end waterways, which were part of the agricultural land purchased, provided the basis for the secondary road system of contemporary Bangkok and created bottlenecks once they connected to larger thoroughfares. This *soi* system, spreading out like slender branches into the agricultural landscape without connecting one to the other, followed a different logic from roads in comparable car-based cities, more fit for boats than for cars and buses. Once again, previous layers of the urban palimpsest lingered into its present, haunting and orienting its future.

Inside this scant and disconnected road network, the number of vehicles in Bangkok grew rapidly. Traffic jams became a symbol of life in the Thai capital and called into question the dream of the efficient and smoothly developed city. Against the backdrop of this dream, the reality of Bangkok's circulatory system was a bundle of a functional web of elevated highways and giant multilane streets that clashed with the confusing and dysfunctional maze of long, narrow, and often dead-end *soi*. It was this convoluted network of roads that created the excruciating traffic jams that set the scene for the diffusion of motorcycle taxis in the early 1980s. By that time, all the conditions of possibility of their emergence were in place: government officials able to use of their state authority to control and operate businesses in a gray legal area the dominated the streets of the clogged city; millions of rural migrants who flooded Bangkok looking for jobs; affordable motorcycles which spread in the 1970s in the Thai countryside and offered the only viable mode of transportation inside the growing traffic jams; and finally, a dysfunctional road system that had become impervious to cars and buses and blocked the city's arteries.

A SOLUTION TO TRAFFIC: MOTORCYCLE TAXIS

In the era of *phatthanā*, Bangkok boomed both geographically and economically. Its area almost tripled from 125 square kilometers in 1955 to 330 square kilometers in 1981. The urban population expanded even faster, rocketing from just over a million in 1957 to over five million in 1981, owing to increased birth rates, life expectancy, and internal migration. By the early 1980s, more than 50 percent of the migrants who were flowing into the Thai capital came from the northeast regions. In 1983, when the first newspaper article reporting on motorcycle taxis came out, 11 percent of the nation's population lived in Bangkok. The capital now housed a population fifty-five times larger than that of Chiang Mai—the second biggest city in the country. Seventy-five percent of the nation's phones were in Bangkok, 32 percent of its GDP was produced in this area, and 61 percent of the national electricity consumed here. More than 50 percent of country's motor vehicles were in the capital, with more than four hundred thousand motorcycles and around a million cars. In this period, Bangkok emerged beyond doubt as the heart of the Thai nation pumping human, agricultural, and economic resources out of the countryside, an heart threatened by traffic increasingly clogging its arteries.

By the late 1970s, Bangkok had risen to global infamy as a traffic disaster. The small *soi* operated as bottlenecks for traffic along larger roads. Private cars lined up in long winding queues at the entrance of these alleys. Buses and vans often did not even fit into the *soi,* which could hardly accommodate two cars traveling in different directions. Hours and hours were lost every day walking along these long roads to reach a bus stop or waiting in a queue of cars and buses. Millions of dollars were poured into foreign consultancies to create reports titled "Traffic Disaster" and "Bangkok Chaos" which continued to propose solutions that the Thai government was unwilling to implement. It was in these gridlocks, which came to characterize life in Bangkok, that the contradictions and contingencies of the new order imagined in the era of *phatthanā* were most evident. As public transport remained hindered by a lack of investment, the elimination of trams and rickshaws, and the impenetrable *soi* system, local government struggled to find a solution for the everyday mobility of a city with the highest car ownership per capita and the lowest road pavement per car in Asia.[58] By the early 1980s, in the confused palimpsest of Bangkok, traffic had become unbearable. Out of necessity, a response started to emerge: a new informal solution that allowed people to cut through the traffic jams characteristic of life in Bangkok, to move, like water had once done, by finding gaps and rivulets in the midst of traffic. This solution was motorcycle taxis.

58. Between 1961 and 1967 the population of Bangkok grew by 40 percent, the number of vehicles by 125 percent, while the road surface only extended by 5.4 percent (Sternstein 1971, 214).

TWO

The Dangers of Mobility

> Cities are characterized by incessantly flexible, mobile, and pro-
> visional intersections of residents that operate without clearly
> delineated notions of how the city is to be inhabited and used.
> These intersections . . . have depended on the ability of residents
> to engage complex combinations of objects, spaces, persons, and
> practices. These conjunctions become an infrastructure—a plat-
> form providing for and reproducing life in the city.
>
> ABDOUMALIQ SIMONE, *"People as Infrastructure"*

BANGKOK SEEN FROM ABOVE RESEMBLES an octopus, scarred on its
left side by the sinuous bends of the Chao Praya River and squeezed in the
middle, with its tentacles distending sideways. From the central shopping
and leisure district that clumps around Siam Square, where the city's elevated
railway lines cross, large multilane roads spread radially, reaching deep into
the hinterland. Zooming in, the tentacles start to break off and contort into
cramped and convoluted patterns. Long boulevards wriggle into a maze of
small roads; roundabouts and radial streets narrow into slender *soi* that
branch out and writhe in the space between them. The result is a confusing
mesh of roads that coil and entwine, reaching out to one another and then
suddenly stopping a few meters before connecting, interrupted by buildings,
gardens, and parking lots. This infuriating topography reveals the doomed
audacity of multiple attempts to plan, organize, and impose order over
Bangkok's organic and unruly expansion.

A crossroads since its origin, the city still preserves the thrown-together
feeling of a harbor, even if its central areas are now far away from water. The
land zoning and spatial segregation typical of European and American cities
never took over the Thai capital. Along the convoluted and narrow *soi*, architectural structures mix according to complex histories of booms and busts that
left untamed shrubs next to upscale residences, crumbling shop-houses beside
international shopping malls, small slums in the shadows of skyscrapers.
Behind the Princess Palace and the elevated square of one of Bangkok's most

glamorous shopping malls—Siam Paragon—two small slums survive, next to condominiums and small garment factories.[1] From there, a six-lane street overshadowed by the concrete rail of Bangkok's Skytrain connects the commercial core of the city to its financial district, extending along Silom and Sathorn Roads. Even in this area, where land reaches prices comparable to New York or London and new skyscrapers constantly pop up, dilapidated apartment buildings covered with rusty grating overlook low-rise villas with vistas on fake Greek and Roman sculptures. Moving further away from the center, shophouses modeled after their Singaporean counterparts mix with neoclassic neighborhoods where the nouveaux riches live. Decrepit wooden houses on stilts mold away in the shadow of glassy skyscrapers and single-family homes dressed up as Gothic churches. Buddhist temples sit next to Dutch-looking palaces that provide all the pleasures of the red-light district of Amsterdam. Small mosques on sleepy canals and half-empty Portuguese churches doze beside bustling shopping centers, Chinese shrines, Hindu temples, and massage parlors. At the edges of the city, crossed by lonely but busy highways, a few enormous mosques, financed with money from the Gulf, pepper upscale residential complexes that mimic the architecture of major international metropolises. The compounds carry the names of their inspirations: London, Paris, all the way to the Grand Canal, a Venetian-themed neighborhood that screams Las Vegas more than Bangkok. As the city dissipates, these gated communities morph into giant industrial estates, unfinished townhouses abandoned after the 1997 economic crisis, lush waterways, and swampy rice fields.

In the morning Bangkok wakes up from there, the octopus reviving from the tips of its tentacles. Workers and their children flow into the city, where most of them work but cannot afford to live. Small vans, collective taxis, and buses ferry them through the maze of radial roads and branching streets, all the way to their workplaces. Those who can afford it ride taxis or their own personal cars to the mass transit terminus and continue their commutes inside air-conditioned trains, either through the elevated urban corridors that cut the business district or below ground, on the two subway lines. People living along the few remaining navigable canals jump on slim longboats and endure the pungent smell of the waterways in exchange for bypassing traffic. Even if the city provides transportation to different locations, wallets, and urgencies, motorcycle taxi drivers alone are able to reach deep into the maze of *soi* where most of Bangkok's city dwellers reside.

1. Ünaldi 2014a.

Every day at street corners, transportation hubs, parking lots, and housing complexes all around Bangkok, two hundred thousand of these drivers, for the most part young men from rural areas, travel an estimated four to five million trips, more than ten times the number of trips traveled by Bangkok's subway and elevated Skytrain combined.[2] Without significant state investments, legal support, or a formalized organization, motorcycle taxi drivers have become indispensable to the city. Day after day, hour after hour, trip after trip, they connect the threads that weave together the urban territory, its daily activities, and its dwellers. Through their trajectories the city is ceaselessly produced and held together, consolidated both as a concrete and an imagined entity: an economic and social machine.

The following pages are an attempt to understand the drivers' role in this process as urban infrastructure and as producers of the channels through which the city moves. To explore how they weave Bangkok together, I move away from the logic of the urban historian, interested in layering, toward that of the drivers, less concerned with origins and more attuned to the modalities of navigating gaps and finding passages in those layers. Their channel-making labor requires the drivers to adjust and synchronize to the multiple rhythms of nature, urban capitalism, and city life, rather than consciously attending to the historical transformations they themselves are a part of. Bangkok, in fact, is not only the product of epochal processes of construction, destruction, and layering but also of continuous assembling and reassembling, through the actions of a variety of networks and actors. The drivers are pivotal to this everyday production: they weave the city together as they strive to move their own lives along the channels they create. Sometimes they succeed and set their own futures in motion. Others they do not and find themselves stuck and exhausted at the side of the road, ready for their last ride, all the way back to small cramped rooms in the urban periphery. It is in one of these rooms that this story begins.

WEAVING BANGKOK

It is Friday night. Wud sleeps next to me on a thin mattress thrown on the concrete floor of a damp shack on the eastern side of Bangkok, across the

2. These numbers are an estimation generated by the author in collaboration with the Association of Motorcycle Taxis of Thailand.

river from the central business district and his motortaxi station. Only the static noise of his minifridge and the occasional barking dog down the road pierce the silence. A small alarm clock plastered with a sticker of the United Front for Democracy against Dictatorship (UDD)—a political group protesting the government of Prime Minister Abhisit Vejjajiva—reflects the time on the floor. I grope for my glasses: 3:49. Next to me Wud snores soundly, taking advantage of the few hours of sleep that his work as a motorcycle taxi driver allows. A few objects adorn the musty walls: a poster of Carabao, a country music band that narrates the stories of migrants like him,[3] a small radio, a water heater, a few boxes of instant noodles, and a couple of protective amulets that he respectfully takes off every night and hangs on a solitary nail sticking out of the wall. In a few minutes the alarm will go off and, as every morning, Wud will wake up, run across the tiny courtyard into the small toilet in front of his room, and shower, scooping buckets of cold water from a big cement tub. Back in the room he will put on a mentholated powder to fight the daily sweat and get dressed, before walking silently out of the small courtyard, a big leather saddle bag on his shoulder, to jump on his bike.

BEEP BEEP BEEP ... BEEP BEEP BEEP ... the alarm goes off.

The scene plays out, but Wud does not kick-start his bike in the *soi*. We walk our bikes out of the alley so as not to wake his sister and her family in the house next to his shack. From there we drive into the quiet night. A few people sit in the street, placidly enjoying their last drink, next to a street vendor who prepares northeastern food for a couple of aging sex workers courted by a taxi driver, bathed in sulfurous street lights. In a few minutes we are merging onto a major highway, our heads tucked down to fight the chill of the night while we speed toward the other side of the city where Wud works, next to Bangkok's financial center. Before crossing the river, as he does every weekday morning, Wud turns in to an industrial area. Here the day is already fully in operation: sounds of machinery and diesel trucks drone over the rattle of our bikes. We stop in front of a large iron door that opens into a depot. The shop floor is raised to facilitate the movement of big loads directly from and into delivery trucks. Wafting over from the back, the smell of ink and the rhythmic sound of cylinder printing machines fills the warehouse.

3. Carabao is a popular rock band in Thailand. Their name means "buffalo" in Tagalog and was chosen by the band members while they studied in the Philippines to refer both to the hard working and patient animal and to the insult people in Bangkok use to refer to migrants from the countryside.

An older man drops a bundle of newspapers into Wud's arms, silently going through the motions that he repeats every morning. Wud sticks them into the saddlebags that hang across his bike and leaves behind the din of mechanical production, returning to the quiet of the predawn city.

We ride across the Chao Praya River over Taksin Bridge and enter the nearly empty streets of Bangkok's financial district, heading toward Silom Road, one of the few streets still crowded at this time of the night. During the day, the road offers a scene nearly indistinguishable from any other global business district: office workers frantically going in and out of work, vendors on the street, international shopping malls and subway stops. Late at night, however, the area reveals its peculiar—and some would say fitting—double life as a prostitution hub. Off the main road, the alleys of Patpong and Thanniya teem with cheap T-shirts, clothes, and fake watches. Behind them, the heavy doors of massage parlors and pole-dancing clubs open onto scores of half-naked bodies dancing in heavily air-conditioned rooms to the beat of loud music, surrounded, watched, and often groped by drunken western and Japanese men. Wud stops at a motortaxi group outside one of these alleys, where the drivers continue to ferry a regular flow of clients. He greets Pon, a young driver from his village, and we sit down to eat a bowl of noodle soup, glittering with the purple reflection of a giant neon sign of a club called Super PUSSY. Pon, who has just visited their village, fills us in with news from their hometown: weddings, deaths, and the construction of new houses. As we take our leave, Wud agrees to call him the next time goes back home and bring back a jar of fermented fish, a delicacy from their native northeastern region.

As we drive away, the music dissipates quickly. We ride through back roads and parking lots, against the direction of traffic and across four-lane roads, following a mental map that Wud activates every day, a sequence of landmarks that he has internalized but that means almost nothing to anyone but him. At every stop he pulls out a small stack of magazines to leave on shops' doorsteps before driving to the next one, in a regular sequence. As soon as the sun comes up, Wud stops to put on a balaclava to protect his skin from tanning, a small sacrifice to the altar of urban living. "I already have dark skin," he tells me with a mix of irony and affliction. "No matter what I do I look like a *khon bānnǫk* [redneck]. I always look like I work in the field. Women do not like that. It may work with *farang* [white foreigners] women.[4] They like dark people, but I cannot speak English so I am left with Thais, and

---

4. *Farang* is the word used to refer to foreigners, particularly Caucasians.

we Thais, we prefer white skin." With the sun up, racial, class, and regional biases emerge through skin care and sun exposure.[5]

In the meantime, the city around us awakens. Vendors push lonely carts to street corners, the first buses start to move, and more cars fill the streets. Continuing along Wud's path, we deposit the last bundle of magazines and head finally to his station in a *soi* off Sathorn Road. On the way we stop at one of the more than three thousand 7-Eleven shops in Bangkok, for the first of many energy drinks that keep Wud awake and alert during his interminable days of work. "When I worked in construction it was methamphetamines," Wud remembers. "The boss used to put it in the water we were given to drink. All of us, we worked high, we never stopped working. You feel like you have boundless energy, until you come back home and your whole body hurts." Although nowadays no one is drugging drivers like Wud, a system of exploitation, operating primarily on their *bānnǭk* bodies, still structures their lives in the city and leaves them exhausted at the end of the day, with just a few hundred baht in their pockets.

By the time we reach Wud's station—a few meters of road pavement confined by two crash barriers where drivers park their bikes at an angle—his colleagues are starting to arrive from their cramped apartments in the urban periphery to which they have been displaced by growing land prices and sprouting condos. Each of them arrives, parks his bike, and stares around for his first client as the street, drowsily, reanimates. Around us food vendors set up their carts, light the grills, and pack their products into one-portion plastic bundles, greeting each other with mellow morning voices, almost covered by the crackling of charcoal. Once the street economy is set up, the store economy gets ready. Shopkeepers hoist up their roller shutters, office buildings open their glass doors, the small school down the road unlocks its gates. Suddenly the rhythm of the city picks up and thousands of vehicles enter the scene, as if on cue, with their regular roar and acrid smell. In the concert that repeats every day, buses are the percussion, their failing engines grumbling along traffic and occasionally bursting into a hit of bass drum. Private cars, taking up most of the road pavement and the soundscape, provide the wind instruments, with their harmonic and hypnotic progression. Finally, motorbikes, darting through traffic, take the role of the strings, creaking and vibrating as they swerve through the other vehicles

5. This complex politics of skin color is marked in Thailand by ethnic and class belonging. Whiter skin, in fact, besides pointing to Chinese origins also indexes a life of privilege away from the rice fields. For this reason, skin whiteners are very popular cosmetics in the country, advertised by famous actors or models.

and bringing the ensemble together, one trip at a time, allowing the city to move, commodities to circulate, and urban dwellers to reach their destinations.

Wud's newspaper delivery provides a remarkable entry point into the drivers' roles in creating and sustaining the channels through which the Thai urban and national communities are constituted, consolidated, and preserved. Newspapers, as Benedict Anderson famously argued, play a central role in the creation of the imagined community that is pivotal for the operations of modern nation-states.[6] Every day, as citizens engage in the simultaneous mass ceremony of reading the news, these national communities are rooted in everyday practices.[7] While scholars of nationalism agree on the role of print capitalism in the creation of a unified national community, few have directed their attention to the people who allow the circulation of its products and to the work they perform to keep them moving. People like Wud, in fact, do not just participate in the imagined community; they also sustain the channels through which such imagination occurs. It is through their labor, along with that of other workers, that newspapers circulate across the urban and national landscape and are made available for daily consumption, allowing the maintenance of a unified national community.

The same is true for the entity called Bangkok, a community that needs an equal leap of imagination to scale up from the limited spaces any urban dweller experiences to the totality of an ever-expanding city. Every morning, at a similar time, millions of people wake up, get dressed, leave their home, and begin to move, work, discuss, shop, and act in ways that make them feel part of this larger urban community. In so doing, they adopt a variety of comportments and rituals—from skincare to sneakers, from food to modes of transportation—which turns them into urban citizens while creating and consolidating the imagined community they recognize as Bangkok.

Wud is among them and, as other drivers, he occupies an often invisible yet crucial position as a producer, mediator, and gatekeeper of the channels

6. Anderson 1983, 36.
7. As he showed, newspapers "create this extraordinary mass ceremony . . . the significance of [which] is paradoxical. It is performed in silent privacy, in the lair of the skull. Yet each communicant is well aware that the ceremony he performs is being replicated simultaneously by thousands (or millions) of others of whose existence he is confident, yet of whose identity he has not the slightest notion. . . . At the same time, the newspaper reader, observing exact replicas of his own paper being consumed by his subway, barbershop, or residential neighbors, is continually reassured that the imagined world is visibly rooted in everyday life. [It] seeps quietly and continuously into reality, creating that remarkable confidence of community in anonymity which is the hallmark of modem nations" (ibid., 36).

through which people, commodities, and ideas travel around the city. After quietly performing his newspaper round, Wud heads back to his station and starts ferrying clients, documents, and other commodities, creating multiple channels through which the city, its dwellers, and economic flows circulate.[8] Without people like him the city would come to a halt. Letters and documents would stop being delivered and people would remain helplessly stuck in traffic. In this sense, the drivers perform essential forms of labor for the city, not just as service workers, transportation providers, and messengers, but also as *phatic labor,* workers who produce "communicative channels that can transmit not only language but also all kinds of semiotic meaning and economic value."[9] The concept of phatic labor, proposed by Julia Elyachar, builds on an early observation in anthropology. In 1914, a young scholar named Bronislaw Malinowski was given the chance to travel to New Guinea from his home institution, the London School of Economics. On the way there, Malinowski, an Austrian subject, got caught in the First World War. Stopped by British authorities, he was offered two solutions: he could wait out the conflict from a prison in Australia or pitch his tent in the Trobriand Islands, in Melanesia, and stay there. Unsurprisingly, he chose the second option and, stuck in his tropical prison, he *invented* ethnographic fieldwork. During his years in the Trobriands, Malinowski became fascinated, among other things, with the long time the islanders spent in apparently insignificant linguistic interactions, such as polite small talk, salutes, gossiping, and chitchat. Those apparently aimless interactions, he pointed out, actually played a role in creating and sustaining the local community through a *phatic communion,*[10] a unity made by talking.[11]

8. Surely, one could argue that Wud's moving a few newspapers, passengers, and objects is hardly what makes up Bangkok. After all, in such a ponderous and complex assemblage his acts seem too small to matter at all. If his life is significant to the city, that person would say, it is as a pawn in a larger game of mobility, capitalism, and urban politics, a tiny cog in a giant machine. While this view forgets that machines often stop working because of tiny cogs, the critique may be fair if Wud were to be considered only as an individual. He is, however, just one of the two hundred thousand drivers who dart through the city and collectively operate more trips than any other forms of transportation in Bangkok. Their apparently minuscule acts, when considered as an ensemble, assume a different significance.

9. Elyachar 2010, 453.

10. Malinowski 1994, 468. The world *phatic* comes from the Greek *phanai*—to speak, say.

11. Four decades later, the linguist Roman Jakobson—one of the main influences on Levi-Strauss structuralism—used this concept in his theory of communicative functions. One of the six functions he individuated was focused on the preservation of channels of communication, which he called phatic (Jakobson 1962). The humming or nodding that you hear

Exploring the role of women's conversations, trips, and home visits for the success of workshops in Cairo,[12] Julia Elyachar drew together Malinowski's observations with a Marxist analysis of labor and showed how those apparently mundane acts generate channels for economic transactions, political discussions, and physical mobility.[13] Wud's trips, and those of two hundred thousand other drivers, play a similar role: they create and sustain the community of Bangkok through apparently mundane small acts. They weave the threads of the spatial, social, economic, and political entity that people come to imagine as Bangkok, rooting it in everyday life. In so doing, they define what urban life is, what spaces are reachable and unreachable, and mediate the economic and social relations among its dwellers, the urban territory, and a variety of objects. Their phatic labor, with its swerving mobility, provides a functional—yet largely decentralized—infrastructure of transportation and delivery. An infrastructure as forgotten as the electric wires that hang over people's heads or the pipes below their feet, yet as essential to the everyday life of a city that state-run mass transportation has failed to connect either spatially or socially. If at the end of any water infrastructure, however big, there is a tap, then at the end of any transportation system in Bangkok there probably is a motorcycle taxi driver like Wud. What does it mean, however, to see Wud as part of an urban infrastructure?

(IN)VISIBLE URBAN INFRASTRUCTURE

In the last decades, attention to infrastructures has dominated anthropology and social sciences at large.[14] This nascent literature has helped bring to the forefront questions of materiality, technologies, ecologies, nonhuman actors, as well as to uncover the social, economic, and political processes that determine and are determined by infrastructures. As often is the case, however, new intellectual trends tend to follow the law of the instrument: if all you have is

---

and see in classrooms around the world, for instance, accomplish a phatic function. In other words, it tells nothing about the process of signification but rather it marks that the channel of communication is still open and the public is not completely tuned off.

12. Elyachar 2010.

13. Marx 1906, vol. 2.

14. Anand 2011; Carse et al. 2016; Graham 2010; Harvey and Knox 2012, 2015; Jensen and Morita 2015; Kockelman 2013; Larkin 2008, 2013; Latour, Hermant, and Shannon 1998; Morita 2016; Ong and Collier 2005; Rao 2014; Simone 2004.

a hammer, everything looks like a nail. Down this road, every object that enhances human actions becomes an infrastructure: that hammer, its nail, even this very book. To dispel this risk of expanding a definition so widely as to make it insignificant, it is worth pausing a moment to ask what an infrastructure is and why it makes sense to describe motorcycle taxis in Bangkok as one.

Three elements are central to infrastructures. First, an infrastructure is an ever-changing system. It is not just a thing, an object, or even a network, but an assemblage of material, economic, symbolic, legal, political, and technological processes that, by acting as a system, "enable[s]—and disable—particular kinds of actions."[15] Second, the kinds of actions that infrastructures allow or restrain always revolve around circulation. Whether of energy, waste, water, people, commodities, ideas or data, infrastructures, by definition, are below—*infra*—structures and allow those structures to operate and survive by connecting them and moving matter through them. Therefore, infrastructures are not just assemblages, as many scholars have noticed, but are also assembling devices: they create entities through circulation. Third, infrastructures are defined by a complex relationship between visibility and invisibility. A megaproject such as a new high-speed railway or a fiber optic system may be, during its construction, the center of public attention, national pride, or self-congratulatory celebrations, but it will soon become mundane, settle into everyday life, and start performing its work away from the spotlights, only to return to visibility in the case of scandals, ameliorations, or failures. Seen in this light, motorcycle taxis are one of Bangkok's main infrastructures.[16] Both an assemblage and an assembling device, Wud and his colleagues operate as a system that connects the city together and weaves its threads, undergoing moments of high visibility and complete obfuscation. These characteristics are nowhere more evident than in the relations between the drivers and the ultramodern elevated Skytrain, the main public transportation infrastructure in contemporary Bangkok to which Wud delivers most of its clients.

15. Graham and McFarlane 2014, 1.

16. The idea of looking at people as urban infrastructure is not new. Most notably AbdouMaliq Simone has used this concept to analyze the functioning of African cities in which, in his words, state and civil administration lack the political and economic power to manage the city. Their survival, therefore, depends "on the ability of residents to engage complex combinations of objects, spaces, persons, and practices. These conjunctions become an infrastructure—a platform providing for and reproducing life in the city" (Simone 2004, 408).

The Bangkok Transportation System (BTS), commonly known as Skytrain, opened on December 5, 1999, on the king's birthday, after decades of failed attempts to create an elevated train system. The idea of realizing such a network to ease the road traffic had been proposed multiple times but its realization was undermined by an endless string of shady business deals and bankruptcies. This time the project was carried out by a state agency and, using cement acquired from a company owned by the Crown Property Bureau, it enjoyed unprecedented support from the palace as well as from prominent business conglomerates.[17] The elevated tracks would run through the city's business districts, where new shopping malls were mushrooming. According to one of the engineers who designed the Skytrain, the stations' location was decided precisely to connect directly into those shopping malls. During those years, Bangkok was trying to leave behind the economic crisis that brought the city to its knees in 1997. The new, imposing infrastructure was to be the symbol of the renewed metropolis, where well-dressed, white-skinned middle-class clients would travel comfortably to their shopping malls in air-conditioned carriages, above the chaos of street-level traffic where the darker, poorer, and filthier population—such as the motorcycle taxi drivers—lived and thrived.[18]

This plan, as many previous urban interventions had done, splintered as it encountered the reality of life in Bangkok. The elevated train overlaying on the mazelike structure of Bangkok allowed only for a condensed system that ran along major thoroughfares, miles away from where the majority of people lived. Clustered around the central business districts, the Skytrain simply did not tap into these residential areas. The *soi* system that had limited the diffusion of other forms of mass transportation proved just as impermeable to the Skytrain. As a result, the new elevated railway was—at least for the first years of its operation—a failure: an expensive infrastructure that created an urban artery disconnected from its capillaries, never managing to become part of the city's everyday life.

Things started to change when thousands of workers who were laid off after the 1997 crisis joined the ranks of motorcycle taxi drivers. The new movers of Bangkok connected the new artery to a larger circulatory system. Suddenly the flow picked up. Motorcycle taxi stands appeared at each station.

17. Bengtsson 2006; Peeradorn 2007.
18. For a treatment of elevation and hierarchy in the Skytrain see Jenks 2003, and for an analysis of white-washing in Thai urban planners' renderings see Herzfeld 2017.

From there, they operated the final or initial legs of a Skytrain trip, connecting the station to the travelers' homes, workplaces, or offices. Even drivers like Wud, whose group is not close to the Skytrain, end up operating as feeders for the new system, dropping off most of their passengers outside one of its stops. Paradoxically, as the motorcycle became indispensable for the operation of the ultramodern mode of transportation, public opinion and urban planners continued to cast the drivers as remnants of a previous Bangkok, shameful leftovers of a city that the Skytrain and the new shopping malls were supposed to replace.

Wud, who entered this occupation right at that time, never failed to point out this paradox. "People in Bangkok use us every day, they need us to go around or to transport their kids, but look at us like we are bandits or thieves." He tells me as we sit at his station. "Not to me personally, all of my clients are polite. But all the stories on TV or magazines about motorcycle taxis are about how dangerous we are, how we are not good people. But if we are so bad, how is it that they all run to us? Sure some of us drive like crazy, some sell drugs, and some steal, but is it not the same among people of Bangkok? They have their good and bad people, just like us." Whether these views were based on actual events or a widespread bias against rural migrants, the backward and unruly motorcycle taxis proved essential to mass transportation, allowing passengers to reach the station to and from their homes, deep into Bangkok's dysfunctional urban texture. The Bangkok subway, which opened in 2004, learned this the hard way; it started to work well only when motorcycle taxis appeared at its stations. Mindful of these experiences, the State Railway of Thailand (SRT) contacted motorcycle taxi drivers even before opening their Airport Link in 2010 to make sure no initial inconvenience would limit access to the new line. They had realized, in other words, that the *modern* infrastructures needed the *backward* drivers to attract its middle-class passengers and operate a far-reaching system. It simply could not function without them.

Their highly formalized, untaxed, and diffused infrastructure supports the functioning of state-run multimillion dollar projects, defying clear-cut distinctions between formal and informal economies and questioning its usefulness. More broadly, it reveals the drivers' function as an infrastructure with a systemic internal organization, a central role in fostering urban circulation, and a complex relationship with visibility. Most of the time, this infrastructure operates invisibly, at least as long as the drivers continue to deliver people and commodities. On few occasions in recent decades, however, it attracted popular attentions, particularly when the system first emerged in Bangkok in the 1980s, when it saved the Skytrain from bankruptcy in the late 1990s and when it became the field for a political and economic struggle over the profits coming from the street economy in the mid-2000s.[19] By the time I began my research, however, those moments had past and the drivers had settled into the inglorious life of infrastructures, basic and essential to our lives yet taken for granted. As a result, people like Wud quietly blended into the urban background.

Their invisibility operated on multiple levels. Spatially, they were stationed in dead areas between buildings or next to Skytrain ramps, bus stations, or boat piers. Socially, as young migrants who are often registered residents of their villages, they remained invisible to the statistical eye of the state and to Bangkok' municipal administration, which since the 1990s had stopped investigating their operations or attempting to resolve their legal status. Politically, many of the drivers retained their housing registration in their home villages and therefore they did not even appear as an electoral constituency in the city. Economically, as self-employed service workers with murky legal status, they operated mostly unnoticed by tax collectors and cut off from social provisions. Finally, as a diffused system of transportation, they remained largely invisible to urban planners, scholars, and city dwellers who rarely reflect on the work that the drivers perform in connecting and mediating the city until they fail to perform it, get into a road accident, or keep enraged passengers waiting for them at an empty station.[20]

Seeing the drivers in this light, one is tempted to say that they remain invisible as long as they carry out their work proficiently and become visible

19. This particular moment and its significance for the drivers' collective action are explored in chapter 5.

20. This invisibility has been a characteristic of workers in capitalist cities across the globe. As more and more people became flexible, new forms of invisibility emerged based on the destruction of daily routines. As Giuliana Commisso has argued, this shift has brought the destruction of "the urban geography of the city-dormitory, of the city-barracks, in which compact masses and uniform individuals move according to predefined runs, rhythms and times regulated by the time of the factory around which everything swarmed. The new factory designs a different architecture, a different human geography. The compact mass of the Fordist city is replaced by an unstable aggregate of bodies. The spatial separation of the factory from the city determines a kind of 'immaterialisation' of the labour force, here meant in the sense of the social invisibility of the worker's job. For the workers, this means destructuring/restructuring of the daily routines. The work experience, the daily condition of the workers' existence is translated into a condition of continuous subtraction of their bodies from the social context in which they live" (Commisso 2006, 183).

only in case of failures, a platitude often repeated about infrastructures. If we look more carefully, however, we realize that visibility and invisibility are only the "extreme edges of a range of visibilities that move from unseen to grand spectacles and everything in between."[21] Like other infrastructures, the drivers live somewhere in between the two, locked in a complex game of visibility and invisibility—a game that allows them to build the channels through which the city circulates. After all, in order to move through the city the drivers need to move unnoticed against the direction of traffic, through private parking lots, and on sidewalks, but also to be recognized by traffic police as taxi drivers and thus not be stopped or fined. It is through this continuous negotiation of their visibility and invisibility that the drivers are able to keep up with the shifting rhythms of capital, urban life, and nature around them, even when everybody else gets stuck in traffic.

RIDING THROUGH BANGKOK

Organizing and policing the complex relation between rhythms and workers' bodies has been a central concern of capitalism since its origins, and even more clearly since its Taylorist turn. Labor management and workers' struggles revolved around discipline of labor, the former trying to enforce it, the latter to resist it. Whether in response to the despotic mechanical repetition of factory assembly lines or to the ups and downs of urban life, economic production, and nature, this struggle sits at the core of the capitalist system. Early analysts of capitalist production, both those who condemned its effects and those who tried to increase its productivity, understood very well the centrality of this struggle and realized that the worker's body and its rhythms were the field on which it would be fought. Both Taylor and Engels knew that political economic transformations, productivity, and exploitation were enforced or challenged on this terrain.[22] Bodily practices and disciplining rhythms, they understood, were situated within particular configurations of capital and labor and were both shaped by them and shaping them.

Unfortunately, over time this understanding faded from academic analysis while it remained central to the management of labor. Production manag-

21. Larkin 2013, 334.
22. I am referring here to Friedrich Engels's *Conditions of the Working Class in England* and Frederick Taylor's *The Principles of Scientific Management* (Engels 1968; F.W. Taylor 1914).

ers continued to explore and exploit their entangled nature, increasingly including in their considerations bodies, mind, and creativity. Social scientists, on the contrary, largely disentangled the political-economic and phenomenological analysis that overlapped in Engels's analysis of the British working class. On one side, orthodox Marxism drifted toward economistic materialism, which relegated perception and experience to the realm of superstructure. On the other side, phenomenology moved toward a transhistorical dedication to the body, rather than insisting on situating embodiment and experience in relation to capital and labor. The few scholars who refused to accept the primacy of one aspect over the other were often ostracized and seen as unable to pick a side.[23] The drivers' everyday lives bring this divergence into question. If in Engels's analysis of the British working class, factory and life rhythms were where structural political-economic conditions and the workers' everyday practices faced each other, for people like Wud, rhythms are where the wheels of everyday life meet the road of political economy and shape the relations between the drivers' bodies and the city around them.

In concrete terms, for the drivers this means adjusting or failing to adjust their bodies and minds to the circular rhythms of nature and to those of the urban economy. Sun up, morning peak hours, slow midmorning, lunch rush, slow afternoon, after-job peak hours, sun down, evening leisure, active nightlife: long days that repeat endlessly, with some variation, depending on the period of the year, day of the week, location, and weather conditions. Below these larger rhythms are those of the drivers' trips: the multiple paces of a ride, with its accelerations, braking, traffic lights, and meandering in between cars, always different in its destinations, always returning to the same station. A driver's success, both as earner and as an urban infrastructure, relies on his ability to read and synchronize the three rhythms: of nature, of urban capitalism, and of his own body.

Yet, keeping the city moving requires more than just temporal discipline. It also demands concentration that alerts the body to its relations with a variety of elements around it. Riding puts the drivers in an intimate relation

23. The prime example of this reaction is the inexplicably obscure Henri Lefebvre's magnum opus, *Critique of Everyday Life* (Lefebvre 1991a). While his *Production of Space* (1991b) obtained popular acclaim and long-lasting fame, his main opus, an attempt to reconcile theoretically Marxist political economy with phenomenology, remains largely ignored and got him expelled from the Communist Party of France. The attempt was so ostracized that Lefebvre included in the text a whole section responding to the accusation of walking into nonmaterialist territory (1991a, 2: 50–58).

with the bike, the tension of its brakes, the pressure in its tires, as well as the strength of its engine. Similarly, it requires a constant awareness of other vehicles, which could swerve and come crashing at any moment or suddenly brake. And finally, it creates a physical closeness to the city, its roads, and their surface, always potentially causing an accident due to gravel, slippery paint, engine oil, or slippery asphalt covered in rain.[24]

Avoiding accidents presents additional considerations to the drivers, starting from the gendered passenger on the backseat. While male passengers are socially permitted to ride astride, women are supposed to ride on motorcycle taxis seated side-saddled, with their legs crossed one on top of the other and gracefully rested on the exhaust pipe. Such a posture, learned from other female passengers, is devised to limit the uncomfortable contact with a stranger but also puts them at greater risk of hitting something or falling off the bike, a risk the drivers need to be particularly aware of, the same awareness they must have in relation to the bike, the terrain under it, and the moving city around it.

Even if drivers take every possible measure to limit those risks, riding the city remains a dangerous game. Every swerve, acceleration, or brake could result in a crash. Even more certain, their presence at street corners, immersed in the chemical and sonic pollution of a city, and their riding posture takes a toll on their bodies and well-being. To reduce the risk of accidents and take control over the potentially deadly contingencies of their jobs, the drivers often appeal to amulets or magic tattoos to seek protection.[25] Wud often told stories about his multiple accidents and how the small object hanging from his neck never failed to save his life.

24. This feeling has been masterfully described by the British novelist John Berger. In *Keeping a Rendezvous* he describes: "Except for the protective gear you're wearing, there's nothing between you and the rest and the world. The air and the wind press directly on you. You are *in* the space through which you are travelling. There is no vessel around you. But also, because you are on two wheels and not four, you are much closer to the ground. By closer I mean more intimate with the surface of the road, for instance. You are conscious of all its possible variations, whether it offers grip or is smooth, whether it's new or used, wet, damp or dry, where there's mud or gravel, where it's painted white (painted surface is always more slippery), where there's metal, where the wind blows dust, where ruts are being worn—all the while you are aware of the hold of the tyres or their lack of it on the varying surfaces, and you drive accordingly" (Berger 1991, 194–95).

25. On the use of amulets among northeastern population see Pattana 2012b; Tambiah 1984.

My first accident wasn't too bad. I crashed with the car, but my hand was still holding the motorcycle when I was down on the pavement. I got hurt just a little, my leg broke the handle of my motorcycle.

Did you have any amulets with you?

Yes. I wear them every day. Buddhists believe in Buddha amulets. I think they saved my life twice.

How did they save your life?

I had two big accidents. The second one was particularly bad: I was driving back to my hometown in Korat at 160 kilometers an hour when a car changed lanes and I hit it full speed. I flipped over the car, did a 360 and slid for twenty meters. My wind jacket was torn. I thought either my leg or my arm must have broken. But no, I held up my motorcycle, and rode back home. I really respect amulets and I believe they protect me but our job is dangerous, no matter what we do.

Holding on to their amulets and trying to remain concentrated on the road, motorcycle drivers carry out their dangerous work reading the movements of vehicles around them and the small spaces emerging between them. To someone perched on a bike, Bangkok reveals the open-ended malleability of its history. It presents itself to the driver as a moving entity, a mutable maze of vehicles, traffic lights, road signs, and traffic rules that can be ignored and manipulated to forge a new channel—or misread only to run into an accident. In the midst of thickening traffic, the street is in front of the drivers, ready to be taken, but is often blocked, clogged, occupied. New paths constantly need to be found through the maze of cars, buses, trucks, pickups, and tuk-tuks. Riding a mile down a big street may take them along back roads with just enough space for them to squeeze in, against the regular flow of traffic, or through a parking lot that links back to the street, always with the risk of choosing the wrong detour and remaining stuck. In this sense, the drivers' experience of riding through Bangkok resembles the progression that directed the birth and growth of the city: an unpredictable and tentative journey in which solutions emerged through side roads and the appearance of unexpected paths where chaos seemed to dominate.[26] Nonetheless, while

26. This mobility follows different configurations from equally meandering circulation presented in Michel de Certeau's famous essay "Walking the City" (de Certeau 1984, 91–111). Focusing on parallelism between walking and speech acts, de Certeau analyzes the phenomenology of moving on foot. For de Certeau, walking the city resembles the performative linguistic acts described by J. L. Austin (Austin 1962). Riding the city, though, lacks the linear and predictable nature of Austin's performative acts. Riding winds, diverges, reinstates, deviates, and swerves, making the felicitousness of such navigation less subjected to a series of discernable criteria or requisites and more open to the unpredictability of Ludwig

this piecemeal progression infuriated the city's planners, it provides a reason to exist and a source of wealth for the drivers, a mode of engagement with the city that marks their effectiveness as phatic labor and urban infrastructure.

Not every aspect of the drivers' operations in the city, however, is as nerve-racking as their zigzagging through traffic. Their life at street corners is divided between swift slaloms through traffic and long waiting times at their stations. Sitting there, the drivers become privileged sources of local knowledge, from food recommendations to directions, from shortcuts to shops in the areas in which they operate, while they also provide occasional help to local dwellers in need of assistance, be it help moving furniture or keeping an eye on someone's house while they are gone. Even when the drivers are not busy moving people, goods, and documents through Bangkok, they continue to build the channels that connect local neighbors, shop owners, street vendors, office workers, and police officers. In this context, patience, endurance, and the ability to sit with the boredom of waiting become skills, virtues, and forms of engagement in the social life of the neighborhood, as important as their movements to the drivers' phatic labor. As the life of the street unravels in front of their bored yet vigilant eyes, the drivers engage in a sociality of proximity, apparently mundane interactions that become central to their operations in the city and to the preservation of the channels that weave the neighborhood together (see fig. 4).

Theirs, however, is not the bored waiting of people who are stuck.[27] Rather—much like the productive boredom analyzed by Michael Herzfeld in his study of Cretan artisans[28]—it is fecund with expectations and interactions, as well as with learning and discussions.[29] If waiting became for the

Wittgenstein's language games that "see the straight highway before it, but of course cannot use because it is permanently closed" (Wittgenstein 1953, 25). A language game, he shows, "is so to say something unpredictable. I mean; it is not based on grounds. It is not reasonable (or unreasonable). It is there—like our life" (Wittgenstein 1969, 559). Equally the drivers' engagement with the city is not based on a preexisting reasoning, but rather relies on on-the-spot decisions and attempts to find their ways through Bangkok.

27. In the last decade, anthropologists have written extensively on waiting, boredom, and being stuck in relation to unemployment, migration, and economic stagnation (Hage 2009; Jeffrey 2010; Mains 2007; O'Neill 2014; M. Ralph 2008). While many of these authors stress the nature of waiting as a form of wasting time, holding on to a future that fails to arrive, in my case waiting is revealed as a productive time, a time necessary for the making of that future.

28. Herzfeld 2004.

29. This is also the time for them to engage with larger national publics. Given the rhythm of the drivers' life on the sidewalks, for instance, reading newspapers and magazines, as well

FIGURE 4. Waiting at a motorcycle taxi station. Photo by Agnes Dherbeys.

artisan's apprentice a time for stealing the craftsman's skills with the eyes, for the drivers, waiting is a time for mapping the neighborhood around them, sustaining the channels through which their social relations with local state officials, street workers, and residents are forged, and attempting to make use of them to move up the social ladder. Their lives on the streets, they hope, retain a transformative potential not just for the city around them but also for themselves, as they get accustomed to urban life, a trip at a time, its marvels and its sorrows, its excitements and its crushing oppression. The channels that their presence maintains, in fact, also offer pathways for their physical, social, and economic mobility. Much like in their riding, however, taking

---

as chatting with colleagues, plays a central role in their daily life. This configures them, in relation to other service workers, as well-informed and eager readers of anything that comes into their hands and therefore often closely involved in the "public" that these newspapers create, and often active and vocal political commentators.

these roads is always a gamble,[30] one that can project the drivers into another life or keep them stuck in their place.

CONVERTING MOBILITIES

Kong is a middle-aged driver who operates inside one of the many new developments mushrooming on the outskirts of Bangkok. Hidden away from the main road and framed by a cement arch that delimits its border, the neighborhood preserves the enclosed feeling of an old community shaded by mango trees. A few steps beyond the arch, however, the view opens out onto two rows of modern concrete townhouses with adjacent garages, clustered around an L-shaped dead-end road. At the street bend, underneath a wooden gazebo, sits a group of five drivers, the only nonprivate means of transportation available in the area. Despite their secluded location and few potential customers, Kong and the other drivers make a good income—up to 1,000 baht ($30 USD) a day—by delivering documents and paying bills for the middle-class residents. Even more important, and potentially more remunerative, during their waiting time they sustain relations with local dwellers that can open unexpected routes of social and economic mobility.

The first time I visited Kong, he was sitting on his bike drinking some beer that an older woman in the neighborhood had offered to his group to thank them for watching her house while she was away visiting her son and grandchildren in the northern city of Chiang Mai. As we started chatting, Kong's astute eyes kept looking away from me, checking on two local children who biked on the road beside us to make sure they did not go onto the main road, a few meters away. It was clear that Kong was immersed in a bundle of daily interactions that were all predicated upon his reliable and consistent presence at the corner. These interactions guaranteed him regular offerings of food and drinks—such as the beer we shared—as well as, I would discover, more significant and empowering forms of access. This mesh of social relations, however, was not built overnight. It was the result of sustained and long-term interactions that occurred mostly in the time spent waiting at his corner. Drivers who operate in larger and more crowded roads, and therefore have

30. Gambling in this sense provided a model for the relation between risk taking and masculinity among the drivers. For a treatment of their interplay in gambling culture (Malaby 2003).

less waiting time, can rarely claim the same immersion in the life of their neighborhood. Kong, on the other hand, had established his reliable presence over his ten years of operations in the area. He mediated local dwellers' relations with post offices, utilities companies, and banks. He had become an informal security guard for their house and children. And he had built relations of reciprocal trust that guaranteed a continuous flow of documents, bills, and checks in and out of the community on his wheels. "They see me here every day. I saw their kids being born, their parents die. We are a community and we help each other. If they need something they know they can find me here, sitting on my bike. I help the neighbors take care of their gardens. I look after their houses or give them a hand to moving furniture. They know they can trust me. Sometimes they even trust me more than I would like," Kong told me during my first visit.

Puzzled by his allusion to excessive trust and attracted by the calm of his neighborhood, I kept coming back to see Kong whenever I needed a rest from the chaos of the city and wanted to drink with him. During these visits I saw him managing the complex sociality of proximity that defined his daily presence and social standing in the neighborhood. One day, passing by, I stopped at his station but Kong was not there. The other drivers directed me to a small apartment in a crumbling construction building right outside the arch. Kong was sitting with a group of friends, without his vest and visibly drunk.

"What happened?" I asked.

"I am celebrating: my daughter has been admitted into a private school of accountancy. We fought, but now finally she can have a better future, not like her father working all day in the street." He laughed.

"Does she have a scholarship?" I inquired, curious about how he could afford the school tuitions.

"No, Mr. Pong will pay," he said raising his chin toward the biggest house in the neighborhood, at the end of the road.

Kong had talked to me before about Pong and their shady business deal. After years of using Kong to deliver documents around the city and keep an eye on his house, the wealthy businessmen, involved in construction, had started to ask him to deliver envelopes with money around the city in exchange for a generous fee. Over time, the amounts inside those envelopes grew from a few thousand baht to hundreds of thousands, well beyond Kong's monthly and at times even yearly income. Kong diligently carried the money to their destinations without asking questions about its provenance and keeping to himself his fear of being caught with piles of cash by local police, criminals, or the common overlapping of the two. "At the beginning, I was so scared when I had to carry this money," he said. "What if I get attacked? I thought all the time. What if I get stopped? I used to tuck the envelope inside my pants, on the back, and cover it with my shirt and vest. Then I found a better method. I parked my motorbike inside Mr. Pong's garage and unscrewed the front part of my scooter. I put the money in and closed everything up so no one would know that I had money and where it was." As Kong's deliveries continued without glitches, the sums kept growing to a one-time peak of three million baht ($100,000). "I was so scared," he recounts. "I had never seen so much money. I had no idea where to put it: the whole bike was full of money, in the front, in the back, behind the lights, I was a moving bank," he laughed.

Over time, Kong and Mr. Pong created an increasingly tight circuit of reciprocal favors in which the former became a delivery man for the businessman as well as a handyman in his house, while the latter sponsored Kong's son's ordination ceremony into monkhood. This exchange of favors solidified over the years. When Kong's daughter passed the admission exam to a local private accounting school, leaving him to find money to fulfill her dreams, Mr. Pong stepped in to help. During a chat with Mr. Pong outside his house, Kong had mentioned his financial conundrum and the businessman had offered to pay his daughter's tuition, opening up a new channel for social and economic mobility for Kong's family. Through his sustained and regular presence in the neighborhood, the establishment of reciprocal trust and a circuit of favors, Kong was able to create new channels through which Pong's cash traveled around the city and his daughter entered a prestigious and expensive college in Bangkok, a school well beyond Kong's financial reach. He was able, in other words, to convert his presence in the neighborhood, both in terms of transport and waiting, into other forms of economic and social mobility for his family.[31]

31. These dynamics have often been analyzed in the context of Southeast Asia in terms of patron-clients relations (Eisenstadt and Roniger 1980; Kemp 1982; Ockey 2004; Scott 1972a, b). Nonetheless this framework poses three main problems. First, it is engrained in an outsider gaze. It is not by chance, in fact, that what in the American context may be referred to as building social capital, in the context of Southeast Asia becomes framed as patron-client relations. Second, it stresses power imbalances and oppression rather than acknowledging the open-endedness and mutual importance of these relations. Third, patron-client relations are often presented as the only game in town, a form of sociality in which clients are forced to engage in order to survive. The drivers' actions question such depictions. For them engaging in this work of channel making is a decision, one that many of them decide not to take, and is often predicated upon a refusal of the hierarchy of so-called patron-client relationships.

A similar successful transformation of forms of mobility was performed by Boon, another driver who operated in a small *soi* along Sukhumvit Road that houses a mix of office workers, local elites, and expatriates. In the neighborhood Boon was renowned as a reckless driver, ideal if you had to get to your destination in record time but otherwise to be avoided. Speeding on a bike, however, was not Boon's only claim to local fame. His fast tongue and taste for gossip made him a popular source of local information, the more embarrassing the better. In March 2010, right after the end of the school year, the son of a wealthy local family became the talk of the street. It was said that he failed his primary school final exams and thereby jeopardized his chances for a good education. The gossip, mixed with the sadistic pleasure of seeing a well-to-do family put to shame, spread like wildfire around the *soi* and reached Boon's ears. Waiting at his station, he listened carefully to this story and the half-muttered jokes that the local street vendors repeated every time the kid's parents drove past them. Boon became himself a teller of this story to other local residents who stopped to chat with him on their way home, as he sat at the street corner waiting for clients. One of them, who often used Boon as a messenger, told him that he knew a school headmaster who could—for an appropriate sum—find a way to get the kid into a good school regardless of his academic results. After a few days of reflection, Boon decided to pay a visit to the family and offer his services as a go-between to put the family in contact with the headmaster. After they worked out a deal, which probably entailed a conspicuous bribe, Boon received a generous fee of 30,000 baht ($1,000). With this money he took another gamble and invested in a shoe stall that his friend had been setting up in a local market and that, it turned out, would grant him an extra income for the following years. Boon's economic mobility, in other words, was enhanced through a dense mesh of channels and social relations that he had established over time, which, in turn, allowed for the creation of new channels for social and economic mobility, both for him and for the young boy. Through these channels, the child entered a good school and Boon created a debt of gratitude toward himself, as well as an actual payment, which in turn solidified his position in the neighborhood and, potentially, his future economic and social status.

The complex relation between riding and sitting in their neighborhoods and an ability to create new channels and move along existing ones allowed Boon and Kong to transform and activate social relationships into paths for their economic and social mobility. As in Bourdieu's theorization of the convertibility of economic, social, and cultural capitals,[32] they transformed different forms of mobility—physical, social, and economic—one into the other. These exchanges, as Bourdieu has argued, "in contrast to the cynical but also economical transparency of economic exchange, in which equivalents change hands in the same instant, . . . [presuppose] a much more subtle economy of time."[33] As in their riding, the drivers' life in the city relies heavily on their ability to master this economy of time. First, they need to synchronize the rhythms of their labor—with its long waits at the street corner and speed of movement through the city traffic—with those of nature and the urban economy to become mediators of movement in their neighborhood as well as reliable presences and trusted helpers. While this ensures their success as drivers, it does not guarantee the success of their conversion of forms of mobility. This secondary mobility, on the contrary, requires a longer game, one that does not play out in the daily routines of rides but over years, in the times between rides. Kong created the connections that had allowed for his daughter to enter the private school over the course of years in the neighborhood, years during which he established a close relation to Mr. Pong. Similarly, Boon heard about the child's difficulty and the headmaster through connections built over years of services in the neighborhood. The conversion of mobilities, in other words, happens over a much longer timescale, in which particular relations and channels, such as the one between Kong and Mr. Pong, are developed, nurtured, and solidified before they can allow for the transformation of physical mobility into more empowering forms of economic or social mobility.

Like the drivers' trips constantly balanced on a few inches of rubber tires, however, these forms of mobility are equally threatened by accidents and failures: dangers that amulets are not always able to ward off. Years of phatic labor, personal relations, and trust can disappear in a moment, carried away by an external occurrence, a wrong move, or a death. In most cases, in fact, being able to create channels and find paths and to spend time in them does not create new trajectories or mobilities, but rather reveals the fragilities of the drivers' attempts.

Id, a driver who worked not far away from Wud's station, learned this lesson the hard way. Id was born in the northeastern province of Sisaket and, like many of the drivers, had a wife and kids back in his hometown. At the

32. Bourdieu 1986.
33. Ibid., 54.

time of my fieldwork, Id's daughter Fai was finishing school in the country-side and was expected to move to Bangkok after her graduation. Her father's plans, however, were not to see his daughter swell the ranks of the urban working class but rather to find a way to get her into Saint Louis College, a prestigious school near his station where she could study as a nurse. Id's pref-erence for this college was not only due to its reputation. Over time, he had built personal channels with an older French priest who was appointed to the school's church as a form of retirement from four decades of missionary life in remote parts of northern Thailand. Carrying local clients to the church or the adjacent school, Id met the priest multiple times and started to run errands for him. Over time a solid friendship developed, a friendship anchored in intergenerational circuits of patronage and care that made Id proud of calling the priest *phǭ,* father. "He reminds me of my father," Id told me one time. "You know we respect elders here in Thailand, so I take care of him." Particularly after the priest's health took a turn for the worse, Id visited him every day, spent some time with him, and brought him some groceries that the congregation would not provide, such as cigarettes and a regular bottle of Cointreau, an expensive French orange-flavored liqueur for which Id himself had developed a taste. These visits, filled with care, attention, and concern, became a regular part of the two men's daily routines, slow hours in which Id would take off his vest and sit at the priest's bedside.

Over time, Id came to see this sustained relation as a potential channel for the realization of his daughter's dreams. In their conversations, he talked about her aspirations and hopes. Slowly the priest became sympathetic to Id's struggles and eventually promised to take care of her once she was done with school. For most of the period of my fieldwork this seemed like a successful story of Id's ability to convert forms of mobility and provide new access to his older daughter who was waiting in the village to move to Bangkok and get on to her life as an urban dweller. A few weeks before I left Thailand, however, the old priest unexpectedly died, taking with him his promises and revealing the fragility of Id's aspirations. Id never spoke to me again about the priest's promises and never bad-mouthed the old man for what amounted to empty promises. Yet it was clear that the priest's silent departure had set him years back in his search for a better future for his daughter and had forced him, in the meantime, to send her to a high school in the district capital instead of the expensive private nursing school in Bangkok, leaving her stuck—her channels closed—in the provinces.

THREE

The Unresolved Tensions of Migration

Instead of taking social categories such as rural and urban . . . at face value as elements of culture, [we should] demonstrate what these categories do, how people deploy them to achieve material gains, construct meaningful identities, and carve a space for themselves within society.

ERIK HARMS, *Saigon's Edge*

IT IS GETTING DARK. The city lights color the winter dusk and reflect on the pavement of the train station, through dozens of moving legs. Two blocks of plastic chairs, on both sides of the hall, overflow with people, mostly internal migrants taking advantage of a long weekend to visit their homes. The crowd is dotted with foreign travelers wearing Thai fisherman pants, an item of clothing that locals would never wear in public. On the balcony above, wealthier travelers sit outside small restaurants and coffee shops that serve western food and drinks, pastries, and donuts. The smell of baked goods mixes with that of grilled chicken down below.

Suddenly the crowd comes to a halt, called to a pause by the national anthem broadcasting from the station's speakers. It is six in the afternoon and the Thai nation-state is synchronizing its citizens. Everybody stands still, head up, facing a giant portrait of King Chulalongkorn that overlooks the scene from a neoclassical arch connecting the hall to the tracks. The tourists, still sitting on the ground, are puzzled by the sudden immobility, indifferent to the state's interpellation. "Hail the nation of Thailand, long last the victory, hurrah," concludes the broadcast, snapping everybody out of their stasis. I look around but there is no sign of Adun, a driver whose village I am supposed to visit. Conscious of his propensity to drink too much on nonworking days, I begin worry he will not show up. Adun calls me an hour and a half later. "I'm already on the train," he slurs with his thick northeastern accent. "I have kept a spot for you. Come in."

The platforms overflow with people. Sellers run up and down to supply travelers with food and drinks. Bags are passed to hands sticking out of the trains' windows, behind which passengers take their seats according to their tickets and class. I get into the carriage and walk down a narrow corridor between wooden benches covered in thin gray plastic pads. Adun sits on the bench he reserved for us, slightly bent. He wears dark blue jeans and a black T-shirt, a small backpack and a purple belt bag with his documents and a few thousand baht. "Already drunk," he smiles. He takes a small bottle of rice whisky out of his backpack and passes it to me. "Get used to this," he tells me struggling to keep his eyes open. "No whiskey and soda at home. And no ice either. In the village, we are not developed yet [*yang mai phatthanā*]." He pauses. "But no worries, you will not need anything. You can eat for free anywhere, just knock at somebody's house and they'll feed you. Not like in Bangkok where everything is money. After I save enough here in Bangkok, I will go back to the village, open a vegetable farm there, and sell my products in the city."

As Adun finishes his sentence, the train slowly moves out of Hualampong Station, a few minutes after eight in the evening. In the crowded car, people settle in, cradled by the rocking locomotive. Some put luggage on the racks, some set up for the night, other pass around small packages of food. A few curious people stare at us, puzzled by our odd pairing. Indifferent to those gazes, Adun launches into one of his drunk tirades. His favorite targets are the usual ones: the Oxford-educated Prime Minister Abhisit Vejjajiva, who, he remarks with disgust, does not even know how to grow rice and yet wants to run the country; and Bangkok's police officers who constantly demand bribes to allow motorcycle taxi drivers pick up passengers, occupy public land, and ride without a helmet. The train moves through industrial compounds toward the ancient capital of Ayutthaya before making its way east into the pitch-black darkness of rice fields and further still to the light of the provincial cities of the northeastern plateau. Adun continues with his alcohol-fueled invectives, increasingly rambling and blunt. We get through the first bottle of rice whiskey and our conversation follows meandering routes. As he puts the empty bottle back in his backpack, a box of Kentucky Fried Chicken peers out of his bag. "What the hell is that?" I pry. "This is all my kids want from Bangkok." "What?" I ask puzzled. "Yeah, all they want from the city is KFC and pizza. They must have seen it on TV and they cannot shut up about it." "Isn't that just very expensive fried chicken?" "I know"— Adun replies, frustrated—"and I don't even think it is good. It is greasy, tasteless, and costs me five times the price of a piece of normal fried chicken, but this is what they want from the city so I buy it. I have no fucking idea why they want it, but they are my kids," Adun concludes breaking out another bottle of rice whisky.

These pieces of KFC chicken, together with the "not-yet-developed" rice whisky we have been drinking and Adun's dream of returning to the village, illustrate the paradoxes of the drivers' mobility between city and countryside and the tensions they create, enfolded within—to use the words of Henri Lefebvre[1]—everyday objects: KFC, an urban commodity whose image traveled to Adun's kids through multiple circuits of media-produced and parent-indulged desires that cast the city as a space of progress and development but also of unnecessary needs; rice whisky, a rural product that comes to symbolize the village as a space of backwardness but also of pristine calm and sharing, both *before* and *away* from the city and its urban modernity.

These imaginaries are critical to economic policies and temporal depictions which position Bangkok as the developed and modern core of the nation and Isan as the quintessential space of the "not yet": not yet developed, not yet disrupted by modernity, not yet educated, not yet capitalist, not yet ready to partake in democratic electoral politics.[2] In between the two are people like Adun, who reproduce narratives of development and their lack of it that open a temporal gap between the village and the city. At the same time, however, they also move between these two spaces and bring them closer in the hope that one day they will be able to carry just enough urban development back to the village—a vegetable farm in Adun's case—while retaining the city as a market for their products. This tension, present in all Thai internal migrants, is particularly pronounced among motorcycle taxi drivers who, more than other urban workers, move regularly along the channels between the social, economic, and aspirational landscapes of Thai villages and those of Bangkok. Along these channels the drivers become vessels for urban commodities (e.g., iced whisky, KFC), lifestyles, and narratives (e.g. on modern commodities, developed tastes). Here lies the predicament of the drivers' mobility and that of migrants the world over. On the one hand, their experiences, stories, and trajectories contribute to reproducing narratives in which Bangkok and the village sit at opposite ends of the spec-

1. Lefebvre 1991a, 1: 134.
2. "While its residents and citizens have been pivotal in the production of Bangkok—its urbanization, its industrial capacity and its economic dominance over the country—they often remain stuck in the realm of the not yet" (Elinoff and Sopranzetti 2012, 331). For other debates on the relation between modernity, or modernities, temporality, and futures see Appadurai 2013; Bear 2014; Comaroff and Comaroff 2001; Fabian 2014.

trum of development and modernity. On the other, the drivers modulate between the two spaces, constantly attempting to draw them together, connect and mediate them, struggling to find a place for themselves in between the two.

In the pages that follow, I analyze the complexities of this position. While most studies of migration focus on the economic, spatial, and social dimensions of mobility, the numerous trips I took with the drivers back to their villages were dominated by questions regarding its temporal reality—in terms of imagined temporalities of development, rhythms of everyday life, and expectations.[3] The recurrent theme was a feeling of being pulled in opposite directions and struggling to reconcile them. Drivers like Adun often remain torn between participating in reproducing a narrative of distance between the city and the village and attempting to reconcile them through their life trajectories. These unresolved tensions reproduce an exploitative relation between Bangkok and the Thai countryside, pushing people to reorient personal, economic, and political aspirations toward the city but also limiting their full realization. Adun tries to deal with these predicaments by dreaming of setting up a farm in the village and selling its products in the city. Other drivers try to mediate the opposite pulls though an array of strategies, whether attempting to bridge the two spaces, accepting the gap between and becoming fully urbanized, or expanding the gap to find pride in the village's backwardness. Whichever the strategy, in migrating they all take the same gamble they accept while riding through the city: a gamble that makes them both aware of and concerned with the fragility of their lives and the material effects of these unresolved tensions on their families and villages.

UNFINISHED VILLAGES

At the break of dawn, after ten-plus hours of our drunken dozing off in third class, the train approaches Udon Ratchathani, our final destination. Adun sleeps on the hard bench as people around us start to move, getting ready to alight. I wake him up and we exit onto the crowded platform: Adun, two pieces of greasy deep fried chicken, and myself, all three equally melting in the morning heat. The town seems to contradict Adun's depiction of Isan as

3. For a treatment of this blind spot in studies of migration, see Griffiths, Rogers, and Anderson 2013.

backward. Shopping malls occupy the roads around the station and local markets overflow with international commodities. Among the Isan food stalls are hamburgers, frying bacon, and strawberries. These exotic goods cater to the older foreign men brought to Udon by the American military base or their Thai wives, often met in go-go bars in Bangkok or in the sex-trade hub of Pattaya. Adun precedes me through the market's narrow lanes. Soon we jump on a rickshaw headed to the nearby bus station, a large clearing surrounded by small shops clustering around a concrete shelter. Adun walks to a small shop. "Do you want a beer?" he offers. "I am OK," I reply, wary of drinks before eight in the morning. "*Tong thǫn*," Adun tells me, humming the melody of a catchy Isan song that praises the virtues of the hair of the dog. We sing for a minute, laughing. He buys a big jar of biscuits, another *developed* commodity that goes into his backpack next to the KFC box. In a little while we get on a local bus in the direction of Bandung, Adun's district capital, an hour away. This time Adun does not sit next to me, but two rows in front. From my seat I can see him savoring the air of home as we slowly go deeper into the countryside. Dry rice fields pass by as the street gets less crowded and more unkempt. His eyes examine the familiar landscape with a new light, the light that shines in the eyes of people returning home, eyes whose gaze moves across the familiar landscape and attends to its places, counting landmarks like the beads of a rosary.[4] As for many returnees, this almost religious act brings silence. Adun is no exception, his eyes locked on the window and his chin high in the air. We get off at a small intersection, a few miles before arriving in town, and walk to a nearby shop: Adun is home.

The shop owner comes out to greet him and fill him in on the village's recent events and rumors. Someone has died, someone else got married, a new cohort of teenagers moved to Bangkok after completing secondary education. Above our heads, former Prime Minister Thaksin Shinawatra—who still retains wide support in the region even after a military coup removed him from office in 2006—looks over the scene from a big banner: sitting, elbows up on a large wooden desk. "We love Thaksin," the old seller tells me, echoing

4. This dynamic has been extensively described by Keith Basso. In his fantastic ethnography of place making among the Apache he said: "By now and again, and sometimes without apparent cause, awareness is seized—arrested—and the place in which it settles becomes an object of spontaneous reflection and resonating sentiment. It is at times such as these, when individuals step back from the flow of everyday experience and attend self-consciously to places, when, we may say, they pause to actively sense them, that their relationships to geographical space are most richly lived and surely felt" (Basso 1996, 107).

a show of love normally directed exclusively toward the king. "He did so much for us. He brought money and development to our region, he ——" Adun interrupts him, impatient to get home. "He knows. You don't have to explain." The shop owner laughs. "Good." A large battered Yamaha motorbike makes its way toward us. Gai, Adun's wife, drives it and their younger daughter stands in the front, between her and the handlebar. The bike, without a license plate, stops before us. The small girl runs toward Adun and leaps into his arms, in a physical display of affection rarely seen in the Thai capital. A few minutes later, all crammed on the motorbike, we drive on a street that was asphalted in 2004 with money the government of Thaksin Shinawatra gave the village. "This is all that a government has ever given us," Adun shouts, turning his head, "Since the coup [of 2006], they once again stopped caring about us. They just left us here. This road and the village school that was built by students from Bangkok forty years ago are the only two times in my life I saw the government doing something for the village."[5] We drive toward Adun's house slowly, greeting everyone we meet. The village is clustered along the street, a clump of scattered houses covered by the red dust that spreads over everything: buildings, motorbikes, fields, people. Small kids run around or sit outside their houses. Most adults seem to have disappeared, migrated to join the ranks of Bangkok's workforce. We pass an unfinished temple, the small concrete school, and an empty square where middlemen come to collect rice during harvest season. Finally we arrive at Adun's home.

The compound, like most in the Thai countryside, comprises multiple houses. At the entrance, behind a rudimentary arch, stands a small *salā*, a traditional wooden gazebo on stilts, under which two dogs lie drowsily. On the left, small vegetable patches provide for basic daily consumption. On the right, a small shack houses Adun's sister on the rare occasions when her family visits from Rayong, a regional center in eastern Thailand where her husband works as a doctor. A few meters away is Adun's home. Originally a wooden structure on stilts, the house, like many in this village, shows the material effects of urban remittances, lifestyles, and architectural tastes. The ground floor, traditionally left open to provide air circulation, a refuge during floods, and shelter for cattle, has been enclosed in cement walls, interrupted by two doors and four wooden windows. "See," Adun tells me, "we just finished the

5. This school was part of a program of education and development sponsored by the Thai government between 1974 and 1976 that sent university students from Bangkok around the country.

house a few years ago. I had to save money for many years but now the house is beautiful." The concrete walls cost the family 70,000 baht ($2,300) and were built, unlike the upper part of the house, by hired skilled workers. Outward migration has not just changed the materiality of Isan houses and their architectural styles; it has also revolutionized labor practices in the village. House renovations now require specific skills and, like the agricultural work from which migration has subtracted able bodies, rely on hired daily laborers—often landless laborers from slums in the regions' growing cities—to carry out the jobs formerly executed by household members.[6]

Adun's parents live beyond the yard in a larger wooden house with small decorative engravings on the roof. "Their house is not finished yet," Adun tells me as if he heard my unspoken romantic appreciation of the wooden structure.

"What do you mean?" I ask, confused.

"You see the lower floor, it doesn't have concrete. I promised them I will finish it but I don't have money. Besides, my father almost never sleeps there. We built a raft and now he lives on the river, fishes . . . He likes being alone there, it is calmer."

All around the village, old traditional wooden houses are now seen as *incomplete* houses, waiting to be contained by cement walls.[7] As a consequence, urban remittances are invested to retrofit them to include a concrete ground floor so to *finish* them, even at the cost of eroding the area below the elevated floor and destroying its traditional systems of air circulation. These work-in-progress houses with only one wall up and unfinished pavement display the tangible effects of the narrative that Adun voiced on the train, a narrative that distances city and village. In these houses, rural tradition is reframed as unfinished while waves of modern necessities and desires arrive to fulfill and complete it, reconfiguring their economic, spatial, and temporal locations. Throughout the rural landscape of Thailand, things that were accepted in the past are now seen as unfinished, incomplete, to be rethought and updated.

The ascription of development to a specific urban location and consequent reframing of villages as *not yet developed* is by no means peculiar to this context. On the contrary it resonates with Raymond Williams's analysis of the

6. Elinoff 2013.
7. For an extensive treatment of the significance of house architecture in Isan, see Elinoff 2016.

relation between Britain's city and countryside.[8] Even more poignantly, it echoes what Dipesh Chakrabarty, in the context of colonial relations, has called historicisms: linear narratives that posit a modern and liberal Europe as the necessary and desired destination of all nations.[9] The forms these narratives take in the Thai context, however, are specific. Here historicist narratives, such as those of *phatthanā* (development) and *siwilai* (civilization) that organized the growth of Bangkok in the twentieth century and continue to orient the way in which millions of Thai citizens perceive, describe, and ultimately live the reality around them, replaced Europe with the Thai capital. In so doing, the narratives sustain a regime of internal colonialism and uneven development that has reorganized the whole country as a reserve of resources, material and human, to be extracted and directed to Bangkok. This regime has shaped and still shapes the relation between Bangkok and its provinces, as well as the personal trajectories of millions of migrants from those provinces.[10] Its power does not only lie in reorganizing the economic and spatio-temporal continuum of the Thai nation and inspiring expensive

8. R. Williams 1975.

9. Chakrabarty 2000.

10. This relation—analogous to what Gramsci has described in the Italian South (Gramsci 1988)—started during the reign of King Rama V. As I showed in chapter 1, a completely new set of techniques of governance, modeled around colonial administrations in the region, was introduced by the Siamese absolute monarchy and continued to be actively implemented long after absolutism fell in 1932 into the Cold War period, by the Thai developmentalist state. These new techniques ranged from territorial constitution and penetration to forms of governance and administration, from religious conversion and proselytism to racial politics and resources extraction. The persistence of such regimes has been showed by a number of scholars (Reynolds 1987, 2002; Thongchai 2000), and most prominently voiced by Rachel Harrison, Peter Jackson, and Michael Herzfeld (Harrison and Jackson 2011; Herzfeld 2002). Paradoxically, this recognition of colonial structures continuing to operate in Thailand and specifically in Isan has not just been voiced by critical intellectuals. One of the most public contemporary formulations of internal colonialism in Thailand was provided by General Sayud Kerbphol, an ultraroyalist military official, first director of the CSOC (Communist Suppression Operations Command) and central figure in the later renamed ISOC (Internal Security Operations Command) between 1966 and 1983, supreme commander of the Royal Thai Army between 1981 and 1983, vocal member of the conservative yellow shirted PAD (People's Alliance for Democracy), and actual president of the People's Network for Election and the Bangkok Vegetarian Society. Gen. Sayud Kerbphol was quoted saying that avoiding colonization by Europe simply meant that we colonized our own people. This internal colonialism, in which officials appointed by the metropolis rule and drain the country-side like conquered provinces, has led to obvious differences among the Thai. It is interesting to note that his words echo a Marxist analysis that he personally worked to suffocate during the Cold War.

architectural renovations, but also in creating in the migrants a yearning for the present, imagined as urban, capitalist, and modern.[11] For Adun, as for many other drivers, this thirst for new commodities, lifestyles, and forms of participation can only be quenched by directing his personal trajectory toward the city—a city that extracts from the provinces its most productive human capital by creating, to paraphrase Marx, the compulsion to move.

Adun's *finished* home reveals the complexities and anxieties that drivers and other migrants experience in trying to satisfy this compulsion while remaining connected to the village. As Adun walks into his enclosed home he straightens his whole body, adjusting it from the marginal existence of a motorcycle taxi driver on the streets of Bangkok to his rural status as a relatively successful man who works in the city. The interior space of the house, organized around six concrete pillars, is sober but filled with commodities that display his urbanized tastes and economic potential to support them. Beside the entrance, on the right, two sewing machines sit idle, surrounded by small colorful dresses that his wife is preparing for the upcoming temple fair. Facing the machines hangs a picture of Adun's colleagues at his station: five northeastern men in cowboy hats at a bar in Bangkok stand in front of a fake background with an image of the American Wild West. As I stop to look at the picture, Adun points out his nametag for the United Front for Democracy against Dictatorship (UDD), a political organization that was formed in 2006 to oppose the military coup that removed Thaksin Shinawatra. In the previous four years, the group had become the core of the Red Shirts, a social movement that was gaining momentum around the country. This popular mobilization demanded another form of mending the tears between city and countryside through democratic elections and an end to the political, economic, and legal double standards (*sǫng māttrathān*) that keep the country's lower classes in poverty and prevent their representatives from governing. The laminated nametag hangs in front of a curtain that separates a small corner area of the room where the family sleeps on thin mattresses, next to the wooden stairs that lead to the second floor. What used to be the core of the house—the upper floor—is left empty and rarely used, abandoned as a space of the past, of wooden rural life unfit for the developed, concrete-framed present.

11. Talal Asad has analyzed how European power operated in colonial settings "not as a temporary repression of subject population but as an irrevocable process of transmutation, in which old desires and ways of life were destroyed and new ones took their place" (Asad 1991, 314).

If in the city's history past and present maintained porous relations, in their home Gai and Adun are trying to cast the past away and replace it with a frantic pursuit of urban modernity. Their attempt, however, much like that of urban planners to impose order on Bangkok, remains largely incomplete. The urban commodities that fill their house are a constant reminder of the doomed audacity of their chase. They symbolize both their desire to be urban and their inability to bridge the gap. The secondhand giant leather sofa that Adun brought back from a karaoke bar he patronized now dominates the downstairs living room and remains largely unused by his family, who are accustomed to traditionally Thai houses that do not have any collective seating. The house appliances remain constantly out-of-date, the fans a step behind the air conditioners common in the city, the TV bulkier than those in Bangkok. At the same time, the house renovations Gai and Adun undertook create new needs, setting them further back in their attempt to keep up with the city. The cemented walls that *completed* the house made the place stuffy, blocking the free circulation of air and light. As a result, other appliances had to be introduced to keep this more urbanized place livable: two florescent tubes, constantly on, hang from the roof; a fan rotates, taking advantage of the sole electric plug in the house. Its mechanical sound mixes with the low buzz of the neon and the sounds of the country outside—neighbors chatting, the indefatigable tractor's engine, buffaloes herded from field to field, and the occasional passing motorbike or truck.

Overall, both the soundscape and the objects inside the house reveal the overlapping and intertwining of urban commodities and rural life, once again bringing the urban and the rural together but also distancing them, condensing the experience of urbanized villagers like Adun.[12] The carefully manufactured design both projects the house into a developed future and punctures it with challenges it cannot overcome, revealing the impossibility of fully keeping up with the progress of Bangkok.[13] First, the infrequent rhythms of remittances and Adun's trips back mean that house renovations progress too irregularly and slowly, backlogged when compared with the rapid march of urban modernity. Every step forward is followed by a long

12. Naruemon and McCargo 2011.

13. Tania Li has analyzed precisely the same dynamic in relation to the discourse of development and the self-defeating desires and aspirations that it creates (Li 2007, 11).

pause before the next remittance, the next rice harvest, the next buffalo sold. Second, the gap between the village and the city that Adun tries to bridge is a force well beyond his reach, a narrative central to the construction and preservation of contemporary Thailand. The development of Bangkok, in fact, relied on the material, economic, and discursive production of rural backwardness. Much like the introduction of the rice premium tax in the 1950s, which raised the levy on rice production in order to extract resources from the countryside to develop Bangkok, the narrative production of rural backwardness and urban development is a zero-sum game. It is only by reframing the village, its architectural traditions, and social practices as a thing of the past, incomplete and unfinished, that the city could become the space of the present, developed and in continuous evolution.

For Bangkok to remain the center of development, desires, and glamor, the village needs to remain the space of backwardness, calm, and tradition. In other words, even if the two spaces may be depicted as discrete social, spatial, and temporal realities they are two sides of the same coin, configuring each other by opposition. It is through their mutual production that a national geography of uneven development, migration, and exploitation is preserved. Drivers are well aware that in this process they are condemned to get the shorter end of the stick. As a consequence, their lives are a constant struggle to find a workable middle ground. Adun's circular migration, his concrete walled house, and much of what happens inside it are attempts, as desperate and meaningful as any, to undo the country's geographic and temporal inequality and mend the gap it generates by bringing city and village closer and, ideally, reconciling their opposition. Even though these attempts may not succeed, their failure has material effects. They are precisely the unresolved tensions between city and village, in fact, that fuel and orient much of the life trajectories of villagers, including those of Adun's own children.

In front of Adun's unused sofa, a TV broadcasts images of a wealthy household somewhere in the suburbs of Bangkok where a family drama unravels before the attentive eyes of Nam, Adun's older daughter. Nam sits on the ground leaning against the sofa. Her eyes are glued to the screen, lost in a popular soap opera set in the faraway reality of Bangkok's middle classes. Attentive to their language, demeanors, and social intricacies, Nam is learning to yearn for that lifestyle and the city in which, it seems, it needs to take place. Through the show's depiction of life in Bangkok and the roles of darker-skinned Isan house workers, she is learning to see and accept a distance that her father has already accepted. This distance propels Nam to imagine herself in Bangkok and leap to the other side of the spectrum.[14] Nam, lost in the TV starlets' secret love story with her handsome white-skinned boyfriend, quickly *wais* (salutes) Adun before sinking her teeth into the piece of KFC he brought back for her, temporarily fulfilling her craving for a different life, one with urban settings, lifestyles, and tastes.

Adun is not indifferent to her desires, which mirror the yearnings that drew him to Bangkok three decades before. She is, he tells me, increasingly voicing her intention to migrate to the city, an intention that has been—consciously or unconsciously—cultivated not just by exposure to a variety of media, but also by the commodities and stories that Adun carries with him to the village. All around Isan, sitting in poorly lit houses in the northeastern countryside, kids and older people listen with widened eyes and ears to the tales of the city that migrants bring back. These stories fuel imaginary trajectories and desires of urban life among rural dwellers, imaginations that oscillate between the celebration of urban life and its advantages, and the dismissal of urban experience, its perils, and struggles. In this sense, Adun acted for Nam as culture broker and mediator of life in the metropolis and its goods, from cellphones to KFC chicken. These circulations that Adun channeled, whether with presents, stories, or by buying her a TV, orient Nam's future towards Bangkok, the endpoint of personal and collective linear trajectories of development. This, in turn, has made her only more conscious of her present distance from that future. Through this kind of awareness, "the harshness of peasant life and the squalor of the farmyard . . . appear intolerable. . . . [T]hey seem even more so once we become aware of the magnificent, grandiose character of the works they have produced with their labor. Our awareness of this contradiction becomes more acute, and we find ourselves faced necessarily with a new imperative: the practical, effective transformation of things as they are."[15] Munching in front of the TV, Nam sees this imperative solidify and the awareness of her exclusion grow.

14. As Mary Beth Mills has observed: "Widespread images of Bangkok (particularly on television which is widely available in rural areas) highlight the city as the focal center of modern Thai life, the pinnacle of 'national development' and 'progress'. By contrast media images, as well as most attitudes fostered by the centralized Thai state, commonly identify rural agriculturalists with the national periphery; they are *khon baan nohk,* literally people of 'outlying' communities, located on the nation's social and cultural margins. As such they hold significantly lower status and power than their better educated and more sophisticated urban compatriots. Consequently many young men and women in the countryside are drawn to Bangkok in part out of desires to enhance their own knowledge and status" (Mills 1999a, 35).

15. Lefebvre 1991a, 1: 134.

The drivers' mobility between city and countryside intersects at a variety of different angles with those imperatives, the desires they configure, and the failures they prefigure. First, the drivers, as urban migrants, are products and victims of the temporal distancing between the village and Bangkok: a distancing that directs the extraction of human, natural, and economic resources from the countryside and attracts millions of people to the city in an attempt to bridge the gap. Second, they are proponents and diffusors of this distancing, through their stories from the city, their talk of development and incompleteness, and their circulation of urban commodities. Third, they challenge this separation with their trajectories and imaginations of a future in which the two realities are reconciled. While this analysis may sound like an artificial dissection of everyday realities, drivers are constantly discussing the tensions that these three dynamics create in their lives, the challenges they raise to future aspirations, and their plans to reconcile them. Some opt to save up in the city and eventually go back to the countryside. Others leave the village behind forever and never look back, struggling to be fully accepted as urban citizens. Finally, some others continue to move between the two spaces but take pride in their status as backward villagers, turning urban biases and temporal trajectories on their heads.

HONG AND THE CHALLENGES OF RETURN

The midday August sun blazes down on us, unforgiving. Fields are covered in lush rice sprouts ready to be transplanted. Hong and I spent the last twelve hours on an interminable bus ride punctuated by multiple breakdowns. At each stop Hong, used to the rapid zigzags on his bike in Bangkok, proposed to get off and make our way back to the city. Resisting his frustration with arrested movement, we remained on the bus that, forty minutes after passing through the provincial town of Nong Bua Lamphu, leaves us at a street corner, at the entrance of the small asphalt road that leads to Hong's village. There we hop on a tuk-tuk and head past the roundabout toward Hong's house. While this district has the lowest per capita income in the country—and the highest proportion of votes for pro-Thaksin parties—the village looks relatively affluent, and almost all of the houses have been walled in concrete and *finished*.

The front of Hong's home has been transformed into a small shop, a small attempt to collapse the village and the city. The family calls their tiny corner store Family Mart, a hat-tip to the chain shop that, together with 7-Eleven, dominates the streets of Bangkok. Hong's older sister, who recently moved back from Bangkok for health reasons, runs the shop. Outside, a large wooden table occupies a shaded area where patrons sit for a cigarette or a few glasses of rice whisky after a day of work in the fields. Once in a while somebody else stops by, mostly on motorcycle, and orders something. The top sellers are petrol, coffee, cigarettes, and alcohol. In front of the shop, life repeats as a regular cycle synchronized with nature. Hong's family wakes up at five in the morning, showers, drinks a cup of instant coffee, and heads to the small field where, at this time of year, they pull rice plants out of dry ground and plug them into larger wet fields. Grab, pull, shake, gather, tie, cut. Small bunches of plants pile up at the side of the dry field. Grab, pull, shake, gather, tie, cut. When a couple dozen bunches are ready, they gather them up one by one and hang them over a long bamboo stick, to carry them over the shoulder the few steps to the wet lots. There the bunches are transplanted into straight rows. Grab the bundle, pierce the soil with the thumb, and insert the small bunch in the ground. This cycle repeats over and over again until lunch break.

When the sun becomes too strong, Hong's mother walks into the bushes to harvest spices or vegetables for the daily meals. "We don't have to buy anything here," everybody repeats, especially Hong. As Thai urban migrants often do, Hong stresses the communitarian and precapitalist nature of the village, repeating a narrative that confirms the distance between the city and the village, but this time celebrating the morality of the village over that of the city. Through this narrative, which pretends to ignore the crude reality of rural debt, financial insecurity, and personal conflicts, Hong declares a nostalgia for a life that he himself has a difficult time adjusting to, even just for a few days. "He is having more problems getting used to this and working with me," Hong's mother tells me when he is too far away to hear. "He has been in the city too long, he cannot do anything with his hands anymore and he doesn't want to. He gets bored so fast. He cannot do with the way of life in the village. He is used to a fast life. Here every day is the same, slow. It is hard for him."

After lunch, the family goes back to work while Hong and I fall asleep, overloaded by food and physical work—insignificant compared to what seventy-year-old farmers around us sustain. "It is in our body already," Hong's grandfather tells me with an encouraging voice. "Sit down and take a rest, otherwise tomorrow your back will hurt." Hong rests next to me, out of boredom more than physical exhaustion. After the nap, I wake up and walk into the field where Boi, Hong's older brother, is working in silence. The skinny forty-year-old man entered monkhood when he was a child and came out a religious scholar twenty years later , the former abbot in the local forest temple where all of the boys of the family were ordained. Fed up with monastic life and ready to settle down with a woman, Boi disrobed, went back home, and lodged in a small shack in the field where he takes great pleasure in rural silence and calm. From there, he works alone, eats small amounts of food, and is treated by the family with the mixture of distance and respect normally reserved for monks. I start working by his side, the water coming up to our knees. After a few minutes of silence he raises his head, stares for a moment at Hong still sleeping at the side of the field, and begins to talk. "This is Hong," he says with a soft voice, interrupted by deep long pauses. "Living in speed and making a living out of it makes it really hard to go back to slowness." Bent over the rice field Boi continues, "especially if you are thirty years old and spent fifteen of them in the city." He pauses reflexively while slowly pushing another bunch of plants down into the inundated field. "Hong needs to go, to change activity, to feel like something is happening. Maybe someday he will find calm again."

If not as eloquently, Hong also voiced his hopes to find that calm someday, a dream that orients his present life in the city and his future plans to come back to the village. While Adun dreams of a vegetable farm, Hong's plan is to build a few wooden shacks in the field and transform them into home-stay guest houses for tourists. "There are a lot of *farang* like you who want to see the real Thailand." Hong ruminates. "They don't want to go to the islands and the Full Moon Parties. They want to see the countryside, learn how to grow rice, take pictures of the fields. You see the rice, it is something special and you don't have it back home. I talked to many tourists in Bangkok. They are all looking for something different from the usual experience. Sure, I will have to learn English, but that's not too hard, my sister speaks it a bit." Like Adun, Hong envisions a return based on money and experiences he accumulated in the city and plans on bridging its distance to the village by bringing tourists in. Hong's plans, however, seem to lose focus rather than gain clarity at each day he spends in the city. First, since he is young and single Hong struggles to save even a little money in Bangkok. Second, having lived in the city half of his life, Hong would need to readjust to the different rhythms of life in the village; something he himself knows would be hard. Used to the fast pace of urban life and to a job that values speed and uninterrupted mobility, Hong is frustrated and jaded by the slow pace of the village. In the city, even his waiting time at the motorcycle station is rife with expectations and interactions. Here in the countryside, waiting means having nothing to do and nothing to anticipate. The slowness of rural life, as much as the continual interruptions we experienced in the bus ride from Bangkok, grates on Hong's nerves, as it does to those of many other rural migrants.

A marvelous rendition of this feeling is offered in the film *Citizen Dog* (*Maa Nakorn*) directed by Wisit Sasanatieng, one of the main representatives of the Thai New Wave cinema. The 2004 box office hit narrates the story of Bod, a young Isan migrant who moves to Bangkok and falls in love with Jin, another migrant worker. Through a surreal mix of a cryptic discussion of urban class relations and a classic boy-meets-girl narrative, the story follows Bod's failed attempts to get closer to Jin. Halfway through the movie, Bod, ignored by her, finds no other way to get her out of his head than to go back to his native village. His return begins with a bucolic scene of Bod's mother sifting rice in slow motion. The whole time that Bod is in the village, everybody moves in slow motion while he moves at a normal speed. "Bod notices that everything moves more slowly in the country," the narrator explains. "His dad said that the reason it was like this was that Bod had been in Bangkok. Time in Bangkok must move faster than in the country. His Dad said he had just gotten there, but he'll get used to it. Many days passed by, but Bod didn't get used to it. Time passed slowly, making him hurt even more. Every breath, when thinking of Jin, took half the day. Bod decided to return to Bangkok."[16]

Both Hong and Adun mirrored Bod's feelings, minus the lover's yearning. They both commented on the difficulties of adjusting to this change of pace and the challenges it creates for their dreams of returning. The rhythm of village life appears to them as a thing of the past, both collective and personal, while at the same time their aspirations frame the village as a space of return, the ultimate locale for their personal futures. In between the two, the city operates as an interim space, one that is only functional, both economically and in terms of status, to that return. Yet as Hong spends more time in Bangkok, his urban experience undermines his ability to get reaccustomed to life in the countryside and potentially threatens the viability of his imagined return, eroding the very thing he longs for. Hong is eaten up by this contradiction. "I don't know if I will ever be able to really leave Bangkok, it has become part of me," he confides looking up at the tall building growing

16. Wisit 2004.

above his motorcycle taxi station. "It's strange. I like it and don't like it at the same time. Maybe I will get trapped here, like in a prison."

NOK AND THE ATTEMPT TO LEAVE
THE VILLAGE BEHIND

While Hong fears remaining stuck in the complex mesh of aspirations, experiences, and dreams that he lives in Bangkok, Nok, another driver who operates in one of the up-and-coming residential neighborhood in the city, embraces urban life and fully accepts the vision of the village as a space of the past, leaving it behind to never look back. Born in the central province of Lopburi, Nok arrived in Bangkok in 1992 to find a city in its prime, booming with economic growth, conspicuous consumption, and a construction bubble. "The first time I arrived in Bangkok," he recounts with shining eyes, "I knew this was it. I knew I had finally arrived at my place. The colors, the noises, the buildings, I loved every bit of it. Boring life in the village was not for me. I wanted something else." Even when the 1997 economic crisis pushed many migrants back home without an occupation, Nok was not discouraged. "I would have done anything to stay in Bangkok. It was where life was, where development was." Soon after the crisis, Nok started to drive a motorcycle taxi and to recraft his body and demeanor to fit in with urban life. He stopped going back to the village and basically cut off connections with his family there. He considered himself lucky enough to have been born in the central province so that his rural accent was easy to lose, but his skin tone was a different matter. Day after day Nok religiously relied on whitening creams to acquire the pallid tone so popular in the city. He cut his hair in fancy shops to emulate the various waves of Japanese and Korean pop stars that had surged and receded over the previous decade, and followed urban fashion trends with absolute dedication and great creativity. By the time I met him in 2010, it would be impossible to tell him apart from the fashionable office workers he carried around the city, were it not for his occupation as a driver which continued to mark him as an outsider. Nonetheless, no matter how hard he tried—Nok complained—people in Bangkok continued to look down on him as a backward villager. "I know what they think of me, but I don't care," he repeats unconvincingly. "I have been here for ten years. I know I will never become a Bangkok person for them, but I know this city better than they do. There is no point trying to convince them that I am more from

Bangkok than they are. It is like playing violin for the buffaloes to listen to," he concludes using a famous Thai proverb and subverting the epithet (buffalo) used normally to insult villagers by using it to refer to Bangkokians.

Nok accepts that his attempt to leave the village behind will never be completely successful in the eyes of locals. He nonetheless attempts to distance himself from the countryside and accepts its depiction as a not yet developed space. This is most clear in his interactions with other migrants, especially newcomers. During the low agricultural season, it is not uncommon to meet young migrants hanging out at motorcycle taxi stations around Bangkok, scouting for the possibility of moving to the city. New migrants almost always move to the city through existing social networks of fellow villagers who relocated to Bangkok before them, as was the case for Adun, Hong, and Nok himself. Motorcycle taxi drivers, owing to their phatic labor in the city and their connections with local dwellers, office workers, and factory owners, are privileged nodes of these networks. Over time, they solidify those connections into a full-fledged infrastructure of migration, one that allows young migrants to transform their dreams of moving to Bangkok into realities. In it, drivers operate as bridgeheads for the new migrants, hosts for their first weeks in Bangkok, guides to potential job opportunities, and facilitators to adjusting to life in the city.

In mid-March, Kon, a nineteen-year-old boy from Isan, arrived at Nok's station, taking advantage of one the drivers' hospitality to explore the city and try to find a job. During his trip, Kon often hung out at the station. There, he sat at a small iron table on the other side of the *soi* from the drivers. In the heat of midday, reclining on a plastic chair, Kon showed the toll that the city was taking on his body, nerves, and liver.

"The city is getting to his head," Nok tells me with a knowing smile. "We all lived this during our first years here. Drinking too much, visiting prostitutes, staying up late. It is the way of life of country people in the city. There are not many occasions to have fun in the countryside and here in the city there are too many. But this is not how people of Bangkok live. He will never find a job like this, he is drunk with life. Look at him, you could see from far away that he is a county bumpkin. His clothes don't fit him. Look at that military jacket; he is not in the jungle. And look at what he is drinking." Nok laughs. "Rice whiskey as if he was in the countryside."

While superficially these remarks show Nok's adoption of common urban bias against villagers, its tone reveals also his own discomfort, masked behind irony, in looking at a person who could be a younger version of himself. In the young Kon, Nok finds confirmation of the distancing narratives that oriented his lives, of the distance he himself has covered to become who he is today, and of how, to people in Bangkok, he will always remain closer to Kon than to them, no matter how expensive his haircut looks or how much whitening cream he puts on.

BOON AND THE PRIDE OF BACKWARDNESS

Doomed to never be fully accepted as urban dwellers, other drivers go the opposite way and transform urban bias into a source of pride, wearing them as badges of honor. Boon, the driver who negotiated the entrance of a local child into a good school, was one of them. Boon came from an uncharacteristically prosperous cluster of villages in northeastern Thailand. The area was selected in the 1990s for a pilot agricultural project to expand rubber farming from southern Thailand. The results were, at least at the time of my research, remarkable.[17] Each house had a pick-up truck parked outside, roads were paved, the village school had a computer room, and a steady flow of returnees from Bangkok joined the remunerative agricultural business. Boon was not, and would not be, among them. He had migrated to Bangkok in the 1980s looking, like thousands of other migrants from the northeastern region, for a good income, entertainment (*pai thīeo*), and a modern life (*chīwit bǽp thansamai*).[18] However, since rubber was introduced in his village, the modern technology of the plantation cut him off from home. During his family's first harvest, Boon discovered he was allergic to the chemicals used to transform rubber into latex. He started to visit only occasionally and accepted he could never go back to work there. Boon's life in Bangkok had been a sequence of low-paying jobs, some decent and some remembered with contempt, which came to a halt with the 1997 crisis. Unable to go back to his village, Boon bought a bike and became a driver. Income was not a central concern to Boon, as a share of the family farm ensured him a regular cash flow. Nor, it seemed, was personal safety, as testified by his upper body, scarred by the signs of multiple road accidents, the most serious of which shattered his forearm, leaving his right arm slightly bent, unable to distend fully. He was, however, a prideful man, determined to not let the city, where

17. The global price of rubber has since plummeted.
18. Mills 1997; Pattana 2006b; Walker 2012.

he was condemned to remain, destroy his sense of self-worth and enjoyment of life.

On a torrid Sunday morning of the rainy season of 2009, Boon invited me to ride to the outskirts of Bangkok and go fishing in the marshes that surround the city where the father of one of his friends had built a small wooden shack. Happy to leave the city, I joined them. We rode down empty highways and started to see Bangkok crumbling into a mosaic of wet plots of land and ordered ponds. Feeling hungry and having no experience fishing, I worried that I would not catch anything. My worries were soon relieved. Along the way we stopped at one of the many side-road huts that keep basins full of squids, shrimps, and catfish. We picked up a few kilos of each of them, three bottles of whisky, twelve bottles of soda, three bags of ice, and, just to be sure, a couple servings of duck noodles as a present for the old couple who was hosting us. It was pretty clear that "fishing" was a pretext for gorging on food and alcohol.

The shack faced a crystal clear pond and had a wide veranda extending over the water. A portable DVD player and a large fan sat at the corner of the veranda where Boon's friend's parents were eating. We greeted them, scooped the duck noodles into a bowl we added to their food, and put out three fishing rods that we quickly forgot about as we started to grill the fish we bought. As always in convivial situations in Thailand, everybody sitting around the mat made sure that everybody else was properly served and taken care of. Different dishes were circulated to make sure nobody had to overextend their arms to grab them. Similarly, whenever a glass was nearly empty, one of us filled it with ice, a few splashes of whisky, and a copious serving of soda and passed it back to his owner. In a few hours we went through the first two bottles of whisky and dozed off on the mat.

Seeing us sweat, the older woman begun to apologize for not having any air conditioning. "I really would like to have air conditioning, but the money is never enough." She voiced as she piled away our dishes. "This is our life. We worked hard for many years and now we are retired but still cannot afford the comfort of people in Bangkok. We are not yet at their level, fighting the heat with an old fan while they have air conditioning." Boon jumped up, surprisingly awake. "Screw air conditioning. We are not city people. We are villagers and we should be proud of it. We don't need their things, we have something else, with all their development in the city people of Bangkok don't even know how to survive."

He launched into a parable. "Two men were alone in a dirt road. One was a big professor, an urban person with a Ph.D. He had read many books, he drove a big car, and people greeted him with respect whenever they saw him. The other was a villager. He worked all his life and never went to school. People thought he was stupid, a buffalo. The two had been walking for the whole day without meeting anybody and had no food with them. Night was coming, they were starving, and dangerous animals were beginning to come out, so they started looking for food and shelter. Tell me, Claudio," Boon asked me defiantly. "Who do you think survived?" Before I even had the time to respond, he answered with pleasure: "The villager. He knew what plants he could eat, how animals moved at night, and where to sleep. The day after he woke up and continued to walk to town. The professor spent the night looking for food, ate a poisonous plant, and remained half dead on the side of the road." He concluded with a sneering laugh. "Isn't that true? We villagers may be uneducated, not yet developed, but we know how to survive. At the end, that is the most important thing, not air conditioning."

With this story Boon was not only teasing me on the worthlessness of my academic pedigree but inverting dominant narratives that cast the village as backward and pit it against the developed city. If Adun, Hong, and Nok tried to bridge and mend the anxieties created by those distancing narratives, Boon widened them even further, turning them upside-down, finding pride in the resulting distance, and making the apparent underachiever into the hero. While Boon may have been unique in the forcefulness of his convictions, a collective sense of self-respect and dignity had been growing among the drivers over the previous decade—a confidence not just in their lives as rural migrants but also in their profession in the city and its importance for Bangkok. This confidence had been boosted by the rise to power of Thaksin Shinawatra, a tycoon but also a man from the provincial capital of Chiang Mai, who offered the drivers a social, economic, and political recognition they had never experienced before.

FOUR

The Paradoxes of Freedom

Freedom is a project . . . flanked by the problem of power on all
sides: the power against which it arrays itself as well as the power
it must claim to enact itself.

WENDY BROWN, *States of Injury*

ADUN WAS BORN ON A HOT AUGUST afternoon of 1966 in a village fifty
miles from the Laotian border. He came to the world in a swampy wooden
house surrounded by rice fields. His mother sweated through a whole day of
labor, accompanied by the local midwife. His father waited outside, chain-
smoking hand-rolled cigarettes and nervously listening to his wife's screams,
hoping to hear her voice after Adun's first cry. Too many of his friends lost
their wives in labor but fortunately she was not one of them. She delivered
Adun without problems: a chubby boy, their first son.

His father was a quiet man, a heavy smoker, and a womanizer who often
disappeared for long periods, heading to what Adun later suspected may have
been his second—or third—family. Adun's mother, on the contrary, was loud
and never went anywhere. She was the forceful master of the house, an ener-
getic and at times imposing figure who gave her husband's silence the feeling
of a balancing effect more than a personal trait. "When she walked out of the
house," Adun remembers, "the dogs always stopped barking."

After Adun, two younger sisters were born. They soon became his favorite
playmates as older children in the village became teenagers and disappeared
one after the other, attracted by the swelling Bangkok of the 1970s. Adun
spent his early years running in the fields, catching catfish and mice, gathering food in the woods, and helping to harvest rice and sell it to Thai-Chinese
buyers who came to the village once a year. He was liked by the other villagers
and grew close to the local monk, who saw in him a potential pupil, one

gifted with a talent for deep thoughts. Adun, however, preferred running in the fields to the quiet of the monk's quarters.

In 1974 a group of leftist university students who participated in taking down the ruling military government came to Adun's village to build a school that replaced the temple, where he had studied until then. It was the first time he saw women with short hair and skirts. "Their skin was so white," he remembers, "not like us, farmers darkened by the sun. I dreamed of being like them one day, a university student like them, helping to develop [*phatthanā*] the nation." University, however, was not really an option for a farmer's son and his contribution to development of the nation was to be through manual labor. After finishing his primary education, Adun started to work in the fields full-time. He looked after the family farm and, during harvest season, traveled around the province with a group of seasonal workers as they cut their way through hectares and hectares of sugar canes owned by large agro-business companies that had started to penetrate the region. "The pay was terrible—Adun recounts—but it was a decent job. We went to sleep with a tired body, not with a restless mind as in Bangkok." With his first stipend he bought a small portable radio that he carried everywhere. During the day, Adun listened to news from the city. At night, he dreamed of its big roads, of the giant buildings that grew from the soil above the trees all the way to the sky, and of the unlimited fun to be had there. By the time he turned fifteen or, as he punctuates time, as soon as he got his national ID, Adun had already made up his mind: he would move to Bangkok. In just a few weeks he got everything ready and he jumped on a train in September 1981. "Bangkok was more than I expected . . . it was . . . you know . . . people everywhere . . . traffic, noises, colors, smells . . . " His eyes wander as he struggles to find the words. In the city, he rented a cramped room in one of the many small slums that were popping up to house the steady flow of internal migrants, not far away from where he works today as a motorcycle taxi driver. With the help of a friend from the village, Adun found a job in a small shoe factory and joined the urban working class who manned the booming industrial economy of Bangkok.

This was the era of the Asian Tigers. Between 1986 and 1996, Southeast Asian economies grew exponentially, led by a massive influx of foreign capital and a realignment of national economies toward export-oriented industrialization. Over this decade, the Thai GDP grew an average 9.5 percent per year—faster than in any other nation in the world—as the volume of exported goods rose at a yearly average of 14.8 percent.[1] Following the economic boom, Adun hopped from factory to factory, changing one job after the other. He never thought of becoming a motorcycle taxi driver, even though he must inevitably have encountered the system as it grew from a few hundred drivers concentrated in rare groups in the early 1980s to almost forty thousand a decade later. "If there were motorcycle taxis when I got to the city, I did not even notice them," he tells me sitting on top of his motorcycle. "At that time, we were workers, we wanted to work in a company."

The Thai economic miracle in the 1980s and early 1990s was neither based on a service economy nor on market liberalization and state-retreat as proposed by the International Monetary Fund (IMF) and the United State Treasury under the Washington Consensus. Rather, it was driven by a strong state that managed a gradual liberalization of markets; planned industrial, social, and monetary policy; and brokered compromise between capital and labor along Fordist lines.[2] This meant the expansion of mass industrial production together with the transformation of workers into consumers, through growing salaries. In European social democracies, this configuration was also connected with the development of Keynesian welfare programs; in Thai Fordism salaries remained the main mechanisms for redistribution.[3] Welfare state provisions were never introduced and economic growth went

1. Pasuk and Baker 1996.
2. I rely on Bob Jessop's definition of Fordism as a process that can be analyzed on four levels. "As a distinctive type of labour process [that] involves mass production based on moving assembly lines technique operated by the semi-skilled labour of the mass worker. . . . As a stable mode of macroeconomic growth that involves a virtuous cycle of growth based on mass production, rising productivity based on economy of scales, rising income linked to productivity, and increased mass demand due to rising wages. . . . As a mode of social and economic regulation [that] involves the separation of ownership and control in large corporations with a distinctive multi-divisional, decentralized organisation subject to central controls; monopoly pricing; union recognition and collective bargaining; wage indexed to productivity growth and retail price inflation; and monetary emission and credit policies oriented to securing effective aggregate demand. . . . And, fourthly, as a general pattern of social organisation [that] involved the consumption of standardized, mass commodities in nuclear family households and provision of standardized, collective goods and services by the bureaucratic state" (Jessop 1991, 136–37).
3. In the Thai context, therefore, it is critical to distinguish between Fordism, a specific configuration which organizes the relation between capital and labor (in term of process, macroeconomic growth, regulation, and organization), and Keynesianism, which deals more directly with the relation between markets and states (in terms of incentives, planning, and security).

hand in hand with growing inequality, unhealthy living conditions, and lack of services. Nonetheless, minimum wages kept rising. Between 1982 and 1992 they tripled, from 50 baht per day to 150 ($3 at the time).[4] In this period, to use Adun's words, you wanted to be a worker and the company's floor promised to transform you into a citizen and a mass consumer of urban commodities, lifestyles, and leisure activities.

Over these years, Adun filled his cramped room with small mass-produced luxuries—a better radio, a wall clock, an electric rice cooker—as his urban income contributed to the economic and agricultural life of his family back home, transformed by a small rototiller he brought for them. His wardrobe changed, his haircut changed. By the early 1990s, in his occasional trips back home, Adun sported a newly bought Yamaha motorbike, a leather jacket, spotless white jeans, and a pair of aviator sunglasses. "Look at this," he tells me as he spreads snapshots on a mat in his living room. "I looked like a thug. I thought I was hot shit. Always showing off, always running after women and visiting prostitutes. I looked good, though. Didn't I?"

Adun had become a successful migrant—a worker, a consumer, and a citizen—and the embodiment of the heroic migrant manhood that dominated rural imaginaries at the time.[5] This dominant form of masculinity was characterized by an often unresolved tension between the image of the rogue—drinking, gambling, and smoking—womanizer and that of the moral breadwinner, committed to his family, his village, and his woman back home. While today Adun has fully endorsed the second model, in the early 1990s he was living his womanizer days, which he remembers with a mix of self-dismissal, irony, and nostalgia. In 1991, while he was working in a garment factory in Bangkok, Adun met Gai, a young woman from the northeastern province of Loey. Their love story blossomed against the backdrop of shop floors, where they spent endless hours sewing piles of jeans, and Bangkok's tourist destinations where they took advantage of their new lives as urban worker-consumers and the leisure activities that they entailed.[6] They flew kites in Sanam Luang, the expansive ground in front of the Royal Palace, where many of the internal migrants spent their few free days. They drank beer sitting on Memorial Bridge, feet hanging over the river at dusk. And they strolled

4. Pasuk and Baker 2002; Stiglitz 2002.
5. This concept of the "heroic migrant manhood" has been proposed and extensively explored in the work of the late Pattana Kitiarsa (Pattana 2005a, b, 2006b, 2007, 2008, 2009, 2012a).
6. Mills 1999a, 2012.

through the shiny new shopping malls, cathedrals of the new era of economic prosperity for the country. A year later, Gai got pregnant.

After some deliberation they decided they would get married and that Gai would move back to Adun's village to have the baby, a decision that—when Adun is not around—she admits to regretting. "I miss the city," Gai voices squatting in the outdoor kitchenette in their village home. "I had so many friends there, life was fun. Here there is nobody. The kids are getting older and then will soon be gone. Adun is there, and I am here, alone." The unequal gender relations that dominated Adun's household as a child had gone full circle. Like his father, he was an absent parent, away from home for months at a time. Gai, who had migrated to Bangkok with the same dreams of a more exciting life, was back in the village, raising children, like Adun's mother had done, performing the unpaid care work that allowed him to stay in the city.

Meanwhile, Adun continued to send remittances back home, fulfilling his filial and paternal obligations and crafting his image as a successful bread-winner. From the village, his life seemed almost perfect. In the city, however, he was growing frustrated with the difficult adjustment to the discipline of labor on the factory floor and the constant experience of oppression and personal dismissal. Before moving to the city, Adun, like thousands of other migrants who were flooding to Bangkok, complemented seasonal work in the fields with occasional wage labor. Whether as paid or unpaid labor, their activities in the village were organized according to social hierarchies and relations that went beyond the labor processes. Age, family relations, exper-tise, and status framed a hierarchy that was transparent and navigable to them compared to the division of labor found in the companies where they landed once in the city. To be clear, the village was not some mythological and precapitalist space of free and equitable production in contrast to the egoistic materialism of the city, as implied by dominant discourses in Thai society.[7] Nor was it true that class, bureaucratic titles, and social standing played no role there. Rather, social relations and interactions in the village preceded and extended beyond labor transactions. Disciplining labor, there-fore, could not take the form of direct and frontal dismissal, attack, or

7. John and Jean Comaroff have defined these representations, in which local communi-ties mobilize traditional or precapitalist symbols and practices in response to new forces of material and ideological domination, "poetics of contrast" (Comaroff and Comaroff 1992, 175–76). For an examination of these poetics in the Thai context see Chatthip 1999; Dayley 2011; Vandergeest 1993.

scolding without the risk of jeopardizing social standing, for both the employer and the employee.

The anonymity of urban industrial production subjected rural migrants to very different treatment: factory employers and employees had little at stake in the preservation of good relationships or social reciprocities beyond honoring their working arrangement. While this configuration offered a respite from the expectations of the localized and intimate social hierarchies that organized life in the village, it also created a space in which disdain, scorn, and open derision—forms of engagement that are strongly sanctioned in Thailand[8]—came to color the relationship between workers and employers. To make things worse for rural migrants like Adun, a deeply rooted urban bias against them exacerbated their already uneven interactions in urban factories. In particular, the discourses of the backward and stupid villager (*chāo bān*), often framed in a dehumanizing language that compared migrants to water buffaloes (*khwāi*),[9] provided the framework for the relationship between urban employers and rural employees. "It was terrible," Adun recounts with barely contained anger. "I wanted to walk away so many times. Many others did. But I had a family." His salary grew every year and, with a child at home and another on the way, Adun could not be too picky. "I put my head down, worked hard, and hoped things would change."

Things did change, but not for the better. In 1992, the World Bank published a report entitled *The East Asian Miracle*. This text, while recognizing the central roles that state interventions and regulations had played in the growth of Thailand, presented them merely as *market facilitating*, rather than as an alternative to the IMF's one-size-fits-all free market prescriptions. As a result, the World Bank proposed an agenda consistent with the IMF's approach and advocated for further liberalization of national economies.[10] The newly elected government of Chuan Leekpai, strengthened by international confidence in Thailand's growth, followed these suggestions and liberalized national capital markets with the belief that this would help the economy grow even faster. The country became a laboratory for the application of the structural adjustments peddled around the globe by International

8. For an extensive treatment of the importance of face and the social sanctions associated with being ridiculed and embarrassed in Thai society see Persons 2016.

9. The same language was adopted to describe the descent of rural protesters during the Red Shirts' protests (Thongchai 2010).

10. Robison and Hewison 2004; Stiglitz and Yusuf 2001; Wade 1996.

Financial Institutions (IFI). The effects were tripartite: international capital flooded the country; national companies borrowed heavily from international markets; and the banking system was deregulated, leaving its actors free to invest in whatever sector of the economy they wanted, rather than having to follow the government directives that had dominated the previous decades of economic growth. The Thai economy inflated rapidly, new capital entered the country, and real estate became an enormously profitable market, apparently confirming the IMF's expectations.

As the Thai economy became increasingly financialized, industrial wages stopped growing. Adun realized it was time to move on. Sensitive as always to shifting opportunities, he left the factory floor and got a job in construction. He started roaming the country building tourist resorts. "Traveling was nice," he recounts. "I saw many parts of the country. I liked especially the South, the islands. But the work was hard and dangerous. People fell from the bamboo scaffolding all the time. Many people got injured, some died. We worked so many hours per day. We would arrive somewhere; build huts with corrugated iron next to the construction site; work and sleep. Sometimes we got a day off and we went to the beach, swam a bit, had fun with women. I did not go home very much, but we were all young men from the northeast, so it felt like home. It was a hard life but we were among friends." He sighs. "Then the crisis arrived and we all lost our jobs."

On May 14 and 15, 1997, the Thai currency was hit by speculative attacks. Driven by the financial liberalization pushed by the IFI, capital rapidly flew out of the country, destabilizing the national economy. This was the spark that ignited the Asian financial crisis. In a few days, the baht lost more than half its value. Suddenly most Thai companies that had borrowed in foreign currencies saw their debt burden doubled and went into bankruptcy, provoking an estimated 2 million layoffs in finance, real estate, industry, and construction.[11] Many of the laid-off workers drifted back toward agricultural work, which traditionally offered a security net in times of economic recession, or toward more insecure, informal, service-oriented occupations. Paradoxically, at a moment when flows seemed to come to halt, informal transportation, and driving motorcycle taxis in particular, became one of the occupations that absorbed these workers. In 1994 the city was traversed by an estimated 37,500 drivers. After the crisis, their number skyrocketed. By 2003

11. Pasuk and Baker 2008b.

the ranks of motorcycle taxis had expanded almost threefold, to 109,056.[12] Adun was one of them.

ON THE MEANING OF *'ITSARAPHĀP*

After losing his job in construction, Adun returned to Bangkok, hoping to find something to sustain his family. He reconnected with a friend from his province who was a driver near one of the small factories Adun had worked in. During the previous years, the neighborhood had transformed into an expensive residential area, a few tangled alleys away from Bangkok's financial center. Since the crisis, many had left, pushed away by the rising rent prices and layoffs. His friend was among them. Before heading back to the northeast, he sold Adun his driver's vest, which operated as an informal license to ride a motorcycle taxi. It was 1998 and Adun's convoluted life path had brought him back to the neighborhood he once worked in when he first arrived in Bangkok. This time, however, rather than bent over a factory table, he was sitting on his motorcycle on the side of the road, chin up, waiting for clients.

The following years were harsh for Adun, as they were for the country at large. Bangkok struggled to restart its economic flow and the recovery promised by IFI failed to materialize. Nonetheless, many of the new drivers decided to remain in their new occupation. If a multitude of paths brought them to the job, *'itsaraphāp* (freedom, independence) convinced them to stick with it. Adun was outspoken about the importance of freedom to his personal and work choices. Sitting at his street corner, he told me: "My family and I are happy with this job. It is a free life. You can come and go from home anytime; you can get money fast, every day, without waiting for the salary. I have *'itsaraphāp*."

What is this *'itsaraphāp?* I asked.

"I can go home whenever I want. I don't have to take leave. Don't have to ask anyone. I don't have to come to work if I get sick or get drunk. If I earn enough money for the day and I want to go home to sleep, I can do that. This is *'itsaraphāp*. I used to work for a company, I went home often and I was never promoted. I have to go back home to the village regularly: my family is there, my farm is there. . . . I like my job because it is a free job. I was offered

---

12. These numbers come from unpublished data on motorcycles registered for public use obtained by the author at the Ministry of Land Transportation.

to go back to work in the company I used to work for, but that job in Bangkok is bad for a countryman like me. The boss always looks down on you, always orders you around, always insults you. In the construction company, the boss's son kept insulting me, shouting at me, treating me like scum. A twenty-year-old kid with no experience, just out of university; I could not accept that. So I am happy now, I am my own boss."

Adun was by no means alone in celebrating being his own boss. Almost every single one of the drivers I spent time with echoed his sentiments, even those who did not share Adun's economic struggles. Boon, with his prideful attitude and solid economic situation, was also an adamant defender of the importance of the 'itsaraphāp offered by his new occupation.

"I never liked to follow orders," he told me sitting on his bike, a cigarette hanging from his mouth. "I came to Bangkok to have my own life and I found myself sitting at a table, fixing electric components or sewing bags. Now I have a free profession ['āchīp'itsara], I come to work whenever I want, I leave whenever I need."

"But you always stay until night. I see you here every morning until sundown, you work more than in a factory."

"Yes," he interrupted, "but it's my own decision."

Similar exchanges were repeated, with minimal variations, hundreds of times over the course of my research. If entertainment and modernity had attracted many of the drivers to Bangkok in the 1980s and 1990s and kept them in its Fordist economy, by the early 2010s 'itsaraphāp had taken over both as a motivation for choosing a line of work and as a source of pride and personal dignity, at least among workers who were pushed out of the factory floor and joined the booming service economy.[13] Adun and Boon were just two of the many drivers who claimed human and economic independence from the crushing machine of industrial mass production and its organization of labor, as well as a renewed participation in the economic and emotional life of their villages, through the idiom of 'itsaraphāp. But what did 'itsaraphāp mean to them? Why did the same people who wanted to be workers in the 1980s now strive to be their own free bosses? And what did this shift mean for them personally and, more broadly, for Thai capitalism after the 1997 crisis?

13. Maureen Hickey has pointed out the emergence of the discourse of 'itsara in her study of cab drivers in Bangkok and argued that traditional Thai discourse of 'itsara "stressing free will and responsibility for one's actions, has been reworked to reflect the neoliberal ideals of the autonomous individual and rational economic actor" (Hickey 2011).

The word *'itsaraphāp* is composed by *'itsara* (to be free, independent, sovereign) and *phāp* (state, condition) and derives from the Sanskrit *is'vara,* meaning lord, ruler, chief, or king. In its original meaning the word was used to refer to the supremacy of a kingdom over another or of a lord over his subjects. In this understanding, a ruler had *'itsaraphāp* over his subjects, not the other way around. At the end of the nineteenth century, on top of using the word to refer to the power of a selected group over another, *'itsaraphāp* was first adopted as the opposite of oppression, in particular with reference to Siam's defense of its own sovereignty and independence from French and British colonial expansion in Southeast Asia. Once again, however, the word was not used in relation to individuals of low ranks. It was only as a product of legal diatribes over slavery and family law and the introduction of the 1908 Penal Code that *'itsaraphāp* began to be used to refer to an innate quality of all humans, one that "each person naturally possessed . . . and could not be deprived of."[14] Finally, in the 1930s, as western-educated Siamese elites promoted the idea of individual free will against the authority of the sovereign, *'itsaraphāp* assumed its present-day individualistic connotations of self-reliance and sovereignty over oneself, against exterior oppression.[15]

Adun's and Boon's depictions of *'itsaraphāp*—as that of many other drivers I talked to—retained this meaning in a double sense. Taking up this occupation, even if as a result of post-crisis layoffs, offered them *'itsaraphāp from* the discipline and discrimination of industrial production that infantilized, dehumanized, and forced them to subdue their working hours and their participation in village life to the whims of their boss. Becoming drivers gave them *'itsaraphāp to* decide if and when to go to work, return to their villages, and ultimately to be their "own bosses" and make their "own decisions." In this double territory of positive freedom (as *freedom to*) and negative freedom (*freedom from*)—echoing the classic work of Isaiah Berlin[16]—the new job emerged as a synonym of *'itsaraphāp*. It gave Adun and Boon the opportunity to live a less alienated life by refusing the factory floor and reclaiming ownership over their work and family lives.

'Itsaraphāp, however, did not just offer the drivers personal emancipatory opportunities. It also created the conditions under which an increasing number of unnecessary industrial laborers, laid off after the 1997 crisis, con-

14. Loos 1998, 43.
15. Loos 1998; Thanet 1998; Thongchai 1994, 133–35.
16. Berlin 1969.

sented to move toward more unstable, precarious, and insecure forms of employment.[17] This shift gave them new freedoms but also took away job security, fixed contracts, and the ability to bargain collectively that decades of labor struggles had granted them. In this sense, *itsaraphāp* not only helped the drivers *make sense* of their labor trajectories by claiming pride in and agency over their lives; it also allowed them to *make do* with the post-crisis political-economic restructuring and align their everyday lives, desires, and aspirations to the new configuration of Thai capitalism. Much like what the introduction of rubber plantations had done to Boon's life, or what the 1992 IMF report did to Adun's growing wages in the industrial sector, the 1997 economic crisis shifted the landscape in which the drivers used to live and work and demanded they find new paths through it. *Itsaraphāp* was integral to that transformation as it provided a "common material and meaningful framework for living through, talking about, and acting upon social orders characterized by domination."[18]

FROM WORKERS TO ENTREPRENEURS

The 1997 crisis had a profound effect on Thai capitalism. The crash burst the country's dreams of global prosperity and its faith in economic liberalization. More broadly, it reorganized its model of accumulation. Until 1993 Thai

17. Analysis of precarity have mostly emerged in the context of advanced economies and retreating welfare states (Allison 2012; Molé 2013; Muehlebach 2013; Standing 2011). As a result, some scholars have argued for the validity of the concept exclusively in these contexts (Neilson and Rossiter 2008), while others have retained its usefulness to describe global trends in contemporary capitalism (Kalleberg and Hewison 2013; Lee and Kofman 2012; Munck 2013). I take the second view and argue for its relevance to contemporary Thailand, but I acknowledge that this path would need a clearer definition of precarity in this context. Unfortunately the few anthropologists of Thailand who adopted this concept did so without defining its meaning in a country in which the welfare state has been expanding in recent decades, rather than contracting (Endō 2014; A. A. Johnson 2012). In order to exit this impasse, I here define precarity as an experience created by a variety of forms of unstable, flexible, unbounded, and individualized employment, which is only marginally protected by social benefits, legal provisions, or collective bargaining. These include the informalization of labor, seasonal and temporary employment, homework, flex and temp work, subcontracting, freelancing, and self-employment. While this status emerges out of labor arrangements, the conditions they generate go well beyond the sphere of employment and extend their characteristics of instability, flexibility, and individualization to subjectivities, social relations, or imaginaries of the future.

18. Roseberry 1994, 361.

economic growth had been driven by a Fordist model, characterized by an alignment between mass industrial production and a compromise between labor and capital that incentivized migrants to become industrial workers and modern consumers. Since then, however, wages stopped growing, replaced by speculative financial bubbles as the primary means of capitalist accumulation. When these bubbles burst, the country entrenched the neoliberal transformations that had generated them in the first place. In August 1997, the country entered the IMF recovery program. In the following months, Thailand received $17 billion USD in loans from different sources.[19] As is often the case, the money came with strings attached. Thailand initiated a season of structural adjustments that involved privatization, liberalization of the economy, a push toward macroeconomic austerity, deregulation of financial markets, and unprecedented access given to international companies. Even if the crisis had been the effect of IFI's push toward deregulation, it was presented by the IMF—now holding the reins of the Thai economy through the recovery program—as the effect of crony capitalism and state interventions, "proving" once and for all the superiority of free markets over planned economies.[20] In 1993, IFI had praised Thailand as evidence of the effectiveness of their neoliberal proposals; by 1997 the country was attacked with the patronizing attitude of a father scolding a bad boy who had not followed his directives. Milton Friedman once argued that "only a crisis— actual or perceived—produces real change. When that crisis occurs, actions that are taken depend on the ideas that are lying around . . . alive and available until the politically impossible becomes politically inevitable."[21] This crisis, as the global financial crisis in 2008,[22] became an opportunity for apologists of neoliberalism to present their agenda as politically inevitable. The IMF strong-armed the sinking economy to conform to their credo. Thailand became a laboratory for post-crisis austerity measures, similar to those rolled out in Southern Europe since 2010. The recipe was to reduce regulations on capital flows, strike workers protections, and limit fiscal spending. For workers like Adun and Boon this meant, quite simply, losing

19. The lenders were: Japan $4 billion; the central banks of Australia, China, Hong Kong, Malaysia, and Singapore $1 billion each; the central banks of South Korea and Indonesia $0.5 billion each; the World Bank $1.5 billion and the Asian Development Bank $1.2 billion. Since then, Japan has taken up the contributions of South Korea and Indonesia.

20. Beeson and Islam 2005, Robison and Hewison 2005.

21. Friedman 1962, viii–ix.

22. Mirowski 2013.

their jobs and any form of labor security, collective bargaining, and wage support that they had obtained in the previous decades.

Any attempt to oppose this approach was crushed into conformity by the threat of stopping international loans. Immediately after the crash, Prime Minister Chavalit Yongchaiyudh tried to introduce a mild form of capital control to prevent foreign capital from abandoning the sinking Thai economy. The IMF cornered the government into retracting these measures. The results were disastrous. International capital, free to leave, fled the country as the national economy sank. While neighboring Malaysia refused the IMF's diktat and limited the outflow of international capital, starting its road to recovery, the Thai economy continued to collapse, bringing down its leader. The government of Chavalit fell in October 1997 and Chuan Leekpai, the prime minister who directed the market liberalization after 1993, returned to office in early 1998, with the support of the IMF. The new government was a vane caught in the wind of IFI. Following their directives, Chuan moved to put an end to the Fordist configuration that had driven the country in the previous decades and sacrificed it, along with the country's economic sovereignty, to the altar of neoliberal orthodoxy.

The plan, however, like previous attempts to reorganize Bangkok, remained largely incomplete, haunted by established economic practices, expectations, and alternative models governing the relations between state and markets. The loss of sovereignty provoked by accepting IMF funds generated a pushback by nationalist forces. Public opinion blamed the crisis on a purposeful plan by the United States to destabilize the growing Asian economies through capital speculation and IMF's interventions. Boon, with his love for conspiracy theory and unapologetically nationalist feelings, was adamant in seeing the hands of international powers behind the crisis, and Thai economic performance under the IMF plan hardly proved him wrong. The Thai economy continued to plunge. The national GPD fell by 7.9 percent in 1997, 12.3 percent in 1998, and 7 percent in the first half of 1999.[23] By 2000, Thailand was still in recession while Malaysia, ignoring the IMF's suggestions, had solidly recovered. The pro-IMF government of Chuan Leekpai had lost its popular support, not only for its failure to deliver economic recovery but also for allowing and supporting policies that were largely perceived as an international attack on Thai political and economic self-determination.

23. Stiglitz 2002, 127.

The attempt to introduce market neoliberalism in Thailand had been a failure, both economically and socially. As Friedrich Hayek, the founding father of this economic discipline, argued, the success of any economic theory is predicated upon the acceptance of a social philosophy that is persuasive only if connected to a compelling worldview.[24] Three years after the crisis, the neoliberal worldview of free markets and retreating states was simply not compelling for Thailand—economically, socially, or electorally.

A new electoral alliance started to emerge, opposing the neoliberal agenda proposed by the ruling Democrat Party. It included business leaders who opposed the internationalization of the Thai economy, employees of state enterprises and social activists who opposed privatizations, government officials who saw their power decreased under the influence of IFI, middle classes who had been crushed by the economic crisis and the failed recovery, and—most prominently—rural masses and their urban migrants like Boon and Adun who, more than anybody, were feeling the negative effects of neoliberal policies.[25] These forces brought Thaksin Shinawatra to power in 2001.

Thaksin was elected prime minister with a solid majority and an ambitious plan to reform Thai politics and society. The son of a politically connected middle-class family in Chiang Mai,[26] Thaksin had broken into the business world in the late 1980s, acquiring a large portion of the national mobile communication sector through his personal connections and state contracts. The 1997 economic crisis left his businesses largely untouched, with less liquidity but in a stronger market position. Aside from strengthening his domination over telecommunications, the crisis marked a major turning point in Thaksin's political career. On July 14, 1998, after a series of unimpressive performances in ministerial positions,[27] he founded the Thai Rak Thai (TRT) Party. As the party leader, Thaksin leaned heavily on his advisors' expertise and mixed a strong refusal of the IMF policies with decisive leadership and an almost obsessive reliance on marketing techniques. The strategy worked. He was elected prime minister in 2001 and four years later he went on to become the first premier in Thai history to serve a full term and

24. As cited in Burgin 2012, 51.
25. Glassman 2010b, 1311.
26. Thaksin carefully manicured his narrations of his family background, often stressing its lower class and regional upbringing and hiding the prominent political role his father had in Chiang Mai.
27. Thaksin had unimpressively held three short ministerial positions, once as minister of foreign affairs and twice as deputy prime minister, between 1994 and 1997.

be reelected. Thaksin—a former policeman turned communication tycoon turned populist leader—had become the most unlikely proponent of an alternative to the neoliberal agenda—a hero for Adun and Boon.

Under Thaksin, the country continued its move toward flexible accumulation, a regime that pushed "flexibility with respect to labor processes, labor markets, products, and patterns of consumption, . . . characterized by the emergence of entirely new sectors of production, new ways of providing financial and business services, new markets, and, above all, greatly intensified rates of commercial, technological and organizational innovation."[28] Yet, contrary to the IMF's prescriptions, the new prime minister envisioned a significant expansion of the state's role in promoting economic growth and managing its social consequences.[29] This approach, soon dubbed Thaksinomics, was a mixture of economic nationalism, market advocacy, and welfare state tendencies. It proposed the flexibilization of labor markets, the application of the logic of management to public administration, and the redefining of citizens as risk-taking entrepreneurs—typical of neoliberal doctrine—but coupled it with an expansion of social provisions, not the shrinking advocated by neoliberal forces. In a speech to police officers, Thaksin explained: "Capitalism has targets but no ideals, while socialism has ideals but no targets[, therefore] we need to combine the best of each. . . . I'm applying socialism in the lower economy, and capitalism in the upper economy."[30] The idea was quite simple: the Thai economy would operate on a dual track, the upper one would follow market liberalization, the lower—of which they drivers were a part—would be heavily supported by state interventions, in particular an expansion of the welfare state.[31] Seen in this light, the usual narrative of the expansion of neoliberalism as a result of economic crisis hardly fits the trajectory of contemporary Thailand. Nonetheless, scholars of Thailand continue to refer to his policies and the larger Thai economic system over that decade as neoliberal.[32] Projecting this label onto a country that has seen a wide expansion of the welfare state, not a retreat, is highly problematic. First, it means extending the definition of neoliberalism so widely as to make it analytically useless. Second, it means ignoring local contexts, imposing a Euro-American lens over them, and assuming a uniform

28. Harvey 1989, 1.
29. Harris 2015.
30. Pasuk and Baker 2004, 342.
31. Hewison 2008; Kasian 2002; Pasuk 2004.
32. Hewison 2004, 2010; Hickey 2013; Pasuk and Baker 2004, 2005; Tausig 2014.

and flat response to global capital by national forces.[33] How can we speak of neoliberalism in countries like Thailand where, over the last decades, the state has been expanding its planning presence in the economy and introducing unprecedented welfare schemes rather than cutting them?

The neoliberal doctrine was at its core a Euro-American project. It emerged in the minds of Austrian and American economists in the late 1930s as a middle path between Keynesian state planning and liberal laissez-faire and gained momentum after the Second World War by claiming that excessive state planning would give way to authoritarianism.[34] As a dominant political project—one that advocated for market liberalization, cuts in labor rights, reduction of taxes, trickle-down economics, and retreat of the welfare state—neoliberalism abandoned the original attempt to find a middle path and endorsed market laissez-faire. This model was experimented with in South America first and, in the 1980s, solidified under the governments of Ronald Reagan and Margaret Thatcher before being rolled out globally, under the Washington Consensus.[35] Its basic objective was to tip the scale between state interventions and markets forces, leaving the latter to operate as undisturbed and unregulated as possible. Thailand was one of the countries in which this rollout was attempted between the mid-1990s and the early 2000s.

By the time Thaksin became premier, however, this project had failed and a new configuration started to emerge. Thaksin wanted to allow market forces to operate freely, as the language of 'itsaraphāp suggested, yet he envisioned this happening through the expansion of state interventions. In this sense, his platform was not about shifting the relation between market and state toward deregulation—the core of the neoliberal agenda. Rather it centered on reorganizing the relationship between capital and labor toward entrepreneurialism. This was a post-Fordist transformation, not a neoliberal one. Its objective was to transform workers into entrepreneurs, and welfare state had a big role to play in this transformation.

The new social welfare envisioned by Thaksin, which survived his time in office, had nothing to do with the model most commonly associated with European social democracies. That system was based on fostering the work-

33. James Ferguson has voiced a similar critique of the lack of rigor in the use of the term *neoliberal* (Ferguson 2009).

34. Burgin 2012; Mirowski 2013; Mirowski and Plehwe 2009. This association was first related to a theory of knowledge and later expanded to refer to political organizations (Friedman 1962; Hayek 1944).

35. Harvey 2005; Jones 2014.

ers' consumption and productivity by supporting them during unproductive phases of their lives. Hence it normally focused on education, unemployment child assistance, and retirement schemes. The model Thaksin had in mind was aimed at freeing economic activities and entrepreneurialism. As a consequence, it focused on giving support during productive years in the form of debt relief, financial access, economic literacy, social housing, health assistance, and social insurance. In this sense, if the former was a Kenyesian model—based on anticyclical interventions—Thaksin's system was Schumpterian—based on the idea that economic inequality is best addressed by granting access to resources and credit for entrepreneurship.[36]

Concretely, Thaksin's welfare revolved around seven policies that were implemented during the first six months of his premiership: a debt moratorium for farmers, a Village and Urban Community Revolving Fund, the creation of the People's Bank, the One Tambon (district) One Product scheme, financing for Small and Medium Enterprises (SMEs), a public housing project for low-income people, and universal healthcare coverage.[37] The debt moratorium allowed farmers to postpone their repayments to the Bank for Agriculture and Agricultural Cooperatives, while the Village Fund created a revolving fund for villages or urban communities for cheap loans, promote local community building, and stimulate the entry of farmers and urban poor into the capitalist economy. More broadly, the People's Bank and the SMEs' financing funded low-income people to invest in microbusinesses, while the One Tambon One Product (OTOP) provided government-led guidance to such microbusinesses. Under this policy, the state offered local districts technical support to choose a specific product or service typical of their area and to develop it, both in the production and the marketing side,

36. Joseph Schumpeter was a German economist. Contrary to his contemporary Milton Keynes, Schumpeter focused much of his attention not on state interventions but on individual entrepreneurship, its operations, spirit, and role in innovation. Schumpeter advocated for addressing economic inequality through a system that granted access to credit for entrepreneurs (Schumpeter 1934, 1947). When talking about a Schumpeterian welfare state, therefore, I mean—building on a definition given by Bob Jessop—a system whose economic and social objectives can be summarized as "the promotion of product, process, organizational, and market innovation; the enhancement of the structural competitiveness of open economies mainly through supply-side intervention; and the subordination of social policy to the demands of labor market flexibility and structural competitiveness" (Jessop 1993), as well as, I add, the creation and fostering of individualized entrepreneurship (Sopranzetti forthcoming-b).

37. For a comprehensive analysis of these policies, see Suehiro 2014.

with the purpose of making it attractive to international markets. The social housing scheme provided forty-eight thousand families affordable homes. Finally, and most successfully, the universal healthcare system provided lower-income citizens with health assistance for a flat cost of 30 baht ($1). Overall, this system aimed at fostering universal participation in capitalism by protecting small businesses and low-income people from difficulties which limited their competitiveness, such as outstanding debts and health expenses, while transforming them into free entrepreneurs and granting them access to credit. For millions of workers this meant acquiring *'itsaraphāp* to become their own bosses in exchange for more precarious lives, the reduction of labor rights and collective bargaining, but also for a new welfare state that supported the unleashing of their free entrepreneurial forces.[38]

Adun took great advantage of this system. He saw his agricultural debt—accumulated during years of meager yields—frozen. His village used the revolving fund to asphalt the road connecting it to the main road and the markets of the closest town. And, most significantly, Adun was able to afford costly medical expenses for his father's growing lung problems. What would have thrown him into unrepayable debt just a few years back, or forced him to accept his father's slow death, now cost him 30 baht—less than a dish of noodles. These everyday changes—together with the freedom he obtained by moving from being a worker to an entrepreneur—garnered an unprecedented mass support for Thaksin among rural and urban lower classes who, for the first time in Thai history, saw a prime minister make good on his electoral promises, put them at the center of his agenda, and present his interventions as the government's responsibility toward its citizens rather than as acts of charity or benevolence. This made drivers like Adun and Boon even more supportive of Thaksin's political project and its celebration of entrepreneurship and flexibilization. Nonetheless, it did not blind them from seeing the negative consequences of this transformation.

FRAMED BY FREEDOM

"I have worked hard all my life, it does not bother me." Boon told me as we walked through the rubber tree orchard back in his village. "I know I work many hours every day. But before I had no advantages, if I worked harder I

38. Pasuk and Baker 2008b; Siamwalla 2000; Warr 2005.

would still receive the same money and the same treatment. Now is up to me. I work longer hours, I make more money; I am lazy, I make less."

"Sure," I pushed him, "but you work more than before. I do the same with my work, I thought I would work in the university to be freer, but I end up working all the time without a fixed contract. I need to work just to keep working."

"That's true. I used to have a regular contract and now my life is less safe. But it's different. It's not just work. You are investing in your own development, like you are your own company."

"Sure your own company"—I pushed back—"but what if you have another accident? What if tomorrow you break your arm worse than last time or hurt a client?"

"I am fucked then," Boon replied looking down on his bent arm, "but this is our life. We are motorcycle taxis. We die young, but live free."

Boon was aware that by being his own boss he ended up working longer hours than he did in a company. Similarly he knew that in the factory he at least had a contract that gave him some minimum job security and economic support in case of injury. Yet, having adopted the framework of 'itsaraphāp and the discourse of Thaksinomics, he saw himself as both an entrepreneur and a worker and talked about self-exploitation as a form of sacrifice to build his own capital, making his own decisions, and getting the profit of his own work. This, he acknowledged, meant running all sorts of risks, physical and economic. Risks that both he and Adun were ready to take in exchange for 'itsaraphāp. Adun, a more careful driver, was less concerned about accidents. But for him, without Boon's cash flow, the trap of debt was always around the corner.

Since Thaksin took office in 2001, his consumption as well as that of millions of people around the country had been supported by access to financial services rather than growing wages. During Thaksin's premierships households' debt grew significantly. In 2001, when he was elected, the national average household debt was 68,279 baht. The following year it jumped to 82,485. In 2004 it had reached 104,571 baht.[39] When Thaksin left office in 2006 household debt had arrived to 116,585 and it grew even faster with the following governments.[40] When I talked to Adun about this in 2009, the

39. Chucherd 2006, 6–8; Siriporn, Wanvimol, and Pimporn 2009, 157.

40. Many critics of Thaksin imputed this growth to his pro-poor policies and financial largesse but this trend only accelerated since he was removed from office in 2006. In that year, household debt was 26.8 percent of the country GDP (Siriporn, Wanvimol, and Pimporn 2009, 154). In mid-2016 it had more than doubled to 80.3 percent. Over this period,

average household debt had reached 133,293 baht, almost doubled since 2001. Adun was struck by these numbers when I showed them to him, but, while concerned, he saw taking economic risks in the form of debt not only as an acceptable part of the promises of *'itsaraphāp,* but a desirable one: the ultimate marker of their new lives as entrepreneurs and free men.

"You should see back at the village, they are all buying pick-up trucks now." He commented on the other villagers' financial near-sightedness. "They have benefits, they make life in the countryside easier. But who knows what will happen? Since Thaksin left, the economy is bad. Who knows if they will be able to repay their debts? But it's part of being your own boss, you must take risks."

Both Boon and Adun understood that the idea of turning workers into free entrepreneurs—central for the post-crisis recovery and the transformation of Thai capitalism—came with its own contradictions. On one side, long working hours, income disparity, and work accidents were now seen as the outcomes of individual successes or failures, laboriousness or laziness, rather than of labor conditions or a tyrannical boss against which they could organize collectively. On the other, the new configuration offered them recognition and pride in their decision to escape industrial labor and become their own bosses. Similarly, the freedoms obtained by moving toward self-employment made a significant difference in their lives and those of their families. Yet, they also kept them in a precarious, unsafe, and unstable occupation, relying only on their own free entrepreneurship and risk taking. On the factory floor they had to submit their bodies to the industrial discipline aimed at rationalizing them to the point where every hand would work in unison, reduced to orchestrated and automated movements. On the street, their souls were rationalized to the logic of maximization, self-directed growth, and profit-seeking entrepreneurship. Lenin talked about the first form as the scientific extortion of sweat; the second became the scientific extortion of life

---

household debt rose by 13.4 percent per year, almost double the GDP growth rate (Languepin 2016). While the numbers for the Thai economy are particularly striking, these trends are not unique to Thailand but characterize contemporary capitalism worldwide. The expansion of personal debt, in Thailand as in the United States or in Europe, became necessary to foster consumers' desires while also cutting wages. As Costas Douzinas has argued in his recent study of contemporary Greece, "Post-Fordist economy of services treat people everywhere as desiring and consuming machines" (Douzinas 2013, 9), and debt became the fuel these machines ran on.

itself, "not only as bearers of nerves and muscles, but also of more general social attitudes, intellectual abilities and powers."[41]

By desiring 'itsaraphāp and adopting the language of advantages, investments, and risk taking, Adun and Boon morphed into entrepreneurs, freed from the external discipline of the factory floor and left in the hands of the hardest boss: themselves. In industrial production their failures were seen by the employer as the natural result of their rural stupidity and were brushed off by them as the effects of unbearable working conditions. Now, they became nothing more than their personal inability to be good rational actors, to plan properly, invest wisely, and maximize their profits. In this configuration, they navigated between binds, limited by the framework of 'itsaraphāp but also freed by it, claiming a freedom that provides *both* emancipation from the dictates of their previous oppression *and* the raw material of a new one.

This dynamic is by no means peculiar to these two men, or even to motorcycle taxi drivers in Thailand. The paradox of freedom as both an emancipatory and an oppressive force has been extensively studied, both in social theory and the social sciences. Explorations of the role of freedom as a way to accept and often push for deregularization, flexibilization of labor, and precarity—as well as a means of reducing civil and political rights—have been numerous.[42] These analyses, however, have largely revolved around two established arguments.[43]

The first, derived from Marx's early writings, sees freedom as a tool of exploitation that presents structural relations of exploitation as the result of individual decisions. As Marx said in *The Jewish Question,* exploring the introduction of constitutional rights to liberty, "man was not freed from religion, he received religious freedom. He was not freed from property; he received freedom to own property. He was not freed from the egoism of business; he received freedom to engage in business."[44] In the development of this line of thought, freedom becomes a hook that drags people into a false sense of empowerment while carrying them into accepting and participating in contemporary

41. Commisso 2006, 163.

42. Clarke 2005; Dey and Steyaert 2016; Peters 2001; Roberts 2010; Rose 1999.

43. These are ideal-types of existing arguments, presented in their most extreme versions, which may not be fully endorsed by most, or even any, of their proponents. Exaggerating their characteristics, however, helps us reveal the existing spectrum of explanations and, in so doing, sheds light on underexplored alternative routes.

44. Marx 1992, 232.

capitalism or similarly oppressive projects.[45] When applied to the drivers, this reading would see *'itsaraphāp* operating as a mechanism through which they are not freed from the exploitation of the factory floor, but given the freedom to be their own exploiters by becoming their own bosses—entrepreneurial subjects who accept unstable and insecure employment.

The second explanation, developed out of Foucault's early writings on disciplinary apparatuses but largely ignoring his later explorations of ethics, sees freedom as an apparatus that operates by creating its own subjects, "free individuals [who] become governable . . . as normal subjects."[46] Following this analysis, *'itsaraphāp* has come to provide the ground for the drivers' conceptions of how they should be ruled, how their practices should be organized, and how they should understand themselves and their predica-ments.[47] In it, drivers "are not merely 'free to choose', but *obliged to be free,* to understand and enact their lives in terms of choice."[48]

Adun and Boon—as most of the motorcycle taxi drivers I talked to— would not be satisfied with either of these explanations. They reject the notion that their choices are the product of somebody else's action and plan-ning, something the drivers either *received* or are *obliged to accept.* These formulations, they would argue, are the product of the same mentality that cast migrants and urban poors as stupid buffaloes, unable to make conscious decisions and easily duped: theories developed by people who never spent a day on a factory line and are more concerned with general principles and abstract ideas of freedom than with the profound difference that leaving the factory floor made to their lives.

The problem is precisely how freedom is defined. Both academic theories implicitly compare, and ultimately conflate, whichever local and contextual use of freedom they encounter in the real world with an abstract, absolute, and universal conception of Freedom—with capital F—as something that should

---

45. Althusser 1984; Santoro 1999; Teasdale and Mason 2012; Žižek 1989.

46. Rose 1999, 76.

47. I am here referring to a specific—and possibly incorrect—understanding of subject-formation and freedom. As James Faubion has shown, Foucault himself in the latter part of his life pointed out the fallacious nature of this passive understanding of subject-formation. For him, "ethical practice proceeds after all in the middle voice, actively and passively often at one and the same time" (Faubion 2011, 50). In this sense, Foucault himself, while acknowl-edging his role in allowing this misunderstanding to emerge, showed how subjects are neither un-free to participate in their formation nor fully at liberty in inventing their own technique of the self (Foucault 1984a, b, 1997), but they are not *obliged* to it.

48. Rose 1999, 87.

be *obtained* and not be *given* or *obliged to* exercise. As a result, they always find the former lacking when compared with the latter, and cast passive subjects to explain and justify the gap between the two.[49] Adun and Boon propose a different, less myopic, definition of freedom, one consistent with Wendy Brown's argument that "freedom is neither a philosophical absolute nor a tangible entity but a relational and contextual practice that takes shape in opposition to whatever is locally and ideologically conceived as un-freedom."[50] What they experienced on the factory floor around the time of the crisis was for them the epitome of un-freedom, an oppressive system that limited their mobility, controlled their time, and broke their spirit. In relation to that, post-Fordist *'itsaraphāp* offered a way out, attractive even as it constructs new limitations around them, of which the drivers are painfully aware.

Antonio Gramsci helps us make sense of this dynamic, recognizing the daunting tensions that it suggests. In his prison writings on Italian history and the southern question, Gramsci clarifies how consent and coercion

---

49. While anthropology, with its focus on context-specific constructs, would seem to have a lot to contribute to this debate, it "has [historically] had strikingly little to say [about freedom]" (Laidlaw 2002, 311). Partly, this is due to the fact that anthropologists have been as guilty as other social scientists of turning their attention—however critical—to Freedom with the capital *F*. As a discipline, we have pointed out its analytical shortcomings and unmasked its universalist, normative, and elitist nature (Bidney 1963; Mahmood 2005); we have revealed its grounding in Protestant and western modernity (Asad 2003; Keane 2007), and its centrality to colonial and post-colonial governance (Veer 2001; Viswanathan 1998). In the process, however, we have too often turned our attention away from what contextual understandings of freedom we encounter in our ethnographic engagements. These freedoms are not predicated upon a metaphysical and ahistorical ideal but always developed against a local experience of un-freedom, and therefore much more entangled in the complexity of people's experiences and political-economic transformations. Recently, under the rubric of the anthropology of ethics, a number of authors have argued for a limited, qualified, and restricted understanding of freedom (Fassin 2014; Faubion 2011; Laidlaw 2013). Building on Foucault's explorations of freedom as a necessary condition of ethical practice (Foucault 1984c, 245, 1997, 283), rather than on his analysis of disciplinary power, they have pointed out that degrees of freedom—understood as the capacity to exercise choice and pursue alternatives—are always situated in an existing field of power relations and have called for an investigation of "how freedom is exercised in different social contexts and cultural traditions" (Laidlaw 2002, 311). While resonating with my own argument, their engagements have largely remained at the analytical level. As a result, they have stopped short of exploring local conceptions of freedom ethnographically and revealing how they operate as systems of value, objects of reflection, and compasses that orient people's lives, not just in relation to "local moral worlds" (Kleinman and Kleinman 1996), but also to political-economic restructurings.

50. W. Brown 1995, 124.

sustain each other and how emancipating projects—such as the ones promulgated by the Italian Risorgimento—can also sustain oppressive forms of hegemony. Between the lines of his heavily controlled prison notebooks, Gramsci hinted that consent was not the product of gullible passive agents, tricked into false consciousness,[51] but rather the result of a complex interplay between two forms of control: domination and hegemony. While the first is obtained through the coercive organs of the state, the second entails an intellectual and moral leadership that is exercised through civil society—a composition of educational, religious, and associational institutions. This second form of submission operates through a "spontaneous consent given by the great masses of the population to the general direction imposed on social life by the dominant fundamental group, consent 'historically' caused by the prestige (and therefore by the trust) accruing to the dominant group."[52] For Boon, Adun, and thousands of other laid-off workers after the 1997 crisis, Thaksin emerged in 2001 in opposition to the post-crisis neoliberal governments under the direction of the IMF with an enormous amount of prestige. As the champion of a new dominant group, he proposed entrepreneurship and freedom as new frameworks for success. Adun and Boon adopted the framework of ʾitsaraphāp not because they were duped or obliged to conform to it, but because the precepts of Thaksinomics resonated with their everyday aspirations and their desires to define themselves in opposition to the lives on the factory floor that they experienced before the crisis. This language turned them, as Thaksin liked to repeat, into a new free labor force that chose to leave behind the shackles of dependent occupation to enter the brand new world of self-employment and entrepreneurship. Drivers like Boon and Adun endorsed ʾitsaraphāp because it aligned, if just for a moment, their previous experiences, present possibilities, and future aspirations with the new political-economic relations and state interventions that emerged after the 1997 crisis. This equilibrium, however, remained—as any hegemonic project[53]—

51. As Gavin Smith has argued, "the epistemological bedrock of the ideas contained in the notion of hegemony rejects the possibility of the social person as object, passive recipient, or cultural dupe, just as it minimizes the moments when consciousness can be false" (G. Smith 2004, 99–100).

52. Gramsci 1971, 12.

53. As Stuart Hall has argued, in Gramsci "what we are looking for is not the absolute victory of this side over that, nor the total incorporation of one set of forces into another. Rather, the analysis is a relational matter—i.e., a question to be resolved relationally, using the idea of "unstable balance" or "the continuous process of formation and superseding of unstable equilibria" (Hall 1986, 14).

unstable and constantly challenged by the ever-changing nature of everyday life. Thaksin's attempt to transform the collective identity of workers into that of individualized entrepreneurs, if apparently successful in terms of personal motivation, started to crack as the drivers created new forms of collective organizations to demand more and more recognition.[54] In a few years, these individualized free entrepreneurs would emerge as a collective force, one that Thaksin as well as his successors had to reckon with.

54. In a famous summary of Thaksin's autobiography that was posted as an electoral manifesto around the country, Thaksin stated: "Even today, my friends range from hired motorcycle drivers to the presidents of great countries" (Pasuk and Baker 2004, 85).

PART TWO

Mobilization

FIVE

Fighting over the State

It is not sufficient simply to criticize the abstract, idealist appearance the state assumes. . . . The task of a critique of the state is not just to reject such metaphysics, but to explain how it has been possible to produce this practical yet ghost-like effect.

TIMOTHY MITCHELL, *"The Limits of the State"*

ON MAY 20, 2003, two years after his election, Thaksin initiated a set of interventions aimed at registering, making visible, and managing the drivers' operations. Given the prime minister's support for market economy and free individual entrepreneurship, crafting regulations may have seemed like an unlikely action but it was not. Casting entrepreneurship and regulations, or free markets and state control, in opposition to one another has been one of the many myths invented by apologists of neoliberalism,[1] a position too often taken at face value by scholars.[2] In reality, things are less clear-cut. The multi-billion-dollar bailouts of banks after the 2008 crisis showed that, as Karl Polanyi argued half a century ago,[3] markets do not self-administer, they do not sustain themselves but need institutional actions to be created, preserved, and managed, to harness their profits and mitigate their losses. The same goes for entrepreneurship, whose successes always rely on striking a balance between state support;[4] "the enhancement of the creative potential of people; and its

---

1. Graeber 2007.
2. Aiwa Ong's definition of neoliberalism is a prime example of this analytical slippage. She defines neoliberalism as "(a) a claim that the market is better than the state at distributing public resources and (b) a return to a primitive form of individualism: an individualism which is competitive; possessive; and construed often in terms of the doctrine of 'consumer sovereignty'" (Ong 2006, 6). The same analytical mistake is evident in other authors (Boyer and Drache 1996).
3. Polanyi 1944.
4. Mazzucato 2013.

harnessing the value that results and directs it back toward capital."[5] Motorcycle taxis were no exception.

Thaksin's government recognized them as free entrepreneurs but also registered them, putting them under state control and aggregating their profits into a tax-paying economic sector. After he freed entrepreneurial forces from the binds of the Fordist discipline of labor, Thaksin immediately regulated their entrepreneurship. His plan to impose order was not just directed to the motorcycle taxi drivers but also aimed at controlling the people who extracted protection money from their activities: state officials who used authority (*amnāt*) to exert influence (*itthiphon*) over the gray economy. Aware that elected governments had historically faced significant opposition and resistance from bureaucratic and military forces, Thaksin wanted to take away their financial resources by legalizing illicit and illegal sectors on which they thrived. This, he hoped, would be a first step toward bringing them under his control and establishing his domination over other state forces.

Much like the plans to restructure Bangkok, however, Thaksin's vision encountered significant resistance, both on the streets and inside the corridors of state offices. His policies triggered a series of processes with spillover effects and unintended consequences. At the street level, the formalization of motorcycle taxis ended up pushing these atomized driver-entrepreneurs to mobilize into a significant collective force, one that initially unified to criticize Thaksin and question his leadership. In the halls of power, Thaksin's attempt to bring other state forces under his control ended up unifying them in his opposition, sowing the seeds of his demise. In what follows, I reconstruct both dynamics: the struggle that ensued during Thaksin's time in office and the shifting alliances that responses and pushbacks against Thaksin's visions generated. Once again, my explorations begin at a busy street corner.

THE SYSTEM OF INFLUENCE

In *soi* Ngam Duphli, the narrow alley where motorcycle taxis first appeared in the 1980s, nobody ever walks. The mile-long *soi* branches out of Suan Phlu Road and resurfaces into Rama IV Road, a major east-west thoroughfare in

---

5. G. Smith 2011, 24. This dynamic is by no mean exclusive to economic circulation but extends also to other forms of mobility. Think for instance of the innumerable governments around the world which advocate for deregulation and free markets while tightening control over their borders and strengthening their intelligence apparatus to spy on their own citizens.

the city. For most of the day the alley is one of the many sleepy backroads that make up most of Bangkok. During rush hour, however, it becomes a useful shortcut to bypass the unbearable gridlocks of Sathorn Road. No bus serves it and the road hardly fits two cars traveling in opposite directions. Yet hundreds of motorcycle taxis dart up and down the road with customers on their backseats. Given the high traffic in the *soi,* multiple groups of drivers are scattered along it. Most of them are small and cluster along the road, where drivers watch the traffic go by, chat with street vendors and shop keepers, read newspapers, and wait drowsily for clients. The largest among the groups, however, does none of this. At the corner with Rama IV Road more than a hundred drivers line up in two rows next to the sidewalk. Engines turned off, they push their bikes forward, as a continuous flux of clients hop on the bike at the front of each line. Long wait times do not exist here, making the drivers' connections to the neighborhood scant and the job of the ethnographer difficult. I spent the first weeks of my fieldwork trying in vain to get to know the drivers in this group, walking along the moving lines only to steal a few minutes of conversation before the driver arrived at the top of the line, got a client, and dived into traffic.

As I became a regular presence at the corner, an older woman, the owner of a tailor shop next to the group, inquired about whom I was and why I was asking so many questions. Visibly dissatisfied with my answers, she walked back into her shop and made a phone call. The good-cop approach had not paid off and now was time for its less pleasant partner. A few minutes later a couple of tough guys showed up. "Who are you? Why are you here?" they demanded to know, as the drivers kept moving down the line, looking away. My smile and explanations, once again, did not have any effect. One of the men, putting his hand on my chest, told me that I could not hang around the group, while the other leaned against the wall behind us, smoking a cigarette and staring at the drivers. Clearly I was not the only one whom they intended to scare off: from then on talking to the drivers became impossible. Every bit of conversation was now dotted by impatient gazes toward the tailor shop, raised eyebrows, and half-murmured sentences. Going back there was of no use and would only put the drivers in an uncomfortable position.

Luckily, however, my apartment was not far away from a famous street vendor specializing in northeastern beef salad. A few days later, as I was eating there, I saw Nit, one of the drivers in the group, waiting in line to taste the delicacy of his native region. I invited him to join me. After eating I asked him what had happened at their station.

"You have to understand that we cannot speak there." He warily looked around. "Those people are thugs and they are sent by the group's owner to make sure we pay our rent regularly and create no problems."

"Rent for what?" I asked.

"Yes, rent for our vests and for our right to drive there. Only a few drivers in the group own their vests. You see the name written on this vest, right below the Bangkok Metropolitan Administration [BMA] logo? This is my name but only few of us in the group are really the people our vests say we are. Five or six years ago, when Thaksin formalized the motorcycle taxis, we were all given an orange vest for free and had to register our names and driver's licenses at the Ministry of Transportation. But some of the drivers didn't want to stay in the job or wanted to make some money and so they sold their vests, often back to the same people who controlled the group before the new policy who now collected rent for these vests. So many drivers were back to square one, back to paying them for the vest. I kept my vest and continued to drive, without paying anybody. If the owners came back to bother us we could report them directly to the office of the prime minister and they will be scared off. Since the military coup [which removed Thaksin Shinawatra from power in 2006] I once again have to pay, just to be able to work, otherwise I get kicked out or beaten up. But I still own my vest so I pay less than the others: most of them also have to rent the vest from the group owner, because they are too expensive to buy."

"How much is a vest?"

"Up to 100,000 baht [$3,300]. Think about it. If I had that money I would never have come to Bangkok, I would have stayed in the countryside, built a house, and worked on my own farm. So most people rent, is more affordable. Some people pay 500 baht [$16] a day, some people less. Some people pay up to 1,000. It depends on your connections."

"Connections to whom?"

"To the person of influence [phū mī itthiphon] who owns the group. Everybody knows. They are state officials: police, metropolitan police, soldiers, sometimes business people or politicians."

"And here in the neighborhood?"

"I cannot speak about this, I have to keep working. Let's talk about something else and pass me that beer."

Half-conversations like this filled the first months of my research: gazes into a reality of daily interactions with a system of official authority, patronage, rent, and protection money largely in the hands of local bureaucrats.

Drivers like Nit talked freely about this system but they rarely admitted personal involvement in its circuit of racketeering, illegal payments, and favors. The army personnel, state and municipal police officers, and state officials I interviewed had a similar attitude. All of them were willing to admit that people of influence dominated the inner workings of Bangkok's street economy, and were quick to offer stories and complaints about the rampant corruption of state officers. Yet they never admitted that anybody in their own offices was involved. It was always another official to be corrupt, the other corps who squeezed motorcycle taxis for bribes.

Despite my inauspicious first encounter with his group, in a few weeks Nit and I developed an unspoken agreement, one initially fueled by beer and beef salad. I would not go back to talk to him at his group or ever ask the name of its owner again. But whenever we met in the neighborhood, we would eat together and he would explain the inner workings of the system of influence and control over motorcycle taxis, before, during, and after Thaksin's attempt to formalize their operation. Nit had arrived in Bangkok in 2000 and, unlike most other drivers, this had been his first occupation, one he kept for the previous decade. When he started to work, he told me, every group was organized around a head driver who was often put in this position by the owner. The head collected money from group members and operated as a middle man between them and the various local officials and mechanisms that needed to be oiled for the group to operate smoothly. The main recipient of this money was the person of influence (*phū mī itthiphon*) who owned the group. Owing the group, Nit explained, did not imply any formal property right, it just meant that the person of influence and his paid thugs guaranteed the group, in exchange for the payment, with exclusive operation in their area; made sure that other drivers only picked up clients at their station, not in the middle of the street where they would impinge on the group's routes; and ensured that no new groups would be set up nearby.

In this system of extralegal property rights, the drivers' vests played a central role, operating as de facto licenses, marking ownership over each group, and separating between them. The uniforms were introduced early on in the history of motorcycle taxis precisely for these purposes. Each person of influence created his or her own vests, which often carried their names, and distributed them to the drivers in exchange for a monthly rent and daily operational fees. Especially after the 1997 crisis swelled the ranks of motorcycle taxis, the vests' value grew exponentially. In 2003, just before Thaksin started the regularization of drivers, a local newspaper noticed that "a glamorous evening gown may be worth less than the weather-beaten rag of a jacket worn by Bangkok motorcycle taxi drivers."[6] Over the previous years, the vest not only acquired economic value, it also became a symbol of the system of corruption and racketeering that revolved around motorcycle taxi drivers. Much like the discourse of *'itsaraphāp,* the jackets were two-edged swords: they symbolized the drivers' imprisonment in this system of influence, yet they guaranteed their jealously guarded right to operate in an area.

People of influence protected this right through two methods: direct violence against other drivers who did not respect the rules or people who tried to set up new groups, and connivance with state officials who left alone the drivers who paid protection money regularly and fined and arrested those who refused to do so. State officials, Nit noticed, could use the law to force drivers to pay their owners. As long as you paid your dues, the police officers would turn their attention away from the various illegal aspects of your driving, from the use of public land for parking to the failure to wear helmets or abide by the traffic code. Refuse to do so and suddenly they started to do their job. This ability to use the law to extract illicit profit, as well as the bureaucracy's low salaries, created a set of incentives for state officials to become people of influence and take control over illegal business on Bangkok's streets, from motorcycle taxis to prostitution, from shops' protection money to drug trade. All they had to do was convert their *amnāt*—"authority which derives from any official position or is sanctioned by law"[7]—into *itthiphon*—"power which a man in authority exerts beyond his authority or which a man without an official position exerts."[8] In other words, they just needed to use the formal authority of their office to make a profit for themselves.

This specific configuration determined the economic, territorial, and hierarchical logics of influence in Bangkok. From a monetary point of view, police, army officers, and powerful civil servants—given their official authority and their role in enforcing the law—could avoid legal scrutiny without having to bribe anyone. Business people and local thugs who wanted to become people of influence, on the contrary, had to use bribery to gain influence. As a consequence, state officials were able to turn a higher profit from the gray economy, even demanding a lower protection fee from the drivers. Territorially, state officials were already organized inside the bureaucracy

6. Wassayos and Manop 2003.
7. Tamada 1991, 455.
8. Ibid.

according to established spheres of authority that became easily reproduced into spheres of influence. Each police station and military barrack already had a clear jurisdiction, precisely to avoid tensions and struggles over territorial control. Similarly, each section of the state apparatus had a set of responsibilities that it oversaw. In Bangkok, for instance, the metropolitan police is officially in charge of sidewalks, while the national police controls road pavement. This allowed state officials to split up the large pie of bribes, rent, and protection money by simply retracing their legal authority. As a result, groups that parked on the road were most commonly owned by a national police officer; those parking on sidewalk by metropolitan police; those near an army barrack to a military officers, those close to a government office to a bureaucrat working there; and groups beside a navy housing complex, such as Nit's, to a navy officer. The official relation between state forces in the bureaucratic apparatus did not just determine the geography of the system of influence, it also organized its hierarchy. While over time the hierarchy between state agents could change and be challenged, since the emergence of motorcycle taxis it was generally seen as the military sitting on top, followed by national police, ministerial officers, and, at the bottom, municipal police. On the streets of Bangkok, this meant that a military officer would almost automatically be given priority were a conflict to emerge, as police officers or civil servants would think twice before going after him, both by legal and illegal means. The hierarchical logic organized the whole system of influence, all the way down to the drivers who, as mere citizens, sat at the very bottom. As a consequence, being controlled by someone with institutional authority makes them less likely to organize and fight against the owners, as the very same people supposed to enforce the law would be the ones who illicitly exerted control over the system.

"In the first two years I worked here," Nit remembers, "we tried to organize and fight against the owner. In 2001, we met almost every week at night and talked in secret about our problems. On a Friday during the cold season, when the traffic was at its peak and we thought it would be harder to send us away, we began a protest. Pong, an older driver who had been a labor organizer in a factory, convinced many of us to stop paying our daily fees to the owner and demand that he lower our rent. The rent strike lasted only two days. The owners' thugs went to Pong's house and beat him up. They sent him to the hospital, and Pong was kicked out of the group. He even had to leave the neighborhood. They came to the group and said they would do the same with all of us if we dared not pay again. We were scared but decided to denounce them but the owner was a navy officer. Who would do anything to stop him? We went to the local police station but they were more scared than us. We were alone. No one listened to us. There was no one who could help us. Whether he used violence or the law we were screwed. Who could we complain to?"

WAR ON DARK INFLUENCES

When Thaksin came to power the drivers finally had someone they could appeal to, at least in Nit's eyes. The newly elected prime minister referred to the drivers in his speeches not only as an example of the entrepreneurial forces that were left unutilized by previous governments, but also as an example of the wide variety of classes that supported his program and could call him friend. Following his usually decisive style, Thaksin's words quickly turned into policy. In early 2003, he launched the "War on Dark Influences." The nation-wide campaign aimed at subjugating the system of influence that profited from a variety of illegal activities—from logging to prostitution, from underground lotto to motorcycle taxis—and bring them under the administrative and economic control of the government. If the policy was to succeed it would hit two birds with one stone: it would extend control of his newly elected government over powerful bureaucrats and civil servants; and bring the economic activities from which they had profited into the formal market, amassing new revenues and proving his seriousness in providing assistance to entrepreneurs.

The idea of extending the scope of capitalism by formalizing the underground economy and protecting its entrepreneurial pushes was based on the theories of Hernando de Soto, the guru of third world capitalism whom President Bill Clinton had introduced to Thaksin.[9] In *The Mystery of Capital*, the Peruvian economist argued that capitalism had failed to kickstart in the developing world because in these countries large sectors of the national economy exist outside the purview of the law, in particular outside a uniform and enforceable system of property rights. Under these conditions, he claimed, the majority of the population controls assets that they cannot transform into capital and remain locked in the extralegal sector—according to his calculation up to $10 trillion USD worldwide.[10] In order to allow these

9. Pasuk and Baker 2004, 117.
10. Soto 2000, 212.

assets to become productive capital, de Soto proposed, they needed to be brought inside the formal economy, so their owners could use them as collateral to raise more capital.

In November 2002, Thaksin invited the Peruvian economist to Bangkok and, after paying de Soto's usual hefty consultancy fee, began to draft a policy to formalize illegal economies with the controversial objective of transforming assets into capital.[11] Motorcycle taxis, central to the lives of millions of people in Bangkok and relatively easy to control, were to be its poster children. This entailed making their hardship highly visible before the policy was announced. Government-controlled media initiated a campaign to publicize the motorcycle drivers' struggles and prompt a collective "obsession with a particular and easily-identifiable costume, the ubiquitous taxi vests."[12] The transportation infrastructure that had drifted into invisibility a decade before was suddenly on everybody's mind.

Between April and May 2003, Thai newspapers, TV, and radio programs were flooded with articles interviewing drivers, voicing their pleas, denouncing the role of people of influence and the estimated 1.2 billion baht per year ($40 million) they illegally extracted from the drivers. On May 20, Bangkok's district officers begun to register the drivers operating under their jurisdiction. In late August, the government outlawed the colorful uniforms that group's owner had previously used and distributed free orange vests to all registered drivers. The standardized uniform symbolized that the drivers now had a new protector: the government of Thaksin Shinawatra. These vests operated as personal licenses and, at least in theory, provided an asset that could be transformed into capital and used as collaterals for loans.[13]

The disproportionate focus on the drivers' vests and their distribution soon showed the limits of Thaksin's intervention. Without reorganizing the internal organization of motorcycle taxis' groups or legislating their use of

11. For detailed critiques of this approach see M. Davis 2006, 79–82; Gilbert 2001, 2012; Kerekes and Williamson 2008; Roy 2013, 149–52; Woodruff and de Soto 2001.

12. Haanstad 2008, 275.

13. These vests were paid with money from the General Lottery Office (GLO), which, during Thaksin's government, was entrusted to a former police officer and his classmate. The GLO was used as a sort of cash bank for Thaksin's social agenda and credit policies. Thaksin, in fact, had brought part of Thailand's massive underground lottery system into the legal fold by operating a frequent national lottery run by the Government Lottery Office. Lottery sales of approximately 70 billion baht ($2 billion USD) were used for social projects, including the "One District, One Scholarship" program, the village fund, and the formalization of motorcycle taxis (Pasuk 2004).

road pavement, the formalization became little more than the distribution of a precise amount of free vests (exactly 109,056) to already-operating drivers. As the city continued to grow, however, new drivers would be forced to operate illegally. As a consequence, vests immediately assumed a high value on the black market. Many of the drivers, finally seeing an opportunity to cash in, sold their vests to the highest bidders, often the same person who previously controlled their group.[14] The newly created black market was one indication that not all drivers were on board with Thaksin's attempt to bring their system under government control and make them visible, controllable, and ultimately taxable. Boon—adamant in his defense of his personal independence—was very much aware of the risks involved in this process and refused, as he still refuses today, to put on one of the government's official vests and register with the local administration. "I chose this job because it gave me 'itsaraphāp. I am not going to give them my name and location so the government can control me." Boon's refusal, however, was a drop in a sea of popular support for the new policy.

Nit was a stalwart supporter of the campaign. "Suddenly everybody was talking about us. The prime minister talked about us in his speeches, he mentioned our struggles, he told us that our taxes were paying state officials' stipends and therefore no one could ask us for protection money. And he gave us this vest," he said, proudly tapping his hand on the orange vest. In Thailand any official position, from taxi driver to security guard, from porter in a market to masseur, is identified by a standardized uniform, a source of identity and pride. The motorcycle taxi drivers were now getting their own. While, as could have been predicted, no bank would accept the motorcycle taxi vests as collateral, the orange jackets embroiled with the city's insignia were still a concrete recognition of the drivers' importance for Bangkok and their roles as stakeholders in the Thai state as free entrepreneurs, rather than good-for-nothing lazy country bumpkins, as many Bangkokians perceived them. Even if the policy did not completely eradicate people of influence from the business, as Thaksin had promised, it supported the drivers' struggles to claim 'itsaraphāp from their meddling and allowed motorcycle taxis to operate also outside the direct control of people of influence.

14. Given that vests failed to operate as collateral, selling them was the best way to transform assets into capital. This dynamic is strikingly similar to other contexts in which de Soto's ideas were applied, particularly to individual land rights. There, as with the drivers, many slum dwellers sold the land title, often to the same people whom they used to pay rent to, and moved elsewhere (M. Davis 2006, 79–82).

"Bureaucrats, civil servants, they are the problem of this country," Adun said as we sat at the Ministry of Transportation to renew his driver's license. "Look at how they treat us. They order us around as if they owned us but they are the ones who steal from our work. It is like Thaksin said, when we go into an office in the district or our province it should not be for us to *wai* (salute with palms pressed together) the officers, it should be they who *wai* us.[15] We pay for their salaries, for their desks, and for their computers; we are the owners and they need to learn to work with us and for us, not the other way around.[16] Instead, Thai people always feel like we are asking them a favor and we need to be nice to them." While traditionally citizens had to approach bureaucrats with the attitude of subjects asking for help or paying to be able to continue to do their job, Thaksin—adopting the language of entrepreneurs and clients—advocated for the opposite dynamic, one in which bureaucrats must address citizen-clients with respect and deference. Whether or not Thaksin had this objective in mind, the drivers saw in his words a basic reversal of the hierarchy that dominated the system of influence. If citizens sat at the bottom while different layers of officials took advantage of them, in Thaksin's declaration they envisioned a system where elected governments were in charge and ensured that state officials respected and served the people who put them there.

This inversion struck a chord with migrants like Adun and Nit, who experienced the indifference and rent-seeking of state bureaucracy each day.[17] They both frequently talked about the Kafkaesque experiences of navigating offices and being sent away and invited to return on a later occasion, or of being asked for money by bureaucrats, both in the city and in the village. Thaksin's reform, in their eyes, questioned bureaucratic indifference and abuses. "The formalization made us feel like we were not alone anymore." Nit told me, visibly emotional. "A government that we elected was finally work-

15. On the social significance of the *wai,* see Aulino 2012.

16. Adun was referring to a famous discourse that Thaksin delivered on September 11, 2002. In it he declared: "most important task for us is to reform the old culture of work together with a new one at the levels of government officers, the relationship between public sector and a country, and the relationship between public sector and the people. We need a new culture of work together" (Pran 2004, 1: 300–301).

17. As Herzfeld has shown, state bureaucracy operates by "treating the clients like dirt" and professing indifference to the citizen's requests through "petty harassment and especially the often repeated advice to 'come back tomorrow,' the endless sets of more and less identical forms, the bureaucrat's professed inability to predict outcome and duration" (Herzfeld 1992, 161).

ing for our interest, not that of rich people in Bangkok. And we loved Thaksin for it."

Sad as it may be that being formalized and putting themselves under the patronage of Thaksin represented the only available form of recognition, this feeling was echoed by many drivers. As it happened with the acceptance of precarious work to get out of the factory floor, whatever people are deprived of, they end up longing for. The drivers experienced a profound invisibility and indifference from the state's apparatus and now they developed an ardent desire for statehood and seemed enchanted by the promises of participating in it.[18] Workers who mastered the art of moving freely both in Bangkok and between the city and their villages by finding invisible paths and zigzagging through these spaces—a contemporary version of what James Scott has called "the art not being governed"[19]—were willing to fight to be included and made legible in the state apparatus. While this may seem contradictory—and indeed it was for Boon—for most of the drivers Thaksin's offer of visibility was the fulfilment of their desires for recognition or, to use Nit's words, for not being alone anymore. To reach this objective, most of the drivers were happy to be positioned within a new system of registration and control that allowed a variety of state forces to monitor their location, take away their license in the case of accidents or drunk driving, and limit their numbers. Proximity to state power, even if it meant being under its control, made them feel powerful. The drivers were now determined to "devise strategies to position themselves closer to what they imagine to be the centre."[20]

UNINTENDED CONSEQUENCES: THE DRIVERS' COLLECTIVE ACTION

Resolved to see their presence in the city fully regularized, many of the drivers did not simply submit to Thaksin's plans. They started to mobilize to force him to live up to his promises. While occasional protests against the roles of particularly exploitative owners, like the one Nit took part in, had previously erupted in various locations, discontent had never coagulated into a citywide attack against people of influence. Toward the end of 2003, new local leaders

18. On this desire for statehood among people excluded from participating in the state apparatus see Li 2005.

19. Scott 2009.

20. Li 2005, 385.

and a larger network of drivers began to emerge. These would become the basis for the drivers' participation in urban and national politics. As an effect, a mass of individual entrepreneurs who were supposed to activate their assets and compete with one another under the government's protection started to stage a collective struggle against exploitation and influence—a fight for recognition and self-determination.

This shift was epochal. The creation of a collective consciousness—what Marx called the shift from class-in-itself and class-for-itself—requires a basic transformation. On the one side stands a series of individuals—comparable to those queuing at a bus stop who "do not care about or speak to each other and, in general, [only] exist side by side." On the other, a collective of active agents of history, a fused group that "tighten[s] its bonds against an enemy and becomes aware of itself."[21] Thaksin's formalization inadvertently triggered the process that would ferry the drivers from one to the other. Their organizers did much of the work needed for this transformation.

On May 22, 2003, two days after the formal launching of the new policy, a hundred motorcycle taxi drivers drove to Parliament to show their support for the campaign and openly denounce the system of exploitation in which they operated. They delivered documentation proving the full extent of bureaucratic abuses and demanded a rapid intervention. While this first action was to support Thaksin's policies, by the time the vests were distributed in August, the drivers had grown frustrated with the gap between Thaksin's promises and the reality of continual threats they experienced on the street.

"Thaksin gave us the vests," said Nit, "but for all the rest we had to fight ourselves. Vests were the beginning but without law to limit people of influence, they made no difference. People say we chased Thaksin out." Nit laughs. "Well, yeah, in a way we did. We knew he was a good person and was trying to help us, but he just did not go far enough. We had to force him to really implement his policies. Initially we had no legal basis, we could not press charges against the owners nor could we convince anybody to stop them. So we started protesting against Thaksin. We began with fifteen days of protests and suddenly we got his attention."

Over the next few months, groups of drivers rallied at local district offices, the Crime Suppression Division, the Bangkok Municipal Administration, as

21. These are the words of French philosopher Jean-Paul Sarte, who, trying to give an everyday grounding to Marxist theory of consciousness, called the first group a plurality of isolation and the second a unity of individuals in solidarity (Sartre 1976, 256, 346).

well as the Government House, demanding a swift and total crackdown on people of influence and denouncing the role of police and military officers both in continuing to demand money and in rejecting the formalization. Nit and Adun were both among these protesting drivers. "It was the first time we felt like a group." Nit remembers. "Finally officers had to receive us, to listen to us. We started to fight together, to get to know drivers from other groups. It was exciting. It was actually funny. We had met to support Thaksin and a few months later we were protesting against his government because they were not carrying out the policy properly." These mobilizations often remained at a district level and rarely involved more than a few hundred drivers at a time. Yet over the year a network of vocal drivers emerged around Bangkok, under a dozen leaders who organized and assisted groups in their fight with local people of influence and district bureaucracy. This was the beginning of a mobilization that would animate the fall of 2003 in Bangkok. It was there that the citywide network of motorcycle taxi drivers that would become central to national politics in the late 2000s was born.

Among the leaders of this first wave of protests were two twins, Yai and Lek, the ninth and tenth sons of a migrant family from central Thailand. The two brothers grew up in a small slum along Lad Phrao Road. Since their youth they worked as thugs and right-hand men for a local army officer who had close connections to one of the most powerful men in Thailand at that time, General (and former Prime Minister) Chavalit Yongchaiyudh. Chavalit had risen to prominence during the Cold War as an expert of mass mobilization, psychological warfare, and counterinsurgency. Just before the 1997 economic crisis, he was elected prime minister and rapidly lost his office, due to pressure from the IMF. In 2003, Chavalit was once again in a position of prominence, the executive director of Thaksin's War on Dark Influences. Indirectly, the two brothers had followed a similar path from henchmen, to vote canvassers, to drivers' leaders in the struggle against owners. In the late 1980s, Yai and Lek had become motorcycle taxi drivers and managed their group for the military officer. In time, Yai and Lek made a name for themselves in the urban underworld and establishing solid connection with army officers and politicians on all sides of the political spectrum. Over the following two decades, they managed to remain always on the winning side. In the early 1990s, when the Democrat Party dominated Thai elections, the brothers worked as vote canvassers for them. Before the 1997 crisis they shifted to Chavalit's party, which also rose to power. Finally, since 2001 their political allegiance had shifted to Thaksin. Once the formalization was initiated in

2003, Yai and Lek abandoned their affiliation with their group owner and used their extensive network of soldiers, politicians, and drivers to become prominent figures in the struggle against people of influence, mobilizing drivers around the city, first to support Thaksin's reform and then to denounce its shortcomings.

As Yai remembers, "2003 was a busy year. Lek and I almost had no time to work as drivers. We were making no money. Every week we would organize a rally, rent a truck and speakers and head out to some district police station or district office and collect information on the amount of money being paid to people of influence and state officials. It was hard; we received threats and drivers who were collecting information got attacked by thugs sent by the local mafia. Back home our wives were not happy either: we were not bringing back any money. But we were getting to know other drivers in every district who had state officials come to demand payment and wanted to fight back. That kept us going. We started to fight together, we realized five fingers are nothing but if they close into a fist they can fight."

Soon more local protests were organized around the city and more drivers joined in—not only in their own districts but along with other groups. Pin and Samart, two drivers who would become central leaders in the following years, joined in a second batch of organizers. By the end of 2003, two more people joined in: Lerm, an experienced organizer from the eastern province of Buriram who had been a union leader in a local factory; and Oboto, an Isan migrant who had previously worked in a Bangkok hospital and become a political organizer in Klong Toey, the biggest slum in the city. This core group extended its web of contacts throughout the city. "During that time," Samart recounts. "we began to collaborate and get to know each other. Every day we met new drivers, listened to their problems, and gave them support to organize a protest or talk to local officials. We knew who was where, knew who was taking money from them. From then on any time somebody had a problem we called each other, met up, and decided what to do: whether to quietly put pressure on local officers or to organize a public protest. We chose to become drivers because of the 'itsaraphāp this job offered us; now we were fighting to have 'itsaraphāp from people of influence."

Thaksin's hegemonic project of 'itsaraphāp wanted to create workers/entrepreneurs in competition with one another. The drivers used it to develop collective organization. Like other hegemonic projects—as Gramsci shows but careless adopters of the concept often forget—this remained an incomplete and ever-changing process, engrained in contestations that are never completely settled.[22] Rather than creating unified consent, Thaksin's intervention opened up a field of struggle. The prime minister had pushed the formalization of motorcycle taxis as a central piece of his fight against established privileges and his support of low-income populations. The drivers, unsatisfied by an implementation that focused on distributing new vests and left people of influence unpunished, used their renewed visibility as a springboard for collective action. The resulting protests embarrassed Thaksin, who had hoped to use the motorcycle taxis as a model case for his reforms. Nonetheless, rather than repress the drivers, he saw an opportunity to solidify his alliance with them.

Thaksin decided to take matters into his own hands. He acknowledged that ending long-standing vested interests might take some time and would require the drivers' direct involvement. First, he invited drivers to bypass local police and send their complaints directly to him, either at the Government House or to PO Box 1234, which he set up explicitly for their complaints. Second, he incorporated the growing network of drivers' leaders into his team. Yai and Lek were hired as consultants on policy implementation and had biweekly meetings with the prime minister to discuss the drivers' problems, report high-profile officers involved in extortion, and suggest potential interventions. These meetings, immortalized in a large framed picture that dominates Yai's living room, went a long way in solidifying the relationship between the prime minister and the motorcycle taxi drivers. This alliance became an example of Thaksin's vision for a new Thailand, one in which citizens would become involved in supporting the elected government to exert direct control over the operation of state bureaucracy. Under the umbrella of the War on Dark Influences, Thaksin was not just waging war on the illegal structures of the street economies. He was embarked on an all-out fight inside the state apparatus: a fight over state control.

WAR OVER THE STATE

Even though the premier had adopted de Soto's ideas of regulating illegal economies, he understood a few things that the Peruvian economist seemed

22. As Stuart Hall has argued, when we look at hegemony in Gramsci "what we are looking for is not the absolute victory of this side over that, nor the total incorporation of one set of forces into another. Rather, the analysis is a relational matter—i.e., a question to be resolved relationally, using the idea of "unstable balance" or "the continuous process of formation and superseding of unstable equilibria" (Hall 1986, 14).

not to. First, Thaksin was well aware that de Soto's magic wand of offering property titles would achieve nothing if not paired with larger interventions, in this case the Schumpeterian welfare state that he introduced.[23] Second, and more important here, while de Soto argued that his solution entailed an extension of the state's legal framework, protection, and taxability to include informal arrangements previously outside its purview, Thaksin and his advisors knew that there was no such thing as a unified state or an informal sector separated from it.

"Thaksin knew that state officials, and especially police officers, operate as a parallel state. They give permission, protect property rights, and collect taxes," Nipon Poapongsakorn, the then-director of the Thai Development Research Institute (TDRI), explained to me when we met to discuss the War on Dark Influences. "Taxes, that's what this corruption is," he declared, diving into a story. "Some years ago I was conducting research on informal and illegal economies in Bangkok. I was interviewing a police officer, a high official. Halfway through the interview he called another policeman and asked him to bring the register. The guy came back with a big book. 'Not that, the other one.' The officer told him. The next book arrived at the desk and it was a full registry of every prostitute in the area, where they worked, their ID numbers and pictures. It was an informal police registry, their tax registry." A grin spread on his face as he masterfully let the story simmer in the air. "And he said it wasn't the first one, so you can imagine they do this systematically. They have their own system of taxation, just like the state."

Nipon's story illuminates the inner workings of an illegal, yet highly formalized, system of extraction and racketeering run by state officials. His analysis of the police as a parallel state does even more; it questions traditional theories that refer to *the state* as a coherent body in which every section plays a part: the government its mind, the police its repressive antibodies, the military its arms, and so forth. Nonetheless, his view still personifies the state—or in this case, multiple states—as an actor with its internal coherence and shared objectives. This misreading of complex and internally divided organizations as unified states has historically dominated Thai political

23. As Alan Gilbert has argued "the danger inherent in [de Soto's] myth is that it will persuade policy makers that they need to do little more than offer title deeds and then leave the market to do everything else. The market will provide services and infrastructure, offer formal credit and administer the booming property market. In the process every household will get to own their own home and even make money from it. A form of utopia is nigh" (Gilbert 2001, 14).

analysis.[24] Even Tyrell Haberkorn, the scholar who most eloquently showed "the Thai state [as] a collection of competing actors and agencies and their actions, as well as the ideas and action that citizens, critics, and those actors and agencies attribute to it," maintains that "the state [is] a site, *not only an actor,* of struggle."[25]

Thaksin's War on Dark Influences paints a more complex picture, one in which the state is not an actor, or even a series of actors, but a site of struggle that a number of conflicting forces—governmental, bureaucratic, military, and monarchical—try to conquer in order to obtain control over the others. In this sense, Thaksin's attempt to take control of the state by subjugating other factions resonates with scholarly critiques of the subjectification of the state that have emerged since about the mid-1970s. In 1977, the American sociologist Philip Abrams noticed that, when attempting to study the state, one is often left with empty hands, as if trying to catch a mirage. Get closer to the so-called state, Abrams pointed out, and you will be left with government officials, bureaucrats, ministries, board of directors, or parties. This is because the state is anything but a unified entity that operates as an actor. Nonetheless, he concludes, we remain attached to a false idea of the state, a unified image of an actual disunity that tricks citizens and scholars alike into believing in its existence. "Political institutions," he continued, "conspicuously fail to display a unity of practice—just as they constantly discover their inability to function as a more general factor of cohesion. Manifestly they are divided against one another, volatile and confused. What is constituted out of their collective practice is a series of ephemerally unified postures in relation to transient issues with no sustained consistency of purpose."[26] Faced with the ephemeral nature of *the state* and the concrete actions of its constitutive elements—government, bureaucracies, military, and propaganda apparatus—Abrams proposed to stop wasting time on the state and focus on these institutions and their conflicts.

A decade later, Timothy Mitchell, an up-and-coming political scientist, adjusted the aim of the analysis. Acknowledging that *the state* is little more

24. The personification of multiple states, one living next to the other, has dominated contemporary Thai political analysis. Until the 1990s, the debate revolved around the so-called bureaucratic polity, in which unelected civil and military officials controlled elected forces (Riggs 1966). In the early 2000s, it became the network monarchy, a system of actors and organizations revolving around the palace and using its name as a legitimizing tool to control and direct governmental actions (McCargo 2005). More recently, the idea of a deep state that, behind the curtain, directs political transformations in the country (Mérieau 2016).

25. Haberkorn 2011, 131–32.

26. Abrams 1988, 79.

than an ideological and cultural construct, he pointed out that what Abrams called a "unified posture" does nonetheless affect our lives, the way we identify ourselves, the language we speak, the food we eat, the borders we can and cannot cross, the rights and protections we have access to or don't have access to. Even if its existence may be illusionary, Mitchell showed, its effects are real. By focusing on its effects, he argued, "one can both acknowledge the power of the political arrangements that we call the state and at the same time account for their elusiveness. One can examine how it is that the state seems to stand apart from society and yet see this distinction as an internal arrangement."[27]

The drivers understood this duplicity of the Thai state better than anyone. They knew, as Nit said, that officials who controlled their system received their strength from this ideal state authority (*amnāt*) and could convert it into concrete influence (*itthiphon*) to be exerted outside the formal system, all the way from national politics to the street economy. They also learned, through their mobilization, that the faceless state meant nothing when they tried to get Thaksin's policies implemented and that they needed to align with one of its forces in order to get something done. The state authority that these factions were able to invoke may have been an imagined and ephemeral construct that covered and obscured internal division—as Abrams pointed out—but it allowed people of influence to control and impose an order over the street economy. By formalizing their activities and allowing themselves to be registered and organized, the drivers hoped to do the same: obtain control over their own lives by claiming proximity to the metacapital of the state,[28] "its hallowed form commanding an imagery of power and a screen for political desire as well as fear."[29] In this sense, *the state* operated for people of influence and drivers alike as the conch in William Golding's *Lord of the Flies*—an empty shell that gains power from collective acceptance of its role, allowing whichever faction holds it to act as if it has obtained complete and unified control.[30] Thaksin was now determined to become its holder, claiming the strength of electoral support to enforce his own influence over state forces.

A fight of this proportion was a lot to take on for the newly elected prime minister. As a consequence, the battle needed to be waged swiftly and publicly to support the carefully crafted image of Thaksin as a resolute leader who always had at heart the people's interests. The first move had taken place a few

27. Mitchell 1991, 94.
28. Bourdieu, Wacquant, and Farage 1994.
29. Aretxaga 2003, 394.
30. Golding 1983.

months before his attack on the system of influence. Under the guidance of General Chavalit Yongchaiyudh, Thaksin declared a controversial War on Drugs, which turned out to be a violent and extrajudicial attack against drug users. In a few months, almost three thousand people were killed at street corners, local bars, and badly lit alleys. In this war, Thaksin used public performances of violence "to threaten Thai citizens with [his] capacity for coercive force."[31] In the new War on Dark Influences, again under Chavalit's control, "the threats were turned more inward and were increasingly leveled on state agents themselves."[32]

Thaksin presented this struggle over the state as a moral fight, one in which the government was the upholder of an ethical conception of bureaucracy, while officers, police generals, and army personnel were the villains, taking advantage of their position to accumulate wealth to the disadvantage of citizens. The War on Dark Influences was conceived as a spectacle of efficiency and anticorruption that relied heavily on filling the media with statements regarding the roles played by bureaucrats, police officers, and military officials in the illicit economy. Creating the appearance of a broader attempt to eliminate networks of favoritism, corruption, and influence, Thaksin planned to hit other state forces where it hurt: their wallets.

Motorcycle taxis and illicit economies were important sites from which the bureaucracy and the military drew their economic resources. Yet the real bulk of their funding came from the state budget, over which each ministry had control, independent from government policies. Thaksin decided to change this system. In late 2002, Thaksin took decision-making power over budget expenditure out of the ministries' hands, where it had been since a budget reform carried out two decades before.[33] Budget allocation decisions now had to be ratified by the prime minister and the ruling party, and needed to be consistent with their political agenda, rather than being based on ministerial planning. Each expense, in other words, had to be justified against the backdrop of the government agenda. The effects on budget allocation were striking. Over Thaksin's five years in office the percentage of the national budget controlled by central funds more than doubled, from 9.6 to 20 percent, while those controlled by ministries decreased from 77.4 to 65.6 percent. The most affected was the defense budget, which decreased from 8.4

31. Haanstad 2008, 264.
32. Ibid.
33. Suehiro 2014, 325–27.

percent of the total when Thaksin took office to 6.3 percent in 2006, the last year he controlled the national budget. Satisfied with how things were progressing, in 2005 Thaksin ordered a full-fledged revision of the 1959 Act of the Budget with the objective of writing into law the new agenda-based budgeting. Thaksin had managed to mobilize unprecedented popular support; he had publicly attacked and put to shame state bureaucrats and officers for their immoral behavior and lack of efficiency; now he was after their money. Those state bureaucratic, military, and royal state forces were not going to roll over without putting up a fight.

GROWING DISSENT

Thaksin had come to power with the support of a motley alliance of heterogeneous groups that were unsatisfied with the neoliberal policies of the post-1997 governments. Over the course of his premiership, his popular support continued to grow. The upper layers of this alliance—bureaucratic, military, monarchic traditional elites, urban middle classes, Buddhist conservatives, and intellectuals—began to realize that they were getting more than they bargained for. Thaksin's brusque and authoritarian style of government and his capitalist but pro-poor policies, together with his attempt to subdue their allies, enraged many of them.

The first significant opposition to Thaksin was mounted in response to the bloody War on Drugs, which adopted the language of antiterrorism and employed extrajudicial methods and violated civil and human rights to tackle drug trafficking.[34] As soon as the government declared the victorious end of this war, the same iron fist and violent repression were applied to the ongoing insurgency in southern Thailand. Once again, hundreds of dead bodies started to appear. The effects on the region were disastrous; the local population grew increasingly disenfranchised with Bangkok and the numbers of attacks and bombings against local state officials, bureaucrats, and police and military officers rose steadily. NGOs, academics, and activists denounced the government for its approach to both of these issues, its violence, and its disrespect for

34. Thaksin's language here echoes former U.S. President George W. Bush's policies and statements, including labeling drug dealers as part of the "axis of evil" and mounting a war on them.

basic human rights. Meanwhile, a large portion of the population, including military officers and the king himself, praised Thaksin's iron fist.

If his brutal violence did not distance state officials from the prime minister, his pro-poor policies, expansion of capitalism to the lower classes, and style of leadership began to open a fracture. Thaksin's social policies and invitation for the poor to partake in capitalism conflicted with a romantic depiction of the poor as exemplars of precapitalist communal life, a view at times shared by the drivers as well. While the drivers attempted to reconcile this narrative with their desires of migration and participation in state capitalism, monarchists, Buddhist thinkers, and urban elites viewed this process as an erosion of Thai "local wisdom."[35] As a consequence, they saw Thaksin as the moral corruptor of pristine villagers, feeding their greed in order to buy their electoral support.[36] On top of this, Thaksin antagonized both the media and academics by attacking everyone who dared to criticize him or mention the fact that his personal wealth was growing significantly during the course of his first premiership—his main business endeavor, Shin Corporation, tripling in value.

Thaksin had already been losing support from ranks of the state bureaucracy, but his attempt to control them and go after their money marked the final rupture. Chatichai Choonhavan, the last elected prime minister who had tried to dominate other state actors' involvement in illegal economies, had been removed from power by a military coup in 1991. Now, the same forces—bureaucratic, military, and monarchic—that staged that coup were growing increasingly irritated with the new prime minister.[37] By the time Thaksin concluded his first term in office, it became clear they were no longer going to watch Thaksin exerting his control over them passively. They

35. The concept of "local wisdom" emerged in the 1990s as a central tool for antiglobalization movements in Thailand, pushed by environmental NGOs and engaged Buddhists who argued for the preservation of Thai genius against the flattening logic of capital (Jungck and Kajornsin 2003; Phatthanā 1994; Sulak and Swearer 2005; Tinnaluck 2005; Wisalo 1999). Nonetheless, much like the doctrine of Sufficiency Economy, by the mid-2000s the same concept, and often the same people, became central to a conservative movement that saw the villagers' desires as sign of their moral corruption, pitted against ideal noble savages who should remain attach to their "local wisdom" (Elinoff 2014b; Somchai 2014). This is one of the reasons why during my fieldwork people in Isan often see the NGOs as their enemy, trying to keep them behind.

36. Anek 2006 [Buddhist year 2549]; Chookiat 2011; Kriengsak 2006; Sangsit 2005 [Buddhist year 2548]; Thitinan 2006.

37. Kriengsak 2006; Pasuk and Baker 2004.

remained, however, a small minority in the face of Thaksin's popular support, which continued to rise.

Although his government was marked by authoritarianism, blunt disregard for human rights, and murky business deals, his first premiership had delivered the first universal healthcare program in the history of the country, instituted new crop subsidies, boosted access to credit, and led Thailand back to the economic prosperity experienced before the crisis, while reducing the country's international debt. In short, he had shown the effects of a government attentive to its people. As a result, Thaksin's popularity grew massively, both in the countryside and in the capital, attracting more and more citizens into his party machinery. The network of motorcycle taxi drivers that previously emerged to protest his implementation of the War on Dark Influences had become, by the end of his first premiership, part of his electoral machine, operating as vote canvassers and organizers of support rallies whenever the prime minister was criticized by opposing parties. On February 6, 2005, Thaksin was reelected with almost 60 percent of the Parliament seats, marking the first one-party majority in the history of Thailand.

Despite the overwhelming electoral support, soon after his reelection the timid political tide that opposed Thaksin during his first term grew exponentially. In September 2005, Sondhi Limthongkul, a former business associate of Thaksin who had fallen out with him after Thaksin refused to grant him a large loan to save his failing business, started an anti-Thaksin TV program and a small protest group. Shortly thereafter, in January 2006, Thaksin provided an opening to his critics. He announced that he would sell his company—Shin Corporation—to a Singaporean media conglomerate. Not only would a national leader in the communications industry fall into foreign hands but, through a holding company based in the Virgin Islands, Thaksin's family would avoid paying $2 billion in taxes on the sale.[38] Driven by popular anger over his actions, the anti-Thaksin movement gained tremendous momentum. Bureaucratic and military elites saw their opportunity to get rid of him.

Sondhi was joined by prominent public figures, including religious leaders, NGO activists, public intellectuals, and Chamlong Srimuang, the politician who had initiated Thaksin's political career. Together they founded the People's Alliance for Democracy (PAD) in 2005, also known as the Yellow Shirts, and organized popular protests calling for a royal intervention to remove Thaksin from office. The people who took to the streets were an

38. Funston 2009.

agglomeration of civil servants, state enterprise labor unions, urban middle classes, conservative Buddhist groups, southerners, and monarchic elites. While the prime minister invoked his electoral mandate as the justification for his attempt to control and subdue other state forces, the PAD saw his large popular support as a sign of the masses' corrupted morals and vote-buying practices, especially among the rural voters who, in PAD's vision, were bought or brainwashed by Thaksin. The Yellow Shirts' discourse latched on to decades of mistrust and bias by the urban intelligentsia, political activists, and elites toward the Thai rural masses, their political struggles, and electoral choices, the same bias that the drivers experienced every day in the factory floors and later on the streets of Bangkok.

Pressured by mounting PAD protests, on February 24, 2006, Thaksin, with his usual decisive hand, dissolved Parliament and called for new elections, which he envisioned as a plebiscite on his premiership. All opposing parties announced their plans to boycott the vote. In the polarized situation, a pro-Thaksin demonstration was organized on March 3 in Sanam Luang— the large ground in front of the Royal Palace. Among the two hundred thousand protesters thousands of motorcycle taxi drivers, headed by Yai and Oboto, figured prominently.

Adun and Nit were in the crowd that day. "We could not accept that the only government that ever listened to us and defended our interests was being pushed out," Adun raged, recounting the events. "It was the first time in my life that I saw a government giving us something, a democracy we could make a living with. So we took to the street to show our support. We wanted to show that the Yellow Shirts did not represent the Thai population."

The drivers' collective action moved beyond the protection of their own interests as workers; they now defended their role as citizens. In this protest, the drivers showed their potential as political mobilizers, a potential that Thaksin wanted to keep at his side. "On March 3 we brought thirty thousand motorcycle taxis," recounted Yai, the leader of motorcycle taxis in that protest. "Thaksin himself was surprised and asked us: how could you mobilize some many people? We talked at the central office of his party and he asked: 'How can we help you? What would you need?' We requested only things we could use: food and water. We were there because we believed in him, not because we were looking for a handout. During that period we met various times with Thaksin. One time I was seated at a table and talked to him backstage at the election campaign. I said if you wanted to step down as prime minister, please inform the motorcycle taxis a day in advance and we will create chaos around the city against the Yellow Shirts, we will shut the city down. He didn't tell me to do that—I told him we could do it. But he understood the role of the motorcycle taxis, he knew we could bring the country into turmoil and bankruptcy by blocking Bangkok."

While Thaksin was organizing his supporters, on the other side the PAD continued to protest. On March 25, they mobilized three hundred thousand people in a counterdemonstration along Ratchadamnoen Avenue that called on the king to appoint a new prime minister. The ultraroyalist, nationalist, and anti-democratic agenda of the Yellow Shirts started to reveal itself in these requests. The PAD reiterated that they were defenders of the monarchy, hence their decision to dress in yellow,[39] accusing Thaksin of trying to undermine the king's authority and of selling out the country to foreigners. Furthermore, while the movement advocated for democracy, what they meant was a local version, based on "good people" who were largely handpicked by the palace, the army, and NGOs, rather than on one-person-one-vote elected representation that, in their view, only favored the election of corrupt and populist politicians.[40]

Despite mounting protests, new elections were held on April 2, 2006. Thaksin's party won, running unopposed in many constituencies. In Bangkok however, the "no votes"—basically an anti-Thaksin vote—outnumbered those in his favor. This election shattered the alliance between urban elites, the middle class, and the rural population that had emerged in 2001 against the IMF-driven policies of Chuan Leekpai and sustained Thaksin's rise to power. It became clear that the urban middle and upper classes, NGO activists, urban intelligentsia, and large portions of the bureaucratic and military establishment were done with Thaksin, while in the countryside—especially in the north and the northeast—and among the urban lower classes large portions of the population continued to support the prime minister.

39. Yellow is the color associated with Monday, the day of the week in which the king was born. As a consequence, yellow has long been closely associated with the monarchy.

40. The concept of Thai-style democracy was developed by conservative forces soon after the end of absolute monarchy in 1932. Building on colonial historicist and culturalist arguments, its proponents argue that Thailand, with its contextual specificity, is not ready for western-style democracy, which therefore needs to be administered through a localized form of democracy, one not based on one-person-one-vote, but rather on the "good people" shepherding the nation. For an extensive treatment of this concept see Connors 2011; Ferrara 2010; Hewison and Kitirianglarp 2010; Pattana 2006a; Surin 2007.

Thaksin's attempt to control and conquer the state had backfired, generating a fracture inside the state apparatus deeper than the one he inherited. The period after the election was one of deep uncertainty and polarization. The Yellow Shirts continued to demand a royal intervention, while Thaksin—elected but under popular and judicial pressure—took an unprecedented leave of absence as prime minister. The courts were pressured by the palace to arbitrate the political dispute. On May 8, 2006, the three highest courts in Thailand—administrative, constitutional, and supreme—decided to annul the previous election and schedule a new vote for October of that year. Thaksin was furious. Attacking the courts, he claimed that his authority and Thai democracy were threatened by *phu mi barami nok ratthathammanun* (an individual with moral charisma outside the constitution). These words unequivocally referred either to the king—himself considered the maximum holder of this kind of charisma *(barami)*—or to General Prem Tinsunalonda, a former general, prime minister, and current head of the Privy Council and considered the closest political figure to the monarchy—legally defined as above the constitution *(nok ratthathammanun)*.[41] This was a giant mistake on Thaksin's part. Everybody acknowledged the ongoing struggle between the prime minister and state military and bureaucratic forces and many supported it, even inside the state administration. Behind closed doors, many even whispered that the palace was itself threatened by Thaksin's ever-expanding support among rural masses and lower classes, traditionally the core of the king's popularity. Until now, Thaksin's attempt to control other sections of the state had been openly directed only towards the bureaucracy and the military. Thaksin' words dragged the monarchy into the struggle.

UNINTENDED CONSEQUENCES: THE 2006 COUP

In July 2006 and August of 2006, Prem Tinsulanonda reminded soldiers and students that "the military's alliance belonged to the king and the country rather than to the government of the day, that leaders must be moral and ethical people, and that wealth—especially if gained through improper means—was an inappropriate basis for political power."[42] It did not take long for the army to receive the message. On September 19, 2006, while Thaksin

41. Montesano 1998.
42. Funston 2009, 8.

was in New York preparing to address the United Nations General Assembly, military tanks rolled into Bangkok, largely welcomed by the urban middle classes. The army took power and was soon endorsed by the monarch on national television. Thaksin had tried to use his unprecedented electoral support to unify state forces—bureaucracy, military, and the monarchy—under his control. These forces had responded by pushing him out of the country and discrediting the electoral process as a legitimate system for the selection of the country's leadership. It was now their turn to hold the conch of state power and try to expel Thaksin. This time it was up to the forces sympathetic to Thaksin to stage a response.

Although the removal of Thaksin Shinawatra signaled the return to power of the same forces that had previously governed Thailand and exerted influence of the street economy, the popular network that had emerged during the previous years around Thaksin's party and policies did not disappear. Motorcycle taxi drivers were among them. Their leaders and organizing capacity remained very much in place and oriented the drivers' political presence in the city after 2006. During years of being inscribed into an institutional setting, their leaders had developed an extensive web of connections and personal relations with state officials, from people in the Bangkok Metropolitan Administration and high-ranking police officers to army personnel, which guaranteed channels for future negotiations and demands. Now that they were left without institutional protection, they adopted the same meandering and path-seeking progression that directed their circulation in the streets of Bangkok to move through the corridors of government administration. While the coup of September 19 struck a significant blow to their formalization, Thaksin's ouster did not mark the end of drivers' newly acquired pride in their jobs or of their shared identity and organizational cohesion in the face of outside attacks on their livelihood.

Some of them who, like Nit, became pessimistic about the future went back to paying local officers and quietly driving their bikes, content with the slightly better conditions they had obtained. Others, like Boon, who had not even supported Thaksin's formalization, became enraged with the profound injustice of Thaksin's removal from power. The vast majority of the drivers, however, simply continued to oppose the unfairness of not being allowed to choose their own leaders and losing the recognition that Thaksin had once given them. Adun and Hong were among them. In conversations at their stations and in occasional street protests, many of the drivers refused to stay silent in the face of the military takeover. As a result, their leaders—in particular Yai, Lek, Lerm, and Oboto—became even more prominent public figures and power brokers of street politics in Bangkok, negotiating relations with national political parties, Thai governments, local police, and army personnel.

Thaksin's heavy-handed attempt to control illegal economies, challenge the power of bureaucratic, military, and monarchic forces, and instigate an unprecedented boost in political participation seemed to have failed. However, its unintended consequences survived and would come to color the role of motorcycle taxi drivers as political actors in Thailand. Thaksin's attempt to unify state forces under the control of an elected government responsive to the demands of its constituency had opened Pandora's Box. What came out was beyond Thaksin's plan—and, most probably, his expectations. Now that these forces had toppled democratic rule with the excuse of toppling him,[43] the authoritarian Thaksin was transformed into the most grotesque of democratic heroes. During his premierships, Thaksin had shown a tendency to authoritarianism, a poor human rights record, and a low tolerance for criticism. He violently dismissed and often silenced any form of dissent, whether from journalists, NGOs activists, or public intellectuals. He saw any criticism as illegitimate, anti-national, and potentially a betrayal of his electoral majority. Given his enormous popular and electoral support, he argued, every action he took, even if illegal or questionable, had to be accepted and could not be scrutinized.[44] Once his popular support was silenced by the coup, Thaksin became a symbol of the suppression of democratic politics, a man whose aspirations were being hampered by national elites, exactly as they were those of millions of people, including the drivers.

This paradox sits at the center of the figure of Thaksin Shinawatra, what he came to represent after the 2006 coup, and the political instability that Thailand has lived since. In the course of his political life, former friends and patrons became his archenemies while harsh critics would end up marching in the streets with his face on their T-shirts. Journalists, commentators, and citizens described him alternately, or simultaneously, as a populist handing

43. On the tension between toppling democracy and toppling Thaksin, see the verbal crossfire between Thongchai Winichakul and Kasian Tejaripa (Kasian 2006; Thongchai 2008b).

44. This became clear since the first days of his premiership during his trial for hiding assets, only to become more evident and vocalized in the case of the extrajudiciary killings during the controversial "war on drugs" or the bloody handling of the southern insurgency.

money to the poor, a commoner from the countryside vindicating centuries of Bangkok's domination, a neoliberal media tycoon protecting the interests of big businesses, and a developmentalist leader with a proclivity for authoritarianism. Some saw him as a breath of fresh air for the country, a republican at heart, and the first Thai politician to develop and implement holistic policies for the poor. Others viewed him as a profit-minded capitalist who turned to politics only to expand his wealth and power, a challenge to the nation so vile that it required abandoning electoral democracy and calling back the military and the palace to take control of the country.[45] Thaksin himself contributed to this confusion with chameleonic policies and speeches. When he founded the Thai Rak Thai political party, Thaksin ran for office as the spearhead of nationalist business groups who wanted to put an end to the IMF agenda post-1997 crisis. By 2003, he was promoting extrajudicial killings, passing unprecedented welfare provisions, and championing rural and urban masses while also attempting to bring military, police, and civil servants under his direct control. Now, all of his plans seemed in shambles.

Nonetheless, when everything seemed lost, his political stature continued to grow. In his absence, the former prime minister became a ghostly presence, a mirror which allowed different portions of Thai society to see in him whatever they wanted: for some a hero of democracy and the small people, for others an immoral villain who threatened to destroy the country's foundations. Behind this hall of mirrors, however, probably stood a man like many others who got caught in his own plans, who engaged in a fight larger than he could take on and learned how reality often ridicules grandiose machinations but also presents new and unexpected openings.[46] His economic policies and welfare provisions continued to garner mass support from the rural and urban lower classes who had seen for the first time a prime minister making good on his promises, extending their access to state services, and offering them social, economic, and political recognition. This, in turn, sustained new forms of political participation and desires among the drivers and millions of

45. Anek 2006 [Buddhist year 2549]; Chaiyawat 2010 [Buddhist year 2553]; Chookiat 2011; Funston 2009; Hewison 2010; Kriengsak 2006; Looney 2004; McCargo 2002; McCargo and Ukrist 2005; Nithi 2010 [Buddhist year 2553]; Pasuk and Baker 2004; Pye and Schaffar 2008; Sangsit 2005 [Buddhist year 2548]; Thitinan 2006.

46. A less sympathetic reading has been proposed by two prominent Thai scholars who concluded that "as a man of no real principles, ethical and political, he has reflected the forces swirling around him" (Baker and Pasuk 2009, 354).

others in a similar position. Without him, those desires brewed and became something larger and more intense than the ousted prime minister had ever intended. While for him they were the natural expression of free entrepreneurship and the road to economic prosperity, in the hands of its supporters they became personal and political demands—demands they would not stop fighting for, even once Thaksin was gone.

SIX

Transforming Desires into Demands

Men do not fight or die for tons of steel, or for tanks and atomic
bombs. They aspire to be happy, not to produce.

HENRI LEFEBVRE, *Critique of Everyday Life*

AT THE END OF 2009, I traveled to the northeastern province of Udon
Thani, where I planned to spend some days helping Adun and his family with
their glutinous rice harvest. On the train I met Id, a man in his fifties from
Korat Province.[1] Id sat in third class and stared out the window at the boun-
tiful rice fields. His hands revealed the marks of a rural upbringing but also
suggested an atypical softness. As the train moved out of the station we
started to talk. Naturally, the conversation swerved to the country's political
situation. The Thai Supreme Court was about to rule over the seizure of
Thaksin's assets, while he remained in exile abroad. Nearly four years had
passed since the military coup that removed him from power. During his
premiership Thaksin had gone after the military and bureaucratic forces'
money. Now it was payback time.

"Democracy is justice," Id began. "For the most part we don't have legal,
political, and educational justice. It is a matter of opportunity and double
standards [*sǫng māttrathān*]. Look at the case of Thaksin. Maybe he is corrupt but who isn't in Thai politics? Why are they going after him and not all
the others? Why are they trying to confiscate all of his money, even what he
made before taking office? This is what double standards means. It is the
same for us, people from Isan. Every time we elect someone who listens to our
problems and takes care of us, they take him down and replace him with a

Parts of this chapter have been previously published in *South East Asia Research* 2 (3)
(September 2012), published by Sage Publishing. All rights reserved.

    1. The city of Korat, officially known as Nakhon Ratchasima, traditionally marked the
fuzzy boundary between the Lao and Siamese territories. The city is often referred to as
the "gateway to Isan" for its strategic geographic position along transportation routes, both
streets and railways, ascending to the northeastern plateau.

soldier or an unelected government that follows the interests of rich people in Bangkok. There is no point in voting under this system. So we have to fight for our kids, for our nephews and nieces, for the population at large."

Listening to Id's grievances, I asked him about life in the Isan he grew up in, before the accelerated neoliberal transformation of the 1990s, the 1997 crisis, and Thaksin's policies. Id told a familiar story of growing up in a small wooden house crowded by his grandparents, parents, and five siblings, next to the rice fields and forest which provided most of their food. He talked of a simple but hard life, of regular days made more exciting in the 1970s by the arrival of politicized university students who opened local schools and then, driven by political repression, escaped into the forest and took up armed struggle. He recounted how, a decade later, those same students laid down their weapons and returned to their lives as urban elites while villagers were left behind, with the same lack of opportunities they had before the students arrived. Id wanted to study but, short on money, he became a day laborer in sugarcane fields. Id's dreams, however, went beyond using his hands to slash sugarcane. Following the 1997 crisis that destroyed local agribusiness, he became an apprentice barber in his village, as part of a government training program for laid-off workers. He loved the job and, helped by the easy access to credit and the wave of support for entrepreneurial forces during Thaksin's premiership, he opened his own shop in 2004.

"Compared with when I was a kid," Id concluded, "now we have everything in the countryside. We have motorcycles, TV, cell phones. Now things are better than twenty years ago. We have asphalted streets; we have electricity, everything..." He paused. "But life today is harder. The whole world has developed and Isan too. But we are slower than Bangkok so we remain behind. We know in which direction the world is going, we just can't keep up. My father did not study, yet he still had a job; my nephew finished high school and cannot find anything to do. We have new needs, new things we want. The whole world is developing, we must follow that development. Cell phones for instance, we never had them twenty years ago, but now you cannot work without them. If you live in the city, they are the only way to talk to your family and not lose contact, to remain connected. How can we live without them? We need them to progress. Now the government of Abhisit tells us we should not want them, that we should be moderate. They are slowing us down. They want us to remain undeveloped villagers. They call us stupid, they call us greedy, and they take whatever they want. It is their mindset. We need to take to the streets and we need to kick them out. If they remain in power we will always be kept behind."

After this long conversation, Id excused himself and went to the train's toilet to take a leak. As he walked down the crowded railroad car, his words lingered in my mind and brought me back to a conversation I had a few days before with Yai, one of leaders of the motorcycle taxi's mobilization during Thaksin's premiership. We had been talking for a few hours about the early days of the drivers' struggle against local people of influence and, as usual, once the conversation became casual Yai shifted from high-sounding political proclamations to his more concrete and everyday demands as a worker, a citizen, and a father.

"Things have changed," Yai said, eyes locked on his son playing a few meters away from the street. "This society is fucked. People with power always look ahead and never realize what is happening around them. Whenever things start to change in this place they always look to the middle class and high society, as if the country was only them.[2] But now the issue is with the lower class, with us. We don't have enough money for our family; we can't open a business, can't buy toys for our kids or send them to a good school. Thaksin saw us and gave us the possibility to get that money, to get opportunities. But since then no one thinks about us. They say we followed Thaksin because he bought our votes, because we are stupid, because we are buffaloes. Do they really think that is the cause of the problem? A few coins for a vote? It's Thailand, every party comes around to give money away before elections. We take from both sides and then we vote however we want. If you want our support first thing you need to do is make sure that people have enough money to survive and give their kids an education, to give them a job, to give the opportunity to fulfill their desires. Then everything will be easier. Thaksin was doing that, but now they are telling us that wanting those things is not good, that we should not dream of a better life. They tell people to be self-sufficient, to be happy with what we have. What is that? How can you be self-sufficient when your kids have no money, when they have no education? How can we be happy when our lives are not getting better?"

Id's and Yai's words resonated with those I heard almost every day at motorcycle taxi drivers' stations: voices that lamented their long-standing

2. Unfortunately this attitude has also dominated the work of scholars of Thai politics. With a few significant exceptions (Ferrara 2015; Glassman 2010a; Nostitz 2009, 2014; Somchai 2006; Sopranzetti 2012b), most of them have explained political transformation from the Bangkok-centric perspective of intra-elite struggle, power-brokers networks, and movement's leaders (Hewison 2010; Kasian 2006; Marshall 2014; McCargo 2005; Mérieau 2016; Nithi 2010 [Buddhist year 2553]; Pavin 2014; Pye and Schaffar 2008; Thongchai 2014).

exclusion from the legal, political, and economic opportunities that are available to the rich and the powerful but seem to escape them and their children constantly. Ousted Prime Minister Thaksin Shinawatra, they said, had not just extended these opportunities to them, recognizing them as free entrepreneurs and protecting them from the influence of state officials. He had done something even more significant: he recognized them as citizens and saw their aspirations and desires as legitimate.

As all these voices overlapped in my head, it was clear that their desires were not just directed to new phones, a bigger TV, or a better bike as objects of conspicuous consumption. Rather, these commodities materialized their struggles to keep up with the pace of urban development and claim participation in it, the same struggles that they experience in their lives between the city and the villages.[3] Through them, these people were not only asking to be allowed to prosper economically. They were demanding recognition: recognition of their roles of citizens, recognition of their rights to choose representative which their interests at heart, recognition of their struggles to give better educational opportunities to their children or obtain a fairer treatment from the bureaucracy. When Thaksin rose to power, he recognized those desires as legitimate forces. The military government established after the 2006 coup and, even more clearly, the government of Abhisit Vejjajiva which came to power in 2009 dismissed them as the immoral effects of their greed and Thaksin's handouts. This shift made the drivers only more aware of larger systems of injustice and double standards that never questioned the desires of urban elites but rejected all of theirs as greed. In the period between 2009 and 2010, faced with a government unwilling to hear their voices, the drivers and millions of other citizens transformed those desires into political demands.

Thus far, I have analyzed how the drivers operated as connectors for the diffusion of desires and lifestyles between the city and the countryside, how this role related to Thaksin's discourse of entrepreneurship and freedom, and how his plan to control other state forces ended up creating a citywide network of drivers and getting him out of office. Here, I explore how these processes generated the spark that would ignite the largest political mobilization in Thai history. Once again, the conditions for its existence emerged as unintended consequences of Thaksin's policies and the actions of the governments that replaced him. Yet its specific features were molded by people, like the

3. For a treatment of the importance of cell phones to the social life of migrants in Bangkok and their attempt to bridge their villages and the city, see Mills 2012.

drivers, who pushed Thaksin's promises far beyond the limits he had set for them and transformed his capitalist desires for individual prosperity into condemnations of inequality and collective demand for justice. In order to understand how this shift happened, however, we need to go back to 2000, to Thaksin's first address to the assembly of his newly created party.

UNLEASHING DESIRES: THE SHINAWATRA LEGACY

A few months before the 2001 election, Thaksin presented the platform that would eventually become known as Thaksinomics to his party members. The program, Thaksin told them, was the result of months of work in which party members roamed the countryside and villages to listen to the needs and desires of the people. Nidhi Eoseewong, a leading Thai intellectual, ironically remarked that Thaksin's plan was "just somebody taking the dreams of Thai society and making them into policy."[4] He could not have been more right. Thaksin knew that mapping and satisfying people's desires had been the core of his business success. Now, unleashing and legitimizing them would become the central pillar of his government and the economic recovery that it promised. His plan was to obtain economic recovery by fostering consumption. Under Thaksinomics Thai capitalism thrived. In two years, consumption rates had returned to pre-1997-crisis levels and continued to grow.

The idea of recovering from an economic crisis by fostering consumers' desires was hardly a novelty. Its roots were planted almost a century before on the pages of a prestigious American business magazine. In a 1927 issue of the *Harvard Business Review*, Paul Mazur, one of the first nonfamily employees at Lehman Brothers, wrote: "We must shift America from a needs to a desires culture. People must be trained to desire, to want new things even before the old had been entirely consumed. We must shape a new mentality in America. Man's desires must overshadow his needs."[5] Two years later, when the 1929 crisis hit, provoked by massive overproduction, Mazur's words sounded prophetic. The preservation of the capitalist system now hinged on this transformation.

Karl Marx had pointed out that crises of overproduction—where supply overshadows demand—were one of the main weaknesses of the capitalist system. The 1929 crash seemed to prove him right. The only way to fix them

4. As reported in Pasuk and Baker 2008a, 73.
5. As reported in Curtis 2002.

was to turn workers into perennially hungry consumers, indulging desires beyond providing for their material needs. Fordism, a new form of routinized labor organization aimed at increasing production while raising workers' wages, was a first response. Previously, as Marx showed, wages were calculated in relation to the cost of the survival and reproduction of labor force; now they were determined by the need to transform workers into mass consumers.

This system dominated the part of the world under American influence after the Second World War, including Thailand. It created an unprecedented period of economic growth and prosperity, deeply unjust and unfair but at least slightly more distributed. Another crisis, however, changed this dominant paradigm. After the 1973 petrol crisis and the subsequent economic downturn, a new model emerged, one that saw profit making increasingly connected to financial services rather than industrial production.[6] As a consequence, the industrial wages that had supported mass consumption stopped growing. Workers' buying power stagnated and their consumption needed to be fostered through different mechanisms. Attention turned to manufacturing consumers' desires and supporting them through access to debt.[7] While the latter required the creation of a new financial infrastructure,[8] the former relied on the collaboration that emerged after the Second War World between the advertisement industry, the new name of the American propaganda machine after the end of the war, and psychoanalytic theory.[9] The objective was to connect consumers' behaviors to their unconscious desires, imbuing commodities with meanings well beyond their function. It was not the mass object that the workers needed to desire but the lifestyles that those objects stood for.[10] Consumption was no longer about what people wanted to have but also about whom they wanted to be.

6. For a treatment of the effects of this crisis on capital flows and financialization, see Harvey 1985, 2001, 2005.

7. Bear 2015; Graeber 2011; James 2014; Lazzarato and Jordan 2010; White 2012.

8. Bryan and Rafferty 2006; Klein 2007; Lapavitsas 2009; Merton 1995; Reinhart and Rogoff 2011; Schein et al. 2001.

9. M. H. Anderson 1984; Ewen 1996; Tye 1998.

10. This was a radical transformation. In Fordism, as Pierpaolo Pasolini argued, "the individual cannot be the consumer that producers want. In other words, he can only be an occasional consumer, unpredictable, free from choices, deft, in some case even able to refuse, to refute the hedonism that has become the new religion. The notion of the 'individual' is by its very nature irreconcilable with the needs of consumption. The individual needs to be destroyed. He needs to be substituted by the mass-man" (Pasolini 1975, 36). In post-Fordism, it is precisely the unpredictable individual that becomes the ideal consumer, one for whom new products can always be developed.

This transformation began in the United States but rapidly spread to its allies during the Cold War. In the context of Thailand, the making of these desiring subjects was not just an economic project to foster consumption but also a central tool for American imperialism and its counterinsurgency against the spread of communism.[11] A local version of Fordism had emerged in the country since the late 1950s under the ideology of development (*phatthanā*). This configuration, similar to its American counterpart, revolved around the new worker-consumer, a *modern* citizen who lived by the slogan "work is money, money is work that gives happiness."[12] A newly created local advertising industry had a central role in connecting work and consumption with happiness, thereby stimulating consumers' desires while preventing them from developing sympathies toward the neighbouring communist experiments in Laos, Cambodia, and Vietnam. Between 1963 and 1965, advertising agencies from Japan and the United States opened branches in Thailand. By 1967, the country had its own advertising association and the industry grew over the next two decades as workers' wages rose steadily. As many of the drivers' personal stories showed, citizens were transformed into mass consumers, especially those who lived in the capital city. Bangkok saw a rapid diffusion of shopping malls, the temples of the new society of ever-desiring mass consumers.[13] Standardized goods flooded Thai households, beginning from those of workers in Bangkok and rapidly spreading throughout the country. Something, however, began to change in the mid-1990s. Wages stopped growing and many workers left the factory floor while the business elites and new middle classes, provided with unprecedented access to credit, went on a spending spree. This mass consumption and spending bubble, fueled by debt and financial speculation, burst with the 1997 crisis. The economic crash, however, did not bring the manufacturing of consumers and desires in Thailand to an end. Quite the contrary.

After the crisis, Thai capitalism entered a post-Fordist phase that turned millions of people, including many of the drivers, away from their previous lives as mass workers on factory floors toward new ones as individualized, free, and precarious entrepreneurs.[14] This individualization was not limited to labor practices, but also shaped consumer desires and advertising. Following international trends, the Thai advertising industry moved toward

11. M. H. Anderson 1984; Phillips 2015.
12. Sunate 2006, 127.
13. Peeradorn 2007.
14. I analyzed this dynamic in detail in chapter 4.

the manufacturing of desires by creating an association between commodities and individual emotions and aspirations. Over this period, "the task of advertising thus becomes not only to inform the consumer of the availability of a particular product on the market, but to build and expand his need for that product."[15] Consumption was no longer presented as a way to obtain the social status and lifestyle that the commodity stood for; it expressed who you were as an individual.[16]

The drivers did not passively accept the new model. Thaksin might had seen unleashing their desires as little more than a way to restart the stagnant Thai economy by allowing the economic potential of rural masses and urban poor, who were traditionally excluded from the capitalist feast, to flourish under the protection of his government.[17] Yet over the course of his premiership, and particularly after the 2006 coup, the drivers interpreted Thaksin's policies in their own terms. To them, Thaksin was not just offering commodities but inclusion in the state apparatus, an end to bureaucratic indifference and oppression, and recognition of their legitimate participation in the nation and in the market. For the drivers, in other words, desires for commodities and services provided a language to articulate demands for social, economic, and political participation, equality, and recognition.

Whether or not these outcomes were part of the prime minister's intentions, his premiership gave the drivers a taste of the positive effects that a government relying on their electoral support could bring to their lives. When the 2006 coup took place, many of the drivers did not see the military takeover as bureaucratic, military, and monarchic forces pushing back against Thaksin, but rather as an attack on their own desires to have a better life or simply keep up with the development of Bangkok. With Thaksin out of the country, those unleashed desires did not just disappear. Rather they gained momentum, this time championed by the will of popular masses, not by an authoritarian tycoon.

15. Sunate 2006, 155–56.

16. Prime examples of this dynamic are Apple products. The American multinational has managed and spearheaded, maybe better than any other corporation, this post-Fordist consumption modality, making its product into a status symbol and a way to declare the owners is, indeed, "a Mac person."

17. As McCargo and Ukrist have argued, under Thaksin "popular participation was limited to a consumer mode" (McCargo and Ukrist 2005, 14).

TAMING DESIRES: THE POST-COUP
UNELECTED GOVERNMENTS

The centrality of desires to Thaksin's political project did not go unnoticed by the military, bureaucratic, and royal forces that were struggling with him for control of the state. This fight, they understood, did not only play out in the streets, offices, or courtrooms but also entailed a much more personal dimension. Their strategy was to reframe the popular desires that Thaksin had unleashed as deleterious and un-Thai, pitting them against the idea of self-sufficiency advocated by the Thai monarch. The promulgation of this narrative started even before the military coup. In early 2006, to celebrate the sixtieth anniversary of the king's reign, a book titled *The King Who Is Number One in the World* was printed and immediately became a best seller. The text offered a fairytale-style popularization of the sufficiency narrative. "In a far off place," the book states, "the king came across a village that had almost no one living there. Where has everyone gone? The king asked the small group of remaining villagers. The villagers answered their king: a demon of the dark called Greed came and visited and asked the people to leave the village. Most of the villagers abandoned the village and went to live in the City of Extravagance. The king thought for a moment and then gave the villagers a radiant seed. The villagers took the seed and planted it and it grew into a radiant tree that grew large branches and spread its radiance in all directions. The king told the villagers that the radiant tree is called Sufficiency. The radiance of the tree shone to far off places, as far as the City of Extravagance. And many of those who saw it travelled back to return to their village."[18]

In a single paragraph, decades of rural migrations and personal struggles to obtain better access to resources, education, and commodities were reduced to the effect of seduction by the dark demon of greed that attracted the gullible villagers to the City of Extravagance, otherwise known as Bangkok. The life trajectories of all the drivers I talked to, the aspirations that directed their migration, the struggles they experienced in the city every day, their claims to freedom and recognition, and their sacrifices to give a better future to their families—basically all the tensions that this book narrates—are reduced to a vacuity, an act of greed that the glorious king undid with the use of his seed of sufficiency that persuades the villagers lost in the City of Extravagance to start flocking back home and to abandon their

18. As cited in Walker 2010, 251.

struggles.[19] Unfortunately this story was more than an offensive fable sold inside 7-Eleven stores; it was symptomatic of the military government's post-coup agenda. The junta led by General Surayud Chulanont was determined to use this seed of sufficiency to curb popular desires and demands.

On October 24, 2006, thirty-five days after the coup, General Surayud formally endorsed the Sufficiency Economy, an economic philosophy that had been formulated by the King Rama IX in a famous speech delivered immediately following the 1997 economic crisis. The Sufficiency Economy advocated a scaled-down moralized economy in which Thais should be happy with whatever little they have. Mixing Buddhist metaphysical repression of desire, nationalist nostalgia for a rural past of self-reliance and communal living, and the discourse of sustainability, this theory promised to offer a path through which individuals and communities could take care of their own well-being without being trapped in the contradictions of capitalism. The royal doctrine revolved around the concepts of moderation, immunity, and ethics, and offered an alternative view of economic processes that bore little resemblance to both Thaksin's post-Fordism and the neoliberal model that had dominated Thailand for a few years before and after the 1997 economic crisis.[20] By echoing the call by Bhutan's monarchy to consider gross national happiness (GNH) above gross national product (GNP), the Sufficiency Economy offered a radical corrective to market-driven economic theories and proposed to forego economic growth for the psychological and moral well-being of the nation and its people.[21]

The shift necessitated curtailing the desire for commodities and services that Thaksin had fostered. Peter Calkins, an economist at Chiang Mai University, was the main academic reference for the framing of the new theory of a sufficient economy in collaboration with the National Economic

19. This fable is also a prime example of the duplicity of the national discourse I analyzed in chapter 3 that framed the countryside both as a place of backwardness and corruption and as a place of harmonious returns.

20. As reported in a booklet published by the National Economic and Social Development Board (NESDB): "Sufficiency means moderation, reasonableness, and the need of self-immunity for sufficient protection from impact arising from internal and external changes.... In addition, a way of life based on patience, perseverance, diligence, wisdom and prudence is indispensable to create balance and be able to cope appropriately with critical challenges, arising from extensive and rapid socioeconomic, environmental, and cultural changes in the world" (NESDB 2006, 12–14).

21. For a sympathetic analysis of the Sufficiency Economy as viable model for a more sustainable world see Avery and Bergsteiner 2016.

and Social Development Board (NESDB). In an essay called *The Sufficiency Economy at the Edges of Capitalism,* Calkins provided the clearest statement of the relation between this theory and people's desires. "Moderation," he argued, "challenges the very first sentence in the Parkin and Bade book—['all economic questions arise because we want more than we can get']—by saying that wants are not unlimited, they can be satisfied. In fact, one will be happier if one can control one's desires. 2500 years ago at Mrigadava Forest in Vanarasi [*sic*], the Buddha explained that life is full of suffering precisely because we are tempted by the unlimited desires now enshrined in the Western definition of economics; and that the only way to avoid suffering is to avoid greed for things and situations we don't need."[22] Professor Calkins rejected what he saw as the dominant discourse of western capitalism and bridged Buddhist teachings with a vague concept of moderate economics to advocate for the unquestionable moral superiority of a model that reconfigures desires for commodities and services as temptations.

Whatever Calkins's intentions might have been, after the 2006 coup the military junta adopted the Sufficiency Economy using the language of sustainability and happiness to legitimize their actions and repress the popular demands that Thaksin's premiership had unleashed.[23] First, their endorsement of this philosophy had the purpose of legitimizing the coup as the virtuous act of removing an immoral leader.[24] In this view, Thaksin and his policies—much like the demon of Greed in the fable—had undermined the morality of local economic and political systems. Now the military forces were bringing back a higher order of morality represented by the king and his Sufficiency Economy. Second, the junta saw, as many of the drivers did, a direct correlation between desires for commodities and services and larger economic, social, and political demands. While, for Thaksin's supporters, the objective had been to assist both of them, for the men in uniform controlling

22. Calkins 2007, 5.

23. This proposal was so appealing that the UNDP endorsed it in 2007 and celebrated it in their "Thailand Human Development Report: Sufficiency Economy and Human Development," completely ignoring the conservative agenda behind it (Baker 2007).

24. At the same time as they were endorsing this rhetoric of a scaled-down economy and "being happy with what you have", the junta behind his government, which went under the name of Council for National Security (CNS), was receiving salary payments totaling 38 million baht ($1.26 million) a month, six times higher than the payment of the corresponding bodies after the 1991 coup. Moreover, the new "sufficient" government raised the military budget, which had been stable since 1999, by 35 percent in 2007 and by another 24 percent in 2008.

the desires unleashed during Thaksin's premierships became pivotal for the suppression of political and economic demands voiced by rural and urban masses.[25] The Sufficiency Economy showed those desires as illegitimate and immoral, intrinsically un-Buddhist, and ultimately un-Thai. The junta's expanded this notion of immorality with people's larger demands. Social and bureaucratic hierarchies and inequalities were no longer something that hampered the development of the nation, but rather had to be accepted and submitted to, according to the moral behavior of self-sufficiency. Striving to create opportunities and better lives, whether through migration, entrepreneurship, or political participation, was no more a legitimate and useful impulse but rather an immoral behavior, motivated by greed or short-sightedness. By adopting Sufficiency Economy, in other words, the junta attempted to legitimize the preservation of class differences, the disciplining of dissent, the withdrawal from providing social service and resources to the villages, and the furthering of political conservatism.[26]

In order to succeed in their strategy, however, state military, bureaucratic, and monarchic forces needed to make sure that this approach would be adopted by their citizens. In 2007, the Sufficiency Economy was written into a new constitution drafted by the military government, cementing it into state policy and requiring future governments to organize state administration and economic policy around its principles.[27] At the same time, a militarized propaganda machine was set in motion. The ISOC (Internal Security Operation Command), a military division infamous for its violent repression of leftist politics during the Cold War, was resuscitated to advance the philosophy of Sufficiency Economy. In an attempt to win back the people's sup-

25. As Andrew Walker has shown, "not only were the rural people to be shielded (or excluded) from full and active participation in the national economy but their participation in electoral democracy was delegitimized and the power of their elected representatives was constrained" (Walker 2010, 261).

26. Elinoff 2014a; Glassman 2010b; Hewison 2008; Ivarsson and Isager 2010; Rossi 2012; Wah and Öjendal 2004.

27. In the months before the draft was voted through a referendum, the ISOC was ordered by the coup maker General Sonthi to use its seven hundred thousand nationwide staff to "promote proper understanding of the constitution" among rural people and to use door-to-door tactics in their campaign to "educate" people, so they would not be "tricked" into rejecting the draft. Despite the military's "educational" campaign, the rural masses of Isan refused to "learn" and, faced with a referendum, rejected the constitutional draft by 62.8 percent, though it was approved nationally.

port and take back control over the state, the army and the ISOC shared responsibilities. While the former focused on businesses and the middle class, the latter played a crucial role in mustering support from people at the grassroots level. The Center for Poverty Eradication and Rural Development under the Philosophy of Sufficiency Economy was set up in late 2007 under the supervision of the ISOC. Once again, as they had done during the Cold War, the ISOC presented its repressive operations as an attempt to educate the population, this time to the principles of sufficiency.

The military, bureaucratic, and monarchic forces understood that taming the desires and aspirations that had been so central to Thaksin's unprecedented electoral success was essential for the repression of the political forces that had brought him to power. Leaked documents dating back to a meeting marking the retirement of coup leader General Sonthi in September 2007 reveal the existence of such a calculated plan. In the meeting Sonthi spoke of a deliberate scheme to fight what he called "the war for the people," a struggle similar to the one waged by the same institution against radicals and communists during the Cold War, but which now pitted the military and the palace against elected politicians. In Sonthi's words:

> Whether in the pre-war era, the Cold War era, or the era of capitalist democracy, their activist struggle to win over the people has not changed at all. . . . They have not lost their inclinations or ideology. . . . They win over the people through elections in order to take state power and have the ability to make changes they want at an appropriate time. One party, that was founded in 14th July 1998, with a secret organization of this group in the background, is a mix of capitalism and populism. . . . It is our duty, as soldiers of the King, to understand these matters, to understand the war for the people, both in the era of Cold War and in the era of populism. . . . So all of us must contest with them to win the grassroots back for the King. . . . Our most important aim is that all the masses in the territory must be ours.[28]

In this struggle to make the masses theirs, both sides unsheathed their best weapons: for Thaksin, capitalist desires and pro-poor policies; for the army, a combination of the monarchy's Sufficiency Economy and Cold War repressive

28. This document was leaked on the Pro-Thaksin website www.hi-thaksin.com, as report 0402/513 of the army's Policy and Planning Department on September 26, 2007. The legitimacy of this document was discussed for a while until General Sonthi himself admitted the validity of the document, declaring to the *Bangkok Post* that the plans were intended to guide the public down the "proper" path to democracy.

organizations.[29] Both, however, underestimated the ability of the people they were battling over to absorb the impact of their propaganda and deflect it toward their own economic and political objectives. If in pages of *The King Who Is Number One in the World* the villagers' immediately accepted the seed offered by the king, in real life the villagers understood well that they needed to be wary of the shining tree of sufficiency. The popular response to the army's offensive was complex and varied, ranging from ironic dismissal to tepid adoption and fanatic support. Among the hundreds of drivers I met, almost nobody related to the doctrine of Sufficiency Economy: it simply had little to do with their life experiences, struggles, and aspirations. The most critical drivers felt that it was enacted with the direct objective of limiting their economic, social, and political growth, though these individuals were careful to voice their opinions only in private, given the presence of a *lèse-majesté* law that punished anybody who criticized the monarchy and its opinions with three to fifteen years of jail.[30] Others simply found it irrelevant.

Wud, sitting outside his house back in the village was among them: "What can we do? We went to Bangkok to support our families, to send our kids to school and now they tell us that we should accept our situation, we should accept double standards, we should accept people looking down on us or we should come back here, to the countryside. If I want to stay in the countryside what could I live on? See, everybody is sitting in front of their houses. There is no water in the field. There is nothing to do. I need to save first to give a good education to my children. I have to buy them shoes, uniforms for school, to have them study English, to buy a computer. With what money? Should I just give them the same life I had, working in a field for no profit, without the opportunity to study? What should I do?"

Wud let these questions go unanswered, leaving space for the sounds of the countryside around us. One of his neighbors, also a motorcycle taxi driver in Bangkok, sat next to us filling the day with glass after glass of rice whisky. He added, "We struggle every day, we fought all of our lives. Now we fight the government because we don't accept double standards anymore. We are

29. In reference to this war, Andrew Walker has argued: "In General Sonthi's more militaristic vision, there was a 'war for the people' going on, and the Sufficiency Economy philosophy had to be used by the army to win the population back from the populist appeal of 'Thaksinomics'" (Walker 2010, 261).

30. *Lèse-majesté* law has been a main tool of political repression in Thailand since the 2006 coup. For a treatment of its nature, role, and use, see Streckfuss 1996, 2011.

done accepting. We've had enough of people ordering us around. We want democracy and we want the opportunity to choose who governs us."

Their words show that the desires that the drivers see trivialized by the Sufficiency Economy agenda are not just the capitalist desires advocated by Thaksin, but rather larger demands for social, economic, and political participation through formal education, English fluency, access to the internet, and democratic representation. Caught between dreams of a return to an idealized precapitalist village life and the desire for economic, social, and political advancement, people like Wud are faced daily with the impossibility of fulfilling either fairy tale. In this sense, the discourse of sufficiency played a major role in isolating the rural electorate and the urban poor from the unelected governments of General Surayud and, after December 2008, Abhisit Vejjajiva. Both governments, as Id told me on the train, represented a step back from the changes initiated by Thaksin and contributed to the impossibility of fulfilling the desires that the ousted prime minister had legitimized and sheltered. It was in this gap between unleashed, tamed, and unfulfilled promises that the drivers' desires for commodities and recognition turned into the political demands that would push them toward the Red Shirts, a growing social movement that promised to defend their demands to be treated fairly and to achieve what Thaksin had promised them: *prachāthippatai kin dai* (democracy you can eat), a democratic system that would also grant their livelihood. But how did the drivers transcend this rhetoric that portrayed them only as consumers or entrepreneurs and transform their desires into political demands?

FROM DESIRES TO DEMANDS

During one of the many excruciatingly slow afternoons spent at his station, Adun talked to me at length about a lucrative scheme in which he was involved when the iPhone 3 was first released in Thailand in 2009. A shop located in Lad Phrao, on the other side of Bangkok from his drivers' group, had received a large shipment of the phones and was selling a limited quantity of thirty units a day. Each buyer was allowed to purchase no more than one phone, priced at 20,000 baht ($660). A shop owner in Adun's neighborhood, for whom the local drivers operate as messengers, asked them to queue every morning in front of the shop in Lad Phrao and buy as many as they could. For each one they brought back, they would receive 500 baht ($16) and the shop owner would sell the phones in his store for 25,000 baht each. The arrangement made the drivers some money, solidified their relationship with a local merchant, and showcased their role as mediators and phatic labor for the city. The effects of this mediation, however, did not end at the shop counter: playing with the costly phones as they waited in line and shuttling them across the city sparked long discussions among the drivers about their own outdated machines. Chatting on the sidewalk while sipping ice-cold beer after a long day of work, Adun and his colleague made note of all the features that were not included in their phones. They dwelled on the unequal distribution of wealth that makes a month of their income insufficient to buy a single phone.

"Fuck, man." Pond, a twenty-year-old driver wearing a New York Yankees hat, burst out. "You can do everything with this phone and it's so fast. Music, internet, photos. I get them on my phone but they are so slow. I have to go to an internet point if I really want to get online."

The other older drivers, none of whom had internet on their phones, spoke of what it meant to be excluded from it. Adun, an eager reader, told them: "You can find everything there, it is like the biggest library in the world and we cannot use it. It is like when we were in school, we got older books, we had worse teachers than in Bangkok, we had to drop out because our families could not afford it. With these phones is the same, we are kept out and left behind."

A few weeks later, as we sat with some friends outside Adun's village on the riverbank waiting for fish to nibble at our bait, the same conversation traveled with us to the countryside, now tinged with a sense of personal pride that came with the knowledge of and contact with the new phone. Narrating the story of the transaction, he told two older men who sat with us, "There is everything in a small phone. You can do everything with it, take pictures, see the weather, find every kind of information. It is like having the whole world in your pocket. I would really like to have one of those but I will never be able to, it costs more than what I make in a month. If I buy one, who's going to feed my kids?" Adun's desire for the new product was closely connected with wanting to partake in conspicuous consumption and express his individuality as an urban citizen, one that keeps the world in his pocket. Yet it also became a way to articulate a critique of the larger systems of exclusion and exploitation under which he and his family are forced to live.

Discussions of this sort are all too common among motorcycle taxi drivers. Wealthy private houses, glamorous offices, and high-end shops figure in the landscape of their mobility as much as slums, tiny rooms, rural villages and Isan bars. On the one side, this puts them in contact with spaces and objects of privilege and wealth, from which other lower-class urban workers are often excluded. On the other, this experience makes them only more aware of their relative deprivation and the larger structural barriers that keep them from fully accessing and enjoying services and commodities available to their clients.[31] During Thaksin's premiership, the drivers had experienced a government that was questioning those barriers. Following the 2006 coup, they saw a military junta adopting Sufficiency Economy to raise them even higher. The new governments thought that a nostalgic call to a romanticized past of self-sufficiency and social harmony could control popular desires and could curtail their political demands. The opposite happened.

The drivers' inability to fulfill those desires provided a material language to articulate political demands for social justice, equality, and better representation. This process ran opposite to the one famously described by Karl Marx as commodity fetishism. The German philosopher showed how commodities conceal social relations by substituting a "definite social relation between men themselves [with] the fantastic relation between things."[32] Here, on the contrary, the impossibility for drivers to access commodities revealed and demystified the system of exploitation and exclusion under which they operate. For Marx, commodities became "products of the human brain [which] appear as autonomous figures endowed with a life of their own, which enter into relations both with each other and with the human race."[33] For the drivers, unobtainable commodities unveiled the social relations that marginalize and cast them away from the promises of both capitalism and democratic politics.

The drivers' roles as mediators put them face to face with their exclusion, made even more intolerable by the proximity to privilege and the realization of their role in circulating objects and traversing spaces that will always remain unattainable. Everyday realizations, such as that a phone may be worth more than one month of their labor, went a long way toward raising awareness among the drivers and advancing their political mobilization.[34]

31. For a study of the role of relative deprivation in political revolts, see Gurr 2015.
32. Marx 1906, 1: 165.
33. Ibid.
34. This relation was understood more clearly by Henri Lefebvre. In his magnus opus he argued that "to overestimate the 'motivations' of desire and desires themselves is to fall into subjectivism, psychologist and classic idealism. To disregard them is to fall into simplified and vulgar materialism and determinism, in which we forget man's obscure depth and his development" (Lefebvre 1991a, 2: 7).

After all, political struggles take place in the world of people who battle every day to make ends meet. They pertain to people who work and save money to send their children to decent schools, to provide them with opportunities, and to have some extra cash to drink, eat out once in a while, or bet on sports on the weekend. The people who engage in these everyday struggles "are often mythologised as Prometheans, but Hamlet would equally serve as a model. [They are the result of] people's midnight ruminations about a daily humiliation they suffer, about the shame they feel, about the claims to honor they would like to make."[35] These were the concerns voiced by people like Adun. It was not the desire to own commodities like the iPhone to make them reflect on exclusion, but rather the realization of the impossibility of ever owning one given their socioeconomic position and a political leadership that dismissed their aspirations as immoral and irresponsible.

While the centrality of unfulfilled desires to political consciousness and mobilization was evident in the words of motorcycle taxi drivers, this dynamic has been largely overlooked by contemporary scholars of social movements. This, however, has not always been the case. Both Spinoza and Hegel analyzed the role of desire in the creation of individual and collective consciousness.[36] After their early observations, however, desires and political consciousness diverged. On one side, the Marxist tradition elevated them to the realm of superstructure. On the other, psychoanalytical literature pushed them down to that of the unconscious. Desires, those voices argued, can be part of the manufacturing of consent or the acceptance of voluntary servitude, but not of any liberatory politics.[37] This reading has dominated the intellectual debate in Thailand. Prominent conservative public intellectuals have referred to desires as effects of globalization, un-Thai, emblems of the ungenuine nature of the rural and urban poor' political demands, or disruptions to the traditional self-reliance of village life.[38] Similarly, Marxist scholars have also been quick to reject the desire for commodities and services as an oppressive form of false consciousness or an ill-informed market practice of the Thai villagers.[39] Both groups, in other words, have continued to see desires as an illegitimate basis for political action because of their alleged

35. Metcalfe 1980, 56.
36. Butler 2012; de Spinoza 1970; Hegel 1965, 1998.
37. Freud 2003; Lordon 2014.
38. Sulak 1999; Sulak and Titmuss 1988; Wisalo 1999.
39. Chatthip 1999; Kasian 2006.

artificial nature, as opposed to an abstract and romantic idea of authenticity that often slips into both Thai conservative and radical discourses. This view provides a problematic ground from which to dismiss their political significance. Just as the artificial and imagined nature of nationalist passions or statehood does not make them less real, significant, and effective in rallying political participation, the same can be said of desire.[40]

This argument is particularly fraud in the context of post-Fordist capitalism, a system predicated upon the connection between desires and personal identity and values. In this configuration, the impossibility of fulfilling them becomes a denial of people's worthiness, a denial of recognition. It is not by chance that in conjunction with the development of post-Fordism in Europe a number of scholars have argued for the necessity of including desire in our theorization of political action.[41] It was in this context, in fact, that Deleuze and Guattari showed that repressed desires have the potential of "calling into question the established order of a society."[42] Around 2009 in Thailand, that dynamic was in full development. Unfulfilled desires had begun to heat up, slowly burning inside, eroding their own foundations and even destroying the very objects they long for, along with anyone standing in the way. The Red Shirts' mobilization was the end result of this process and would call into question the whole order of Thai society, as military forces, bureaucratic elites, and royalists would quickly learn.

40. B. R. Anderson 1983. Interestingly Marx himself made a similar argument in his analysis of commodities. In opening *Capital* he stated, "the commodity is, first of all, ... a thing ... which satisfies human need of whatever kind. The nature of these needs, whether they arise, for example, from the stomach or from the imagination, makes no difference" (Marx 1906, 1: 1).

41. This has been the case especially among French theorists—most prominently Deleuze, Guattari, and Lefebvre (Deleuze and Guattari 1977, Lefebvre 1991a). In the context of Southeast Asia, over the last decade, a number of scholars have pointed out the relevance of desire to understand political economic and social transformations (Brody 2006; High 2014; Li 2007). These theorizations, however, rarely have been applied to the study of social movements.

42. Deleuze and Guattari 1977, 5. Deleuze and Guattari have argued that the desire-machine needs demolition in order to be assembled. Desire-machines work only through continuous breakdowns, and in those they reveal their explosive potential. In this sense, the desire-machine, or more accurately its breakdowns, experienced as an impossibility to fulfill those desires, became a force that called for the demolishing of an existing political system. What pushed people to question this established order, in other words, was not desire itself but its repression.

BURNING RED DESIRES AND THE MAKING
OF THE RED SHIRTS

On November 1, 2006, one and a half months after the military coup and a week after Sufficiency Economy was endorsed as a policy by the military junta, a lonely protester dramatically showed his frustration with the new political order. Nuamthong Praiwal, a taxi driver who had driven his car into a military tank at Royal Plaza the day after the coup, hanged himself under a pedestrian flyover on the Vibhavadi-Rangsit Highway, leaving a note opposing the military intervention. A few weeks later, three anti-coup groups composed largely of university students, radicals, and Thaksin supporters staged small protests of a few dozen people, lone screams into the silence of militarized Bangkok. Soon, however, their voices gained volume. By December 10, Constitution Day, a crowd of a few thousand people protested in Sanam Luang, the enormous grounds in front of the Royal Palace. The leaders of the 2003 drivers' mobilization—Yai, Lek, Lerm, and Oboto—were among its organizers and used this occasion to expand their network and get closer to the group of people who would eventually lead the Red Shirts. Although Adun, Hong, Boon, and Wud were not together, they were all in the crowd that protested the army's new constitution. It was not, however, until June 15, 2007, that the United Front for Democracy against Dictatorship (UDD) was created. Tellingly, its offices were located in the Imperial World working-class shopping mall along Lad Phrao Road, a space of reachable desires for the people who were to become the movement's urban supporters.

From the central office and myriad local meeting places across the country, the UDD organizers feverishly set up small protests and sit-ins. On September 2, the Red Shirts clashed with the opposing Yellow Shirts that had driven Thaksin out of office and laid the ground for the military coup. After the violent confrontation, the UDD halted its rallies, waiting to hear the results of the December 2007 elections, the first since the coup. The vote was easily won by Samak Sundaravej, a proxy of Thaksin, himself known for his authoritarian tendencies. Other state forces, however, were determined to exclude Thaksin and its allies from reentering the struggle over the state. Almost immediately the Yellow Shirts revived protests and a series of complaints were submitted to the Constitutional Court, which, in September 2008, forced Samak to resign because of a conflict of interest, based on his participation in a TV cooking show while he was prime minister. The premiership was given to Somchai Wongsawat, an uncharismatic bureaucrat and

Thaksin's brother-in-law. His rise to power was encountered with extensive mobilization among the Yellow Shirts, who saw in him a puppet guided by their archenemy.[43] On October 6, 2008, they blocked the Parliament and Government House, demanding the resignation of the democratically elected yet, in their eyes, illegitimate government. On November 25 a few thousand Yellow Shirts supporters marched toward Suvarnabhumi International Airport with the declared objective of preventing Somchai from returning to Thailand after an international forum. A convoy of hundreds of Yellow Shirts blocked the two ends of the road in front of the airport's terminal building and the main road to the airport. Boosted by the army's rejection of the government request to intervene and clear the airport, on November 27, the Yellow Shirts protesters moved to occupy Don Muang, the other international airport, effectively arresting air-based transportation in and through Bangkok. After protesters had blocked the nation, their bureaucratic allies proceeded to remove its elected government. On December 2, 2008, the Constitutional Court dissolved all three parties of the government coalition on questionable charges of electoral fraud.[44] The next day the Yellow Shirt protesters, satisfied with the outcomes of their actions, left the airports.

This charade that Jim Glassman has dubbed "provinces elect, Bangkok overturns,"[45] escalated a few days after in the creation of a new government headed by Abhisit Vejjajiva, the leader of the opposing Democrat Party, thanks to the defection of twenty-two MPs from Samak's party. Red Shirts immediately took the streets again, demanding the resignation of a government that had never received a popular majority but was the result of a game of military and judicial pressures, elite alliances, and cabinet reshufflings. The movement coalesced around a wide and vague agenda of returning to electoral power and a motley crowd of groups, symbols, and demands. Nowhere was their heterogeneity more evident than on the bodies of the thousands of protesters who protested the new government. On their heads, red-star-emblazoned Maoist hats; on their chests, shirts with the face of the former prime minister and capitalist tycoon, Thaksin Shinawatra; and underneath their flip-flops, the face of Prem Tinsulanonda, the most powerful member of the Privy Council who advises the king and was rumored to be behind the 2006 coup.

43. Nostitz 2009.
44. Funston 2009.
45. Glassman 2010b.

The protesters had articulated quite clearly their desires to change established relations of power, put an end to the military and bureaucratic interference in democratic politics, and to rebalance the political-economic and legal inequality that divides Bangkok from the countryside, the rich and powerful from the poor and helpless. Yet their visions diverged and lost clarity as to how these changes should be brought about. Indeed, this vagueness was fundamental in allowing collective action among a wide range of factions and actors who had often been in open conflict during the governments of Thaksin Shinawatra and who, even once unified in the Red Shirts, continued to operate under diverging political trajectories. While functional, this heterogeneity posed a challenge for observers as well as for the movement, which struggled to keep its different currents unified and to present itself to the press in a consistent and coherent way.[46] Up until this point, the multiplicity of actors, motivations, and objectives that came together under the umbrella of the UDD had clustered and dispersed in the streets of Bangkok. During this period of mobilization three streams started to emerge.[47]

The first stream, which I call the Thaksinites, was largely composed of Thaksin Shinawatra's acolytes, former allies, and voters of the Thai Rak Thai party. Its main exponents were former party members who were banned from electoral politics following the 2006 coup. The Thaksinites' objectives, with significant internal variations, revolved around the erasure of the political changes brought by the military coup, the return of Thaksin Shinawatra to Thailand, and the revocation of the 2007 constitution drafted by the military junta. The second stream, the democracy activists, gathered together people who had often opposed the government of Thaksin Shinawatra, its policies, and authoritarianism, yet considered unacceptable any political change brought about by military, judicial, or bureaucratic interventions. Their goal was the establishment of liberal democracy in Thailand, with a system of checks and balances and direct control over military interventions in the political sphere. Its main exponents tended to be established personalities in

46. The multiplicity of representations was particularly evident in international media—especially BBC and CNN—which covered the Red Shirts alternatively as a peasant movement, a rented mob under the control of the media Tycoon Thaksin Shinawatra, or a socialist uprising, depending on their sources in Thailand.

47. This distinction is a gross oversimplification of a segmented multiplicity of forces. I divided them up for the purpose of analytical clarity. I do so with the awareness that this is just one of many possible artificial sectioning of a movement that has retained a fluid and multidimensional nature.

street politics, former student activists, and community organizers who saw the Red Shirts as a new phase in the long and incomplete history of Thai democratic struggles. The third stream was composed of radicals. Their numbers were difficult to estimate given the potential legal consequences of voicing their opinions in public. The radicals' agenda coalesced around a call for the restructuring of political-economic relations between traditional elites and citizens and the withdrawal of the monarchy and the military from any active role in politics, putting them at risk of arrest under the increasingly used *lèse-majesté* law. In their vision, the Red Shirts needed to move beyond their connections to the ousted prime minister and its representative democracy and become a truly revolutionary movement.

Among the motorcycle taxi drivers I met, all three streams were present and often mixed. Adun was the closest to the position of the Thaksinites, and often put his support for the ousted prime minister over other considerations. Boon and Hong, younger and more directed by political demands than by love of Thaksin, identified with the democracy activists; while Wud had developed a more radical agenda.

These three streams, however, were currents rather than clearly established and discrete groups or organizations. During the protest they often mixed into one another, condensed, and then parted again. Most of the protesters I encountered voiced an idiosyncratic and at times contradictory mixture of demands and objectives. Similarly, the protest leaders and most visible political actors sat at the confluence of these streams, often riding multiple currents at the same time or drifting toward a different stream as the protest evolved. Nonetheless, by the end of 2008, the Red Shirts began to work toward the creation of a unified "social imaginary."[48] This process was not the premise of their political mobilization but rather emerged through it. The adoption of the color red—a reference to the national flag—was one of the first signs of this new process of unification. The Thai flag is composed of three colors: the center horizontal stripe is blue, which represents the monarchy; on either side of this are white horizontal stripes that stand for Buddhism; and on the top and the bottom are red stripes, symbolizing the nation. Claiming to be the expression of the people, the Red Shirts began to reformulate the desires and demands expressed by Id, Yai, and Adun—along with hundreds of other people I interviewed—into a collective identity, an

48. Abelmann 1996, 6.

interpretation of contemporary Thai society, and a definition of their enemies and demands.

On December 30, 2008, Nattawut Saikua, one of the protest leaders, delivered a historic speech at the Government House, which began to solidify this imaginary. Standing in front of thousands of Red Shirts protesters, Nattawut stared into the crowd. "We're denied many things," he began, echoing what Id, Yai, and Adun had told me. "We're denied justice; respect in the way governmental bodies treat us; accurate and direct reporting about us in the media. We're denied the chance to declare our fight openly, to declare openly and directly, with clarity and sincerity, what it is that we are fighting for. For sure, we don't have connections"—he paused as the crowd cheered. "What's most important for us all to remember, brothers and sisters, is that we are the salt of the earth. We are the people with no privileges. We were born on the land. We grew up on the land. Each step that we take is on this same land. We stand, with our two feet planted here, so far away from the sky." Nattawut looked up. "Tilting our heads upward, we gaze at the sky, and we realize how far away that sky is. Standing on this land, we only have to look down to realize that we are worth no more than a handful of dirt." A deep silence descended on the crowd. "But I believe in the power of the Red Shirts. I believe our numbers are growing day-by-day, minute-by-minute. Even though we stand on this land, and we speak out from our place in the dirt, our voice will rise to the sky. Of this I have no doubt. I have no doubt." He repeated as the crowd roared. "The voice we're making now—our cries and shouts—is the voice of people who are worth only a handful of dirt. But it is the voice of the people who were born and grew up on this land, and it will rise to the level of the sky. Of this I have no doubt. No doubt. We, the Red Shirts, want to say to the land and sky that we too have heart and soul. We, the Red Shirts, want to remind the land and sky that we too are Thai people. We, the Red Shirts, want to ask the land and sky whether we have been condemned to seek, by ourselves, a rightful place to plant our feet here." The crowd roared and cheered. "No matter what happens, we already have the greatest thing in our lives: the democratic spirit. For this great spirit, for the greatness of all of you, the only thing I can do is this." He concluded by kneeling down on stage and bowing to the crowd.

This speech, with its focus on the inequality in Thai society, its coded reference to monarchic elites (the sky), its denunciation of the protesters' mistreatment by bureaucratic forces (governmental bodies) and of the reduction of the Red Shirts' demands to worthless dirt resonated with what the drivers had been repeating and became the template for their political mobilization. Yet it did not solidify the Red Shirts' political discourse. Over the course of the following year, the movement's identity, opposition, and relations continued to evolve and remain open to transformations of discourses, agendas, and tactics.

On March 26, 2009, the Red Shirts set up a permanent protest camp in front of the Government House and demanded Abhisit's resignation. On April 8, a crowd of more than a hundred thousand joined the camp and rallied there and at the adjacent Royal Plaza, while parallel rallies were held in a dozen provincial centers. Overnight, mobility through the transportation hub of the Victory Monument was brought to a halt by a crowd of taxi and motorcycle taxi drivers. Circulation in the city, the quintessential characteristic of capitalist systems and the main function of motorcycle taxis in Bangkok, was blocked by the very people who were supposed to operate it. Symptomatic of the importance of motorcycle taxis to these protests were the threats by the chief of the metropolitan police and by Prime Minister Abhisit Vejjajiva to revoke their licenses and take away their vests if drivers were found protesting with the Red Shirts. Despite these threats, the drivers continued to play an active role in the protests.

On April 11, a group of Red Shirts broke into the ASEAN (Association of South-East Asian Nations) summit being held in Pattaya, effectively bringing the meeting to an end and forcing Thai and foreign heads of state to flee. On April 13, ten thousand military troops were moved into Bangkok to clear the streets and reestablish usual urban flow. In the first serious clash between state forces and Red Shirts around Victory Monument, at least seventy people were injured and the army seemed to have won the confrontation: the protest at Government House dispersed and many observers thought that would be the end of the Red Shirts.

The movement, on the contrary, began to reorganize its forces. The Red Shirts rebuilt their local branches, extended their presence in rural Thailand, and trained their members. More than 450 Red Shirts' schools opened all around the country. These schools, a tactic developed by student activists in the 1970s, were central to the elaboration of the movement's demands and rhetoric. It was during this period, in fact, that two of the central tenants of the Red Shirts movement emerged: the discourse of double standards, which Id used in our train ride to talk about the exclusions of villagers from legal, economic, and political rights; and their self-identification as commoners, or *phrai*. The terminology of double standards had entered Thai political discourse in 2001 when it was used, in English, to criticize a court decision to acquit the newly elected Prime Minister Thaksin Shinawatra of proven accusations of failing to declare the full extent of his assets when entering politics.[49] Few would have guessed that this term would become so central to a movement that begun by protesting Thaksin's removal by the military coup. After the 2009 crackdown, the Red Shirts adopted the term in its Thai version, *sǭng māttrathān,* to point out the difference in treatment between the violent repression of their protest and the complete lack of repercussions and persecutions, legal and military, when the opposing Yellow Shirts blocked Bangkok's airports.[50] Soon, however, this formula was used not just to refer to judicial bias but also to describe larger political economic inequality, regional disparities, and exclusion in Thai society, on par with the word *phrai.*

The opposition between *phrai* (commoners, serf) and *'ammāt* (aristocracy) dominated feudal relations in Siamese society until the 1892 administrative reform that created the modern Thai bureaucracy. Red Shirts resuscitated this distinction to define themselves and their enemies. They conceptualized their political struggles as a fight between *phrai,* represented by their supporters, and the *'ammāt,* composed of the military, bureaucratic, and monarchic elites as well as the governing party led by Oxford-educated Prime Minister Abhisit Vejjajiva. As Thongchai Winichakul has argued,

49. Immediately after his election as prime minister in 2001, Thaksin was charged with illegally concealing the full amount of his assets while deputy prime minister in 1997. The Thai Constitutional Court, in a ruling which seemed to rely more on Thaksin's vast electoral support than on firm legal ground, dismissed these accusations without explaining in detail the reasons behind their decision. As a result the National Counter corruption Commission (NCCC) pointed to a "double standard" in the ruling when compared to similar cases against other public officeholders.

50. Interestingly, however, the legal origins of this phrase, *sǭng māttrathān,* evidence of the centrality of the relationship between authority and influence to inequality Thai society, is the dynamic I explored in chapter 5. As Chiang Noi argues: "In Thailand there is a close connection between power and illegality, between social status and defiance of the law. Often, laws seem to exist precisely to allow certain people the very special privilege of being able to flout them. . . . The growing political significance of the judiciary over the last few years has given this trend a new twist. While the judicial system may not in fact perform in the service of equity, the justification for the importance of the judiciary is that there really is a rule of law that applies to all. . . . The idea of equity under the law is now very prominent in public debate, yet the political structure still in place is designed precisely to preserve privileges by the evasion or manipulation of the law" (Chiang Noi 2010).

The UDD discourse of their struggles as the *"phrai"* against the *"ʿammāt"* reveals as much as belies the configuration of class and hierarchy in Thai context. Many Thais and foreign reporters translate the word *"phrai"* as serf, or bonded subject in the Thai feudal society. The pro-government scholars argue correctly that such a feudal social order no longer exists. But the *"phrai"* in the Reds discourse does not mean the historical bonded subjects. *"Phrai"* and its opposite, *"ʿammāt"* (the noble, the lords) in the UDD discourse targets the oppression and injustice due to social class and hierarchy such as the one in Thai political culture. The struggle of the Reds is a class war in this sense of the revolt of the downtrodden rural folks against the privileged social and political class, the *"ʿammāt."*[51]

This war, however, was predicated upon a very specific notion of class. When talking about *phrai,* the Red Shirts were not referring to themselves only as the poor, the peasantry, or the working class but rather as a new category, one defined by exclusion from services, such as education or access to credit, consumption, and fair legal and political treatment. In this sense, the language of *phrai* resonated deeply with the drivers' experiences, struggles, and everyday lives, both in the city and in the village: invisible infrastructure excluded from enjoying the product of their work; migrants stuck between rural backwardness and urban poverty; entrepreneurs torn between a new freedom and new forms of exclusion and exploitation; formalized service workers who had fallen back into the clutches of people of influence.

Conservative commentators responded to these claims by dismissing them with sarcasm. In an article in the pro-Yellow Shirts *Bangkok Post,* Voranai Vanijaka joked that *"phrai* need not be poor, they say. *Phrai* can have money, they insist. *Phrai* are only *phrai* in that they don't have the power, they say."[52] Although aimed at dismissing the Red Shirts' discourse, this observation actually provided one of the most perceptive analyses of the movement to appear in Thai mainstream media. When seen in this light, a movement of *phrai* led by a billionaire was not a contradiction, but rather it revealed the extent of the oppression and exclusion perpetrated by the *ʿammāt.* No matter how rich you were, the Red Shirts seemed to say, those people would try to disenfranchise and oppress you, whether you were the majority of the population or a democratically elected prime minister.

51. Thongchai 2010.
52. Voranai 2011.

This discursive shift had a double effect: first, it transformed a rarely used derogatory term (*phrai*) into a term of self-representation and a source of pride. As Isan anthropologist Bunthawat Weemoktanondha argued, the Red Shirts "[were] breaking a cultural taboo by using this word so openly to describe themselves without feeling ashamed of being *phrai*. It is well known that this word indicates class discrimination. [The word] '*phrai*' is so sensitive that its use to describe a person could lead to serious consequences, even physical attack. This word is not used frequently because it means the speaker is calling a person low-class, ignorant, stupid."[53] The Red Shirts were now reclaiming it and wearing it as badge of honor, equating the oppression and unfair treatment they experienced with that against *phrai* in feudal Siam. Second, it bound the movement together around a shared sense of injustice and unfairness that affected very different groups—from rural poor to economic elites, from former politicians to rural organizers, from urban working classes to radical intellectuals. Their unity was funded on submission to the same structural relations of exclusion to the '*ammāt*, an equally generic term that stood for everything and everybody who oppressed the Thai population and constrained its full democratic potential—from the military to the government, from the Privy Council to the palace. As Weng Tojirakarn, one of the key leaders of the Red Shirts explained to me: "*Phrai* simply explains everything. We are *phrai*. Nobody wants to be treated like a dog. Everybody must be treated equally as a human being. For the *phrai*, they only fight to let society accept that they are human. This society dehumanizes people, so that is why the majority of the people now understand what the Red Shirts are fighting for. It is only the '*ammāt* that is fighting against this."

Scholars of social movements have argued that "social movements have three dimensions: (a) Identity, the definition which the social movement actor gives himself [*sic*]; (b) Opposition, the definition of his [*sic*] adversary; and (c) Totality, the stakes over which the movement and its adversary are in conflict."[54] The social imaginary that the Red Shirts developed between 2009 and 2010 accomplished all three objectives: they defined an identity for themselves as *phrai*, construed their adversary as '*ammāt*, and traced the stakes of the conflict as the end of this system of oppression and exclusion, condensed around a discourse of *sǭng māttrathān* (double standards). Strong

53. Weemoktanondha made this declaration to Inter Press Service News (Macan-Markar 2010).

54. Hannigan 1985, 445.

from their newly defined worldview, on March 12, 2010, the Red Shirts' leaders called on supporters to descend over Bangkok. Thousands and thousands from villages all over the country started to move toward the city as urban Red Shirts, among whom motorcycle taxi drivers figured prominently, took control of the city. The geography of Bangkok was to be radically transformed, as it was its political history.

SEVEN

Unraveling the Thai Capital

Analyses of the relations of force cannot and must not be an end
in themselves, but acquire a significance only if they ... reveal
the point of least resistance, at which the force of will can be
most fruitfully applied.

ANTONIO GRAMSCI, *Prison Notebooks*

ON MARCH 12, 2010, the United Front for Democracy against Dictatorship
(UDD) declared a "Million People March." Hundreds of thousand supporters from northern and northeastern Thailand descended upon Bangkok.
Once in the city, they merged with their urban comrades to stage a protest
that would last sixty-eight days.[1] During this period the Red Shirts took
Bangkok hostage by blocking mobility in its commercial and political centers.[2] Motorcycle taxi drivers were pivotal to these actions and the citywide
network they had been building since 2003 proved its strength. The drivers'
organization was originally developed to put pressure on Thaksin's attempt
to regularize their operation. Now it became a platform to express their
political demands. The drivers had been part of the Red Shirts since the
beginning of the countrywide mobilization against inequality, exclusion, and
double standards. When the movement called for a shutdown of Bangkok in
2010, they took center stage by contributing to take over, slow down, and
interfere with the circulation of people, goods, and information that they
normally facilitate.[3] If in their everyday lives the drivers worked as a quiet
infrastructure, weaving the city together, in protest they unraveled it.

1. For a detailed recounting of these days, see Sopranzetti 2012b.

2. Other significant protests and political actions took place outside Bangkok, particularly in the cities of Chiang Mai, Nong Khai, and Khon Kaen. However, I here focus mostly
on a Bangkok-centered reading of the Red Shirts' protests as my fieldwork was for the most
part based in the Thai capital at the time of the mobilization.

3. This was not the first time in the last two decades in which spaces of transit became
central loci of mobilization. For an historical analysis of the development of these tactics in
contemporary Thailand see Sopranzetti 2012b, 2014a.

In the pages that follow I explore this dynamic and show how drivers transformed their mobility and invisibility as urban connectors into political tactics, posing a significant challenge to state forces and ridiculing the pretense of state control over the city and its flows. The drivers—to use the words of Oboto, the man who led the largest group of organized motortaxis in the protest—embodied their role as "owners of the map," holders of an unmatched knowledge of the urban terrain and gatekeepers of its channels. During three months of protest, the drivers emerged as unrelenting and uncontrollable political actors: invaluable allies and dreaded enemies, able to chart and move through the terrain of the protest better than anybody else, making it readable to their allies and opaque to their enemies. Moving through back roads and parking lots, collecting and circulating information and directives, appearing and disappearing in the urban landscape—skills they developed in years of moving through Bangkok's impenetrable traffic—the drivers managed to raise a formidable challenge to apparently unbeatable state forces.

It would be a mistake, however, to think of drivers who joined the protest as a unified force with a coherent strategy. As Yai explained, the drivers were divided into four main groups. "One section simply benefited from the rallies," he clarified. "They worked at the protest as taxis and made an income transporting Red Shirts supporters. They joined to make money and the protest was good for their livelihood. 'The longer it lasts, the better for me,' they thought. Then there was a second larger group of motorcycle taxis, composed of drivers who had a Red heart. These people joined in because they wanted democracy and justice. A third group was composed of drivers who were relatives of the Red Shirts from rural areas. Their folks from Isan came to Bangkok, so they went to the protest too. 'The Isan people love Thaksin, I love Thaksin, so I'll go, too.' These people thought. Finally," Yai continued, "there was the group I was part of: the organized drivers. We had been involved in the struggle for formalization since 2003, we continued to fight after the 2006 coup, and in February of 2010 we established the Association of Motorcycle Taxis of Thailand (AMTT) and joined the Red Shirts.[4] So you see," he concluded, "each section had different reasons to join, but one thing unified us all: we all wanted to take control of our future. Since the coup, state authorities and Abhisit's government forgot about us: they chased

4. The association was modeled after trade union. Nonetheless, according to Thai law self-employed workers—like the drivers—cannot formally establish a trade union. Membership in the AMTT is voluntary and requires drivers to register and pay a small fee. The association's officials are chosen through election, which normally take place every four years.

the people we loved out of power, they destroyed justice. When they took power they oppressed the motorcycle taxis and they blocked our development. They wanted to take over our business and give it to their party's friends and to people of influence. Motorcycle folks had to decide which side they were on, and they decided to join the Red Shirts."

While this decision unified the drivers, in protest they hardly were an organized ensemble. The same was true for the Red Shirts. Heterogeneity, continuous twists and turn of tactics, overlay of multiple demands, and reliance on improvisations, missteps, and strokes of luck are characteristics of mass collective actions, too often ironed out in scholarly work. This is one of the reasons why protests and social movements have proved such an elusive subject for social scientists: alive, emotional, ever changing, and colorful in the streets, they often become dry, calculated, mechanistic, and tedious in academic books.[5] The drivers' actions in 2010 stubbornly refuse to be pigeonholed in any neat description or static analysis. Their swerving and tentative mobilization, much like their meandering everyday mobility, revealed the doomed absurdity of any claim to order, whether imposed by academic studies or by state forces. Their actions exposed those claims for what they are: an all-too-human pretence to channel and control the flow of life. For analytical clarity, in the following pages, I embark upon one such illusion and divide the protest into four periods, exploring in each of them the drivers' tactics. While the protest unfolded, these partitions were neither clear nor discrete. On the contrary, events chaotically and unpredictably flowed into one another; apparent game-changers were revealed as nothing more than peripheral occurrences; and tactics that seemed successful were suddenly abandoned while marginal practices remained in place, enriched and expanded by a new arsenal of actions.

MOBILIZING BANGKOK (MARCH 13–APRIL 14, 2010)

On March 13, 2010, more and more trains, buses, trucks, and cars filled with protesters reached Bangkok. They set up a stage at the end of Ratchadamnoen

5. The two dominant theories of social movements—the New Social Movement (NSM) school (Castells 1983; Touraine 1981) and the Resource Mobilization/Political Opportunity (RM/PO) approach (McAdam, McCarthy, and Zald 1996; Tilly 1978; Tilly and Wood 2009)—are examples of this shortcoming.

Avenue, the grandiose boulevard that was built a century before to emulate the European capitals and had since become the theater of political protests in Bangkok. Red Shirts began to build shelters and tents, effectively blocking traffic through the main arteries of Bangkok and transforming it into a reclaimed space. The atmosphere was that of a temple fair or a rural festivity, filled with Buddhist blessing ceremonies and merit-making rites, amusement park tents with games, dances, musical performances, and political speeches.[6]

While Ratchadamnoen Avenue offered a base camp to go back to at the end of the day, for the following two weeks large convoys of protesters drove and rode almost daily through the city, bringing normal traffic to a halt and inciting local dwellers to join in and show their support for the movement. Drivers were omnipresent, both in the caravans and along Ratchadamnoen. At the base camp, they became the only viable means of transportation through the thick crowds. Around the city, they directed the convoys, scouted the surrounding areas to track the movement of police and military forces who tried to contain them, and reported this information back to the Red Shirts leaders, who readjusted the protest route. With their help, the caravans continued to traverse the city and bring its traffic to a halt, undisturbed by police roadblocks or attempts to stop them. If in their everyday lives the drivers needed to adjust to the rhythms of urban flows, now they took control over them (see fig. 5).

In order to bring urban circulation to a halt, create widespread traffic congestion, and challenge attempts by state forces to control and contain a truly mobile protest, the parades needed to progress slowly enough to remain compact, but fast enough to prevent state forces from surrounding and blocking them. Oboto and his group of drivers were in charge of this task. Riding on his red bike with a Thai flag attached to it, Oboto always headed the caravans. From there, he paced its speed while his collaborators zigzagged in and out of the protest and took advantage of their familiarity with the city's back roads to make sure the path was clear of riot police. While this group of drivers operated as vanguard, another section rode on the side of the convoy, speeding up and down and carrying directives between Oboto and the leaders' truck, protected in the belly of the caravan.

6. For an analysis of the soundscapes of the Red Shirts' protest see Tausig 2013, 2014.

FIGURE 5.   Red Shirts' caravans entering one of Bangkok's highways. Photo by Nick Nostitz.

Over the following weeks, the drivers not only made the protest mobile, modulating its rhythms and managing its information flows. They also acted as political mobilizers, inciting city dwellers to join the protesters and transforming their vests, bodies, and bikes into itinerant political boards.[7] During the protest, the city became sectioned into Red areas and Yellow areas, usually indexed to the level of wealth of their residents and their regional provenance.[8] These invisible spatial divisions determined levels of comfort for drivers who carried political messages on them. Poorer areas inhabited with migrants from northern and northeastern Thailand were safe. Richer ones populated by Bangkokians or southerners could be a problem. A failure to recognize them and to act accordingly—by hiding political mes-

7. This was not the first time that political groups had used the drivers as mobile boards. Politicians running both for national and city elections, in fact, have used the vest as mobile advertisement since the early 2000s (Wassayos and Manop 2003).

8. While, generally speaking, income level is a good predictor of political affiliation in Thailand, significant exceptions exist. In particular, it is worth noting that the poorest sections of Bangkok's urban population—slum dwellers—were extremely divided. Those who reside illegally in land owned by the Crown Property Bureau tended to support the Yellow Shirts. Those who resided on land which belongs to other owners, such as Klong Toey, the largest slum in Bangkok, tended to support the Red Shirts.

sages when entering a hostile area—could put the drivers in danger and provoke a fight over political affiliations.[9]

On April 3, 2010, the Red Shirts' strategies changed.[10] The leaders decided it was now time to take over another protest site and cement their territorial control, rather than continue to move through the city. On that day, thousands of protesters moved from Ratchadamnoen Avenue to the Ratchaprasong intersection, the city's upscale commercial center (see map 1).[11]

Ignoring the government's threat of arresting anyone who moved to the new zone, the Red Shirts took over an area of two square miles at the core of Bangkok central business district. They set up a stage underneath the elevated Skytrain and in front of Central World, the third biggest shopping mall in Asia and a symbol of middle-class consumption. Now, one of the main transportation nodes in the city was closed off. The up-scale hotels, shopping malls, and retail shops that dominated the area shut down, frightened by the rising tide of protesters. For the next eleven days the protesters and their leaders moved between Ratchadamnoen Avenue—the traditional space of street politics, where large protests had taken place in 1973 and 1992—and the Ratchaprasong intersection—a new political arena in the city.[12] The Red Shirts' mobilization was starting to spill over into spaces of middle-class pacified consumption, where no previous protest in Thailand had dared to go. Struggling to control the two areas, the protest's leaders decided to stop the caravans, which until that point had been largely successful in embarrassing the government and exposing its inability to limit and control a mobile protest.

While the new static phase of the protest may have challenged the drivers' importance for the protest, the contrary happened. The expansion on two fronts opened up a space for them to step into the spotlight. On the evening

9. While some of the drivers I met refused to adjust their bodies and gadgets to this political geography, many of them wore easily removable signs, such as red scarfs and wristbands, which they could take off when carrying clients outside their *soi*, or whenever they enter "yellow areas." It was not long, however, before the larger Bangkok public started to identify motorcycle taxi drivers with the protest, regardless of the symbols they carried.

10. This change took place after a series of media-driven protests around the city, which most poignantly included the symbolic pouring of huge quantities of human blood in front of Government House and an unproductive round of televised negotiations between the protest leaders and the government (J. Taylor 2012).

11. On the contested history of Ratchaprasong, see Ünaldi 2014a, b.

12. Jim Taylor has described it as "a one-stop shopping and amusement park of hyperconsumption, of pleasure and unlimited desires in reproduced bourgeois play-space" (J. Taylor 2011, 6).

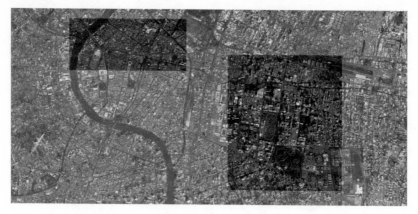

MAP 1. Location of the protest camps: on the left the Ratchadamnoen area, on the right Ratchaprasong. (Map by Carla Betancourt.)

of April 3, as the second stage was being built in Ratchaprasong, the leaders of the drivers' association (AMTT) went onstage in Ratchadamnoen. Ignoring the threats by both the prime minister and the governor of Bangkok to revoke their licenses if they participated in the protest, Yai, Lek, Lerm, Oboto, and sixteen other motorcycle taxi organizers stood in front of the oceanic crowd of Red Shirts. Yai spoke for all of them and pledged their support for the movement as the protesters cheered. This moment, they discussed that night over cold beers, marked a turning point in the history of the motorcycle taxi drivers' collective action. Until now they mostly had played a logistical role in the pro-Thaksin protests. Their vests were nowhere to be seen backstage or at leadership meetings. Their voices were nowhere to be heard in the political declarations or under the spotlight. On April 3, 2010, the drivers were recognized as legitimate political actors, an important part of the movement standing proud on its stage. This event galvanized more drivers to join the protest. Yet, at the same time, it also put their leaders on the map, making them potential targets of state repression.

Four days later, with both Bangkok's historical center and its business district solidly in the hands of the Red Shirts, a group of protesters attempted to raise the stakes and stormed the Parliament. That night, the government declared a state of emergency in Bangkok and surrounding provinces. This declaration outlawed any gathering of more than five people; shifted the responsibility of crowd management from the police, considered sympathetic to Thaksin, to the army; and gave unprecedented powers to the newly created

Center for the Resolution of the Emergency Situation (CRES), a committee of senior military officers, security officials, and government ministers headed by Suthep Thaugsuban, the secretary-general of the ruling Democrat party. From that point on, until the end of the protest, CRES operated as a shadow government, often wielding more power than the prime minister himself.[13] The first CRES action was to issue arrest warrants against the main Red Shirts leaders. Carrying out this order, however, proved impossible, as the leaders remained protected by the huge crowd of Red Shirts around them.

Frustrated by the situation, on April 10 the CRES ordered a military intervention to disperse the protest from Ratchadamnoen Avenue. The first clashes began at one in the afternoon as soldiers hit protesters with water cannons. Soon after, troops from the First Infantry Division—under the command of General Prayuth Chan-Ocha—advanced along Ratchadamnoen Nok Road. Along with antiriot shields and batons, these soldiers also carried automatic weapons (see map 2).

As soon as the soldiers came into contact with the Red Shirts, they started firing tear gas without any warning. The violence escalated rapidly and the military began to shoot rubber bullets directly at protesters. A few dozens were injured, including a motorcycle taxi driver. By four o'clock in the afternoon the soldiers had cleared Ratchadamnoen Nok and prepared to move into Ratchadamnoen, while protesters gathered around the stage preparing to weather another attack. Motorcycle taxi drivers were riding off to track the soldiers' movements in the surrounding area and find possible exit routes. The news was not good. Troops were descending on the protest area from Dinso and Tanao Roads as well as from the end of Ratchadamnoen, armed with automatic weapons. Six armored personnel carriers waited in the back, ready to move in. Some small roads remained opened but, were the army to attack, many of the protesters would be trapped. About an hour later, as the tensions grew, a military helicopter circled over the protesters, spraying tear gas indiscriminately.

As dusk fell on Bangkok, the Red Shirts were nearly surrounded. Motorcycle taxi drivers, with their unmatched knowledge of the terrain, were still able to move in and out of the area but, no matter where they went, they saw soldiers moving in. At about six o'clock in the afternoon, army speakers started to blast John Lennon's "Imagine." Then, in the most bizarre of synchronizations,

13. These provisions, if largely ineffective in preventing the Red Shirts' mobilization, would remain in place for the following eight months, to be lifted only in December 2010.

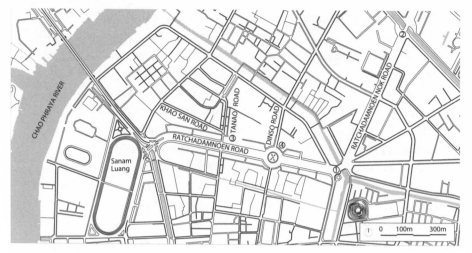

MAP 2. Events in the Ratchadamnoen area on April 10, 2010: (1) Red Shirts' stage; (2) Ratchadamnoen Nok: first army attack; (3) Tanao Road: second wave of army offensive; (4) Dinso Road: clashes between soldiers and Red Shirts; protesters conquered armored vehicles. (Map by Carla Betancourt.)

soldiers opened fire. Rubber bullets hissed through the defenseless crowd while live ammunition flew over their heads. People ran away, unhinged, as a few protesters threw fire crackers, stones, and sharpened sticks at the soldiers. Every few minutes came a new round of rubber bullets and a new rush of protesters tearing away from the army line. Then, about an hour later, two loud explosions resounded right outside the protest area and sent the army into a frenzy. Soldiers immediately moved in on the protesters, prompting the crowd to run away from Dinso and Tanao Roads, seeking shelter. At the time, nobody knew what had happened, but later it became clear that a small armed group sympathetic to the Red Shirts had launched two grenades from the roof of a nearby school behind the army lines, killing the five highest-ranking officers on site. All hell broke loose.

The soldiers, without their field commanders, advanced haphazardly. A few privates stepped out of the lines and fired M-16 live ammunition at the Red Shirts, while the helicopter continued to hover over the crowd. The number of dead and injured started to grow. Most of the protesters desperately ran for their lives but a few thousand remained in place, throwing Molotov cocktails and stones to block the soldiers from advancing. Suddenly, five or six cars drove full speed through the crowd, into the army lines. A few hundred meters away, two armored personnel carriers were blocked by protesters, who destroyed their caterpillars, leaving the soldiers stranded inside at the mercy of the Red Shirts.

At around eight o'clock in the evening, the CRES contacted the Red Shirts' leaders and worked out a mutual retreat. The army moved back and the soldiers trapped in the armored vehicle were handed over to police officers after being stripped of their uniforms and weapons. The protesters, armed with stones, bottles, sticks, and vehicles had managed to contain the army, with the help of armed sympathizers. Local motorcycle taxi drivers, taking advantage of their knowledge of the area, had provided invaluable assistance, guiding the protesters through the maze of small *soi* and helping them to surround and ward off the army.

The Thai Royal Army's attempts to disperse the protest, which became known as Cruel April, had been a clumsy and bloody affair. Twenty-six people were killed—including the five high-ranking military officials hit by an M-79 grenade—and 860 people were injured. The soldiers lost hundreds of rifles and other heavy weaponry to the crowd. And two armored vehicles were taken apart, covered in antigovernment and antimilitary graffiti, and left dismantled in the middle of Ratchadamnoen Avenue (see fig. 6).

In the following days, a mixture of excitement and fear permeated the protest. They had succeeded in pushing back the military but at the cost of nineteen supporters' lives. Both protest areas were covered with pictures of the dead bodies—men and women hit by high-speed bullets that deformed their faces and left their gray matter splattered on the asphalt. Even if the protest continued, nobody wanted this to happen again. It became clear that keeping up this defensive strategy on two fronts was unfeasible. On April 14, the protesters picked up their tents in Ratchadamnoen and moved to the Ratchaprasong intersection.

THE VILLAGE IN THE MIDDLE OF THE CITY (APRIL 14–22)

The decision to move the base camp to Ratchaprasong was both strategic and symbolic. "Ratchaprasong is not just a space of shopping malls," Veera Musikhapong, one of the protest's leaders, told me, "it is a symbol. A symbol of inequality and double standards, a symbol of the relation between aristocracy [*'ammāt*] and commoners [*phrai*] and now we are taking over this space to show that commoners can decide for themselves." Unfulfilled desires for

FIGURE 6. Protesters stand on armored carriers after blocking the army's offensive on April 11, 2010. Photo by the Author.

commodities and recognition had played a central role in the Red Shirts' mobilization. Now its location moved away from the old politics of the palace, the military, and the bureaucracy and took over high-scale hotels and branded glass skyscrapers, fancy cinemas and shopping malls, symbols of inequality, consumption, and desire. This relocation also promised to keep the Red Shirts safe.

Disoriented by the violence that had taken place on Ratchadamnoen Avenue, many protesters believed that the army would never wage an attack that risked destroying the commodities that surrounded them. Those commodities—they seemed to imply—had the power to protect them from a military offense. Sun, a young bookseller who spent every day at the protest sitting behind a small table filled with radical books, wearing his Maoist shirt, explained: "The owners of these shopping malls are the 'ammāt, the people behind this government and the aristocracy. The army has no problem with destroying lives but they don't want to destroy their property. We are safe here, protected by Louis Vuitton's bags."

Once again, instead of mystifying social relations, highly coveted commodities such as Louis Vuitton bags revealed social relations and the collaboration between state forces and economic groups. Aware of the link between the owners of such commodities and the Thai army, the Red Shirts used them to their advantage, turning high-end fashion items into shields from military intervention. Whether the change of location had any actual effect on preventing another immediate dispersal remains unclear, and in the long run the protective power of these commodities would not be enough to stop the military. Nonetheless, at that time the CRES abandoned its violent dispersal strategy, allowing the protesters to establish full control over the Ratchaprasong area.

Over the following weeks, spaces of desire and consumption, from which many protesters felt excluded, were appropriated and made into places of mobilization and dwelling. Many of the drivers talked to me about the feeling of having reclaimed the city that had been taking their lives and sweat. "I come here every day to transport passengers," Boon told me, referring to the adjacent Skytrain station. "Now I come to meet my friends from my village, I sit where cars normally run, I sleep where normally I can stop only for a moment to get the money from my clients. I feel like I own this city. I come back every day to my village, my village in the middle of the city."

Again, as in the Red Shirts' caravans, control over the city and ownership of its spaces revolved around taking charge of its rhythms, to which normally the drivers were forced to adjust. Now, they were the ones in charge, transforming the rhythms of Ratchaprasong into those of a rural village. The tension between the multiple temporalities that haunted the drivers' movement between the city and the countryside were put to rest—if just for a short period—by transforming the most fast-paced section of the city into a slow village, a village in the middle of the city. Boon, the driver who refused to accept the hierarchy between village and city that many around him took for granted, proudly voiced this transformation. For many among the drivers, these reclaimed rhythms were a source enjoyment and another reason to participate in the protest. Adun was among them.

On April 15, after his usually long day of work on the street, Adun stretched his back, took off his vest, and invited me to join him. After a few drinks at his station, we headed toward Ratchaprasong. Adun, three other drivers, and I entered the protest area on bikes, waving to two other motorcycle taxis who patrolled the barricades. We rode slowly through the protest, enjoying the feeling of being in a small convoy. A stenciled sign inside the protest area declared in English: "Red Land." As the crowd thickened around us, we parked and walked into a large gazebo that housed Adun's fellow villagers. Mats covered the ground where a group of older men and women sat in a circle. Younger protesters lingered outside the circle, occasionally passing food and cold water to their elders. As if inside a house, everybody took off their shoes before entering the gazebo and bowed slightly at the elders before greeting the person they had come to see.

At one corner of the tent, a small crowd gathered around a large TV screen that showed pictures of bullets and bullet wounds. A well-dressed man in his fifties talked into a microphone, describing each bullet type, its range and deadly potential, and showing pictures of the damages they caused to protesters on April 10. Like a vendor at a village fair, he rode the feelings of the crowd with great empathy, alternating information with pictures and real bullets passed around in sealed plastic bags. Not far from the TV, an aluminum saucepan sizzled over a small fire burning inside a clay pot, spreading a strong smell of wild herbs. Next to the fire, large bags of papayas, nuts, and an enormous quantity of chilies lay on the floor. An older woman, sitting on these bags, held a peeled green papaya in her left hand, rhythmically plunging a knife into it with her right, cutting narrow strips. As the knife found its way into the fruit, just before being raised again, her left hand slowly turned the papaya around. All the while, she chatted effortlessly with her nephew, a taxi driver in Bangkok. Adun and I sat down at the opposite corner.

Immediately, grilled chicken and hot sticky rice were brought to us. A young man handed us some beers, hidden in small plastic bags. "Drink," he told me, "but keep it in the bag. The guards don't want us to get drunk." Adun looked at him with a mixture of respect and derision. "I have known him since he was a kid," he told me with a half-smile. The young man sat next to us and asked Adun if he had any suggestion of where he and his friend could go to party that night. Tired and bored by long days of uneventful political tirades at the protest site, many of the protesters from the countryside used the time to visit family friends, famous city landmarks, or experience some of the thrills that Bangkok had to offer. Drivers like Adun operated as guides, directing the rural protesters around the city to good restaurants, convenient markets, or affordable nightclubs. While the people who came to Bangkok to protest look for enjoyment outside the barricades, for Red Shirts who lived in the city the protest site was the attraction, an urban village in which to meet friends from the countryside, sit, eat, and chat with them, as inflamed political speeches floated through the background barely distinguishable through all of the conversation.

"I have heard [these speeches] before," Adun told me, smiling. "They always say the same thing. I agree with them but I'd rather talk to people from home, hear news of what is going on back there, and have nice food. I am here anyway and I am ready to help if something happens." Many like

Adun have supported the movement for a long time, both ideologically and by becoming members of the UDD, but seldom joined their protests before the arrival of their fellow villagers. Now that the Red Shirts had taken over the space and its rhythms and transformed them into something that resembled a village, the gravitational attraction of acquaintances brought the drivers in, swelling the ranks of the movement.

At times, all that is needed to galvanize active participation in a protest is the presence of a friend you have not seen for a while, a distant aunt who is sleeping there, or a longing for homemade food. While these motivations may seem mundane, they do not detract in any way from the political significance of drivers' and other internal migrants' participation in the protest. Political ideals, democracy, equality, and unfulfilled desires brought them there as much as a home-cooked meal, the desire to be part of history, the chance to go on a date with a romantic interest from the shop next door, or the possibility of going home, as Boon said, without having to take a twelve-hour train ride. Surely, many people marched to the Bastille just because their neighbors invited them to come along or participated in the anti–Vietnam War protests hoping to get laid. Such everyday personal dimensions of political struggles provide movements with their texture and the soil on which political passions can grow.

As we finished our beers, the tent slowly got quieter as one elder after another fell asleep. Adun, tired from his day of work, was next. Soon, I too closed my eyes, comforted by a soft Isan song and the whirring of a fan. A few hours later, Adun woke me up. "It is time to go back to work." Around us other urban workers were moving silently through sleeping bodies scattered everywhere, getting ready to go back to the city beyond the barricades, largely unaffected by the protest. There they would open shop doors, prepare breakfasts, and deliver people and commodities, only to come back again after their shift, creating a cyclical compression and swelling of the protest. The smell of burning charcoal, breakfast soup, and steaming sticky rice filled the road underneath the immobile Skytrain. As we rode out of the Red Shirts' area, Adun stopped in a small parking lot, a few hundred meters away from the army checkpoint that divided the protest area from his station. He put his vest on, transforming himself back into an innocuous motorcycle taxi driver, and passed through the soldiers' line unnoticed, making his way toward a long day of weaving through traffic.

As soon as we arrived at Adun's station another driver called. Wud, who had joined Oboto's group in the previous month and had left his work to become a full-time member of the Red Shirts, wanted to know if I had time to join him in a bizarre rescue mission. A few days before, the CRES had issued new arrest warrants for the protest leaders. On the morning of April 16 the target was Arisman Pongruangrong, a pop singer turned activist who was in hiding in a small hotel across town. "I need to go with some other drivers to get him out of there," Wud told me with excitement. "The police are coming to arrest him, but first they called me," he laughed. Since April 10, a number of drivers I knew were hired by the Red Shirts' leaders as personal guards, selected precisely for their knowledge of the urban terrain, familiarity with escape routes, and ability to disappear into the confusing landscape of Bangkok. Wud was one of them. This time, however, it was not his ability to move through the city that made him into an invaluable ally, but rather his long-standing personal connections with local police officers. As the officers were gearing up for the arrest, a low-level policeman, Wud's friend and fellow Isan migrant, tipped him off. The news ran fast along the Red Shirts' chain of command and a rescue team was rapidly organized. In the escape—as incredible as it was clumsy—chubby Arisman climbed down from his hotel room balcony with a rope made of electric cords. On the ground he was greeted by a crowd of Red Shirts and journalists before jumping onto Wud's backseat and disappearing from the scene, leaving the police empty-handed.

Arisman's escape was an embarrassing and highly visible failure for the CRES, one that they refused to repeat.[14] Furious, they increased the pressure on political mobilizers around the city. In the afternoon of the same day, all the drivers' leaders who had gone on stage to support the Red Shirts found CRES officers waiting at their houses. The officers try to intimidate them into abandoning the Red Shirts. If seen again at the rallies, the drivers were told, they would be arrested and banned from their profession. More broadly, if their association continued to show its support for the movement, all negotiations about protecting their livelihood would be suspended, driver's licenses would be taken away from all members, and strict implementation of traffic laws would make their work impossible. If, on the contrary, the AMTT left the protest and joined the opposing side, the CRES officers promised, the government would resuscitate the war against people of influence who extracted money from the drivers. None of the leaders were willing to take the second offer. Yet the prospect of closing all negotiation with state

14. The video of his escape can be found at www.youtube.com/watch?v=Gc8T5_5aHFo.

forces could jeopardize years of labor organizing and acquired rights. Yai, whom the soldiers visited first, reconstructed this difficult moment.

"I was at the intersection when the shooting happened and I was at Arisman's hotel. After it was over I went back home and they were waiting for me. They asked why the bikers had helped the violent sections of the Red Shirts. I said that we had no role in the violence and that we did not want that to happen. Nonetheless, the Red Shirts'. leaders were not taken into custody but I was. I knew then and there what would happen to my members. Our detentions meant that the government agencies looked at our group as if we instigated the violence. They needed to arrest us first, to weaken the protesters."

The members of the association started to discuss internally what their priorities should be. Everybody agreed that Thaksin had done a lot for them and that they shared objectives with the Red Shirts. The majority of them believed, however, that their purpose as an organization should be to gain concessions for the drivers as a professional group, and not for the social movement that they supported. As Lerm, the AMTT president, told me, "We are Red at heart, but our vest is orange and we need to stand united as Orange Shirts. Our duty is to the drivers not toward the Red Shirts." Yai felt the same. "We discussed what to do and we decided that, as an organization, we had to leave the protest, otherwise we could not move on. The association cannot take a side. It has to be in the middle. But we could not forbid any individuals to take part in the protest. In fact, I myself continued to go." While all of them continued to provide assistance and support to the movement personally, the association formally exited the scene. Oboto strongly disagreed with their view and left the group, effectively becoming the sole leader of the organized section of motorcycle taxi drivers and the main liaison between the movement and the motorcycle taxi drivers. Yai, Lek, and Lerm did not take his decision well and claim to this day that Oboto remained because he got money from the Red Shirts.

The fracture among the drivers, if significant in terms of street-level organizing, was only a minor side effect of the CRES's new strategy. More significantly, the humiliation of Arisman's escape induced a change in its leadership. Even if Suthep formally remained in charge, the actual decision-making power shifted toward the military. General Anupong Paochinda, the army commander in chief, became the de facto head of CRES and was authorized by the prime minister to use force to ensure peace and order. The time for a civilian running the operations was over; it was now time for the army to lead.

The CRES declared Ratchaprasong a dangerous area and invited the protesters to leave immediately. The Red Shirts responded by declaring their intention to extend the occupied area toward Silom Road, the core of Bangkok's financial center. The Red Shirts, having occupied and brought to a halt the main node of commercial exchange in the city, were now threatening to take over also the core of its financial circulation. Anupong was determined to not allow this to happen. On April 18, a military contingent marched into Silom Road, blocking the area and setting up army checkpoints around the protest area to limit the spillover of the protest and put pressure on the occupants. In response, the Red Shirts fortified the area under their control, raising intricate bamboo barricades. Day after day, the makeshift barriers grew taller and wider, soon enclosing the entire protest site. On one side of the barricades, crowds of protesters armed with bamboo sticks and slingshots waited for an attack. On the other, thousands of menacing heavily armed soldiers surrounded the area, ready to move in. In this stalemate, the tension became palpable and grew by the day.

BARRICADES AND FILTERS (APRIL 22–MAY 13)

On April 22 four grenades exploded in the middle of Silom Road, where a small crowd of anti–Red Shirts protesters had coalesced behind the army lines. One person was killed and seventy-five were injured. As the whole country pointed fingers, security was elevated on both sides of the barricades. On the red side, the guards took over the area behind the convoluted mesh of bamboo and barbed wire that sealed off the protest. The barricades were covered by car tires soaked in petrol, ready to be set on fire in case of a military offensive. On the army side, camouflage fabric was laid out to cover their movements, growing stacks of weapons, and a half-dozen armored vehicles. Soldiers established more and more checkpoints around the city. The Red Shirts filtered movement in and out their occupied area. Getting through the barricades with a motorbike now meant having to stop at the entrance, get off, and allow the bike compartment to be checked by Red guards, many of whom were motorcycle taxi drivers. Since the beginning of the mobilization, the drivers had kept the protest mobile and managed the movement of protesters. Now, they also filtered flows in and out of the occupied area.

Although the Red Shirts seemed to be secure and in complete control of the protest site, fear began to spread inside the barricades. Rumors of an imminent dispersal circulated among the protesters. National media increasingly talked about them as terrorists and demanded an end to the occupation of Ratchaprasong. Business leaders lamented the economic disaster that the mobilization was bringing to the country, both by blocking its commercial core and by hurting the country's image and flourishing tourist industry. Responding to these calls, the army commander in chief moved ten thousand troops to Bangkok. The bureaucratic, monarchic, and military forces that the Red Shirts mobilized against had had enough challenges to their power and were closing in on the protest. Running the risk of remaining trapped inside Ratchaprasong, the Red Shirts once again tried spreading the protest.

On April 27, the leaders declared they would organize a new caravan the following day, an attempt to expand beyond the confines of the Ratchaprasong area and prevent the looming military crackdown. Prime Minister Abhisit immediately replied that the government would not allow Red Shirts protesters to leave their protest site and cause confusion in the rest of city. Anupong, the army commander in chief, echoed him. The following day, ignoring these exhortations, thousands of motorcycles and cars converged on the eastern side of the protest camp, potentially safer because of its proximity to the U.S. embassy. Once again Oboto, recognizable from afar by the large Thai flag attached to his bike, headed the mobile protest. The convoy left in the late morning, directed toward Talad Thai, a large wholesale market about thirty miles away, in the industrial outskirts of northern Bangkok. Proceeding under a merciless heat, the caravan grew in size as more and more bikes and cars joined in. Motorcycle taxi drivers, as usual, took care of keeping the group compact and choosing the best routes to take. As the convoy entered Vibhavadi Rangsit Highway, a four-lane road that leads to the market, it enveloped the usual traffic without disrupting it. Just beyond Don Mueang International Airport, however, the parade came to an abrupt stop, provoked by an unusual traffic jam.

A few drivers were sent out to check and see what the problem was. They zigzagged through cars to see what created the blockage. A few minutes later the scouting vanguards came back with bad news: less than a mile ahead a line of soldiers in antiriot gear were blocking the road. Oboto sent more drivers off into side roads to check for possible exit routes. In the meantime, more soldiers were moving in on the roofs and flyovers above. Police officers advanced from behind, leaving no way out. Fear traversed the caravan as people snapped tree branches and advertising boards to set up makeshift barricades. A round of tear gas canisters broke the standstill, filling the air with its pungent smell, too far away to make breathing painful. Oboto, too important a mobilizer to be left in the thick of conflict, took off the vest that made him recognizable and disappeared into a small *soi* on the back of a local motorcycle taxi.

Not realizing the seriousness of the danger, I rode though the traffic jam toward the army lines. I barely made it to the top when the soldiers opened fire. The first rounds of rubber bullets were shot into the air but ricocheted off the bottom of the flyover and came pouring back to the ground. Soon after the first rounds, the soldiers started to advance, this time shooting at eye level. Confusion took over as they moved in our direction, covered by a shower of rubber bullets coming from the flyover, where other soldiers had taken up position. I rode into a small *soi* with other protesters, looking for a way out. Local dwellers told us that there was no exit from this *soi* and urged everyone to move away before the army advanced, closing the only exit route. Scared by the army's progression, we rode back toward the crowd, rubber bullets whistling around us. Three hundred meters away, a large group of Red Shirts was setting up defenses, creating small barricades in the middle of the street and breaking off anything that could be used as a weapon, from light poles to balconies' iron bars. A second round of tear gas reached us, this time hitting the crowd with its full effect. A group of protesters hid behind the barricades, using them as shields to push the military back. Suddenly, the sound of the shots changed. As they had done on April 10, the soldiers started to use live bullets.

The first injured protesters were rushed back from the front lines and rapidly put into ambulances that sped off, passing through the line of police officers who blocked the road behind us without intervening. Above us a few soldiers moved furtively on roofs, confirming rumors that the army was deploying snipers.[15] Caught between the army and police, we were terrified, envisioning a massacre. Then, suddenly, heavy rain started falling, cooling spirits and stopping the fight. We remained under the pouring rain for an hour, waiting to figure out what would happen next. A few protesters negotiated with the riot police while the others looked around with anxiety. Time seemed to slow down, dripping like the rain from the flyover. Suddenly hordes of uniformed police officers—without weapons or protection—came

15. The only victim of this confrontation was a soldier who was killed by friendly fire, most probably by one of these snipers. He and a fellow private were riding at full speed back from the front toward the army line and were shot down, mistaken for Red Shirts' protesters.

out of vans hidden on side roads. They walked past the riot police and the crowd of protesters and took position between the Red Shirts and the army, effectively shielding the protesters and offering an exit route. The crowd in the street cheered them as they made their way back to Ratchaprasong, still headed by a small vanguard of motorcycle taxi drivers who directed the convoy through flooded side roads. An hour later we were back. Even though the caravan had returned to the protest safely, it was clear that the army would not tolerate mobile protests anymore and that they were willing to use live ammunition to keep the protesters at bay. A violent dispersal of the protest camp, everybody seemed to agree, was just a matter of time.[16]

The day after this confrontation, in an attempt to expand the struggle outside of Bangkok and prevent the movements of troops to the city, the Red Shirts established roadblocks around the country and set up smaller stages in regional towns. In the Thai capital, however, the protest was de facto contained within the two-square-mile area they had already taken over. Security forces closed all major roads around the rally site. Moving in and out the protest area became more difficult. Motorcycle taxi drivers were among the few Red Shirts unaffected by this change. Their ability to move through blockages and their invisibility as urban infrastructure, which oriented their daily operations in the city, now allowed them to continue to move despite the military checkpoints. This was done in two ways: by avoiding them through alternative routes or by going through them while pretending to be simple transportation providers.

Finding alternative routes was easy for the drivers even after the army sealed off the protest area, and became fundamental for moving the bags of rice necessary to sustain the tens of thousands Red Shirts who remained in Ratchaprasong. Their knowledge of the urban terrain was far greater than that of any other urban dwellers, let alone that of the soldiers, most of whom were normally stationed outside of Bangkok. The army saw the city as if they were automobile drivers in traffic: once the pavement was taken the road was blocked. To the drivers, instead, paths were everywhere: through underground parking lots, inside the small left spaces in between buildings, in forgotten walkways along the canals.

---

16. On April 29, the Yellow Shirts gave an ultimatum to the government demanding a dispersal of the Red Shirts in one week's time, or they would take matters into their hands. What was paradoxical about this was that two of the Yellow Shirts' main leaders, who had risked their lives in 1992 to oppose military interventions in politics, were now demanding a violent military dispersal against their opponents.

While this avoidance technique relied on their knowledge of the city, the second strategy—crossing military checkpoints unnoticed—took advantage of their invisibility as an urban infrastructure. Any of the Red Shirts drivers could get on their bike, take up a fake passenger, and be allowed through army checkpoints. This did not work with the ones closest to the protest area—which could only be dodged—but it did with the ones that were further away. It allowed the drivers to move behind the military lines, collect information on the movement of state forces around the city, and report back inside the protest area. Such ability was predicated on the tactical use of their vest as a tool of struggle: taking it off—as Oboto said—made them anonymous in a crowd; putting it on—as Adun did after his daily visits to the protest—made them invisible transportation providers in the eyes of the soldiers and protesters alike.

A similar dynamic has been described in Frantz Fanon's analysis of the roles of women in the Algerian War and their use of the veil as a tool of struggle.[17] During the battle between liberation forces and French colonial officers, Fanon showed, wearing a veil in the kasbah assured women invisibility to French soldiers, while not wearing one in the European city allowed "the unveiled Algerian woman [to] move like a fish in the Western waters."[18] Much like the veil, the driver's vest "removed and reassumed again and again, . . . has been manipulated, transformed into a technique of camouflage, into a means of struggle."[19] By manipulating their clothes, both groups played with the complex relation between visibility and invisibility that structured their presence in the city.

The invisibility that marginalized the drivers in their daily operations as an urban infrastructure provided them, in protest, with the potential of challenging the power of state forces and their ability to control and manage territory and people. After all, as a number of scholars have argued, state power performs its mastery over spaces through sight, by making its subjects visible and legible.[20] This strategy, however, does not just configure its strength but also manifest its weakness: it bounds power to its ability to see.[21] Eluding the gaze of the state forces, therefore, means posing a significant challenge by blinding them, taking away their ability to read and control

17. Fanon 1980.
18. Ibid., 58.
19. Ibid., 60.
20. De Certeau 1984; Scott 1998.
21. De Certeau 1984, 37.

their terrain and their people. In this sense, the drivers posed a double challenge to state forces: first, by reclaiming their position as owners of the map, they questioned those forces' control over territory; second, by remaining invisible to the state apparatus, they revealed their inability to dominate their own subjects. While this potential became clear during this phase of static protest, it acquired even more prominence once the stalemate broke and the protest turned into an urban guerrilla confrontation.

URBAN GUERRILLA AND MOBILE
FIGHTERS (MAY 13–19)

On May 13, a high-speed bullet tore apart the curtain of tension, uncertainty, and expectation that had descended over the protesters and the country at large. After two weeks of feverish negotiations, calls for dispersal, and failed resolutions, the bullet pierced the head of Major-General Khattiya, aka Seh Daeng, a renegade army specialist and a prominent Red Shirts strategist, leaving him in a pool of blood. This was the beginning of a military attack. Signs of the imminent dispersal had been accumulating. The previous day, electricity, water, and phone services had been cut off from the area and security had become even tighter. Once Seh Daeng was hit, the incubating tension broke open. Scores of Red Shirts poured onto the streets around Ratchaprasong, effectively creating an outer ring of protesters behind the army lines. On the opposite side, the soldiers were determined to hold their position and opened fire on anyone who came near their checkpoints, both from within the protest area and from the opposite direction. This military technique, known as containment by fire, basically meant shooting to kill anything that moved (see map 3).

The following morning, the outer ring of Red Shirts erected tire barricades outside the originally occupied area, trapping the soldiers in between Ratchaprasong and the their new strongholds. To prevent military snipers from aiming at them, the protesters set the barricades on fire, hiding behind a curtain of black smoke that enveloped them. From there, protesters threw rocks, Molotov cocktails, and fireworks at the soldiers who replied with endless rounds of live bullets. They shot randomly, succeeding more in keeping the Red Shirts contained but rarely hitting them (see fig. 7).

Day after day the barricades grew higher, the explosions louder, and the rifle rounds closer. As nights descended, the conflict zone became filled with

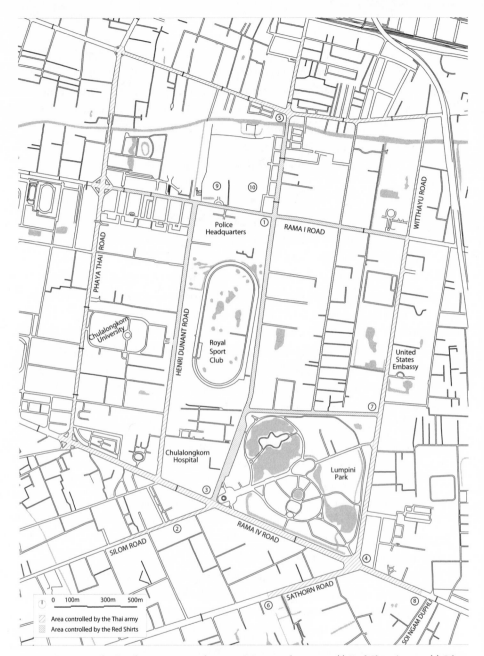

MAP 3. Events in the Ratchaprasong area between May 13 and 19, 2010: (1) Red Shirts' stage; (2) Silom Road: grenade explosion (on April 22); (3) Silom Road: Seh Daeng shot by a sniper on May 13; (4) Lumpini Park: military line shooting to keep the protesters away between May 14 and May 19; (5) Ratchaprarop Road: military shooting to keep the protesters away between May 14 and May 19; (6) Sathorn Road: military shooting to keep the protesters away between May 14 and May 19; (7) Witthayu Road: military shooting to keep the protesters away between May 14 and May 19; (8) Soi Ngam Duphli: Red Shirts guerrilla fighting with Molotov and tire barricades; (9) Wat Pathum: designed by the CRES as a safe area came under military attack on May 19; (10) Central World: set on fire after the military dispersal on May 19. (Map by Carla Betancourt.)

FIGURE 7. Tire barricade on Rama IV Road, erected after the army attack to cover protesters from snipers' fire. Photo by the author.

fast-moving shadows. The number of fatalities and injured grew and was noted on a macabre bulletin presented every morning by national media: 16 dead and 141 injured by May 15; 24 dead and 198 injured by May 16; 36 dead and 258 injured by May 17. For the next several days, the Bangkok central business district resembled a war zone with almost uninterrupted live ammunition shots, grenade attacks, sniper hits, and guerrilla warfare tactics, from walls of burning tires to an endless game of cat-and-mouse between soldiers and protesters in the maze of Bangkok's *soi.* Buildings' halls, small hidden gardens, and abandoned houses became invaluable hiding spots and hidden paths for the Red Shirts fighters, while big roads became the space of the army that occupied them and unloaded round after round of gunfire toward the flaming barricades in the distance. The maze of Bangkok's alleys was now the protesters' best ally.

Once again the motorcycle taxi drivers' knowledge of the territory and their ability to move unnoticed became fundamental to directing the protesters' actions and maintaining their upper hand inside the *soi.* Their roles were multiple. First, the drivers provided the provisions—water and fuel— necessary to keep the barricades burning and to fill Molotov cocktails, both inside the protest area and behind the barricades. In between the two they moved like fishes in water, slipping through the army's clutches only to appear where the protesters needed them. Second, they became personal taxis for the Red Shirts' military strategists who circulated from one front to the other distributing directives on where to establish new barricades, how to move through the *soi,* and how to prevent the soldiers from advancing or retreating. Third, the drivers became inseparable from the Red Shirts' leaders who, blockaded inside the protest area, waited for an all-out army attack, knowing that their chances of getting out alive depended largely on their drivers' ability to move furtively out of the sealed protest area. Fourth, as the number of injured started to grow, the drivers operated as rescuers and first-aid workers, picking up injured protesters, mounting them on their bikes, and driving them out of the protest zone into nearby hospitals. Nonetheless, no matter how many trips they made to refuel the barricades or to deliver directives to the frontlines, by May 18 it was clear to everyone that the battle was lost and there was nothing that could be done to contend with the army's arsenal.

That night, I sat in the darkness of my apartment in the heart of the area where the army had cut electricity. I was unable to sleep through the night punctured by continuous rifle shots, when suddenly someone knocked at my door. Scared, I looked into the peephole and saw Hong and a friend of his, a young woman who worked in an office near his station. The terror that kept me awake had impelled them to get drunk. It was as good an approach as any to make it through the night. I grabbed the bottle they brought with them and we walked upstairs to the rooftop. Hong knew that my apartment over-looked the area of the protest and that from there we could get a sense of the fight without risking our lives. The night was dark, thick with clouds cover-ing a lonely moon. Without electricity, the skyscrapers around us were mon-strous creatures, lit up by the sparse light of the burning barricades. The three of us sat up there for seemingly countless hours, filling the time between gunshots with dishonestly masculine talk of fighting, weapons, sniper rifles and their mechanics, blathering about things we knew nothing about; talk-ing just to not feel alone, to not hear our own thoughts, to not think about the people who were being killed below us. As the sound of military snipers and automatic weapons picked up, however, we all drifted into silence. The situation and the alcohol put all of us in a strange mood.

"Seeing what we have seen in these days, living in this situation makes me sick. I want to do something to support my brothers but I don't know what I can do," Hong whispered, sipping the last gulp of whisky. Silence fell over us, an interminable silence. At every long series of shots, Hong stood up and scanned the landscape of the neighborhood he knew so well, trying to figure out where the shooting was taking place. His friend put her hands together and started praying in a soft and monotonous tone, and I checked my phone for Twitter updates, trying to make sense of the unfolding event. Without realizing it, I fell asleep in the perceived safety of their company. At dawn, when a phone call woke me up, Hong and his friend were already gone. "They are moving in with tanks," Yai told me from the other end of the phone line. "It's over."

Early on the morning of May 19, the army entered the protest area from Silom Road. The bamboo barricades were quickly torn down by tanks and assault units. During the course of the day, the soldiers continued their progress toward the Ratchaprasong intersection, leaving behind a dozen dead protesters. By the time they began to move into the area, the motorcycle taxi drivers had already left, slipping through the closing grip of the army. The soldiers advanced slowly, fearing the presence of bombs and significant armed fights. The resistance, however, was scattered: a violent group attempted to keep the soldiers at bay for a few hours, but soon gave up to the incommensurable power of the army, its tanks, and snipers. These fighters, more able than other Red Shirts to understand army operations, fled the area, leaving the army advance unopposed. The soldiers, now in charge, fired indiscriminately as the remaining protesters converged around the stage. At one o'clock in the afternoon, with the army now closing in on the Ratchaprasong intersection, the protest leaders invited their supporters in the area to surrender, in order to prevent more casualties. The small crowd of five thousand hardliners still present around the stage booed, voicing their willingness to sacrifice their lives for the cause. Meanwhile the Red Shirts' leaders left the area and walked to the nearby National Police headquarters to surrender, aware that the army would be much less kind to them than the police.

The hope maintained by the young bookseller and many others that commodities would protect them from an army attack were dashed—their protective spell proved ineffective. When the objects of desire, condensed in this space of consumption and its shopping malls, revealed their powerlessness to protect the protesters from the army, the inflammatory potential of those desires broke free. Aware that nothing was left for them to do, some of the protesters vented their frustration against shopping malls and banks in the area, the symbols of the system of inequality that they came to protest and that was now crushing them. What had been supposed to be shields became the objects of their rage. Protesters entered the shopping malls at the Ratchaprasong intersection. Outside the buildings some of the remaining hardliner protesters plastered the malls with rocks and Molotov cocktails, determined to bring the whole area down with them.[22] Arson attacks took place around the protest camp targeting malls, banks, and retail shops, carefully selected symbols of their unfulfilled desire and betrayed promises.

As in similar riot situations, the violence was described afterward as mindless destruction. On the contrary, this was lucid rage with specific objectives. Attacking these buildings, however, did not mean that the Red Shirts' grievances were part of an anticapitalist struggle. Rather it showed how central unfulfilled desires for commodities and recognition were to their demands of access to an economic, political, and legal system from which they felt excluded. Once this system had shut its door in their face, their rage was directed at those commodities and the buildings that held them. In the following hours, as the army advanced toward the Red Shirts' stage, thirty-four buildings were set on fire in both the protest area and in the zones that had been controlled by Red Shirts. Among them was Central World. Given that the army had cut the water supply in the area, there was nothing to be done to control the fire. The central section of the building became a furnace. Its beams melted and the section collapsed, leaving the rest of the mall intact, as if a giant spoon had scooped through it (see fig. 8).

Chaos spread around the Ratchaprasong intersection. Many of the remaining protesters took refuge in Wat Pathum, a temple that the CRES had declared a no-conflict zone. Soldiers moved into the area from the Skytrain rails. A cross-fire exchange broke around the temple area and high-speed bullets were shot inside the sacred ground from the rails, killing six people, including Kamolket Akahad, a twenty-five-year-old nurse who had joined the protesters to take care of the injured.[23] The Red Shirts' protest was over, and once again, as in previous political movements in Thailand, the army had brutally choked the protesters' voices in blood.[24] As the remaining protesters were rounded up inside the police headquarters, the soldiers left

22. Jim Taylor has argued that the burning of Central World was not carried out by Red Shirts sympathizers (J. Taylor 2011). While I was not personally present at Ratchaprasong intersection on the afternoon of May 19—just as Taylor was not—the report of Thai and international journalists and observers who were in the area, as well as the repeated threat by Red Shirts leaders to burn the malls down in case of a dispersal (Sopranzetti 2012b), are consistent with the assertion that protest sympathizers were the culprits.

23. The Thai army maintains that these shots were not fired by soldiers. Yet photographic evidence shows army personnel moving and firing from the Skytrain railways nearby the temple.

24. For a history of violent repression of political demonstrations, see Ferrara 2015.

FIGURE 8. Central World with the central section collapsed on May 20, 2010, the day after the army dispersal. Photo by the author.

behind a haunted, humanless space, an eerie square filled only by lifeless objects: clothes, fans, TV sets, motorcycles, unfinished food, half-cooked rice, piles of vegetables, half-opened tents, monks' clothes, wallets, documents, bags, red paraphernalia, medicines, and sealed water bottles. Framed by the sound of birds echoing in the emptiness, the three months–long Red Shirts' protest came to an end, leaving behind ninety-two dead bodies and more than two thousand injured (see fig. 9).

FIGURE 9. Protest stage left empty after the army dispersal. Photo by the author.

FRAGILITY OF POWER

On May 20, when the military offensive stopped, the few hundred protesters who had remained in the area until then sat inside the front court of the National Police headquarters, a few steps from the smoldering ashes of Central World. The Red Shirts had failed to remove the government of Abhisit Vejjajiva, suffered significant losses, and now waited to know what would happen to them. Beneath their apparent loss, however, were two significant victories, which Yai readily recognized. "The government accepted having new elections next year. We wanted them gone now, but at least we will have the opportunity to choose our government soon. But, most importantly, we have shown them that they cannot do whatever they want. The people will respond and will not accept their actions. This is surely a sad moment; many of us died. But we proved that if they want to rule us, there will be consequences."

The protest showed that a motivated group of protesters could take over the center of Bangkok, hold it for months, and keep the Thai government, police, and army in check, forcing them into an internationally embarrassing use of force to clear them out. More broadly, they revealed that the apparent mightiness of bureaucratic, monarchic, and military forces, with their laws and procedures, their billionaire resources, and their heavy weaponry could barely disguise the fragility of their power and their control over the city, its territory, and people. The drivers' uses of mobility and immobility, visibility and invisibility, and their ability to bring the city to its knees, push us to question established understandings of how power operates.

Three dominant lines of inquiry have directed analysis of power since the 1970s.[25] The first strand, inspired by the work of Michel Foucault, sees power as a ubiquitous, all-powerful apparatus of governance, operating through mechanisms that produce their own subjects as well as forms of resistance that "exist only on the strategic field of the relations of power."[26] "Where there is power," Foucault argues, "there is resistance, and yet, or rather consequently, this resistance is never in a position of exteriority in relation to power."[27] While invaluable in showing power as a productive, rather than repressive, mechanism, analyses based on these insights largely overlook moments in which this production fails and something else emerges outside its limits.[28] The second current, most famously associated with work of James Scott, acknowledges that power is constantly challenged by everyday acts of resistance. In this view, these small acts constitute emancipatory struggles and demonstrate the popular refusal of consent and resilience in the face of domination.[29] This line of analysis contributes greatly to revealing the importance of an analysis "that is *not* centered on the state, on formal organizations, on open protest, on national issues."[30] Yet, it also flattens the distinction between collective action that poses systematic challenges and acts of resistance that simply do not. In so doing, it relegates political actions to a reactive mode and gives a romantic caste to resistance, one that overestimates the structural significance of these everyday acts.[31] Finally, the third approach, directed by an engagement with the work of Antonio Gramsci, focuses on

25. Gledhill 2009. Here it is important to notice that I am looking at the way in which the work of Foucault and Gramsci was used and adopted, rather than on their own theorizations. These, in fact, are more open-ended and fluid than most of their interpreters have led us to believe.

26. Foucault 1977, 126.

27. Foucault 1978, 95–96.

28. This approach's blindness to these moments has been noticed by John Holloway. In this view, as Holloway has argued, "there are a whole host of resistances which are integral to power, but there is no possibility of emancipation. The only possibility is an endlessly shifting constellation of power-and-resistance" (Holloway 2005, 56).

29. Scott 1985, 1990.

30. Ibid., xix.

31. These two arguments have been made respectively by Sherry Ortner and Lila Abu-Lughod (Abu-Lughod 1990; Ortner 1995).

the hegemonic nature of power. The Italian political organizer argued that power can operate either through direct coercion, what he calls domination, or through social hegemony, a naturalized and spontaneous form of consent given by the masses to the direction decided by a dominant group in society.[32] This process, for Gramsci, remained always unstable and incomplete, though he never stated that directly to avoid prison censorship.[33] His *Notes on Italian History,* in which he developed the concept of hegemony, was in fact written from a fascist jail. In it he tried to understand the inability of progressive forces to create a historical block able to provide an alternative to the bourgeois project of the modern Italian state after unification. While he wrote about the mid-nineteenth century, the unspoken and unspeakable reference was the incomplete hegemony of the fascist state and the difficulty in developing a communist revolution in industrial countries. In other words, by developing the concept of hegemony to explain the unstable and ineffective project of the modern Italian nation-state, he was commenting on the weak and incomplete hegemony of the fascist regime. The point, however, needed to be made transversally. Anthropologists who have engaged with Gramsci's work have contributed to exploring the entanglements between persuasion and coercion and revealing the centrality of civil and political society in the operation of power and its naturalization.[34] While in theory they acknowledged the unstable nature of this process and the coalitions of forces that create it, in their ethnographic engagements they for the most part fail to explore what Gramsci himself showed in his historical analysis but never could stress: the fragility of hegemony.[35]

Over recent decades, the confluence, overlapping, and conflict between these three schools attuned us to the greased mechanisms of power, the production of consent, the making of subjects, and small acts of everyday resistance. With this focus, however, we have turned a blind eye to the faltering of the mechanisms of power, the fragilities of the order it imposes, and the emergence of cracks in his operation. In doing so, we have assumed an over-systematic view of power, one that attributed a hermetic or finished quality

32. Gramsci 1971.
33. Buttigieg 1990, 2002, 2006; Francioni 1984; Piparo 1979; Ruccio 2006.
34. Chatterjee 2011; Comaroff 1985; Comaroff and Comaroff 1991, 1999; Gledhill 2009.
35. This too stable reading of Gramsci has become so normalized that James Scott's critique of hegemony is entirely based on engagement with this literature, rather than with Gramsci himself. A notable exception to this trend has been the work of William Roseberry (Roseberry 1994).

to its mechanisms. As a result, we have either overestimated the grip of power or seen acts of resistance everywhere, pitting one against the other rather than exploring systematic fragilities of power.

The actions of Bangkok's motorcycle taxi drivers in protest takes us down a different path. They invite us to reflect on the rusted mechanisms as carefully as on the greased apparatuses, on the blockages as well as on the smooth circulation. Their actions in protests do not show power in Bangkok as an all-encompassing functional apparatus or as open to subversions through small acts of resistance. They do not suggest that forms of everyday resistance intrinsically have the potential to challenge and overturn domination, nor that these struggles are always inscribed into a disciplinary and security apparatus that does not allow for dissent. Rather, they reveal power as a frail apparatus, brimming with tensions and contingencies, traversed both by lines of force and by fault lines. It is only when attacked at its weak spots that this apparatus reveals its cracks and opens itself to challenges. In this sense, not every act of defiance or resistance retains the potential to question and unsettle power. The ability to do so is the result of tactical considerations, provisional coalitions, and timing that allow those acts to hit just the right spots.

Ratchaprasong, and the flow of people, commodities, and capital through this space, offered one such spot. Throughout the protest, the political mobilization entailed a radical restructuring of the everyday life of the city—particularly of its rhythms and circulation—by the very people who were operating it. Through the multiplicity of their roles, the drivers showed their position as privileged connoisseurs of the city's hidden paths and flows and as an urban infrastructure. Mobilizers and stoppers, operating mobility and operating onto mobility, the motorcycle taxi drivers reclaimed their roles as both political actors and controllers of urban channels of communication, able to perform phatic labor, through which the channels are built and sustained, and its opposite, a political labor through which the same channels are filtered, slowed down, and at times cut off. Through these actions, they unveiled the power of state forces as a shadow on the wall which belies the fragility of the object that casts it and generates the appearance of stability and unity, an appearance that the Red Shirts were able to challenge.[36] The

36. John Holloway has made a similar analysis of capitalism. "[Its] illusion is effective," he argues, "because it belies the fragility of capitalism. It appears that capitalism 'is': but capitalism never 'is', it is always a struggle to constitute itself. To treat capitalism as a mode of production that 'is' or, which is the same thing, to think of class struggle as struggle from below against the stability of capitalism, is to fall head-first into the filthiest mire of fetishism.

Red Shirts' protest, as other moments of political mobilization in human history, marked a significant success precisely because of its ability to poke holes in the ghostly nature of power and "open the eyes" (*tham hai koet tā sawāng*) of its subjects, as many Red Shirts repeated after the dispersal.

Such a revelation, however, does not necessarily presage the overthrowing of a political system, as the army's dispersal demonstrated. Much like other systems in unstable equilibrium, power is not just a fragile construct but also a malleable one, prone to readjusting and finding a new balance as well as new weak spots. This is not just true for the power of bureaucratic, monarchic, and military forces, but also for that of the AMTT. During the protest its leadership had fractured. After the dispersal they tried to recompose once again, this time in negotiation with the military security apparatus. This process proved harder than expected and illuminated a fault line running through Thai society, one that cut across the association as well.

Capital, by its nature, appears to 'be', but it never 'is'. That is important, both to understand the violence of capital (the continued presence of what Marx called 'primitive accumulation') and to understand its fragility. The urgent impossibility of revolution begins to open towards an urgent possibility" (Holloway 2005, 74).

EIGHT

Combining Powers

I am thinking of a school experiment (which no doubt I have got wrong) in which an electrical current magnetized a plate covered with iron filings. The filings, which were evenly distributed, arranged themselves at one pole or the other, while in between those filings which remained in place aligned themselves sketchily as if directed towards opposing attractive poles.

E. P. THOMPSON, *Eighteen Century English Society*

THE MILITARY DISPERSAL, the killing of almost one hundred people, and the burning of iconic buildings around Bangkok left the country hanging on a cliff. This was not the first time in Thai history that a popular protest was drowned in blood. The same had happened in 1973 when urban workers, students, and trade unionists mobilized to oppose the military government of General Thanom Kittikachorn, and once again in 1992 when workers and urban middle classes resisted General Suchinda Kraprayoon's bid for power. On both occasions, the widening rift in Thai society was bridged by an intervention by the palace that, claiming neutrality, adjudicated the disputes and solidified its role as a major power broker in struggles over the Thai state. In 2010, however, the monarchy had lost its claim to impartiality: there was no universally respected institution to bring the conflict to an end and clean up the mess. In 2006, rumors had circulated claiming that the palace was the real force behind the coup that ousted Thaksin. In 2008, in the midst of the fighting between Red and Yellow Shirts, Queen Sirikit had presided over the funeral of a Yellow Shirts supporter. For the Red Shirts this had been a public admission that the monarchy, which had previously positioned itself as external to political struggles, had entered the fight and chosen the opposite side. After the 2010 military dispersal, the protesters repeated that there would be no way back: their eyes were now opened to the role of the monarchy and the cruelty of the *'ammāt's* power. The government called for reconciliation and agreed to anticipate the next election to August 2011, but had no intention of allowing an independent investigation on the army's role in the killings. The

Center for the Resolution of the Emergency Situation (CRES) refused to admit any responsibility and the prime minister maintained that the deaths were the result of the actions of an undisclosed *third party* that wanted to create unrest. All around the country citizens held their breath amid talks of civil war and a deepening crisis in the legitimacy of the monarchy, Thailand's most revered institution. Protesters talked about spreading the struggle across the country and giving up the peaceful methods they had used so far. Responding to this tide of social, economic, and political resentment, the government kept the Emergency Decree in place to prevent protesters from regrouping or commemorating publicly the deaths of their fellow Red Shirts. In the following two months it seemed as though Thailand was in for two long and bloody struggles, one between two social movements—the Red and Yellow Shirts—the other between bureaucratic, monarchic, military state forces and whichever government would emerge out of the upcoming elections. These battles ran the risk of destroying more than shopping malls, taking down established hierarchies exposing political taboos, and sacrificing a multitude of human lives in the process.

On September 19, 2010, the fourth anniversary of the 2006 coup that triggered all of these events, thousands of protesters defied a countrywide ban on assembly and gathered at the Ratchaprasong intersection to commemorate the death of Red Shirts supporters. Jon, a Bangkok-born company owner, invited me to go with him. During the course of the protest, Jon had followed the movement from afar, more sympathetically than his middle-class friends and family but still not committed to join the "poor people," as half-jokingly he described the protesters. The violent army dispersal tipped the balance.

"This is unacceptable," he had told me a month after the end of the protest. "These people were protesting to get a better life and were killed like dogs. I live around the area, I saw the military in the streets, I saw them shooting. On May 17 with a few friends we went to see what was happening. A line of soldiers was shooting in the middle of the empty street. A guy came out of a *soi* and was shot, left bleeding on the pavement. A team of medics ran to pick him up and the army started shooting at them. At the medics . . . can you imagine? Not even in a war do you shoot the medics. These people are crazy."

Indignant at the army behavior, Jon decided to take to the street to commemorate the dead. Upon our arrival, we found the intersection brought to a halt and brimming with Red Shirts. Once again, motorcycle taxi drivers had taken control of mobility and rhythms at the protest site. Not far away from where the Red Shirts' stage used to be, some protesters were drawing chalk outlines of dead bodies on the street pavement while others recounted their stories and the brutality of the military snipers who shot them. Behind them, the remaining ashes of Central World shopping mall were cordoned off by giant propaganda boards put up by the government in collaboration with a design collective. These boards invited citizens to remain peaceful and, in perfect Orwellian style, reminded them that "EVERYTHING WILL BE OK" (see fig. 10).

Very little, however, was okay for the thousands who came out to remember the dead. Two red pieces of cloth covered the sides of the elevated railway, asking, "Who is the killer? Where is justice?" While these questions filled the intersection, protesters started to write tentative answers on placards and on the propaganda wall surrounding the burned shopping mall. Under the gaze of CCTV cameras, they penned words that until then had only been whispered in private conversations: insults to the royal family and the army, accusations of their involvement in the violence, and unspeakable doubts about Thailand's past, present, and future (see figs. 11 and 12).

The political significance of these writings cannot be overstated.[1] Each offense was punishable with three to fifteen years of jail under the *lèse-majesté* law, making the wall a crime that carried several millennia of prison time. Furthermore, in a country in which pictures of the king hang in almost every home, each scribble tore apart the myth of the nation's uniform love for the monarch and raised a visible challenge to state hegemony. Since the early twentieth century, the triad Nation, Buddhism, and the King has been enshrined and naturalized as the basis of Thai identity and its main legitimizing principle, regularly repeated in classrooms, public events, news stories, and history books.[2] In this configuration the king plays a central role as the father and the bearing pillar of the state apparatus. The authority of state officials is materially handed over by the monarch and legitimized by his unquestionable power.[3] Judges, bureaucrats, the prime minister, and soldiers received their post from the king and they are known as *khā rātchakān,* servants of the monarch. Questioning his actions and his virtues meant

---

1. This event, however, went unreported by news agencies. The only existing analysis has been done by Serhat Ünaldi (Ünaldi 2014c).

2. Connors 2005, 2007, 2011.

3. Herzfeld 2016b; Thongchai 2015a, b.

FIGURE 10. Lone passersby staring at the propaganda wall erected around the burned-down Central World complex, six months after the end of the Red Shirts' protest. Photo by the author.

FIGURE 11. Antimonarchy graffiti covering government's propaganda on September 19, 2010. Photo by the author.

FIGURE 12. Graffiti questioning whether King Bhumibol, also known as Rama IX, killed his older brother, Rama VIII. Photo by the author.

questioning the whole structure of the Thai state or, to use the language of William Golding, the effectiveness of the conch.[4]

While thousands of hands scribbled notes, thousands of eyes stared (see fig. 13). Jon was among the observers. He stood next to me, astonished. "I never thought I would see this in my lifetime," he said, unable to take his eyes off the wall. "I used to love the monarchy, I thought the king was a hero. Since the beginning of the Red Shirts I stopped loving him but only on May 19 did I realize who he really is: a killer and the instigator of the violent dispersal, a man who does not want the people to choose their own leaders. I opened my eyes and I awoke [*tā sawāng*]. I never thought I would see these things written in public in my lifetime. This is the beginning of a new era."

As he stared at the wall, Jon began to untangle the Nation, Buddhism, the King triad, pitting one against the others. Like Jon, the Red Shirts who shared his view framed their new realization in the Buddhist language of *tā sawāng,* literally meaning "blazing eyes" or "eyes filled with light." This turn

4. In chapter 5 I analyzed how the idea of a unified state operates as the conch in William Golding's *Lord of the Flies*—an empty shell that gains power from collective acceptance of its role and allows whichever faction in control to act as if it has obtained complete and unified control.

FIGURE 13. People staring at antimonarchy graffiti. Photo by the author.

of phrase refers to moments of enlightenment, moments of realization of truth beyond truth. Over the course of the Red Shirts' mobilization, and particularly after the violent dispersal, this Buddhist terminology emerged as a code to speak about the awakening from faith in royalist hegemony and the realization of the palace's role in the political turmoil. Six decades of state hegemony, based on largely unchallenged royalism, came under question.

The scribbles in figure 14, in particular, revealed the emerging fault lines in state hegemony. The king is represented as an old man in a wheelchair wearing an eye-patch shooting at the population. On the right side of the picture are two bullets, underneath which is written *phrarātchathān* ("given by the king"), an expression used to refer to the titles, bureaucratic positions, and university degrees conferred by the king.[5] This figure made a multiplicity of claims. First, the protesters who wrote on the wall saw the Red Shirts as representing the nation. In this sense, they presented the ailing king as the perpetrator of a violent attack against the nation itself. In this context, the army's bullets were depicted sarcastically as royal gifts, central to the monarch's legitimacy, the

5. The practice of the monarch bestowing titles is central to the role of the king in Thai society and his legitimacy as the source of state power. Every university degree and bureaucratic title is physically delivered from his hands or from the hands of his representatives. Even more prominently, the constitution is seen as *phrarātchathān* (given by the king).

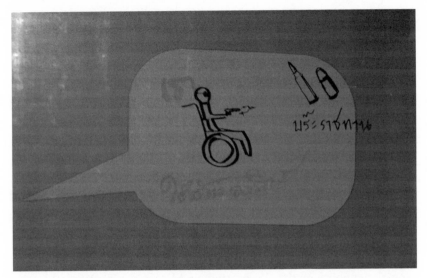

FIGURE 14. Graffiti of King Bhumibol, represented as a man on a wheel chair, shooting bullets. Photo by the author.

operations of the Thai bureaucracy, and popular culture, and now reframed as deadly. Finally, by claiming knowledge of this truth and being *tā sawāng*, the writers were adopting the liberatory Buddhist discourse of awakening to question the king's legacy, doubt his real commitment to the nation, and accuse him of betrayal. Adding this new terminology to the repertoire that dominated their mobilization, Red Shirts supporters took a central tool of state power in the last century—Buddhism—and adopted it as a tactic for the unmaking of state hegemony, which seemed frail, splintering, and destined to fall.

The army's violent responses to the Red Shirts transformed the protesters' challenge to their control over the city into a much deeper fault line, running through royalist hegemony. State forces had stumbled into a crack in their power and, in an attempt to fix it, had widened it. The absurd propaganda wall they erected in Ratchaprasong materially provided the background for those unprecedentedly outspoken attacks. Staring at the graffiti, Jon and other Red Shirts were not only seeing the physical and metaphorical writings on the wall, but were also realizing that many others had done the same and were now condemning the monarchy as one of the state forces behind the repression of their democratic demands, their exclusion from opportunities, and the killings of their comrades in May 2010. Jon was convinced it would be just a matter of time before the people's mobilization would take over.

"We are awakened," he repeated. "It will be impossible to put us back to sleep. More and more people are now seeing the reality between the dispersal, who ordered it and why. The Red Shirts are growing by the day. More and more, even in Bangkok, support them now, even some people like me, middle class, students, office workers." Jon was not alone in his enthusiasm and on the night of September 19, 2010, it seemed as though anything could happen. After just a few months, however, things went back to normal. The growing tide, which had seemed on the verge of washing away the 'ammāt and its system of inequality, exclusion, and exploitation, started to recede.

In the coming pages, I attempt to explain how this retreat occurred and how state forces, after having revealed their fragility during the protest, began to create a new, equally exclusionary equilibrium. This attempt included cutting the motorcycle taxi drivers off from the Red Shirts. The army knew well that this would require a complex negotiation and that winning the support of the Association of Motorcycle Taxis of Thailand (AMTT) would be fundamental. While some of its members, seeing the AMTT's unwillingness to openly support the Red Shirts after the protest ended, had distanced themselves from the association, those who remained seemed to be willing to listen to the army proposal. Behind their apparent unity, however, stood a variety of motivations, lines of reasoning, and conceptions of power that underpinned internal tensions and conflicts inside the AMTT: the same fault lines that ran through the country's political landscape in the previous decade.

RETAKING CONTROL OVER THE TERRITORY: THE ISOC

On May 4, 2010, while the Red Shirts were still solidly in control of the Ratchaprasong intersection, a large AMTT meeting took place in an army school at the other side of town. From the outside, it seemed like one of many meetings between motorcycle taxi drivers, envoys from the Bangkok Metropolitan Administration (BMA) who were trying to upgrade road safety in the city, police officers interested in using the drivers for crime prevention and first aid, and a contingent from Honda hoping to strengthen the company's dominance over the motorcycle market. Something else, however, was brewing. The timing (in the midst of the Red Shirts' protest), the location (an army school), and the presence of the assistant army chief of staff *and* a high-ranking officer from the Internal Security Operations Command (ISOC)—the army division expert in psychological warfare that was resuscitated after the 2006 coup—made clear that this gathering was part of a military strategy to win over the drivers' support and cut them off from the ongoing protest.

I arrived at the meeting with Adun, who was curious to meet the leaders of the association who he had seen on the Red Shirts' stage. After parking our bikes we entered the school from the canteen: a large room filled with formica tables and green plastic chairs surrounded by small cement booths, normally filled by food vendors. Neon lights hung from the concrete ceiling, giving a feeling of staleness to the deserted room. We walked through it and entered a smaller area. There the registration process was being conducted by four young women who gave us a small brochure published by BMA on the role of motortaxis in urban security, a larger booklet of maps of Bangkok, the AMTT's charter, and a small green coupon that guaranteed the participants a free helmet, offered by Honda, at the end of the meeting. A few drivers were hanging around this area, studying the maps and serving themselves coffee and biscuits that were laid out on a table to the left of the registration booth. Adun and I moved upstairs where the meeting had just started.

The large room was ornate with heavy fabrics. At its end, an expansive stage stood against a giant projector screen. The space was filled with chairs for two thousand drivers, delegates from all fifty of the districts of Bangkok that participated in a long day of presentations, gift giving, and pleasantries between the association's leaders and the envoys from BMA, Honda, the Thai Police, and the Royal Army. Of the twenty leaders who had appeared on the Red Shirts' stage a month before to pledge their support for the protest, nineteen were present at this meeting, while the twentieth, Oboto, had refused to use the drivers' role in the protest as a bargaining chip and left the association. "If you see the whole picture, Lerm and Yai are with the army, with ISOC," he told me. "I don't want this. I fight for myself . . . , if other drivers want to go in the street or the Red Shirts' leaders organize something, we go. But I don't want to play politics." Whether his decision was the result of his loathing for the sordid politics of negotiation, as Oboto suggested, or of the large sum of money that the Red Shirts gave him to remain in the protest, as Yai and Lerm maintained, his faction of the drivers was busy manning the protest on the other side of the city while the AMTT was meeting with the army.

The sessions had a conventional structure. One after another, the envoys went on stage and gave thirty-minute speeches on the importance of motorcycle taxi drivers for the city, their plans to fight people of influence, to provide the drivers with a social security scheme, to ensure safety for them and their passengers, and to use their services for the social good. While many of the drivers were attracted to Honda's presence and their willingness to provide free safe-riding certificates to AMTT members, a discount on new bikes, and the free helmet, the rest of the talks was nothing to be excited about—"just the umpteenth round of government officials making empty promises that they had no interest in respecting," Adun pointed out. This time, however, one new element emerged, pushed by the military guests of honor. Their objective, the officers stated quite clearly, was to include the drivers in a new surveillance apparatus, turning them into local informants for crime prevention and drug policing.

Cooperation between police officers, soldiers, and local drivers had existed since the emergence of motorcycle taxis in the early 1980s. Drivers, forced into daily interactions with the state officials who controlled their operations, kept an eye on traffic accidents, fires, and petty criminality and called up police officers in case of trouble. As Lek, Yai's twin brother, told me half-jokingly, "Thai police officers are like the police in American movies, they always arrive too late. Motorcycle taxis, on the contrary, are there even before something happens." In August 2003, a few months after Thaksin's formalization of the drivers' operations, these collaborations became more systematic, motivated by the upcoming Asia-Pacific Economic Cooperation (APEC) Summit. As part of a larger cleanup of Bangkok before the conference,[6] a few drivers from every station in Bangkok were recruited as volunteer informants with the purpose of "help[ing] local forces to watch out for anything suspicious."[7] More than a thousand drivers were included in this scheme and trained in bomb and weapon recognition ahead of the meeting. After this experiment, the cooperation with local drivers was formalized under a policy called eyes-and-ears (*pen hū pen tā*). As the Royal Thai Police deputy commissioner-general declared in 2004 that "motorcycle-taxi stands are located at almost every corner of every street in Bangkok. The riders outnumber traffic-police officers; with their help security in the city will be smoother."[8] Under this policy, training sessions were conducted at police stations, fire departments, and hospitals on weapons

6. Klima 2002.
7. Prasad 2003.
8. Chanunya 2004.

recognition, chase and arrests, fire prevention as well as primary aid and traffic management.

In the mid-2000s the police was not the only institution to notice the motorcycle taxi drivers' unmatched knowledge of the physical and social terrain in which they moved and their potential for the expansion of the surveillance and security apparatus. In 2005, the army also started recruiting and paying motorcycle taxi drivers working in the south of Thailand to "report on unusual and suspicious movements and to identify insurgent activity" in three provinces where a low intensity conflict had turned into a sustained and bloody insurgency.[9] After the 2006 coup, the newly resuscitated Internal Security Operation Command (ISOC) formalized this collaboration into a new policy, called *tā sapparot* (pineapple eyes) (see fig. 15).

The meeting on May 4 was an attempt recruit drivers in Bangkok to join in, before officially launching the policy in Bangkok. Right after the May 19 dispersal the city was flooded with posters of this tropical version of Bentham's panopticon, in which pineapple's dots were replaced by lenses, reassuring Bangkokians that the military gaze would protect them. Similar to eyes-and-ears, the pineapple eyes policy attempted to co-opt the drivers into becoming part of the state security apparatus. Their participation was predicated upon the same omnipresence and knowledge of territory that allowed drivers to weave Bangkok together in their everyday lives and shut it down in the Red Shirts' mobilization. The ISOC wanted to turn these abilities that were revealing the fragility of the military forces into one of its strengths and adopt the drivers as their new instruments of vision, lenses through which the ISOC could collect intelligence and monitor its territory. The owners of the map, in their plans, would go from making the city illegible to state forces to becoming their vicarious vigilantes. "If there are two hundred thousand motorcycle taxis in Bangkok," the highest-ranking soldier in the room told the drivers during his presentation, "there will be four hundred thousand eyes for us, eyes that help us keep the city safe and the country stable." What he neglected to say—but everybody in the room understood—was that even preventing them from carrying out the same function for the Red Shirts would already be a success. The timing of this initiative was so clearly instrumental that there was no point even pretending otherwise.

The ISOC—as Sun, the officer present at the meeting, told me—knew that convincing the association to switch sides and snitch on their fellow protesters

9. Wassayos 2005.

FIGURE 15. Poster of the pineapple eyes policy. The caption says: "Your security is in our eyes." Photo by the author.

would never really be a possibility, but they also understood that limiting the drivers' collective involvement in the protest could weaken the Red Shirts in case of violent confrontations and prevent the spread of the protest citywide. "After the violence in April, the CRES tried to arrest us and told us we should not participate in the protest," Lek told me, looking back at this meeting and on the ISOC's new strategy. "We are working men. Breadwinners day in and day out, we rent houses, buy bikes, and pay for food. Once we are arrested, our families experience great difficulties. But we did not stop anyway. Then the ISOC appointed Sun to manage the relationship with motorcycle taxi drivers.

Sun did not threaten us. He told us he understood why we supported Thaksin and the Red Shirts. He offered us something to make our lives better, to make our families better, and to make our association stronger. They were smart, smart enough to play this way. Even if many of us continued to go to the protest, they cut our network off from the rally."

The terms of this bargain were clear to the AMTT's leadership: they were asked to stop pledging their collective support for the Red Shirts in exchange for the ISOC's assistance.[10] This support entailed two things. First, the ISOC provided a check for 100,000 baht ($3,400 USD) to the association that was struggling to pay rent for their office on the outskirts of the city and provide an income to the drivers who worked there full-time. Second, the ISOC offered to become a patron of the association, a friend who could out-power and out-influence the *phū mī itthiphon* (people of influence) who had come back to extort money from motorcycle taxi drivers since the 2006 coup.

While the first offer was attractive in the short run and allowed the AMTT to pay their bills, the second one—the leaders of the association believed—was pivotal for the growth of their organization. Being able to use such an alliance against people of influence, they argued, would help their members get rid of their exploiters, proving the AMTT to be an effective organization and thereby attracting more drivers to join. Instead of demanding the implementation of existing laws and norms, as they had done since 2003, the leaders of the association now moved to playing different state forces and forms of influence against each other, with strong support from the most powerful of them all: the army. As Lerm explained, "The objective is to have the Army Commander in Chief and the Police Commissioner General on our board. These guys are ranked in the top, above all the police officers and soldiers who exert influence. They will be the best guards for the association and scare off all the people of influence." Convinced by this prospective, the AMTT's leaders decided to accept the ISOC's offer and took a step back from the protest, at least as a collective.

This agreement did not cut off single motorcycle taxi drivers from the Red Shirts, and even people who were present and who organized the meeting continued to join the protest. Yet it succeeded in making this support individual and not collective, thus limiting the post-dispersal chaos in the city. The

10. Their involvement in labor struggles was nothing new for the ISOC. Since the 1970s they have been involved in labor politics through financing some factions of trade unions with the purpose of fomenting "the break-up of the then strongest and most progressive body of organized labour" (Brown 1997, 173).

positive effects for the ISOC were clear two weeks later, when the army moved into Ratchaprasong largely unopposed; the payoff for the association started to become visible a few months later. A group of drivers located in an industrial district at the outskirts of Bangkok became the litmus test for the new arrangement proposed by the army. The group, composed of thirty-six members of the AMTT, had formalized its operations in 2003 and refused to sell their vests or continue to pay the high-ranking police officer who had previously owned their station. After a year of pressure and fight with local police officers, the group had succeeded in getting them off their backs. The situation changed rapidly after the fall of Thaksin Shinawatra, and the officer came back to demand regular payments. The drivers pushed back, remaining united in their refusal to sell him their vests or pay any money. Unable to crack their resistance, the officer set up two new illegal motorcycle taxi drivers groups in the *soi,* one located at its entrance—where the *soi* opens into the main road—and the other at the exit of a local market that provided most of the clients for the legal group. Surrounded by new stations and cut off from potential clients, the drivers tried to voice their discontent and to demand the removal of the two illegal groups. Their plea, however, fell on deaf ears. After all, no other tribunal was offered to them than the local police station, the same station in which their persecutor worked. The drivers found themselves squeezed in the clutches of a local police officer, unable to use the law to voice their discontent.

Now, a new route was opening for the group, one that relied on their membership in the AMTT and its collaboration with the ISOC. The drivers and the AMTT leaders pledged with Sun, the ISOC officer who had presided over the meeting, to intervene. Day after day the local drivers quietly collected pictures, data, and details on the illegal stations, their relationship to the police officer, and the value of his racket. This material was not presented as a formal complaint but was hand-delivered by Yai and Lerm to the ISOC officer who, in the next days, personally called the local police station and strongly suggested that the policeman leave the drivers alone before someone higher in the ranks intervened. What the law had been unable to fix in three years, influence resolved in just a few weeks through this channel. The two illegal groups disappeared and the drivers went back to their business, undisturbed by the police officer who had been told to lay off them. The association could count this as a victory and present it as a demonstration of their effectiveness.

Over the following months, this method became the main strategy in fighting people of influence. Getting the newly created association of motorcycle taxis on the Red Shirts' main stage in Ratchadamnoen on April 3, 2010, had proven to be an important move: it put a barely known labor organization on the map, with enough leverage to play a significant, if localized, role. Suddenly, state forces had noticed their strength and the destructive potential of an uprising of two hundred thousand urban dwellers with an unmatched knowledge of territory. As a result, the association entered a complex game of collaboration, opposition, negotiation with the Red Shirts' leaders, the government, and the army. Never taking sides yet always keeping an eye on all of them, Lerm, the AMTT's president, perfectly synthetized this approach: "We are not Reds, we are not Yellows, we are Orange Shirts, the color of our vests," he liked to repeat. With this clever play on color politics, the association claimed a political middle ground and, in their view, defended the interests of drivers across Bangkok.

While Lerm and Yai, the AMTT's vice-president, seemed in agreement on the association's course of action, their decisions were predicated on two different understandings of how power operates in contemporary Thailand, how legitimacy is built, and what the association's strategies should be. When the protest ended, those understandings aligned. By mid-2011, however, things did not look so positive. The association, seen by many drivers around the city as a sellout, struggled not only to grow but also to keep its members. Oboto had left at the first sign of their propensity to negotiate with state forces. Wud, dissatisfied with the new approach, eventually stopped renewing his membership. And Adun, who had just encountered the association, after seeing the AMTT's leaders shaking hands with the ISOC officers while the Red Shirts were fighting soldiers in the streets, never went back. As the association's numbers dwindled, a rift began to emerge between its two leaders—a conceptual divergence that cut to the core of the political conflict that had played out in the streets. It was not just political-economic shifts, everyday experiences of exclusion and inequality, and the unintended consequences of the struggle between Thaksin and other state forces that had torn the country apart. The fracture also ran along two distinct conceptualizations of how power operates and should operate in contemporary Thailand, which Lerm and Yai embodied.[11]

11. Christine Gray has, more than anybody else in Thai studies, shown how these discursive and political-economic dimensions need to be seen as connected to one another, rather than analytically separated (Gray 1986, 1991).

Lerm was not in the first group involved in the drivers' mobilization around Thaksin's formalization in 2003. He joined the struggle the following year, but rapidly emerged as one of its main personalities due to his mellow leadership style, his readiness to listen to others, and his gentle and accessible language. While Yai roused the drivers with his incendiary speeches, Lerm talked them into being part of the struggle. Once their collaboration was formalized with the creation of the AMTT, Lerm was chosen as the president, both for his pacifying demeanor and for not having a previous criminal record. Yai, without either, became the vice-president. Although Lerm was an adamant supporter of Thaksin and had his profile embroidered on his vest, he was also a strong advocate of putting some distance between the association and the Red Shirts. "As an association we need to build our *barami*," he told me sitting behind his new desk at the AMTT office. "We need to show the population that we are working for the common good, that we are taking care of their kids, that we are cleaning these streets and helping with fire and crime." Whenever I asked him why he thought the AMTT should align with the state forces who had killed fellow Red Shirts protesters, he always ended up referring to *barami* as the way in which power operates in Thailand, and said that building it (*sang barami*) was the association's main objective in his political strategy.

The word *barami* is often translated as moral charisma and refers to a form of effortless power that resides in righteous people and which "results from karmic merit accumulated in previous lives."[12] It derives from the Pali *pāramī,* meaning perfection. In Theravada Buddhism the Bodhisatta—or Buddha-to-be—had to accumulate ten *pāramī* over the course of his previous lives in order to reach the moral and spiritual perfection needed to obtain enlightenment.[13] These were, in order of importance: giving, moral conduct,

12. Jackson 2009, 363.

13. This theory of the Perfections is developed in considerable detail in such Pali canonical works as the *Buddhavamsa* and the *Cariyapitaka,* as well as in the semicanonical but far more popular *Jatakas*—the stories of the previous lives of the Buddha (Jory 2002, 37). In these second stories, "the kings were depicted as being committed to the accumulation of the Ten Perfections, or *barami,* in the same way as Gotama Buddha had done in his previous incarnations as a Bodhisatta. In performing meritorious deeds Thai kings were said to *phoem phrabarami, sang phrabarami,* or *bamphen barami*—all referring to the act of increasing their *barami,* or Perfections, in the hope of attaining enlightenment at some time in the future, and thereby delivering all living beings from suffering" (ibid., 52).

renunciation, wisdom, energy, patience, truthfulness, resolution, loving-kindness, and equanimity.[14] In the context of Thai political thought, people who have *barami* are defined by these characteristics.[15] They are generous and virtuous, detached and judicious, tireless and correct, caring and composed. First among them is the monarch, seen as the embodiment of the Bodhisatta, a Buddha-to-be on his way to enlightenment.[16] The very fact that the monarch was born in this privileged economic and political position is seen as proof of his merit in past lives and this merit justifies his role. Similarly, his moral charisma is responsible for the wellbeing of the reign for Buddhism as a whole, and the reign's prosperity confirms his *barami*. Seen from this light, *barami* is a circular and conservative conception of power, one that equates existing economic, moral, and political hierarchies and legitimizes them by claiming that "the "good" hold a position of power over others due to their superior *barami*."[17] Yet, *barami* is not exclusive to monarch. Commoners can also obtain *barami* over the course of their lives, whether as monks who excel in ascetic pursuits or as millenarian leaders who show command of the ten perfections. This second type of *barami* has played a central role in Siamese and Thai history and has been associated with the leaders of numerous peasant revolts against tyrannical rulers.[18]

Barami, therefore, can be the result of past lives and "karmic debt,"[19] as well as be built over one's lifetime. Similarly, it can both legitimize existing

14. Every Buddhist temple in Thailand has a large mural, normally hung over the entrance, which depicts the ten lives during which Buddha obtained each of these perfections.

15. The concept of *barami* has been historically absent in the work of western scholars of Thai politics, while it has featured extensively in the work of Thai analysts (Kobkua 1988; Likhit 1992; Nidhi 1986; Sirindhorn 1981; Yot 1990). It was Christine Gray's never published yet widely read 1986 dissertation that brought this concept to the attention of international observers (Gray 1986). Since then, a number of scholars have analyzed the concept in detail. In particular see Conner 1996; Jackson 2009; A. A. Johnson 2006, 2013; Jory 2002, 2016; Ockey 2004; Pattana 2006a; Sopranzetti 2014b; Veal 2013.

16. King Chulalongkorn (r. 1868–1910), preoccupied with resisting colonial expansion by showing how civilized Siam was, actively opposed this view. Nonetheless, since the 1970s, the late King Bhumibol over the course of his life cultivated this image of the Bodhisatta-king and based much of his legitimacy on the construction and preservation of his immense *barami*. For a detailed analysis of how this was done through Buddhist rituals, economic investments, and ideological propaganda, see Gray 1986, 1991; Jackson 2010; Veal 2013.

17. Jory 2016, 175. David Wilson, however, has proposed a less cynical reading of this dynamic, arguing that this does not mean that "might is right. It is rather a magico-religious view that right is might" (D. A. Wilson 1962, 74).

18. Ishii 1975; Ladwig 2014; Murdoch 1967; C. M. Wilson 1997.

19. Aulino 2016, 96.

hierarchies and support subversive projects. What defines it, however, are four main characteristics: first, *barami* derives from moral virtue in the form of the ten perfections; second, it is an intrinsic characteristic of the individuals who have it, not the result of a position they hold, and emanates outward from them; third, it does not strive to establish itself but is recognized by others as "byproduct of virtuous leadership;"[20] and forth, it can be accumulated and built (*sang barami*) through pious acts or through proximity or affiliation with a source of *barami,* or lost (*sia barami*) by failing to live up to the ten perfections, been seen as clinging to it, or failing to maintain a position of power. As a consequence, *barami* is never stable and people who have it walk a tightrope, high in the sky of virtue. They draw followings and orient people toward them but they need to be seen as doing so effortlessly. They distribute resources away but they cannot be perceived as doing it to ingratiate themselves with others.

Lerm read the political events unfolding around him and the association strategy through the lenses of *barami:* he understood Thaksin's defeat in his struggle to gain control over the state in 2006 in terms of his insufficient *barami* (*barami mai tung*), revealed by his lack of patience, bad temper, and imposing style; and similarly, he saw the AMTT's failures or successes in its struggle against people of influence as being determined by its *barami.* Building it, therefore, was central to weathering this moment and gaining more power. Political mobilizations and protests could have been a way for the association to attach itself to a source of virtuous power, acquire some of its *barami,* and use it to further social standing. Nonetheless, as the Red Shirts took issue with the ultimate source of such power and lost their high moral ground through violent confrontations, they became something to keep away from. This meant, in concrete terms, realigning the association toward the monarch—the ultimate source of *barami*—and the other actor that was emerging as the new center of power, the army. Lerm was himself the first to be affected by these readjustments. A vocal supporter of the ousted prime minister and the Red Shirts, he stopped wearing his vest with Thaksin's face and his long-sleeve AMTT jacket that Seh Daeng—the Red Shirts general who was shot by snipers on May 13—had autographed for him. In June of 2010, he also refashioned the office of the association. The pictures of a

20. Persons 2016, 33.

protest against the post-2006 coup constitution, which adorned the office, were taken down and replaced by images of the king and the queen.[21]

Although these changes became the object of numerous jokes among the members of the association, they showed a new approach emerging within it, at least under Lerm's leadership. The new closeness to the monarchy, from which *barami* is thought to emanate, however, was not enough to build *barami*. This process required the performance of moral and virtuous acts, such as participating religious rituals, expanding services to the urban community through increasing driver safety, helping victims of road accidents, and supporting the larger security apparatus. Joining the pineapple eyes campaign was, for Lerm, part of this process which also entailed reviving collaborations with local police to train drivers in first aid, crime, and fire prevention, taking part in public events sponsored by the military and the monarchy, as well as raising money among its members for donations to Buddhist temples.[22] Its main objective was to increase the drivers' presence at street corners and their visibility as moral actors who look after Thai society, even if this required the association to collaborate with their former enemies.

AMNĀT AND POPULAR SUPPORT: YAI

In November of 2010, uncomfortable with the association's growing closeness with the ISOC, I made a plan to sit down with Yai and tell him how I felt. I worked up the courage and drove to his house, imagining he would push back and protest my reading of the situation. "Do you think the ISOC's sudden interest in the motorcycle taxis had anything to do with the drivers' roles in the Red Shirts' protest? And if so, how can you ally with the people who killed Red Shirts supporters?" I asked. Yai looked at me and laughed in my face, surprised by my naivety. "It has everything to do with it," he replied. "Politics is a game. The ISOC is helping us for one reason and one reason only: because we went on the Red Shirts' stage. In fact, I wanted to go on stage precisely so that we could negotiate with the government and with the army. When they

21. For analyses of the use of images of the king in political protest, see Baker 2001; Herzfeld 2012, 2016b; Missingham 2002, 2003.

22. For extensive treatment of the cultural, economic, and political significance of donation and merit making in Thailand, see Aulino 2016; Bao 2005; Falk 2007; Gray 1986; Hanks 1962; Jackson 1989; Mulder 1973; Tannenbaum 1995; Terwiel 1994.

saw us, the leaders of the association standing there able to mobilize the drivers, they saw that we have *amnāt*. They wanted to cut popular strength from the protest and they knew we had the *amnāt* to do that, if we wanted to. Politics in Thailand is like this. In Thai we 'play' politics (*len kān mūang*), in English you do not 'play' politics, right? This is how it is: in Thailand, politics is a game, a game of sides and negotiations. And we can play it too."

The distance from Lerm's words could not be more striking. The president of the association relied on *barami* and moral virtue, Yai on *amnāt*, scheming, and effectiveness. *Amnāt* is most commonly translated as authority and it comes from the position one holds inside a formal structure and not from an intrinsic characteristic of his holder. *Amnāt* is much closer of the English term power: it comes from a position of authority, it is "raw amoral power that can be used for either good or evil,"[23] and it is purposeful and calculating. Differently from *barami, amnāt* does not need to appear effortless or magnanimous, it just needs to show effectiveness in making people do things, no matter if out of fear—in which case is seen as *amnāt* of the gun (*amnāt pūn*)—popular support (*amnāt prachāchon*), or a mix of the two. In this sense, *amnāt* operates in a different social order from *barami:* the latter is a religiously oriented power, the former a temporal one. As such, *amnāt* may garner great respect and admiration, fear and submission, but remains a limited resource, bounded by the confines of the position of authority that it is based on and "depleted through use."[24]

When Yai reflected back on the Red Shirts' protest, he saw their failure precisely in their indiscriminate use of *amnāt*, especially in the form of popular support. "They played the game until the end without any possibility of winning." Yai told me. "They consumed too much popular support, they asked the people to risk too much for them. It is acceptable for them because the movement will not be here in ten years but as the association of drivers we could not do the same. We need to play a longer game, we cannot take the side of Red Shirts completely unless we are sure they will win. We need to make sure we grow our popular support, not spend it." For Yai this meant first and foremost entering the game of politics.

The *amnāt* of the association came from its formal structure and the support of thousands of drivers around the city, but it also came from its recognition by other authorities inside the state apparatus. It mattered little if Yai own personal political sympathies were solidly with the Red Shirts. In this

23. Jackson 2010, 33.
24. Conner 1996, 216.

game Abhisit's government and the army were actors that could and should be courted, played one against the other, and never completely dismissed or disenfranchised, as long as that created stronger support for the association. The AMTT's declared neutrality was central to Yai's strategy which relied on the group's ability to play all the different forces involved using both negotiating skills and members' support. The ISOC's support for the drivers' fight against people of influence, obtained thought a show of support on the Red Shirts' stage, was an example of how Yai's game of *amnāt* operated.

Yai not only enjoyed playing this game, he was remarkably good at it. His extensive experience of street politics in Bangkok, first as a thug, then as vote canvasser, and finally as a political mobilizer and as the AMTT's vice-president taught him that power does not reside in charisma or moral virtue but in the ability to mobilize people, to control and direct popular support according to a complex game of alliances, negotiations, compromises, and switching sides. In this field, he applied the same meandering path-seeking approach that characterized the drivers' everyday life in the city. Their mobility through traffic was based on using information and skills to find a route across static traffic. Similarly, Yai's strategy advanced by navigating, negotiating, and adapting to the shifting political terrain, knowing its shortcuts and backalleys, and being able to see a path where others saw blockage. Much like their mobility through traffic, however, playing this game was not without risks.

"Politics is a lie: they talk first and act later. Things are said and agreed upon and then maybe carried out." Yai repeated frustrated. "We have to believe them first. If they keep their word, we picked the right ally. If not, we chose the wrong person. Politics is a lie, a game in which you cannot trust anyone at all." In this game of *amnāt,* every collaboration was laden with potential letdowns, both for the AMTT and for its new allies. The ISOC's plan to transform the drivers into pineapple eyes, for instance, was often ridiculed by the same drivers who were central to its realization. Yai himself liked to repeat that the pineapple eyes would not work because there was no pineapple to start with, no organized institution able to monitor the country, but rather a variety of actors, each with their own agenda, which would, in the long run, break apart and crumble again and again. Their instability and disunity, however, did not mean that collaborations could not bear fruits, quite the contrary. As Michael Herzfeld has shown, in fact, it is precisely the disunity of the nation-state that creates wide room for citizens' to maneuver.[25] That maneuverability, in turn, allows the state to

25. Herzfeld 2016a.

survive by constantly changing its shape. This seemed to be the case for the post-protest cooperation between the AMTT and the ISOC that, with all its potential fragilities and contradictions, was succeeding in granting the army a less violent response to the dispersal and the association a powerful ally in their struggle with people of influence.

THE RISK OF *ITTHIPHON*

By the end of 2011, it had become clear that the AMTT had accepted the army proposal. Lerm's office bore no trace of the Red Shirts movement, the steady flow of cash that the new alliance guaranteed better furniture and a larger space, and prominent army and police personnel were on the president's telephone contacts. Nonetheless, the memberships lagged and the association struggled to grow. Whether the result of building *barami* or of a well-played game of *amnāt,* the decision to collaborate with the ISOC was disenfranchising some of the members and making other drivers suspicious. "I understand this is the only way we can fight," Tong, a member of the AMTT, told me when we met at his station. "When Thaksin was here we could report officers to him and he would take care of it using the law. But now we are alone so we need to use connections. We have only one way: fighting influence with influence. But I don't like this game. I am legal, I pay taxes, I own my vest, and I have registered my bike for public transportation, so why do I have to ask for help from an important person? Why can't I just use the law? Now we depend on Sun. He is better than the people of influence but this is not that different, we are just under a new influence. But this is Thailand." He concluded, disheartened.

Tong despised both Lerm's approach, based on *barami,* and Yai's, based on *amnāt.* He saw both of them as supporting the growing influence of the army over life in the street and believed they should be abandoned as soon as possible. On the one side, Lerm's approach never questioned the idea that power is located in one center and emanates from there. His approach may have disputed which one the legitimate center was—a popular movement or a bureaucratic institution—but never challenged the structural relations between centers and periphery that necessarily create a system of exclusion and inequality. On the other, Yai's strategy may have seen hierarchical relations as intrinsically shifting and unstable, bounded by the ability of whoever occupies a position of authority to obtain results whether through popular support or sheer force. Yet, because of its amoral characteristics, his game always ran the risk of turning formalized authority into a form of influence (*itthiphon*) driven by personal interest, not dissimilar from the one waged by state officials over the drivers. Frustrated with the way the AMTT was going and seeing its relationship with the army grow closer, Tong left the group. "We got together to fight people of influence and to fight the system of influence; we struggled against the people who use their *amnāt* to exert influence over our life and we have become the same as them, we use *itthiphon* for our benefits." he voiced after leaving the association, remarking that the collaboration with the military that ran the risk of corrupting and undoing years of drivers' struggles.[26]

The accusation that Tong was raising is one that people with *amnāt* or *barami* always fear: that of being seen as nothing more than a person of influence, using their *itthiphon* to further their own interest. *Itthiphon*, in fact, is a kind of power that is used to gain personal profit and "can be rooted in socioeconomic force (money), physical force (ability to gain compliance by physical coercion), or psychological force (the threat of using one or both of the former)."[27] If *barami* is moral in nature and *amnāt* is amoral, *itthiphon* is immoral. Nonetheless it has something in common with both conceptualization of power. On the one side, *itthiphon* like *barami* is self-referential: it resides in the person who holds it and justifies itself, without needing to rely on a formal structure for its legitimacy, as *amnāt* does. On the other, like *amnāt*, *itthiphon* is defined by its effectiveness and not questioned for its methods, as *barami* can be. In other words, both *barami* and *amnāt* can be dismissed as sheer *itthiphon,* as Tong was doing with the association of motorcycle taxis and many have done with leaders of opposing factions in the larger political landscape of Thailand.

AMNĀT, BARAMI, AND THE STRUGGLE OVER THE THAI STATE

The two theories of power—as *barami* and as *amnāt*—not only coexisted inside the AMTT at the end of 2010. Indeed, the tensions and contradictions

26. Somchai Phatharathananunth has analyzed extensively the historical role of state forces in proposing these kinds of collaborations with social movements and labor organization as a means of depoliticizing their actions (Somchai 2006).

27. Persons 2016, 137.

between the two social structures they invoked—understood as "a set of ideas about the distribution of power between persons and groups of persons,"[28] and about concrete forms of bringing people to action and governing the nation—cut through the very fabric of Thai society and sat at the core of the political conflict that had been unfolding in the previous decades.[29]

Up until the early 2000s, the equilibrium between these two legitimizing principles revolved around King Bhumibol and his ability to present himself both as the center and ultimate source of *barami,* but also as the holder of *amnāt,* in the form of "super-mandate from the people, one that trumped the electoral mandates of political leaders."[30] This double power had been central to the king's ability to act as a power broker in the political crisis of the 1970s and 1990s and ferry the nation out of them. When Thaksin Shinawatra was elected prime minister in 2001, he managed to mobilize both *barami* and *amnāt,* pairing his unprecedented popular support with the approval of the palace and proximity to other public figures seen as holding *barami.* Nonetheless, during the course of his premiership, Thaksin's authoritarian attitude, disposition to rage, and use of violence in the War on Drugs and the southern conflict resulted in a deterioration of his *barami* (*sia barami*). Moreover, his decisiveness and purposeful attack against state forces took away from him any illusion of *barami,* as Lerm himself recognized. Thaksin was left only with *amnāt,* yet his popular power continued to grow, even without *barami.*[31] When Thaksin was reelected prime minister in 2005 with an unprecedented majority, the supremacy of the king's popular mandate came into question. This shift threatened bureaucratic, military, and monarchic forces and they began to worry that his authority may allow Thaksin to put them under his control. This was unacceptable to the forces he tried to

28. Leach 1954, 4.

29. These two social structures, one based on the idea that power should operate and reside with the holders of *barami* and the other on the idea that power resides in *'amnāt* and the ability to mobilize masses, should be understood as ideal models or, as Leach would have said, "as *if* descriptions [which] relate to ideal models rather than real societies" (Leach 1954, 6).

30. McCargo 2005, 505. Christine Gray in her dissertation reports a conversation with an informant who told her: "the king is like a *thewada* [angel] because he succeeded from *thewada,* from a pure race of men of pure blood. He is not like ordinary people because he has power, *barami* and *amnāt* that common people do not have" (Gray 1986, 152).

31. Sulak Sivaraksa—one of the people seen as having *barami*—criticized Thaksin's arrogance and foolishness. Thaksin, he said, "used his money and [amoral] power, but didn't realize the palace is more subtle than that, and has a lot of quiet power" (McGeown 2006).

control, not only politically and economically as I showed before, but also conceptually.

According to them society should be organized by a moral hierarchy which sees the king at the top as the Buddha-to-be. Right below are the aristocrats, bureaucratic and military leaders, and the commercial elites. Then come the middle class and, finally, urban workers and peasants, including the drivers, at the bottom. In this worldview, Thaksin's call for democratic representation and consideration of people like the drivers as same level citizens was "anathema, since in democracy commoners were equal to Bodhisatta-kings—in fact, they could be superior if they were able to organize themselves into political parties and win power [as they did under Thaksin]. This ... would mean literally the triumph of evil (those of low merit) over good (those of high merit)."[32] Faced with this prospective those forces—as the late Pattana Kitiarsa, whom I quote at length, perceptively analyzed—

> turned to Buddhist morality and principles to justify why people like Thaksin and his infamous "Thaksinomics" (*rabop thaksin*) must be terminated at all costs. Thaksin represented an "amoral capitalist leader/agent," whose five-year regime had abused the country's democracy, corrupted and divided the nation, and been unpatriotic. In this respect, Thaksin had been "dehumanized" as "Mara" (Buddhist personification of evil) and prominently displayed as such in the media. He was often compared to some great demons destructive to both Buddhism and the monarchy.... Thaksin's deep crisis of legitimacy, despite having full control of power, reflects the fact that he had failed miserably to convert his power into the Buddhist ideal of moral and political authority.... The bottom line is that Thaksin has not yet achieved his righteous status in the Buddhist ideal of leadership despite his large-scale state-funded vote-buying. The power which Thaksin possessed was still *amnāt kanmuang* [political] rather than *bun barami* [merit-based].[33]

To use Lerm's words, Thaksin's *barami* was not sufficient to win the war in which he had embarked and the 2006 coup was the result of this weakness.

Since the coup, however, nobody has been able to emerge as both the holder of *amnāt* and *barami,* partly because the two conceptions of power that remain interlinked in Thai political thought started to move apart in the minds of many citizens. A majority of the population, those who voted for Thaksin and supported the Red Shirts, began to argue that, no matter the supposed morality of a leader, he or she should be allowed to govern having

32. Jory 2016, 185.
33. Pattana 2006a, 2–4.

won the majority's electoral support. On the other side, a significant portion of the remaining population took an opposite view and was willing to sacrifice one-person-one-vote electoralism on the altar of moral governance. This process surely was connected to Bhumibol's weakening health, the growing anxiety over the upcoming reign of his son, the palace's uncharacteristic choice to show what side they supported after the 2006 coup, and the heavy-handed use of *lèse-majesté* law to silence questions about the palace's role in politics. At the same time, Thaksin's policies, their effects on a large section of the population, the desires that they unleashed, and their dismissive repression after the 2006 coup played a central role in revealing the effectiveness and usefulness of a model of power based on popular representation rather than on moral hierarchy.

Following this narrative, many political scientists and commentators have interpreted the last ten years of conflict as the painful, yet ultimately destined to succeed, march of a "younger, weaker yet sturdy liberal-egalitarian tradition anchoring state authority in constitutional principles, democratic ideals of popular sovereignty, and pluralist discourse among equal citizens [against] the traditional vision of a paternal state with monarchy and traditional elites heading a stratified hierarchical social order."[34] These linear narratives of an opposition between a traditional and paternalistic mode of governance on one side and a modern and egalitarian one on the other, however, were part of the political arsenal used by the two sides in the conflict, rather than actual representations of how the struggle was unfolding.

Another interpretation of this struggle has been to replace the linear narrative with an analysis of pulsation between *amnāt* and *barami*.[35] In this view, echoed in the anthropological studies of Thailand and Southeast Asia at large, political systems in the area tend to oscillate or pulsate between poles, defined by egalitarianism and hierarchy.[36] This description, however, hardly resonates with Yai's and Lerm's words or with the recent history of

34. Dressel 2010, 463. For parallel versions of this argument see Ferrara 2015; Nelson 2012; M. R. Thompson 2007.

35. I am here purposefully adopting the language of Edmund Leach and Stanley Tambiah, the two main proponents of the kind of analysis I refer to (Leach 1954; Tambiah 1976).

36. Embree and Evers 1969; Gray 1986; Hanks 1962; Tambiah 1976. I myself have previously analyzed the conflict along those lines (Sopranzetti 2014b). The works of Felicity Aulino and Andrew Johnson have provided two remarkable exceptions to this trend, both of which were central in helping me realize my own previous mistake in accepting this depiction of egalitarian and hierarchical tendencies (Aulino 2012, 2016; A. A. Johnson 2014).

Thailand. In them, there is no opposition between hierarchical *barami* and egalitarian *amnāt*. The AMTT's decisions, the conflict between Red and Yellow Shirts, and the struggle between Thaksin and other state forces over state control demonstrate that both conceptions of power imply a hierarchical structure and a pseudo-authoritarian leadership. They are not exactly the same, as the first one legitimizes itself through a claim to otherworldly morality, offering no transparency, while the second needs an external social structure on which to base its actions, whether through popular support or sheer force. Yet presenting *barami* as hierarchical and *amnāt* as egalitarian runs the risk of blinding us and transforming a brutal authoritarian leader like Thaksin, who caused the killing of thousands of people with his War on Drugs and his disastrous management of the conflict in Southern Thailand, into a hero of participation and democracy.

We are not facing a binary,[37] but rather the unresolved tensions and failed attempts to combine two conceptualizations of power that need to coexist, even with their contradicting features. To govern Thailand one needs to have both *amnāt* and *barami,* to claim moral charisma and exert institutional power, juggling both of them always with the risk of being dismissed as *itthiphon,* as Tong did with the association.[38] Since 2006 no political figure has been able to do so.

It would be easy, and cleaner, to take one side or the other, and fill it with all our best aspirations and desires, or look at the present moment as a flick of the tail of a dying older form of power, as many have done both in the country and outside. In my case, it would be convenient to celebrate the democratic nature of Yai's approach and condemn the regressive features of Lerm's. This would be, however, untrue to the experiences of the motorcycle taxi drivers or the Red Shirts I encountered. If there is any side for me to take, it is that of Wud and Tong, who have left the association but keep thinking

37. Michael Herzfeld, in his study of a small slum community in Bangkok, has been one of the few people who have notice this dynamic. In his work he argues that "the oscillation between binary poles does not itself favor a static binarism in political reality; rather, it creates a kaleidoscopic range of possibilities, none of which—attempts to stabilize them bureaucratically or by military force notwithstanding—can be denied in perpetuity (Herzfeld 2016b, 24). Nonetheless, his analysis has only limited itself to *amnāt,* ignoring the centrality of *barami.*

38. For a longer historical treatment of the two conceptions and their relation to political change in twentieth century Thailand, see Baker and Pasuk 2005; Dressel 2010; Gray 1986, 1991; Stent 2010. For an analysis of how the equilibrium was managed by different leaders in modern Thai history see Sopranzetti forthcoming-a.

whether to go back and become more involved; of Adun and Hong, who keep moving between Bangkok and their villages, never completely feeling fully at home in either; of Yai and Lerm, who continue to collaborate while trying to combine their conflicting ideas and use this struggle to propel the activities of the AMTT toward a safer life for its members. My allegiance falls on the side of the book's protagonists: people who zigzag through life striving to survive, to create something better for their children, and to have their demands satisfied, all while being pulled by the irreconcilable tensions between the shifting logics of capital, the concrete reality of their everyday lives, and the aspirational desires of their political struggles.

Epilogue

ON MAY 20, 2014, on the fourth anniversary of the Red Shirts' dispersal, the Royal Thai Army imposed martial law. Allegedly, the military intervened to put an end to seven months of political turmoil that had begun with the creation, on November 29, 2013, of the anti-Thaksin People's Democratic Reform Committee (PDRC)—an organization composed of former elements of the Yellow Shirts, supporters of Abhisit's Democrat Party, and members of the Network of Students and Citizens for Reforms. The organization was led by Suthep Thaugsuban, the former director of CRES who had ordered the April 10 violent attack on the Red Shirts protesters.

The military intervention came as a surprise to most observers.[1] The 2011 election, a result of the the Red Shirts' mobilization, had seen the victory of Yingluck Shinawatra, Thaksin's sister. Once in power, Yingluck had struck an agreement with the military, bureaucratic, and monarchic forces with which her brother had fought. She continued his popular policies but adopted a less imposing and authoritarian leadership style, leaving those other state forces undisturbed to manage their share of power. Furthermore, the threat of another Red Shirts uprising seemed to have dispelled the possibility of another military takeover. This period of peace, however, ended in November 2013. Halfway through her term, Yingluck proposed an ill-conceived amnesty bill that would give immunity to everyone who had been accused of political crimes since the 2006 coup. Seeing this as an attempt to bring Thaksin back to Thailand, those forces jumped to attention, terrified by the prospect of his return. The PDRC was created in a matter of days. Its supporters took to the streets, shutting down a major intersection in Bangkok, a tactic that the Red Shirts had championed

---

1. Hewison 2014.

three years before. They demanded the ouster of elected Prime Minister Yingluck Shinawatra, the complete dismissal of the Thaksin system—a network that according to the PDRC had dominated electoral politics in the previous thirteen years through corruption and vote buying—and the implementation of radical constitutional reforms before a new vote. This time the army remained in their barracks and let the protesters shut down the city.

On December 6, 2013, in response to these protests and the refusal of bureaucratic and military forces to end the protest, Yingluck dissolved parliament. As her brother had done before the 2006 coup, she called for snap elections, hoping they would confirm her popular support and quiet down the protests. The opposition Democrat Party and the PDRC's supporters decided to boycott the polls. Amid disruptions and violence Yingluck won the elections. However, as had happened after her brother's third reelection in 2006, the Constitutional Court nullified the vote and the country remained without an elected government. Prayuth Chan-Ocha, the general who had directed the violent attack on the Red Shirts protesters in April 2010, declared martial law.[2] The following day he invited representatives from the two main political parties and two social movements that had taken the streets under his watch—the Red Shirts and the PDRC—to sit at the negotiation table and resolve their disagreements. Prayuth's patience, however, was short-lived. On the second day of talks, dissatisfied with the way things were going, he stood up and calmly declared, "I am sorry. I must seize power." Many in the room thought he was joking. His words, however, turned out to be a blunt statement of his intentions.

Prayuth staged the twelfth successful military coup in Thailand since the formal end of absolute monarchy in 1932 and took everybody in the room into custody. Two months before, the army commander in chief had denied rumors about an impending coup, calling it an obsolete strategy, unfit for a modern country. He had now changed his mind and plunged the country back into a military dictatorship. Even though they shared the same prison cells, the representatives from the PDRC and Democrat Party rejoiced in the decision while Yingluck's party and the Red Shirts' members denounced the umpteenth military hijacking of the country's democratic process, the second in a decade to remove a Shinawatra from office.

At first, the coup looked like the same tired script that had played out in the 2006 coup. Many assumed it would entail a short-lived military junta

2. Sopranzetti 2014a.

followed by the appointment of an interim government run by either a general or a highly respected figure. The next step would be a new constitution giving more power to independent institutions that would operate as checks and balances and limit the power of elected governments. Finally, elections would be held in a year or so. Following this script, the discussion could quickly move to consider who the interim prime minister would be, what the next constitution might look like, and, behind closed doors, what the role of the monarchy had been in this coup and how this new phase would affect the looming royal succession. The sensation of déjà vu, however, was short-lived.[3] Soon after the coup, it became clear that Prayuth was determined to make a bid for power. If the military, bureaucratic, and monarchic forces had, since Thaksin's rise in popularity, acted as an ensemble, now the army seemed to take the lead in an attempt to take control over the state.[4] Heavy repression, centralization of power, royal silence, restructuring of the relationship between the rule of law and military actions, and Prayuth's appointment as prime minister revealed his determination to subdue other state forces. More than three years after the coup, Prayuth remained in power and was carrying out a deep reform of political and social institutions, a structured attempt to remake a Thai polity that had crystalized into a new constitution enshrining military control over both elected governments and bureaucratic forces.[5]

Life under Prayuth, as under any dictatorship, is divided and often contradictory. On the one hand, it goes on normally. Shopping malls and restaurants are crowded and streets filled with the usual frenzy of vendors and office workers. On the other, people involved in direct actions and critical activities are watched, controlled, and silenced. In these circles, the dominant feeling is one of being inside a perimeter that is slowly closing in around them, while the rest of the society quietly pretends not to see it. The mix of fear and paranoia is not unwarranted. Since this coup, Thailand has gone back to a level of repression and control that had been forgotten since the 1970s. By September 2016 the regime had summoned more than 1,000 people and arrested 561 of them. Two hundred seventy eight people had been tried in military court—which entails being judged without the right to

3. Aulino et al. 2014; McCargo 2014.
4. The alignment of these forces was in fact a recent phenomenon, and since the 1932 abolition of the absolute monarchy their reciprocal weight and power has been shifting and rebalancing. For a treatment of their unstable alliances see Chambers 2008; Chambers and Waitoolkiat 2016; Connors 2007; Ferrara 2015; Gray 1991.
5. For an extensive treatment of the contours of this attempt, see Sopranzetti 2016.

appeal by a jury composed of three soldiers, only one of whom needs to be trained in law.

Hundreds of local political organizers, popular radio hosts, journalists, academics, and activists have left the country for fear of arrest and other forms of repression. The most prominent have made their way to Europe, the United States, Australia, or Japan. Many others, who are less visible and therefore more at risk, have crossed into Laos or Cambodia and are regrouping there, under the threat of becoming victims of extradition agreements between local governments and the Thai junta. Inside the country, any form of criticism has been systematically and harshly persecuted and punished. Political activities are banned and media heavily censored or shut down if they refuse to comply with the junta's orders. At the time of this writing, Thailand had more blocked websites than China and people had been prosecuted for critical Facebook postings and chatroom discussions. Military personnel regularly stop and prevent debates in universities, journalists' clubs, and bookstores, and so far they have charged fifty-eight people for sedition, a crime that carries a punishment of up to seven years in jail. Two years after the 2006 coup, large protests of the newly formed Red Shirts movement were taking place around the country and motorcycle taxi drivers were expanding their roles in street politics. This time minimal resistance has emerged to the coup and most of the drivers keep a low profile and continue to ferry their customers around the city, murmuring their discontent with the new dictatorship only in private.

Adun has aged considerably in the past years but has not lost his infective smile. His wrinkles have transformed into deeper cuts and his belly has swollen. He still works as a driver and still goes back and forth between Bangkok and his village. In 2011 he finally built the cement wall around his parent's house and in 2014 he invested most of his remaining savings in a few acres of land outside his village, on which he started a small sugarcane farm. His first harvests were meager, but he hopes the next will be better. He still dreams of leaving Bangkok and returning permanently to the village. His older daughter, Nam, has not managed to move to Bangkok. She got into nursing school in Loei, her mother's native district capital. Yet, whenever she is on holiday, she goes down to Bangkok to visit him. Adun loves to have her around but fears that one day she will want to stay and he will not have much to offer. His younger daughter has taken her sister's place in front of the television and she also begun to say she wants to move to Bangkok when she grows up. Gai, Adun's wife, is still back in the village but, as their children become older and more autonomous, she is getting increasingly bored, and she would not mind moving back to Bangkok herself. Since the 2014 coup, Adun has not taken part in any of the small protests that have been organized around Bangkok. He continues to believe that Prayuth should step down and that a government chosen by the majority of people is the best form of organization for the country. Nevertheless, he thinks it would be too dangerous to get involved in protest at this moment.

Hong is less and less often at his motorcycle taxi station. His younger sister has married a Frenchman and together they opened a small go-go bar in Bangkok's seedier prostitution street. Hong started to work as a delivery man there in 2013. In a few months, his role in the bar expanded to managing the food and alcohol supply, to making sure no one bothered the sex workers. At first he went to the bar after a day of work at his corner. Fairly quickly, he started hanging out at the bar after closing time, sleeping during the day and spending less time at his station. Hong keeps his vest and occasionally during his free hours picks up clients to make some extra pocket money. Last time I saw him, in mid-2017, he looked sleeker, better dressed, but with the visible signs of his new life. Some of his friends in the city are worried about him and think he has started hanging out with the wrong group of people and possibly picking up a few of their vices. Whether this is true or not, his new life has distanced Hong from politics. "They are all the same," he told me as we sat outside his sister's bar. "Red Shirts, Yellow Shirts, Thaksin, the Army . . . at the end of the day they all cared about themselves, they take care of their own interests, they use us, kill us or get us killed and then, when things get bad, they are nowhere to be seen. That's enough for me." And that was it about politics.

Boon is gone, nowhere to be found. After the 2010 protest, he became a member of the AMTT but, as the association built closer connections to the army, he did not renew his membership and stopped picking up their calls. I last saw him a few weeks after the 2014 coup. We met at a small protest that took place at Victory Monument, the major roundabout in northern Bangkok where in 2009 the Red Shirts had begun a season of massive street protest. This time there were fewer than two hundred people, surrounded by an equal number of police and army officers. Boon was frustrated and demoralized and left the protest after less than half an hour. Since then, he has changed his number and I have not been able to track him down. I hope he is still riding his bike, feeling invincible, and voicing his discontent, as he always did. Once in a while I try searching for his full name on Facebook, which has since become largely available to the drivers, hoping to find him.

But, for a man who refused to register and get a free vest during Thaksin's formalization and who remained until the end in Ratchaprasong risking his life for his convictions, I am doubtful he will ever voluntarily provide his information and whereabouts to an American company.

Lerm is still the president of the drivers' association and the face of its new direction since the Red Shirts' dispersal. With support from the ISOC and Honda, the AMTT has moved its office to a large one-floor building in the outskirts of Bangkok. Lerm is better dressed than ever before, he drives a bigger car, and lives in a small apartment above the new office. He continues to own a vest but rarely picks up clients, buried under the association's administrative load. Since the 2014 coup, contrary to Yai's opinion, the association has become a credit union. This brought a lot more money into its coffers and raised its membership numbers but, according to many drivers, transformed the AMTT into a guild that takes care of its members, rather than an organization struggling to take care of motorcycle taxi drivers in general. Since then, Lerm has become a fairly public figure, often seen with high-ranking military officers, police generals, and local businessmen, always sitting in the first row at public events regarding road safety, making the city clean, and cash-saving programs. Lerm's popularity came to its peak in mid-2016 when the association, in collaboration with the military junta, launched a phone app called GO BIKE, a sort of state-sponsored Uber for motorcycle taxis. Since then, Lerm is regularly on TV, sponsoring and showing the association's involvement in an app that is struggling to obtain the same success as its model. In private conversations, Lerm still says that he supports democracy and misses Thaksin. Yet he continues to believe that drivers need to build up their power in the form of *barami* (moral charisma) in order to gain recognition and advantages. *Barami* works by proximity to the center of power, and so Lerm and the association are now oriented toward the military dictator who holds it.

Yai is formally still a member of the association but he left any official role due to his difference of views with Lerm and his brother's poor health. Lek got terribly sick at the beginning of 2013, as PDRC protesters took the street. When I saw him in the summer of 2015, he had lost a lot of weight and his legs were swollen, making walking very painful. His brain had started to go, transforming a man who had been the glue holding together the meetings at the association into a ghost of himself. Lek, once a soft-spoken man, had become prone to frequent bursts of rage which were partly to do with the fact that he spent most of his days outside his house in the heat on a portable bed.

Lek and Yai, sitting one next to another, looked like a living testament of the theory of parallel universes. One was drying up as his disease advanced, the other swelled in his frustration with the present situation. In September 2016, Lek passed away, after two years of agony.

Between Lek's disease and the military coup, Yai's life has radically changed. Once a man who stood in front of a crowd of hundreds of thousands people who cheered his participation in the Red Shirts movement, only five years later Yai was bitter, aloof, almost depressed. He had, to use his own words, lost his strength. Without Lek pulling his economic weight in the house, both of their families had to leave their home and downgrade to a smaller shack in the same alley where they used to live. In late 2014, Yai was slowly rotting away at his street corner, eaten up by remorse and doubts. Seeing him was painful. Over the course of my previous fieldwork, Yai had always been a force of nature, a relentless organizer, and a forceful motivator for the other drivers. This time, he seemed beaten, wounded to the core. "They fooled us," he told me, referring to the leaders of the Red Shirts, as he carefully dropped some water in Lek's mouth. "People fought, they were wounded and died. How many people died? How many people were injured? Once the military took power, they went silent. What kind of leadership is this? They bury their head in the sand. Good, let's bury them. They talk first and do later. We cannot trust them anymore. But what do we do from here?"

Seeing Yai haunted by these questions forced me to look back and rethink my own work. Some questions in particular kept me up at night: How could state power be so fragile and open to challenges in 2010 and yet seemingly so sturdy and unchallenged today? How could Yai, Lek, Lerm, Oboto, Adun, Hong, and Boon have risked their livelihoods and lives in the streets of Bangkok to demand justice and recognition then, and now sit quietly at their street corners wrapped in new vests given to them by a military dictator? Had the Red Shirts just been a fluke? Had I just been fooled, like Yai, by their rhetoric?

These questions preyed upon me, especially as similar dynamics unfolded in a variety of settings around the world. Egypt had passed from the most inspiring political mobilization of our generation to a regime more repressive than its predecessor. The revolt in Syria spiraled into a disaster, now with two tyrants dividing up the country's territory rather than one. Street protests in Brazil, rather than obtaining a fairer government, had unwillingly paved the way for a takeover by the conservative Michel Temer. As these saddening events unfolded, I was reminded of Hunter Thompson writing in 1971 on the political and cultural mobilization of the 1960s. "Every now and then the energy of a whole generation," he wrote, comes to a head in a long fine flash, for reasons that nobody really understands at the time—and which never explain, in retrospect, what actually happened. . . . There was a fantastic universal sense that whatever we were doing was right, that we were winning. . . . And that, I think, was the handle—that sense of inevitable victory over the forces of Old and Evil. . . . We had all the momentum; we were riding the crest of a high and beautiful wave. . . . Now, less than five years later, you can go up on a steep hill in Las Vegas and look West, and with the right kind of eyes you can almost see the high-water mark—that place where the wave finally broke and rolled back."[6]

Looking back it seemed as though my fieldwork had coincided with the Red Shirts' experience of that sense of inevitable victory, even in the midst of the army's violent dispersal and all the lost lives. Between 2009 and 2011, millions of people rode that wave with the conviction that, no matter what the other state forces would do, their electoral power was destined to win. And now, with a military prime minister entrenching his control over the state largely unopposed, the sea sat still, not a ripple in sight. In hindsight, the graffiti on the wall outside Central World in September 2010 was the high-water mark, a moment in which thousands of people with *tā sawāng* (blazing eyes) simply did not care about the decades of jail time and enormous social repression they faced to vocalize their disillusionment with the Thai monarchy. After that, however, the wave broke and began to roll back, filling on its way the fault lines that the Red Shirts had revealed.

Since the 2014 coup, the junta has been quite systematic in closing those cracks. First they began by blocking political mobilizers. Yai was among them. In the summer of 2015 he told me: "Claudio, these military are here to stay. They understand our weaknesses and they are using them. We are fighters, you have seen that too. They attacked us with tanks and we remained in the streets. We were ready to fight, but we have families. If they attack us, we fight back. But now it is our wives who ask us to stop protesting, it is our kids who are scared for their fathers. Things are changing, now your loved ones are the army's best allies. It is easy to tell the army to fuck off, but to tell your wife that, to tell your kids that, it is really hard."

Since the coup, his family, like those of thousands of other activists, has become the target of unprecedented pressure from the army. His house has been raided multiple times, always when only his wife was inside. A small

6. H. S. Thompson 1971, 68.

group of soldiers has time and again visited his son's kindergarten, asked his teachers' about him and his family, and lingered outside the school as the students are let out. Through these tactics of intimidation directed toward families more than the activists themselves, the junta married, as totalitarian regimes always do, affect and domination, specifically love and repression. The new regime has transformed the activists' families into allies, agents who beg mobilizers to stop protesting and organizing, out of love. Through this move, the junta is transforming dissenters' political actions into a struggle with their loved ones, as much as a struggle with the army.

This is just one of the ways in which the regime started to fill the cracks that emerged in 2010. For people like Yai, both political organizers and motorcycle taxis, the closure came also from another direction. Less than a month after the coup, General Prayuth, having experienced firsthand the subversive potential of motorcycle taxis' invisibility when he directed the army dispersal in 2010, launched another campaign to register them. Once again Yai, with his usual sharpness, pointed out the contradicting tensions involved in this operation. Continuing the previous conversation he said: "They are now registering motorcycle taxis, recording our names, giving us cards so we will all be catalogued and controlled. In a way this is good for us, it will help formalize our operations and it gives the drivers a sense of security, your name on the vest. But we know very well they are doing it only to control us."

In June 2014, military officers started to visit motorcycle taxi groups around Bangkok, and to lecture them about passenger security and their alleged plan to remove people of influence from the drivers' operations. Soon after, they demanded that drivers register with their local municipality office and get a new vest with a visible name and picture. Those who refused were heavily fined, and their driver's licenses were revoked. Adun was one of them. Aware that the junta's actions were aimed at taking control over the drivers, he quietly refused to register. For the first seven months after the new vests were distributed, he managed to continue ferrying customers. By the end of the summer of 2016, he had accumulated so many fines that working as a driver made him lose money. Frustrated, he put down his name and entered the state's archives.

Finally, Prayuth used *lèse-majesté* law with unprecedented frequency to attack political opponents. Since the coup, at least eighty-six people have been charged while, before the coup, only five people were in jail convicted on these charges and five more were awaiting trial.[7] Similarly, the actions that

7. ILaw 2016.

count as criticism of the royal institution and the length of the resulting sentences have been expanded widely to include a sixty-year sentence for six Facebook postings and one of twenty-seven years for "liking" a post mocking the king's dog. The situation would be farcical, if it were not so tragic for the people who are rotting in jail since the coup.

If the drivers' complex management of mobility and visibility during the 2010 protest had showed the fragilities of state forces' power and the political possibilities that emerge in its cracks and fault lines, the military takeover was now revealing the mechanisms through which the Prayuth proceeded to fix those factures by persecuting families of activists, registering motorcycle taxis, and punishing anybody who challenges royalist hegemony. When seen through this lens, the last fifteen years of Thai history have been a struggle between different state forces and factions of its population for the control of the state apparatus, its legitimizing principles, its political economic relations, and its policies: a contingent and unresolved struggle in which every action, taken by either state forces or by other political actors, tries, and always fails, to impose a new order, and, in so doing, creates the conditions for its unmaking. In this sense, the acts of maintenance that Prayuth is performing since 2014, however successful they may seem, are never complete, as Yai reassured me at the end of the summer of 2016. Just before leaving Bangkok, I visited him once again. This time, he looked calmer and his words seemed to come from a scar rather than an open wound. "You don't have to be in a rush when you struggle." He said "Now we wait, we wait until they do something that gets people upset; we wait until they destroy the economy. They are soldiers, they know how to use tanks and to arrest people, they don't know shit about running a country. We wait and they will show their weakness and then, once they do, we will fight again."

Yai's words not only made me hopeful about the future of Thailand, they also remind me of what the drivers had demonstrated in 2010: that whichever form power takes under the current dictatorship, new fault lines will emerge and new fragilities will be revealed. As with all the attempts to impose order that I have analyzed in this book, Prayuth's dictatorship will be revealed as a doomed enterprise, unable to fully dominate its territory and its subjects, and traversed with tensions, contingencies, and fault lines. As state agents try to close them, they will create new ones. Sometimes the cracks simply become too big to be ignored and alternative possibilities emerge. Other times, as is currently happening in Thailand, state forces are able to keep up an appearance of complete control and unity, even as new fractures emerge. In this sense, the weaknesses that Yai refers to are not failures of power but rather one of its defining features which need to be constantly controlled and maintained. After all, much of what state forces occupy their days with is this work of maintenance, through policing, law making, and consensus building. Most of the time—as when a driver refuses to wear the new army vest or when a family takes down the picture of the king from their living room walls—the cracks that emerge are mundane and easily cemented back or simply ignored. Occasionally, they become systemic and may undermine state power, as was the case in 2010, or foment a violent resurgence, as is currently happening in Thailand.

This does not mean that a teleology will direct the future of the country and that these tensions will be necessarily resolved. On the contrary, as I have shown throughout this book, the next phase will be the result of specific political and economic actions, of their unintended consequences, and of their interactions with the traces left behind by previous processes. And it will, in turn, create new unresolved tensions. The Red Shirts' mobilization in 2010, even if it seems to have been swallowed by the 2014 coup, left significant traces in the drivers and people around them. Beyond any political organization, beyond any form of representation or political party, beyond any specific relation between state and citizens, the period I witnessed left them with a new sense of possibility, individual as well as collective. Any speculation on what forms this will take in the future is risible. Some of the events which will determine its configuration may be already in motion, activated simply by the flow of life. On October 13, 2016, for instance, King Bhumibol died, after sixty-six years on the throne, and was succeeded by his son, a scarcely respected yet largely feared womanizer. What this will mean for the country, for the decades-long struggle between elected politicians, military, bureaucratic, and monarchic forces, and for the drivers is too early to say. We have, as Yai suggested, only to wait until new weak spots emerge. Nonetheless, as I came back from my latest visit to Thailand three years after the coup, one thing is clear: no coup, no repression, and no constitutional reform can erase the feeling of possibility that exists in the drivers, precisely because it does not take place in the streets or in Parliament but in small conversations while fishing, in the waiting times at a motorcycle taxi stand, sitting cross-legged around a meal in a village, or lying down at night, staring at the ceiling of a cramped room in Bangkok, unable to sleep.

Postscriptum

THERE IS NO RESOLUTION FOR THE TENSIONS that the protagonists of this book experience and navigate. Like any other form of travel, their lives on the move entail taking risks and continuously devising tactics to make sense and make do with whatever the road presents. In the previous pages, I have attempted to explore the landscape in which they move, the challenges it raises, and the paths that the drivers adopt, re-create, and invent. In particular I showed how their lives are dominated by a Hamlet-like struggle to reconcile the logics of post-Fordist capitalism that pushed them toward more precarious work, their meandering mobility both in Bangkok and between the city and their villages, and their political aspirations, demands, and horizons. In this position, I have argued, the drivers not only create and sustain the channels that keep the city together but also retained the potential to filter, slow down, and—at times—take control over urban flows, as they did during the 2010 Red Shirts' protest. Their political mobilization revealed mobility both as a characteristic of contemporary capitalism and as one of its fragile spots, always prone to disruption by the people who sustain channels of economic, social, and conceptual exchange yet remain excluded from the benefits of this work. By exploiting this apparent contradiction, the drivers exposed the fragility of state power and its openness to challenges by pointed collective actions; challenges that state forces rushed to control and limit. While those forces cast a ghostly shadow, with their power seemingly extending over everything, they are never able to cover and control their subjects fully. Wherever that power does not reach, it reveals its cracks and spaces for its dismissal open up. Blocking circulation in Bangkok was, in 2010, one such space: a space that the military dictatorship of Prayuth Chan-Ocha is trying to control. But what are we to learn from this analysis? And where do we go from here?

When I started the research behind this book, my advisor asked me why someone conducting research in Melanesia or in New York Upper East Side should be interested in my work. I mumbled something and went on with my project. As a final piece of this journey, however, I want to go back to that question, not to attempt some questionable comparison between these contexts, but to draw some concrete political lessons from the drivers' experiences. The purpose is not to develop a grand theory or to provide a ludicrous synthesis of the tensions, paradoxes, and contingencies that the drivers experienced and raised over the course of my fieldwork. Rather, I attempt to use their everyday lives, struggles, and actions in protest to sketch a cursory map of political action, one that looks for spots of weaknesses in the global political-economic system and for emerging spaces of political mobilization.[1] I am aware that I can provide little more than initial jottings taken from the drivers' experiences, offered "as contributions, possibilities—as gifts"[2]— rather than as prescriptions.[3] Yet this project would not be complete without another doomed attempt on my part to bring back as a way of conclusion a too often forgotten dimension of critical theory: praxis.

Whether Karl Marx himself, his followers, or later thinkers who questioned and developed his thought, critical theorists were not just interested in an analysis of the world around them but committed to change it. Their theories had value to them only insofar as they directed political action.[4] Unfortunately, much contemporary scholarly engagement has reduced their works simply to schools of thought, forgetting they were schools of action. This is particularly striking given the times we live in. The whole progression of this book, from its initial conception to its final words, has taken place in the context of worldwide political mobilizations. On the one side, we have been witnessing the rise of regressive politics, racism, sexism, fascism, and xenophobia—whether in the shape of Donald Trump, Narendra Modi,

---

1. Gavin Smith has been advocating for the necessity of such an analysis (G. Smith 2013). This is a partial attempt to provide an answer to his call to action.

2. Graeber 2004, 12.

3. This distinction is central. The first comes with the contributing attitude of a partner in struggle, the second with the condescension of a higher level of consciousness.

4. This is partly why Michel de Certeau's *Practice of Everyday Life* became so popular among social scientists after the 1980s (de Certeau 1984), while Henri Lefebvre's opus *Critique of Everyday Life*, would be largely forgotten during the same period (Lefebvre 1991a).

Michel Temer, Jacob Zuma, Abdel Fattah el-Sisi, or General Prayuth Chan-Ocha. On the other, we have seen a growing number of social movements, political mobilizations, and collective practices that pushed against them and built alternatives, from the Arab uprisings to Black Lives Matter, from the South African student–led movement for free decolonized education to the Red Shirts.

The outcome of each of these struggles remains uncertain and open-ended. As a consequence, as people who perform a social role as intellectuals, this is not the time to sit in our classrooms or offices, satisfied with our rhetoric. Antonio Gramsci wrote, during a similar period of mobilizations in the 1930s, that intellectuals could no longer limit their work to eloquence. This, he retained, was an exterior and momentary mover of feeling and passions. Faced with the rise of fascism, Gramsci thought that the intellectual needed to adopt an "active participation in practical life, as constructor, organizer, 'permanent persuader' and not just simple orator."[5] Analyses, he argued, "cannot and must not be ends in themselves (unless the intention is merely to write a chapter of past history), but acquire significance only if they serve to justify a particular practical activity, [only if] they reveal the points of least resistance, at which the force of will can be most fruitfully applied, they suggest immediate tactical operations, they indicate how a campaign of political agitation may best be launched, what language will best be understood."[6] Michel Foucault agreed with him. Toward the end of his life, he made clear that he had tried all along to say to his readers: "If you want to struggle, here are some key points, here are some lines of force, here are some constrictions and blockages."[7]

Detecting these lines of force, points of least resistance, and blockages has always been a central concern to the project of knowledge as praxis, present in all its prominent exponents from Karl Marx to Vladimir Lenin, from Rosa Luxemburg to Antonio Gramsci, from Hannah Arendt to Frantz Fanon, from Michel Foucault to John Holloway. In these pages, I try to follow their lead and step away from the post-1980s dominant trend of considering academic inquiry as an exclusively analytical project, routed in seminar debates more than in political participation. This is not to say that I do not see any value in that approach, that every scholar needs to be involved in a political

5. Gramsci 1971, 10.
6. Ibid., 185.
7. Foucault et al. 2007, 3.

struggle, or that I deny that this shift was provoked by a war against intellectualism and higher education waged by neoliberal forces. Yet, once pushed into that corner, many self-professed political intellectuals have become content with using radical theories in their analyses rather than living a radical praxis, made of both words and actions. Fortunately, since the turn of the century, this tide has started to change and more and more academic engagement has been driven by concrete and active political engagements. As a small contribution to that tide, I conclude this book by taking a step back and jotting down some of the paths, lines of force, and fault lines that motorcycle taxi drivers revealed, hoping their struggles can provide a map for further analysis and political actions elsewhere. Much like the plans I have analyzed in this book, this overview will remain partial, but I hope that something will emerge from its contradictions and its unintended consequences. The drivers' trajectories, their lives in the city, and their adoption of mobility as tools of political mobilization and a field of struggle raise multiple issues. First, they invite us to a methodological reflection on the role of contradiction in political praxis; second, the urge us to reconsider where accumulation and the production of value is located in post-Fordist capitalism; and finally, they call us to use this analysis to locate points of least resistance and weak spots on which political pressure can be most effectively applied.

THE GENERATIVE POWER OF CONTRADICTIONS

Marx's philosophy of praxis, while providing one of the most powerful heuristics for determining fragilities and points of action, is dominated by a particular Hegelian idea about the working of dialectics which poses contradictions, understood as "a situation when two seemingly opposed forces are simultaneously present,"[8] at the very core of its analysis.[9] Even thinkers who refuse other aspects of Marx's determinism have retained the notion that

8. Harvey 2014, 1.

9. Like Marxist theorists, anthropologists have traditionally aimed at resolving the tensions that seemed to animate the life of their informants by showing that what we may perceive as contradictions were in fact, when seen from the native point of view, something else. Probably the most famous formulation of this approach has been Evans-Pritchard's analysis of the apparent logical inconsistencies and secondary rationalizations with which the Azande avoid putting witchcraft into question (Evans-Pritchard 1972). For a fascinating debate on the treatment of contradictions in anthropology see Berliner et al. 2016.

these oppositions mark the weak spots of capitalism. In their view, their resolution—in particular that of the tension between labor and capital—is a necessary outcome, one that will make capitalism crumble under the weight of its own contradictions.[10] The drivers' lives, however, suggest an opposite dynamic and show unresolved contradictions as the fuel that keeps the engine of social life running, rather than being the basis of its demise. The drivers' arrival to Bangkok as industrial workers was the result of attempts to reconcile the demands of capital, labor, and consumption under Fordism; their move toward their precarious work and their new function as an urban infrastructure was the outcome of another effort to reorganize the relation between those forces after the 1997 crisis; and finally, their political actions were sustained by their frustration with the unresolvable tensions that their position created. In each of these spheres, their lives show how attempts to impose order and resolve tensions rapidly emerge as incomplete, contingent, and doomed. They expose any idea of a necessary resolution of contradictions as simply that: an idea, a fantasy constantly dispelled by reality, its messiness and indomitable contingency. For the drivers, unresolved tensions fueled social life precisely because they could not be surmounted.

Living beings, after all, are defined and kept alive by the irreconcilable oppositions between inhaling and exhaling, contracting and expanding. On our planet, any stable resolution between these oppositions equals death. Reality operates by creating opposite poles and harnessing the energy generated by their tensions and the doomed attempts to resolve them, rather than crumbling under the resulting contradictions. The same is true for capitalism. Contrary to Marx's analysis, this system has demonstrated time and again that its contradictions have propelled, rather than undermined, its diabolic creativity.[11] This is why crises have not marked the end of capitalism but, on the contrary, allowed its continuous renewal. This realization may seem to make any critique of capitalism helpless. On the contrary, accepting that this system will not crack under the weight of its own contradictions invites us to take it down by the pressure of direct action, grounding those in

10. Harvey 2014.

11. In this sense, rather than following the Hegelian routes of Marxist thought all the way to the necessity of synthesis, I stay closer to Adorno's negative dialectics and its stubborn refusal to postulate any positive resolution to oppositions. This whole book, in fact, has not been driven by an attempt to resolve any of the contradictions, inconsistencies, and fragilities I met, but rather to explore the tensions they generate and their roles in producing, reproducing, and sustaining the social world in which collective action takes place.

an analysis of the contemporary capitalist system, one that acknowledges the radical changes created by its post-Fordist turn.

FROM RELATIONS OF PRODUCTION TO
RELATIONS OF CIRCULATION

If Marxist dialectic hardly fits the drivers' experience, similarly much of his conclusions about collective actions are grounded in a configuration of labor and capital that bears little resemblance to that in which the drivers live. Yet, this does not make Marxism irrelevant to their lives. Marxism was never a set of resolved issues and ready answers but rather a method, a mode of analysis.[12] While Marx's specific conclusion may be outdated in some ways, his method still provides some of the most powerful machinery to connect political theory and action. The central mechanisms of this method are quite simple and straightforward. First, it analyzes capitalism to discover where surplus-value—the oil it runs on—is generated. Second, it considers these locations as the spaces where the dynamics of capitalism, both in terms of accumulation and exploitation, are most visible in everyday life. Third, it offers them as privileged loci for collective action, both as points of strength and of least resistance. Without knowing it, this is the path that the drivers' followed in their life trajectories and political mobilization.

After the 1997 economic crisis, people like Adun, Boon, or Hong understood that economic growth, capitalist accumulation, and the creation of value in Thailand was shifting away from the factory floor. While many of the drivers had to live through the crisis to abandon industrial production for the service industry and adopt new forms of entrepreneurship, global capital had been redirecting its flows away from the factory floor already for almost two decades, especially since the 1973 oil crisis. This shift away from the industrial era of capitalism, from which Marx's theories emerged, was not global, immediate, or complete. Just as had happened in the transi-

---

12. This view has been most eloquently voiced by Etienne Balibar. In his *Philosophy of Marx* he argues: "We have the right then to interpret the implications of what Marx wrote. Not to consider the fragments of his discourse as cards to be infinitely reshuffled at will but, nonetheless, to take a foothold in his 'problematics' and 'axiomatics'*/in other words, in his 'philosophies'*/and push these to their conclusions (to find the contradictions, limits, and openings to which they lead)" (Balibar 1995, 117–18).

tion from landed to industrial capitalism,[13] initially it simply meant that more and more value started to be generated away from the factory floor. As David Harvey has argued, the 1973 global economic crisis was solved with a "spatial fix," namely the inclusion of new territories into the capitalistic system by financializing growing economies and outsourcing production, increasingly to South America and Southeast Asia. While in places like Thailand this looked like the heyday of industrial capitalism, the global scale had already tipped in another direction. In two decades, the 1997 crisis would push industrial production to concentrate in a few hot spots—mostly around East Asia—where the price of labor was reduced to a bare minimum and performed under intolerable conditions. According to orthodox Marxist analysis, this should have created an insurmountable contradiction between capital and labor. Unable to reduce any further the cost of labor and hence to create more surplus value, capitalists should have seen their rate of profit fall, creating a systemic challenge. The opposite happened and capitalist accumulation soared.

The post-1973 period had not only witnessed the inclusion of new territories in the capitalist system. It also saw the creation of financial tools that provided a new frontier for capital accumulation, one that, unlike the surface of the globe and its underground resources, was unlimited. That frontier was the financial market, and in particular derivatives. Derivatives are contracts between two parties that specify conditions—in terms of timing, values, obligations, and amounts—under which payments have to be made. As such they have existed for centuries and have been vastly used to hedge risks.[14] In 1973, however, two American economists, Fischer Black and Myron Scholes, developed a mathematical model of a financial market that included derivatives as investment instruments, that is to say as tools of creating profit by speculating on their changing value, rather than using them to hedge risk. This transformation generated a boom in option trading. The growth in value created in the financial market, rather than through industrial production, was staggering. No statistic is clearer in marking this transformation than the relation between financial turnover and gross domestic product (GDP) in the United States in the following years. In 1970 the trading in

13. E. Williams 1944. In fact, under industrial capitalism landed wealth and enslaved labor, the loci of the primitive accumulation that set this system in motion, continued to exist, it just became less important to the preservation of the capitalist system.

14. Appadurai 2015; Bryan and Rafferty 2006; Lapavitsas 2009; McKenzie 2011; Toporowski 2002.

U.S. stock markets moved $136 billion, 13.1 percent of the country's GDP. Twenty years later, the stock market was worth $1.671 trillion and had doubled its weight in relation to GDP. By the year 2000, trading in U.S. equity markets had expanded to $14.222 trillion, surpassing the size of the GDP.[15] In other words, the amount of value created in finance became bigger than that of the real economy. These numbers did not even include derivatives, where most of the global surplus value has been generated in the last decades. In 2007, the international financial system was trading derivatives valued one quadrillion dollars per year, which has been calculated to be the equivalent, adjusted for inflation, of ten times the total worth of all products made by the world's manufacturing industries over the last century.[16] Even if the 2008 crash destroyed much of this value, it did not change this trend. In 2013, the global GDP was around $65 trillion USD and the derivative market $783 trillion, twelve times larger.[17] Clearly, the core of capitalist creation of surplus value had moved away from industrial production.

In order to realize this shift, one does not need to look so far away in the impenetrable world of finance and its unfathomable numbers. This shift, in fact, happened also in microeconomics, through marketing and branding. The tradition of branding livestock to distinguish individuals in a flock has existed since antiquity. Nobody, however, would have paid a different price for a similar piece of livestock exclusively based on its branding. It was not until the early twentieth century that brands emerged as a significant factor in consumers' choices. The capitalism that Marx studied simply did not have this component. Today, on the contrary, much of the value of a commodity resides in this branding. Apple and Dell computers, for instance, are produced in the same Chinese factory, the infamous Foxconn, by equally underpaid workers, in equally exploitative labor processes, and at relatively similar prices. Yet on shop shelves they carry a substantially different price tag. Their different value is not based on Apple's higher ability to reduce the cost of labor, but rather on its branding and ability to create what we call—quite appropriately—added value. As a result, consumers may be willing to spend more money to buy Apple earphones rather than a generic set of similar quality, because of what an association with that brand means to them in terms of fulfilling their needs for recognition, identity, and forms of subjectivity

15. Precisely 144.9 percent of the country's GDP.
16. Steward 2012.
17. *Economist* 2012.

that are implied in owning an Apple product. Once again, value is not generated in production but rather in marketing, advertising, and branding.

This transformation does not mean that industrial production has disappeared or become irrelevant to capitalism. Neither does it mean that significant political, economic, environmental, and social resources have stopped to revolve around production. Rather, all of this is to say that since the 1970s capitalism has reorganized itself and shifted the core of surplus-value creation and accumulation away from production, both at the macro- and microeconomic level. In the first field, it has been moving toward the financial sector; in the second, toward branding and marketing. Overall, if during Marx's time, value was created in production, now it is created in circulation of fictitious capital, whether financial or cultural.[18] But what does this have to do with the everyday lives of the drivers, their political mobilization, and the practical lessons they can offer to social movements outside of Thailand?

This larger global transformation is the background to how the political-economic restructurings of post-Fordism in Thailand interacted with the drivers' everyday lives: their adjustments to its flexible rhythms; their adoption of the language of freedom and entrepreneurialism; their pride in seeing themselves as free economic agents rather than as workers; the expansion of this logic into every aspect of their lives, from job trajectories to politics; and the emergence of desires as a field of political struggle. Each of these aspects resonates with the everyday experience of millions of people around the globe, or at least they do with my own and that of the people around me. Many more examples of parallel dynamics—obviously colored and shaped by the specific contexts in which they take place—are available both in Thailand and all around the globe, from the flexibilization of labor to the financialization of our existence, from the precarization of everyday life to the making of the unemployed, black, disabled, and queer bodies dispensable. This colonization of everyday life by the forces of contemporary capitalism, and the specific forms it takes in different contexts, has been explored by the inspiring work of scholars, commentators, and activists.[19] Less explored, however, remains the third phase of the method proposed by Marx: namely the

18. Amin 2013.

19. Allison 2012; Blyth 2013; Burgin 2012; A. Davis 2015; Douzinas 2013; Edwards 2016; Elyachar 2005; R. A. Ferguson 2004; Fraser 2003; Hill 2016; Karamessini and Rubery 2013; Klein 2007; Knight and Stewart 2016; Lee and Kofman 2012; Mattoni and Vogiatzoglou 2014; Mbembe 2013; Molé 2013; Muehlebach 2016; Vaneigem and Nicholson-Smith 1983; Verney and Bosco 2013.

transformation of the locus of capitalist extraction and accumulation of surplus value into privileged spaces for collective action.

THE DRIVERS' LESSON

This is the lesson of praxis that the drivers teach us. First of all, they refused a politics based on their class position as workers, defined by relations of production, and moved toward a new theory of class based on exclusion from the advantages of exchange, circulation, and mediation, as the language of *phrai* developed by the Red Shirts suggested. Second, they reclaimed everyday life not just as a territory of colonization by those forces but also as the terrain on which to ground its decolonization, or at least reveal some points of lesser resistance in this project, points on which pressure could be most effectively applied.[20] Finally, the drivers found one of these spots in their urban mobility and took control over it. While normally they wove the city together, one trip at a time, during the 2010 protest they decided to unravel it. Motorcycle taxi drivers' roles as connectors made them both essential infrastructures for urban life and street capitalism in Bangkok and serious threats to their functioning. This invites us to reflect on mobility and circulation as significant sites and strategies of political mobilization, and on cities as vulnerable spots for political action.

The drivers are not alone in making this invitation. In 2009, a French collective the Invisible Committee, made an almost identical claim. "It is precisely due to its architecture of flows" they wrote, "that the metropolis is one of the most vulnerable human arrangements that ever existed. . . . Every network has its weak spots, the nodes that must be undone in order to interrupt circulation, to unwind the web. . . . In order for something to rise up in the midst of the metropolis and open up other possibilities the first act must be to interrupt its *perpetuum mobile*."[21] Soon after, other mobilizations around the globe seemed to echo these words. From the beginning of the Occupy movement as an attempt to shut down a financial node to Anonymous's internet attacks aimed at blocking the flow through websites and payment providers; from the visibility of Somali pirates who arrested

20. In this sense, they materialized Henri Lefebvre's call and the core of the Marxist project, which the French theorist defines as "a critical knowledge of everyday life" (Lefebvre 1991a, 3: 58).

21. Committee 2009, 61–62.

ships carrying oil and weapons along the Horn of Africa to the worldwide significance of mobilization by logistics workers, contemporary capitalism is seeing the unfolding of political conflicts in which mobility *becomes* mobilization and shapes its strategies and tactics. In Thailand, operators of mobility and their occupation of shopping intersections and interruption of traffic rearranged the political landscape. Globally, social media, bridges, highways, ports, and financial nodes are figuring more and more prevalently in the global landscapes of mobilization and changing its morphology.

Clearly, blockages of transport, circulation, and mobility as modes of political mobilization are nothing new, just as the creation of surplus value through circulation is not. However, if we compare their present weight in relation to the decreasing number of political mobilizations taking place on factory floors, a clear trend starts to become visible.[22] As a consequence, the significance of mobilizations that involve operators of mobility, make circulation into a terrain of struggle, and show systemic fragilities through blockages are worth reflecting on.

Failing to analyze these fragilities would mean forfeiting the contribution that social analysis can provide in a time of political mobilizations: helping to find points of least resistance and weak spots. This type of conversation and analysis, in fact, is and has always been central to political activists around the globe. Yet, in the last decades this has hardly been at the core of academic discussion. On the contrary, we have too often focused on the sturdiness of power, the invincibility of capitalism, or—at most—on the small and hidden acts of resistance to its triumphal and disastrous march. This has made many of us into the oversystematic thinkers despised by Henri Lefebvre, people who "oscillate between loud denunciations of capitalism and the bourgeois and their repressive institutions on the one hand, and fascination and unrestrained admiration on the other. [Thinkers who] make society into the 'object' of a systematization which must be 'closed' to be complete; [and] thus bestow a cohesiveness it utterly lacks upon a totality which is in fact decidedly open— so open, indeed, that it must rely on violence to endure."[23]

The drivers' actions and the present repression in Thailand tell a very different story, a story of unresolved tensions and continuous attempts to brush them under the rug, of reemerging cracks and fault lines, of collective actions that raise significant challenges when aimed at the right spots, and of

22. For an analysis of this decrease see Biggs 2015; Hetland and Goodwin 2011.
23. Lefebvre 1991b, 11.

opposing orders striving in vain to impose themselves. Failing to recognize and explore these characteristics poses more than an ethnographic and intellectual dilemma. It runs the risk of promulgating a praxis of political immobility, a position that portrays power as unbeatable, curtailing openings rather than fostering them. Taking such a position in times of mass mobilization and fascist resurgence will not only make us irrelevant to social movements. It will eventually put us on the dock, on the side of those who could have helped but decided to do nothing. As a discipline we have made that unforgivable mistake in the past, remaining silent and turning our heads to the horrors of colonialism. Are we going to repeat it?

REFERENCES

Abelmann, Nancy. 1996. *Echoes of the Past, Epics of Dissent: A South Korean Social Movement.* Berkeley: University of California Press.

Abrams, Philip. 1988. "Notes on the Difficulty of Studying the State." *Journal of Historical Sociology* 1 (1): 58–89.

Abu-Lughod, Lila. 1990. "The Romance of Resistance: Tracing Transformations of Power through Bedouin Women." *American Ethnologist* 17 (1): 41–55.

Allison, Anne. 2012. "Ordinary Refugees: Social Precarity and Soul in 21st Century Japan." *Anthropological Quarterly* 85 (2): 345–70.

Althusser, Louis. 1984. *Essays on Ideology.* London: Verso.

Amin, Samir. 2013. *Three Essays on Marx's Value Theory.* New York: New York University Press.

Anand, Nikhil. 2011. "Pressure: The Politechnics of Water Supply in Mumbai." *Cultural Anthropology* 26 (4): 542–64.

Anderson, Benedict R. 1983. *Imagined Communities: Reflections on the Origin and Spread of Nationalism.* London: Verso.

Anderson, Michael H. 1984. *Madison Avenue in Asia: Politics and Transnational Advertising.* Madison, NJ: Fairleigh Dickinson University Press.

Anek, Laothamatas. 2006 [Buddhist year 2549]. *Thaksinā-prachāniyom.* Krung Thēp (Bangkok): Samnakphim Matichon.

Appadurai, Arjun. 2013. *The Future as Cultural Fact.* New York: Verso.

———. 2015. *Banking on Words: The Failure of Language in the Age of Derivative Finance.* Chicago: University of Chicago Press.

Aretxaga, Begoña. 2003. "Maddening States." *Annual Review of Anthropology:* 393–410.

Asad, Talal. 1991. Afterword in *Colonial Situations : Essays on the Contextualization of Ethnographic Knowledge,* edited by George W. Stocking. Milwaukee: University of Wisconsin Press.

———. 2003. *Formations of the Secular: Christianity, Islam, Modernity.* Stanford, CA: Stanford University Press.

Askew, Marc. 1993. *The Making of Modern Bangkok: State, Market and People in the Shaping of the Thai Metropolis.* Bangkok: Thailand Development Research Institute Foundation.

———. 1994. *Interpreting Bangkok: The Urban Question in Thai Studies.* Bangkok: Chulalongkorn University Press.

Aulino, Felicity. 2012. "Senses and Sensibilities: The Practice of Care in Everyday Life in Northern Thailand." Ph.D. diss., Department of Anthropology, Harvard University.

———. 2016. "Rituals of Care for the Elderly in Northern Thailand: Merit, Morality, and the Everyday of Long-Term Care." *American Ethnologist* 43 (1): 91–102.

Aulino, Felicity, et al. 2014. "The Wheel of Crisis." Hot Spots, *Cultural Anthropology* website, September 23, https://culanth.org/fieldsights/582-the-wheel-of-crisis-in-thailand (accessed July 27, 2017).

Austin, J.L. 1962. *How to Do Things with Words: The William James Lectures.* Oxford: Clarendon Press.

Avery, Gayle C, and Harald Bergsteiner. 2016. *Sufficiency Thinking: Thailand's Gift to an Unsustainable World.* Sidney: Allen & Unwin.

Baker, Chris. 2001. "Thailand's Assembly of the Poor: Background, Drama, Reaction." *South East Asia Research* 8 (1): 5–29.

———. 2007. *Thailand Human Development Report, "Sufficiency Economy," and Human Development in Thailand.* Bangkok: United Nations Development Programme.

Baker, Chris, and Phongpaichit Pasuk. 2005. *A History of Thailand.* New York: Cambridge University Press.

———. 2009. *A History of Thailand.* 2nd ed. Cambridge: Cambridge University Press.

Balibar, Etienne. 1995. *The Philosophy of Marx.* London: Verso.

Bao, Jiemin. 2005. "Merit-Making Capitalism: Re-territorializing Thai Buddhism in Silicon Valley, California." *Journal of Asian American Studies* 8 (2): 115–42.

Barker Colin, et al. 2011. "Marxism and Social Movements: An Introduction." In *Marxism and Social Movements,* edited by Barker Colin et al., 1–37. Leiden: Brill.

Basso, Keith H. 1996. *Wisdom Sits in Places: Landscape and Language among the Western Apache.* Albuquerque: University of New Mexico Press.

Bear, Laura. 2014. "Doubt, Conflict, Mediation: The Anthropology of Modern Time." *Journal of the Royal Anthropological Institute* 20 (1): 3–30.

———. 2015. *Navigating Austerity: Currents of Debt along a South Asian River.* Stanford, CA: Stanford University Press.

Beeson, Mark, and Islam, Iyanatul. 2005. "Neo-liberalism and East Asia: Resisting the Washington Consensus." *Journal of Development Studies* 41 (2): 197–219.

Bengtsson, Magnus. 2006. "The Bangkok Skytrain." Master's thesis. Department of Urban Planning, UMEÅ University.

Berger, John. 1991. *Keeping a Rendezvous.* New York: Pantheon Books.

Berlin, Isaiah. 1969. *Four Essays on Liberty.* Oxford: Oxford University Press.

Berliner, David, et al. 2016. "Anthropology and the Study of Contradictions." *HAU: Journal of Ethnographic Theory* 6 (1): 1–27.

Bestor, Theodore C. 1989. *Neighborhood Tokyo*. Stanford, CA: Stanford University Press.

——. 2004. *Tsukiji : The Fish Market at the Center of the World*. Berkeley: University of California Press.

Bidney, David. 1963. *The Concept of Freedom in Anthropology*. The Hague: Mouton.

Biggs, Michael. 2015. "Has Protest Increased since the 1970s? How a Survey Question Can Construct a Spurious Trend." *British Journal of Sociology* 66 (1): 141–63.

Blyth, Mark. 2013. *Austerity: The History of a Dangerous Idea*. Oxford: Oxford University Press.

Bourdieu, Pierre. 1986. "The Forms of Capital." In *Handbook of Theory and Research for the Sociology of Education,* edited by John G. Richardson, 241–58. New York: Greenwood Press.

Bourdieu, Pierre, Loic J. D. Wacquant, and Samar Farage. 1994. "Rethinking the State: Genesis and Structure of the Bureaucratic Field." *Sociological Theory* 12: 1–18.

Bourgois, Philippe I. 1995. *In Search of Respect: Selling Crack in El Barrio*. Cambridge: Cambridge University Press.

Bourgois, Philippe I., and Jeff Schonberg. 2009. *Righteous Dopefiend*. Berkeley: University of California Press.

Boyer, Robert, and Daniel Drache. 1996. *States against Markets: The Limits of Globalization*. London: Routledge.

Brody, Alyson. 2006. "Beyond Duty and Desire: Reconsidering Motivations for Thai Women's Migration to Bangkok." In *Migrant Women and Work,* edited by Anuja Agrawal, 136. London: Sage Publications.

Brown, Andrew. 1997. "Locating Working Class Power." In *Political Change in Thailand: Democracy and Participation,* edited by Kevin Hewison, 163–78. New York: Taylor and Francis.

——. 2004. *Labour, Politics, and the State in Industrializing Thailand*. London: RoutledgeCurzon.

Brown, Andrew, and Kevin Hewison. 2004. "Labour Politics in Thaksin's Thailand." *Southeast Asia Research Center Working Papers Series* (62): 1–30.

Brown, Wendy. 1995. *States of Injury: Power and Freedom in Late Modernity*. Princeton, NJ: Princeton University Press.

Bryan, Dick, and Michael Rafferty. 2006. *Capitalism with Derivatives: A Political Economy of Financial Derivatives, Capital, and Class*. New York: Palgrave Macmillan.

Burgin, Angus. 2012. *The Great Persuasion: Reinventing Free Markets since the Depression*. Cambridge, MA: Harvard University Press.

Business. 1983. "Soi Bikes." *Thailand Business,* October.

Butler, Judith. 2012. *Subjects of Desire: Hegelian Reflections in Twentieth-Century France*. New York: Columbia University Press.

Buttigieg, Joseph A. 1990. "Gramsci's Method." *Boundary* 17 (2): 60–81.

——. 2002. "On Gramsci." *Daedalus* 131 (3): 67–70.

———. 2006. "The Prison Notebooks: Antonio Gramsci's Work in Progress." *Rethinking Marxism* 18 (1): 37–42.

Calkins, Peter. 2007. *The Sufficiency Economy at the Edges of Capitalism.* Chiang Mai, Thailand: Chiang Mai University.

Carse, Ashley. 2016. "Keyword: Infrastructure; How a Humble French Engineering Term Shaped the Modern World." In *Infrastructures and Social Complexity: A Routledge Companion*, edited by Penelope Harvey, Casper Bruun Jensen, and Atsuro Morita, 23–56. London: Routledge.

Castells, Manuel. 1983. *The City and the Grassroots: A Cross-Cultural Theory of Urban Social Movements.* Berkeley: University of California Press.

Chaiyawat, Chatcharin. 2010 [Buddhist year 2553]. *Kāo khām Thaksin kōṇ čha thǔng kān lomsalāi.* Nonthaburī: Samnakphim Krīn-Panyāyān.

Chakrabarty, Dipesh. 2000. *Provincializing Europe: Postcolonial Thought and Historical Difference.* Princeton, NJ: Princeton University Press.

Chambers, Paul. 2008. "Factions, Parties, and the Durability of Parliaments, Coalitions, and Cabinets: The Case of Thailand (1979—2001)." *Party Politics* 14 (3): 299–323.

Chambers, Paul, and Napisa Waitoolkiat. 2016. "The Resilience of Monarchised Military in Thailand." *Journal of Contemporary Asia* 46 (3): 425–44.

Chanunya, Satapanawattana. 2004. "Motorcycle-Taxi Men Help Police with Their Duties." *The Nation.*

Charnvit, Kasetsiri. 2015. *Studies in Thai and Southeas Asian Histories.* Bangkok: Foundation for the Promotion of Social Science and Humanities Textbook Project.

Chatterjee, Partha. 2011. *Lineages of Political Society: Studies in Postcolonial Democracy.* New York: Columbia University Press.

Chatthip, Nartsupha. 1999. *The Thai Village Economy in the Past.* Chiang Mai, Thailand: Silkworm Books.

Chiang Noi. 2010. "Talk about Double Standards." *The Nation,* February 8.

Chookiat, Punasprnprasit. 2011. "Thailand: Politicized Thaksinization." *Southeast Asian Affairs* 2004 (1): 255–66.

Chucherd, Thitima. 2006. "The Effect of Household Debt on Consumption in Thailand." *Bank of Thailand Discussion Paper* (Bangkok), 1–35.

Clarke, Simon. 2005. "The Neoliberal Theory of Society." In *Neoliberalism: A Critical Reader*, edited by Alfredo Saad-Filho and Deborah Johnston, 50–59. London: Pluto Press.

Clifford, James. 1997. *Routes: Travel and Translation in the Late Twentieth Century.* Cambridge, MA: Harvard University Press.

Comaroff, Jean. 1985. *Body of Power, Spirit of Resistance: The Culture and History of a South African People.* Chicago: University of Chicago Press.

Comaroff, Jean, and John Comaroff. 1991. *Of Revelation and Revolution.* Chicago: University of Chicago Press.

———. 1992. *Ethnography and the Historical Imagination.* Boulder, CO: Westview Press.

————. 1999. *Civil Society and the Political Imagination in Africa: Critical Perspectives*. Chicago: University of Chicago Press.

————. 2001. *Millennial Capitalism and the Culture of Neoliberalism*. Durham, NC: Duke University Press.

————. 2003. "Ethnography on an Awkward Scale: Postcolonial Anthropology and the Violence of Abstraction." *Ethnography* 4 (2): 147–79.

Commisso, Giuliana 2006. "Identity and Subjectivity in Post-Fordism: For an Analysis of Resistance in the Contemporary Workplace." *Ephemera* 6 (2): 163–92.

Committee, Invisible. 2009. *The Coming Insurrection*. Cambridge, MA: MIT Press.

Conner, David William. 1996. "Personal Power, Authority, and Influence: Cultural Foundations for Leadership and Leadership Formation in Northeast Thailand and Implications for Adult Leadership Training." Ph.D. diss., Department of Leadership and Educational Policy Studies, Northern Illinois University.

Connors, Michael Kelly. 2005. "Hegemony and the Politics of Culture and Identity in Thailand: Ministering Culture." *Critical Asian Studies* 37 (4): 523–51.

————. 2007. *Democracy and National Identity in Thailand*. Copenhagen: NIAS Press.

————. 2011. "When the Walls Come Crumbling Down: The Monarchy and Thai-Style Democracy." *Journal of Contemporary Asia* 41 (4): 657–73.

Curtis, Adam. 2002. *Century of Self*. Directed by Adam Curtis. London: BBC Four.

Davis, Angela. 2015. *Freedom Is a Constant Struggle: Ferguson, Palestine, and the Foundations of a Movement*. Chicago: Haymarket Books.

Davis, Mike. 2006. *Planet of Slums*. London: Verso.

Dayley, Robert. 2011. "Thailand's Agrarian Myth and Its Proponents." *Journal of Asian and African Studies* 46 (4): 342–60.

de Certeau, Michel. 1984. *The Practice of Everyday Life*. Berkeley: University of California Press.

de Spinoza, Benedict. 1970. *Ethics*. New York: Simon and Schuster.

Deleuze, Gilles, and Félix Guattari. 1977. *Anti-Oedipus: Capitalism and Schizophrenia*. New York: Viking Press.

Dey, Pascal, and Chris Steyaert. 2016. "Rethinking the Space of Ethics in Social Entrepreneurship: Power, Subjectivity, and Practices of Freedom." *Journal of Business Ethics* 133 (4): 627–41.

Douglas, Mary. 1975. *Implicit Meanings: Essays in Anthropology*. London: Routledge and Kegan Paul.

Douzinas, Costas. 2013. *Philosophy and Resistance in the Crisis: Greece and the Future of Europe*. London: John Wiley & Sons.

Dressel, Björn. 2010. "When Notions of Legitimacy Conflict: The Case of Thailand." *Politics and Policy* 38 (3): 445–69.

Durand-Lasserve, Alain. 1980. "Speculation on Urban Land, Land Development, and Housing Development in Bangkok." Paper read at the First Thai-European Seminar on Social Change in Contemporary Thailand, Amsterdam.

The Economist. 2012. "Clear and Present Danger: Centrally Cleared Derivatives (Clearing Houses)." *The Economist,* April 12.

Edwards, Sue Bradford. 2016. *Black Lives Matter.* Edina, MN: ABDO.

Eisenstadt, Shmuel Noah, and Louis Roniger. 1980. "Patron-Client Relations as a Model of Structuring Social Exchange." *Comparative Studies in Society and History* 22 (1): 42–77.

Elinoff, Eli. 2013. "Architectures of Citizenship: Participatory Urbanism and Politics in Thailand's Railway Communities." Ph.D. diss., Department of Anthropology, University of California, San Diego.

———. 2014a. "Sufficient Citizens: Moderation and the Politics of Sustainable Development in Thailand." *PoLAR: Political and Legal Anthropology Review* 37 (1): 89–108.

———. 2014b. "Unmaking Civil Society: Activist Schisms and Autonomous Politics in Thailand." *Contemporary Southeast Asia: A Journal of International and Strategic Affairs* 36 (3): 356–85.

———. 2016. "A House Is More Than a House: Aesthetic Politics in a Northeastern Thai Railway Settlement." *Journal of the Royal Anthropological Institute* 22 (3): 610–32.

Elinoff, Eli, and Claudio Sopranzetti. 2012. "Introduction." *Journal of Southeast Asia Research* 20 (3): 331–38.

Elyachar, Julia. 2005. *Markets of Dispossession: NGOs, Economic Development, and the State in Cairo.* Durham, NC: Duke University Press.

———. 2010. "Phatic Labor, Infrastructures, and the Question of Empowerment in Cairo." *American Ethnologist* 37 (3): 452–64.

Embree, John F., and Han-Dieter Evers. 1969. *Loosely Structured Social Systems; Thailand in Comparative Perspective.* New Haven, CT: Yale University Southeast Asia Studies.

Endō, Tamaki. 2014. *Living with Risk: Precarity and Bangkok's Urban Poor.* Kyoto: Kyoto CSEAS.

Engels, Friedrich. 1968. *The Condition of the Working Class in England.* Translated and edited by W. O. Henderson and W. H. Chaloner. Stanford, CA: Stanford University Press.

Evans-Pritchard, E. E. 1972. *Witchcraft, Oracles, and Magic among the Azande.* Oxford: Clarendon Press.

Ewen, Stuart. 1996. *PR! A Social History of Spin.* New York: Basic Books.

Fabian, Johannes. 2014. *Time and the Other: How Anthropology Makes Its Object.* New York: Columbia University Press.

Falk, Monica Lindberg. 2007. *Making Fields of Merit: Buddhist Female Ascetics and Gendered Orders in Thailand.* Vol. 2. Copenhagen: Nias Press.

Fanon, Frantz. 1980. *A Dying Colonialism.* London: Writers and Readers.

Fassin, Didier. 2014. "The Ethical Turn in Anthropology: Promises and Uncertainties." *HAU: Journal of Ethnographic Theory* 4 (1): 429–35.

Faubion, James D. 2011. *An Anthropology of Ethics.* Cambridge: Cambridge University Press.

Feeny, David. 2003. "The Political Economy of Regional Inequality: The Northeast of Thailand 1800–2000." *Crossroads: An Interdisciplinary Journal of Southeast Asian Studies* 17 (1): 29–59.

Ferguson, James. 2009. "The Uses of Neoliberalism." *Antipode* 41 (1): 166–84.

Ferguson, Roderick A. 2004. *Aberrations in Black: Toward a Queer of Color Critique.* Minneapolis: University of Minnesota Press.

Ferrara, Federico. 2010. *Thailand Unhinged: Unraveling the Myth of a Thai-Style Democracy.* Singapore: Equinox.

———. 2015. *The Political Development of Modern Thailand.* Cambridge: Cambridge University Press.

Filippi, Francesca B. 2008. *Da Torino a Bangkok : Architetti e ingegneri nel regno del Siam.* Venice: Marsilio.

Foucault, Michel. 1970. *The Order of Things: An Archaeology of the Human Sciences.* Translated by Alan Sheridan. London: Pantheon Books. .

———. 1972. *The Archaeology of Knowledge.* Translated by Alan Sheridan. London: Tavistock Publications.

———. 1977. *Discipline and Punish: The Birth of the Prison.* Translated by Alan Sheridan. New York: Pantheon Books.

———. 1978. *The History of Sexuality.* 1st American ed. Translated by Robert Hurley. New York: Pantheon Books.

———. 1984a. "On the Genealogy of Ethics: An Overview of Work in Progress." In *The Foucault Reader,* edited by Paul Rabinow, 340–72. New York: Pantheon Books.

———. 1984b. "Politics and Ethics: An Interview." In *The Foucault Reader,* edited by Paul Rabinow, 373–81. New York: Pantheon Books.

———. 1984c. "Space, Knowledge, and Power." In *The Foucault Reader,* edited by Paul Rabinow, 239–57. New York: Pantheon Books.

———. 1997. *Ethics: Subjectivity, and Truth.* Edited by Paul Rabinow. New York: New Press.

Foucault, Michel, et al. 2007. *Security, Territory, Population: Lectures at the Collège de France, 1977–78.* Edited by Arnold Davidson. New York: Palgrave Macmillan.

Francioni, Gianni. 1984. *L'officina gramsciana: Ipotesi sulla struttura dei "Quaderni del carcere."* Milan: Bibliopolis.

Fraser, Nancy. 2003. "From Discipline to Flexibilization? Rereading Foucault in the Shadow of Globalization." *Constellations* 10 (2): 160–71.

Freud, Sigmund. 2003. *The Uncanny.* Translated by David McLintock. London: Penguin Books.

Friedman, Milton. 1962. *Capitalism and Freedom.* Chicago: University of Chicago Press.

Funston, John. 2009. *Divided over Thaksin: Thailand's Coup and Problematic Transition.* Chiang Mai, Thailand: Silkworm Books.

Ghannam, Farha. 2011. "Mobility, Liminality, and Embodiment in Urban Egypt." *American Ethnologist* 38 (4): 790–800.

Gilbert, Alan. 2001. "On the Mystery of Capital and the Myths of Hernando De Soto: What Difference Does Legal Title Make?" *Internation Development Planning Review* 24 (1): 1–19.

———. 2012. "De Soto's *The Mystery of Capital:* Reflections on the Book's Public Impact." *International Development Planning Review* 34 (3): v–xviii.

Glassman, Jim. 2010a. "From Reds to Red Shirts: Political Evolution and Devolution in Thailand." *Environment and Planning A* 42: 765–70.

———. 2010b. "The Provinces Elect Governments, Bangkok Overthrows Them: Urbanity, Class and Post-democracy in Thailand." *Urban Studies* 47 (4): 1301–23.

Gledhill, John. 2009. "Power in Political Anthropology." *Journal of Power* 2 (1): 9–34.

Golding, William. 1983. *Lord of the Flies*. London: Penguin Books.

Graeber, David. 2004. *Fragments of an Anarchist Anthropology*. Chicago: Prickly Paradigm.

———. 2007. *Possibilities: Essays on Hierarchy, Rebellion, and Desire*. Oakland: AK Press.

———. 2011. *Debt: The First 5,000 Years*. New York: Melville House.

Graham, Stephen. 2010. *Disrupted Cities: When Infrastructure Fails*. London: Routledge.

Graham, Stephen, and Colin McFarlane. 2014. *Infrastructural Lives: Urban Infrastructure in Context*. London: Routledge.

Gramsci, Antonio. 1971. *Selections from the Prison Notebooks of Antonio Gramsci*. Translated by Quentin Hoare and Geoffrey Nowell-Smith. London: Lawrence & Wishart.

———. 1988. *An Antonio Gramsci Reader: Selected Writings, 1916–1935*. Edited by David Forgacs. New York: Schocken Books.

Gray, Christine Elizabeth. 1986. "Thailand: the Soteriological State in the 1970s." Ph.D. diss., Department of Anthropology, University of Chicago.

———. 1991. "Hegemonic Images: Language and Silence in the Royal Thai Polity." *Man* 26 (1): 43–65.

Griffiths, Melanie, Ali Rogers, and Bridget Anderson. 2013. "Migration, Time, and Temporalities: Review and Prospect." In compas *Research Resources Papers,* 1–46. Oxford: COMPAS.

Gupta, Akhil, and James Ferguson. 1997. *Culture, Power, Place: Explorations in Critical Anthropology*. Durham, NC: Duke University Press.

Gurr, Ted Robert. 2015. *Why Men Rebel*. New York: Routledge.

Haanstad, Eric James. 2008. "Constructing Order through Chaos: A State Ethnography of the Thai Police." Ph.D. diss., Department of Anthropology, University of Wisconsin, Madison.

Haberkorn, Tyrell. 2011. *Revolution Interrupted: Farmers, Students, Law, and Violence in Northern Thailand*. Madison: University of Wisconsin Press.

Hage, Ghassan. 2009. *Waiting*. Melbourne: Melbourne University Press.

Hall, Stuart 1986. "Gramsci's Relevance for the Study of Race and Ethnicity." *Journal of Communication Inquiry* 10 (5): 5–27.

Hanks, Lucien M. 1962. "Merit and Power in the Thai Social Order." *American Anthropologist* 64 (6): 1247–61.

Hannerz, Ulf. 1980. *Exploring the City: Inquiries toward an Urban Anthropology.* New York: Columbia University Press.

Hannigan, John A. 1985. "Alain Touraine, Manuel Castells, and Social Movement Theory: A Critical Appraisal." *Sociological Quarterly* 26 (4): 435–54.

Harms, Erik. 2011. *Saigon's Edge: On the Margins of Ho Chi Ming City.* Minneapolis: University of Minnesota Press

Harris, Joseph. 2015. "'Developmental Capture' of the State: Explaining Thailand's Universal Coverage Policy." *Journal of Health Politics, Policy, and Law* 40 (1): 165–93.

Harrison, Rachel V., and Peter A. Jackson. 2011. *The Ambiguous Allure of the West: Traces of the Colonial in Thailand.* Hong Kong: Hong Kong University Press.

Harvey, David. 1985. *The Urbanization of Capital: Studies in the History and Theory of Capitalist Urbanization.* Baltimore: John Hopkins University Press.

———. 1989. *The Condition of Postmodernity: An Enquiry into the Origins of Cultural Change.* Oxford: Blackwell.

———. 2001. *Spaces of Capital: Towards a Critical Geography.* Edinburgh: Edinburgh University Press.

———. 2005. *A Brief History of Neoliberalism.* New York: Oxford University Press.

———. 2007. "The Kantian Roots of Foucault's Dilemmas." In *Space, Knowledge, and Power: Foucault and Geography,* edited by Jeremy Crampton and Stuart Elden, 41-47. London: Ashgate.

———. 2012. *Rebel Cities: From the Right to the City to the Urban Revolution.* New York: Verso.

———. 2014. *Seventeen Contradictions and the End of Capitalism.* Oxford: Oxford University Press.

Harvey, Penny, and Hannah Knox. 2012. "The Enchantments of Infrastructure." *Mobilities* 7 (4): 521–36.

———. 2015. *Roads: An Anthropology of Infrastructure and Expertise.* Ithaca, NY: Cornell University Press.

Hayek, Friedrich A. von. 1944. *The Road to Serfdom.* London: G. Routledge & Sons.

Hegel, Georg Wilhelm Friedrich. 1965. *Philosophy of Right.* Translated by T. M. Knox. Oxford: Clarendon Press.

———. 1998. *Phenomenology of Spirit.* Translated by Arnold Vincent Miller. Berlin: Motilal Banarsidass Publisher.

Herzfeld, Michael. 1992. *The Social Production of Indifference: Exploring the Symbolic Roots of Western Bureaucracy.* New York: Berg.

———. 2002. "The Absence Presence: Discourses Of Crypto-Colonialism." *South Atlantic Quarterly* 101 (4): 899–926.

———. 2004. *The Body Impolitic: Artisans and Artifice in the Global Hierarchy of Value.* Chicago: University of Chicago Press.

———. 2009. *Evicted from Eternity: The Restructuring of Modern Rome.* Chicago: University of Chicago Press.

———. 2012. "Paradoxes of Order in Thai Community Politics." In *Radical Egalitarianism: Local Realities, Global Relations,* edited by Stanley J. Tambiah et al., 146–60. Chicago: University of Chicago Press.

———. 2016a. *Cultural Intimacy: Social Poetics in the Nation-State.* New York: Routledge.

———. 2016b. *Siege of the Spirits: Community and Polity in Bangkok.* Chicago: University of Chicago Press.

———. 2017. "The Blight of Beautification: Bangkok and the Pursuit of Class-Based Urban Purity." *Urban Design* 22 (6): 731–56.

Hetland, Gabriel, and Jeff Goodwin. 2011. "The Strange Disappearance of Capitalism from Social Movement Studies." In *Marxism and Social Movements,* edited by Barker Colin et al., 82–102. Leiden: Brill.

Hewison, Kevin. 2004. "Crafting Thailand's New Social Contract." *Pacific Review* 17 (4): 503–22.

———. 2008. "Thailand Human Development Report: Sufficiency Economy and Human Development." *Journal of Comtemporary Asia* 8 (1): 212–19.

———. 2010. "Thaksin Shinawatra and the Reshaping of Thai Politics." *Contemporary Politics* 16 (2): 119–33.

———. 2014. "Thailand: The Lessons of Protest." *Journal of Critical Perspectives on Asia* 50 (1): 1–15.

Hewison, Kevin, and Kengkij Kitirianglarp. 2010. "'Thai-Style Democracy': The Royalist Struggle for Thailand's Politics." In *Saying the Unsayable,* edited by Soren Ivarsson and Lotte Isager, 241–66. Copenhagen: NIAS Press.

Hickey, Maureen. 2011. "Driving Globalization: Bangkok Taxi Drivers and the Restructuring of Work and Masculinity in Thailand." Ph.D. diss., Department of Geography, University of Washington.

———. 2013. *Itsara (Freedom) to Work? Neoliberalization, Deregulation, and Marginalized Male Labor in the Bangkok Taxi Business:* Singapore: Asia Research Institute, National University of Singapore.

High, Holly. 2014. *Fields of Desire: Poverty and Policy in Laos.* Singapore: NUS Press.

Hill, Marc Lamont. 2016. *Nobody: Casualties of America's War on the Vulnerable, from Ferguson to Flint and Beyond.* New York: Simon and Schuster.

Holloway, John. 2005. *Change the World without Taking Power.* London: Pluto Press.

Holston, James. 1989. *The Modernist City: An Anthropological Critique of Brasília.* Chicago: University of Chicago Press.

ILaw. 2016. *Freedom of Expression Situation.* Bangkok: ILaw, July 2016.

Ishii, Yoneo. 1975. "A Note on Buddhistic Millenarian Revolts in Northeastern Siam." *Journal of Southeast Asian Studies* 6 (2): 121–26.

Ivarsson, Soren, and Lotte Isager. 2010. *Saying the Unsayable: Monarchy and Democracy in Thailand.* Copenhagen: NIAS Press.

Jackson, Peter A. 1989. *Buddhism, Legitimation, and Conflict: the Political Functions of Urban Thai Buddhism.* Singapore: Institute of Southeast Asian Studies.

————. 2009. "Markets, Media, and Magic: Thailand's Monarch as a 'Virtual Deity.'" *Inter-Asia Cultural Studies* 10 (3): 361–80.

————. 2010. "Virtual Divinity: A 21st-Century Discourse of Thai Royal Influence." In *Saying the Unsayable: Monarchy and Democracy in Thailand,* edited by Søren Ivarsson and Lotte Isager, 29–60. Copenhagen: NIAS Press.

Jakobson, Roman. 1962. *Selected Writings.* Gravenhage, Germany: Mouton.

James, Deborah. 2014. *Money from Nothing: Indebtedness and Aspiration in South Africa.* Stanford, CA: Stanford University Press.

Jeffrey, Craig. 2010. *Timepass: Youth, Class, and the Politics of Waiting in India.* Stanford, CA: Stanford University Press.

Jenks, Mike. 2003. "Above and Below the Line: Globalization and Urban Form in Bangkok." *Annals of Regional Science* 37: 547–57.

Jensen, Casper Bruun, and Atsuro Morita. 2015. "Infrastructures as Ontological Experiments." *Ethnos* 10 (1): 81–87.

Jessop, Bob. 1991. "Thatcherism and Flexibility: The White Heat of a Post-Fordist Revolution." In *The Politics of Flexibility: Restructuring State and Industry in Britain, Germany, and Scandinavia,* edited by Bob Jessop et al. Aldershot, UK: Edward Elgar.

————. 1993. "Towards a Schumpeterian Workfare State? Preliminary Remarks on Post-Fordist Political Economy." *Studies in Political Economy* 40 (1): 7–39.

Jetsada, Laipaporn. 2004. "Motorcycle Taxi Service in Bangkok Metropolitan: The Effect of Public Motorcycle Ordering in 2004." Master's thesis, Department of Economics, Thammasat University.

Ji, Ungpakorn. 2003. *Radicalising Thailand: New Political Perspectives.* Bangkok: Institute of Asian Studies.

Johnson, Alan R. 2006. *Leadership in a Bangkok Slum: An Ethnography of Thai Urban Poor in the Lang Wat Pathum Wanaram Community.* Bangkok: Oxford Centre for Mission Studies and University of Wales.

Johnson, Andrew Alan. 2012. "Naming Chaos: Accident, Precariousness, and the Spirits of Wildness in Urban Thai Spirit Cults." *American Ethnologist* 39 (4): 766–78.

————. 2013. "Moral Knowledge and Its Enemies: Conspiracy and Kingship in Thailand." *Anthropological Quarterly* 86 (4): 1059–86.

————. 2014. *Ghosts of the New City: Spirits, Urbanity, and the Ruins of Progress in Chiang Mai.* Honolulu: University of Hawaii Press.

Jones, Daniel Stedman. 2014. *Masters of the Universe: Hayek, Friedman, and the Birth of Neoliberal Politics.* Princeton, NJ: Princeton University Press.

Jory, Patrick. 2002. "Barami and the Vessantara Jataka: The Origin and Spread of a Premodern Thai Concept of Power." *Crossroads: An Interdisciplinary Journal of Southeast Asian Studies* 16 (2): 36–78.

————. 2016. *Thailand's Theory of Monarchy: The Vessantara Jataka and the Idea of the Perfect Man.* New York: State University of New York Press.

Jungck, Susan, and Boonreang Kajornsin. 2003. "'Thai Wisdom' and Glocalization." In *Local Meanings, Global Schooling,* edited by K. Anderson-Levitt, 27–49. New York: Palgrave.

Kakizaki, Ichirō. 2005. *Laying the Tracks: The Thai Economy and Its Railways, 1885–1935*. Kyoto: Kyoto University Press.

Kalleberg, Arne L., and Kevin Hewison. 2013. "Precarious Work and the Challenge for Asia." *American Behavioral Scientist* 57 (3): 271–88.

Karamessini, Maria, and Jill Rubery. 2013. *Women and Austerity: The Economic Crisis and the Future for Gender Equality*. London: Routledge.

Kasian, Tejapira. 2002. "Post-Crisis Economic Impasse and Political Recovery in Thailand: The Resurgence of Economic Nationalism." *Critical Asian Studies* 34 (3): 323–56.

———. 2006. "Toppling Thaksin." *New Left Review* 29: 5–37.

Keane, Webb. 2007. *Christian Moderns: Freedom and Fetish in the Mission Encounter*. Berkeley: University of California Press.

Kemp, Jeremy. 1982. "A Tail Wagging the Dog: The Patron-Client Model in Thai Studies." In *Private Patronage and Public Power,* edited by C. Clapham, 142–61. London: Frances Pinter.

Kerekes, Carrie B., and Claudia R Williamson. 2008. "Unveiling de Soto's Mystery: Property Rights, Capital Formation, and Development." *Journal of Institutional Economics* 4 (3): 299–325.

Klein, Naomi. 2007. *The Shock Doctrine: The Rise of Disaster Capitalism*. New York: Metropolitan Books / Henry Holt.

Kleinman, Arthur, and Joan Kleinman. 1996. "The Appeal of Experience; The Dismay of Images; Cultural Appropriations of Suffering in Our Times." *Daedalus:* 1–23.

Klima, Alan. 2002. *The Funeral Casino: Meditation, Massacre, and Exchange with the Dead in Thailand*. Princeton, NJ: Princeton University Press.

Knight, Daniel M., and Charles Stewart. 2016. "Ethnographies of Austerity: Temporality, Crisis, and Affect in Southern Europe." *History and Anthropology* 27 (1): 1–18.

Kobkua, Suwannathat-Pian. 1988. *Thai-Malay Relations: Traditional Intra-regional Relations from the Seventeenth to the Early Twentieth Centuries*. Oxford: Oxford University Press.

Kockelman, Paul. 2013. *Agent, Person, Subject, Self: A Theory of Ontology, Interaction, and Infrastructure*. Oxford: Oxford University Press.

Kriengsak, Chareonwongsak. 2006. *The Pre-death Phase of Thaksinomics*. Bangkok: Success Media.

Ladwig, Patrice. 2014. "Millennialism, Charisma, and Utopia: Revolutionary Potentialities in Pre-modern Lao and Thai Theravāda Buddhism." *Politics, Religion, and Ideology* 15 (2): 308–29.

Laidlaw, James. 2002. "For an Anthropology of Ethics and Freedom." *Journal of the Royal Anthropological Institute* 8 (2): 311–32.

———. 2013. *The Subject of Virtue: An Anthropology of Ethics and Freedom*. Cambridge: Cambridge University Press.

Languepin, Oliver. 2016. "Household Debts Hit Highest in 8 Years, Filling Pockets of Thai Loan Sharks." *Thailand Business News,* May 2, www.thailand-business-news.com/banking/53291-household-debts-hit-highest-8-years-filling-pockets-thai-loan-sharks.html (accessed May 11, 2017).

Lapavitsas, Costas. 2009. "Financialised Capitalism: Crisis and Financial Expropriation." *Historical Materialism* 17 (2): 114–48.

Larkin, Brian. 2008. *Signal and Noise: Media, Infrastructure, and Urban Culture in Nigeria.* Durham, NC: Duke University Press.

———. 2013. "The Politics and Poetics of Infrastructure." *Annual Review of Anthropology* 42: 327–43.

Latour, Bruno. 2005. *Reassembling the Social: An Introduction to Actor-Network-Theory.* Clarendon Lectures in Management Studies. New York: Oxford University Press.

Latour, Bruno, Emilie Hermant, and Susanna Shannon. 1998. *Paris Ville Invisible.* Paris: Institut Synthélabo pour le Progrès de la Connaissance.

Lazzarato, M., and Joshua David Jordan. 2010. *The Making of the Indebted Man: An Essay on the Neoliberal Condition.* Los Angeles: Semiotext(e).

Leach, Edmund Ronald. 1954. *Political Systems of Highland Burma: A Study of Kachin Social Structure.* Cambridge, MA: Harvard University Press.

Lee, Ching Kwan, and Yelizavetta Kofman. 2012. "The Politics of Precarity Views beyond the United States." *Work and Occupations* 39 (4): 388–408.

Lefebvre, Henri. 1991a. *Critique of Everyday Life.* 3 vols. New York: Verso.

———. 1991b. *The Production of Space.* Oxford: Blackwell.

Levitt, Peggy. 2001. *The Transnational Villagers.* Berkeley: University of California Press.

Li, Tania. 2005. "Beyond 'the State' and Failed Schemes." *American Anthropologist* 107 (3): 383–94.

———. 2007. *The Will to Improve: Governmentality, Development, and the Practice of Politics.* Durham, NC: Duke University Press.

Likhit, Dhiravegin. 1992. *Demi-democracy: The Evolution of the Thai Political System.* Singapore: ISEAS.

Looney, Robert. 2004. "Thaksinomics: A New Asian Paradigm?" *Journal of Social, Political, and Economic Studies* 29 (1): 65–82.

Loos, Tamara. 1998. "Issaraphap: Limits of Individual Liberty in Thai Jurisprudence." *Crossroads: An Interdisciplinary Journal of Southeast Asian Studies* 12 (1): 35–75.

Lordon, Frédéric. 2014. *Willing Slaves of Capital: Spinoza and Marx on Desire.* New York: Verso.

Low, Setha M. 2003. *Behind the Gates: Life, Security, and the Pursuit of Happiness in Fortress America.* New York: Routledge.

Luque-Ayala, Andrés, and Simon Marvin. 2015. "The Maintenance of Urban Circulation: An Operational Logic of Infrastructural Control." *Environment and Planning D: Society and Space* 34 (2): 191–208.

Macan-Markar, Marwaan. 2010. "Anti-Gov't Protesters Use Cultural Taboo as Weapon." Inter Press Service, April 18, www.ipsnews.net/2010/04/thailand-anti-govrsquot-protesters-use-cultural-taboo-as-weapon (accessed May 11, 2017).

Mahmood, Saba. 2005. *Politics of Piety: The Islamic Revival and the Feminist Subject.* Princeton, NJ: Princeton University Press.

Mains, Daniel. 2007. "Neoliberal Times: Progress, Boredom, and Shame among Young Men in Urban Ethiopia." *American Ethnologist* 34 (4): 659–73.

Malaby, Thomas M. 2003. *Gambling Life: Dealing in Contingency in a Greek City.* Urbana: University of Illinois Press.

Malinowski, Bronislaw. 1994. "The Problem of Meaning in Primitive Languages." In *Language and Literacy in Social Practice: A Reader,* edited by Janet Maybin, 1–10. Philadelphia: Multilingual Matters.

Marshall, Andrew MacGregor. 2014. *A Kingdom in Crisis: Thailand's Struggle for Democracy in the Twenty-first Century.* Asian Arguments. London: Zed Books.

Marx, Karl. 1906. *Capital: A Critique of Political Economy.* Translated by Ernest Untermann. 3 vols. Chicago: C. H. Kerr.

———. 1992. *Early Writings.* Translated by Rodney Livingstone and Gregor Benton London: Penguin Classics.

Mathews, Gordon. 2011. *Ghetto at the Center of the World: Chungking Mansions, Hong Kong.* Chicago: University of Chicago Press.

Mattoni, Alice, and Markos Vogiatzoglou. 2014. "Italy and Greece, before and after the Crisis: Between Mobilization and Resistance against Precarity." *Quaderni* (2): 57–71.

Mazzucato, Mariana. 2013. *The Entrepreneurial State: Debunking Public vs. Private Sector Myths.* London: Anthem Press.

Mbembe, Achille. 2013. *Critique de la raison nègre.* Paris: La Découverte.

McAdam, Doug, John D. McCarthy, and Mayer N. Zald. 1996. *Comparative Perspectives on Social Movements: Political Opportunities, Mobilizing Structures, and Cultural Framings.* Cambridge: Cambridge University Press.

McCargo, Duncan. 2002. "Democracy under Stress in Thaksin's Thailand." *Journal of Democracy* 13 (4): 112–26.

———. 2005. "Network Monarchy and Legitimacy Crises in Thailand." *Pacific Review* 18 (4): 499–519.

———. 2014. "Thailand's Army Tears Up the Script." *New York Times,* May 30.

McCargo, Duncan, and Patthamānan Ukrist. 2005. *The Thaksinization of Thailand.* Copenhagen: NIAS Press.

McGeown, Kate. 2006. "Thai King Remains Centre Stage." BBC News, September 21.

McKenzie, Rex A. 2011. "Casino Capitalism with Derivatives: Fragility and Instability in Contemporary Finance." *Review of Radical Political Economics* 43 (2): 198–215.

Mérieau, Eugénie. 2016. "Thailand's Deep State, Royal Power, and the Constitutional Court (1997–2015)." *Journal of Contemporary Asia* 46 (3): 1–22.

Merton, Robert C. 1995. "Financial Innovation and the Management and Regulation of Financial Institutions." *Journal of Banking & Finance* 19 (3): 461–81.

Metcalfe, Andrew W. 1980. "The Demonology of Class: The Iconography of the Coalminer and the Symbolic Construction of the Political Boundaries." *Critique of Anthropology* 10 (1): 39–63.

Mezzadra, Sandro, and Brett Neilson. 2015. "Operations of Capital." *South Atlantic Quarterly* 114 (1): 1–9.

Mezzadra, Sandro, et al. 2013. "Extraction, Logistics, Finance: Global Crisis and the Politics of Operations." *Radical Philosophy* 178: 8–18.

Mills, Mary Beth. 1997. "Contesting the Margins of Modernity: Women, Migration, and Consumption in Thailand." *American Ethnologist* 24 (1): 37–61.

———. 1999a. "Migrant Labor Takes a Holiday: Reworking Modernity and Marginality in Contemporary Thailand." *Critique of Anthropology* 19 (1): 31–51.

———. 1999b. *Thai Women in the Global Labor Force: Consuming Desires, Contested Selves*. New Brunswick, NJ: Rutgers University Press.

———. 2012. "Thai Mobilities and Cultural Citizenship." *Critical Asian Studies* 44 (1): 85–112.

Mirowski, Philip. 2013. *Never Let a Serious Crisis Go to Waste: How Neoliberalism Survived the Financial Meltdown*. New York: Verso.

Mirowski, Philip, and Dieter Plehwe. 2009. *The Road from Mont Pèlerin: The Making of the Neoliberal Thought Collective*. Cambridge, MA: Harvard University Press.

Missingham, Bruce D. 2002. "The Village of the Poor Confronts the State: A Geography of Protest in the Assembly of the Poor." *Urban Studies* 39: 1647–75.

———. 2003. *The Assembly of the Poor in Thailand: from Local Struggles to National Social Movement*. Chiang Mai, Thailand: Silkworm Books.

Mitchell, Timothy. 1988. *Colonising Egypt*. Cambridge Middle East Library. Cambridge: Cambridge University Press.

———. 1991. "The Limits of the State: Beyond Statist Approaches and Their Critics." *American Political Science Review* 85 (1): 77–96.

Molé, Noelle J. 2013. "Existential Damages: The Injury of Precarity Goes to Court." *Cultural Anthropology* 28 (1): 22–43.

Monroe, Kristin V. 2016. *The Insecure City: Space, Power, and Mobility in Beirut*. New Brunswick, NJ: Rutgers University Press.

Montesano, Michael J. 1998. "Political Contests in the Advent of Bangkok's 19 September Putsch." *Copenhagen Journal of Asian Studies* 13: 5–30.

Moore, Alan. 1988. *V for Vendetta*. New York: Vertigo Comics.

Morita, Atsuro. 2016. "Infrastructuring Amphibious Space: The Interplay of Aquatic and Terrestrial Infrastructures in the Chao Phraya Delta in Thailand." *Science as Culture* 25 (1): 117–40.

Muehlebach, Andrea. 2013. "On Precariousness and the Ethical Imagination: The Year 2012 in Sociocultural Anthropology." *American Anthropologist* 115 (2): 297–311.

———. 2016. "Anthropologies of Austerity." *History and Anthropology* 27 (3): 1–17.

Mulder, J. A. Niels. 1973. *Monks, Merit, and Motivation: Buddhism and National Development in Thailand*. 2nd rev. ed. DeKalb: Northern Illinois University, Center for Southeast Asian Studies.

Munck, Ronaldo. 2013. "The Precariat: A View from the South." *Third World Quarterly* 34 (5): 747–62.

Murdoch, John B. 1967. "The 1901–1902 'Holy Man's' Rebellion." *Sciences* 5: 78–86.

Naruemon, Thabchumpon, and Duncan McCargo. 2011. "Urbanized Villagers in the 2010 Thai Redshirt Protests Not Just Poor Farmers?" *Asian Survey* 51 (6): 993–1018.

Neilson, Brett, and Ned Rossiter. 2008. "Precarity as a Political Concept; or, Fordism As Exception." *Theory, Culture, and Society* 25 (7–8): 51–72.

Nelson, Michael. 2012. *Some Observations on Democracy in Thailand.* SEARC Working Paper Series. Hong Kong: Southeast Asia Research Center.

NESDB. 2006. *Sufficiency Economy: Implications and Applications.* Bangkok: Office of the National Economic and Social Development Board.

Nidhi, Eoseewong. 1986 [Buddhist year 2529]. *Kanmueang Thai Samai Phrachao Krung Thonburi.* Bangkok: Sinlapawathanatham.

———. 1995 [Buddhist year 2538]. "Ratthathammanun Chabap Watthanatham Thai." In *Chatthai muangthai baeprian lae anusawari,* edited by Nidhi Eoseewong, 136–71. Bangkok: Matichon Press.

Nithi, Ieosīwong. 2010 [Buddhist year 2553]. *'Ān kānmūang Thai.* Krung Thēp (Bangkok): Samnakphim Openbooks.

Norman, Henry. 1904. *The Peoples and Politics of the Far East: Travels and Studies in the British, French, Spanish, and Portuguese Colonies, Siberia, China, Japan, Korea, Siam, and Malaya.* New York: Scribner.

Nostitz, Nick. 2009. *Red vs. Yellow.* Vol. 2. Bangkok: White Lotus Press.

———. 2014. "The Red Shirts from Anti-Coup Protesters to Social Mass Movement." In *Good Coup Gone Bad: Thailand's Political Development since Thaksin's Downfall,* edited by Pavin Chachavalpongpun, 170–98. Singapore: ISEAS.

Ockey, James. 2004. *Making Democracy: Leadership, Class, Gender, and Political Participation in Thailand.* Honolulu: University of Hawaii Press.

O'Neill, Bruce. 2014. "Cast Aside: Boredom, Downward Mobility, and Homelessness in Post-Communist Bucharest." *Cultural Anthropology* 29 (1): 8–31.

Ong, Aihwa. 2006. *Neoliberalism as Exception: Mutations in Citizenship and Sovereignty.* Durham, NC: Duke University Press.

Ong, Aihwa, and Stephen J. Collier. 2005. *Global Assemblages: Technology, Politics, and Ethics as Anthropological Problems.* Malden, MA: Blackwell.

Ortner, Sherry B. 1995. "Resistance and the Problem of Ethnographic Refusal." *Comparative Studies in Society and History* 37 (01): 173–93.

Parnwell, Mike. 1996. *Uneven Development in Thailand.* Aldershot: Avebury.

Pasolini, Pier Paolo. 1975. *Scritti corsari.* Milan: Garzanti.

Pasuk, Phongpaichit. 2004. *Financing Thaksinomics.* Edited by Chulalongkorn University. Bangkok: Chulalongkorn University.

Pasuk, Phongpaichit, and Christopher John Baker. 1996. *Thailand's Boom!* St. Leonards: Allen & Unwin.

———. 2002. *Thailand: Economy and Politics.* Oxford: Oxford University Press.

———. 2004. *Thaksin: The Business of Politics in Thailand.* Chiang Mai, Thailand: Silkworm Books.

————. 2005. "Pluto-Populism in Thailand: Business Remaking Politics." In *Thailand beyond the Crisis,* edited by Peter B. Warr, 1–27. London: RoutledgeCurzon.

————. 2008a. "Thaksin's Populism." *Journal of Contemporary Asia* 38 (1): 62–83.

————. 2008b. *Thai Capital after the 1997 Crisis.* Singapore: Institute of Southeast Asian Studies.

Pattana, Kitiarsa. 2005a. "The 'Ghosts' of Transnational Labour Migration: Death and Other Tragedies of Thai Migrant Workers in Singapore." In *Asian Migrations: Sojourning, Displacement, Homecoming, and Other Travels,* edited by Nicola Piper et al., 194–200. Singapore: Asia Research Institute.

————. 2005b. "'Lives of Hunting Dogs': Muai Thai and the Politics of Thai Masculinities." *South East Asia Research* 13 (1): 57–90.

————. 2006a. "In Defense of Thai-Style Democracy." National University of Singapore: Asia Research Institute. Available at National University of Singapore website, https://ari.nus.edu.sg/Assets/repository/files/events/pattana%20 paper%20%20edited..pdf (accessed July 27, 2017).

————. 2006b. "Village Transnationalism: Transborder Identities among Thai-Isan Migrant Workers in Singapore." *Asia Research Institute Working Paper Series* (71): 1–40.

————. 2007. "Muai Thai Cinema and the Burdens of Thai Men." *South East Asia Research* 15 (3): 407–24.

————. 2008. "Thai Migrants in Singapore: State, Intimacy, and Desire." *Gender, Place, and Culture* 15 (6): 595–610.

————. 2009. "The Lyrics of Laborious Life: Popular Music and the Reassertion of Migrant Manhood in Northeastern Thailand." *InterAsia Cultural Studies* 10 (3): 381–98.

————. 2012a. "Masculine Intent and Migrant Manhood. in *Men and Masculinities in Southeast Asia,,* edited by Michele Ford and Lenore Lyons. *38- 76.* New York: Routledge 41: 38.

————. 2012b. *Mediums, Monks, and Amulets: Thai Popular Buddhism Today.* Bangkok: Silkworm Books.

Pavin, Chachavalpongpun, ed. 2014. *Good Coup Gone Bad: Thailand's Political Developments since Thaksin's Downfall.* Singapore: ISEAS.

Peeradorn, Kaewlai. 2007. "Modern Trade and Urbanism." Ph.D. diss., Design School, Harvard University.

Peleggi, Maurizio. 2007. *Thailand: The Worldly Kingdom.* London: Reaktion.

Persons, Larry S. 2016. *The Way Thais Lead: Face as Social Capital.* Chiang Mai, Thailand: Silkworm Books.

Peters, Michael A. 2001. *Poststructuralism, Marxism, and Neoliberalism: Between Theory and Politics.* New York: Rowman & Littlefield.

Phatthanā, Khana Kammakān Phæiphr æ læ Songsæm Ngān. 1994. *Seeds of Hope: Local Initiatives in Thailand.* Bangkok: Thai Development Support Committee.

Phillips, Matthew. 2015. *Thailand in the Cold War.* London: Routledge.

Piparo, Franco Lo. 1979. *Lingua, intellettuali, egemonia in Gramsci.* Milan: Laterza.

Polanyi, Karl. 1944. *The Great Transformation.* New York: Farrar & Rinehart.

Porphant, Ouyyanont. 1998. "Bangkok as a Magnet for Rural Labour: Changing Conditions, 1900–1970." *Southeast Asian Studies* 36 (1): 78–108.

Povatong, Pirasri. 2011. "Building Siwilai: Transformation of Architecture and Architectural Practice in Siam during the Reign of Rama V, 1868–1910." Ph.D. diss., Department of Architecture, University of Michigan.

Prakash, Gyan. 1999. *Another Reason: Science and the Imagination of Modern India.* Princeton, NJ: Princeton University Press.

Pran, Phisit-Setthakan, ed. 2004 [Buddhist year 2547]. *Collection of Important Speeches by Thaksin Shinawatra.* 3 vols. Bangkok: Matichon Press.

Prasad, Woradej. 2003. "Vest Doled Out to Motorcycle-Taxi Riders." *The Nation.*

Pye, Oliver, and Wolfram Schaffar. 2008. "The 2006 Anti-Thaksin Movement in Thailand: An Analysis." *Journal of Contemporary Asia* 38 (1): 38–61.

Rabinow, Paul, and Gaymon Bennett. 2010. "Toward Synthetic Anthropos: Remediating Concepts." Available at www.anthropos-lab.net/documents.

Radom, Setteaton. 1960 [Buddhist year 2503]. "Street Administration in the Bangkok Metropolitan Area." Master's thesis, Institute of Public Administration, Thammasat University, Bangkok.

Ralph, Laurence. 2014. *Renegade Dreams: Living through Injury in Gangland Chicago.* Chicago: Chicago University Press.

Ralph, Michael. 2008. "Killing Time." *Social Text* 26 (4): 1–29.

Rao, Vyjayanthi. 2014. "Infra-City." In *Infrastructural Lives: Urban Infrastructure in Context* edited by Stephen Graham and Colin Mcfarlane, 39–74. London: Routledge.

Reinhart, Carmen M., and Kenneth S. Rogoff. 2011. "From Financial Crash to Debt Crisis." *American Economic Review* 101 (5): 1676–1706.

Reynolds, Craig J. 1987. *Thai Radical Discourse: The Real Face of Thai Feudalism Today.* Ithaca, NY: Cornell University Press.

———. 2002. *National Identity and Its Defenders : Thailand Today.* Chiang Mai, Thailand: Silkworm Books.

Riggs, Fred Warren. 1966. *Thailand: The Modernization of a Bureaucratic Polity.* Honolulu: East-West Center Press.

Roberts, Alasdair. 2010. *The Logic of Discipline: Global Capitalism and the Architecture of Government.* Oxford: Oxford University Press.

Robison, Richard, and Kevin Hewison. 2005. "Introduction: East Asia and the Trials of Neo-Liberalism." *Journal of Development Studies* 41 (2): 183–96.

Rose, Nikolas S. 1999. *Powers of Freedom: Reframing Political Thought.* Cambridge: Cambridge University Press.

Roseberry, William. 1994. "Hegemony and the Language of Contention." In *Everyday Forms of State Formation: Revolution and the Negotiation of Rule in Modern Mexico,* edited by Gilbert M. Joseph and Daniel Nugent, 355–66. Durham, NC: Duke University Press.

Rossi, Amalia. 2012. "Turning Red Rural Landscapes Yellow? Sufficiency Economy and Royal Projects in the Hills of Nan Province, Northern Thailand." *Austrian Journal of South-East Asian Studies* 5 (2): 275.

Roy, Dayabati. 2013. *Rural Politics in India: Political Stratification and Governance in West Bengal*. Cambridge: Cambridge University Press.

Ruccio, David F. 2006. "Unfinished Business: Gramsci's Prison Notebooks." *Rethinking Marxism* 18 (1): 1–7.

Sangsit, Phiriyarangsan. 2005 [Buddhist year 2548]. *Tamrŭat, phū mī 'itthiphon læ sētthakit mŭt*. Krung Thēp (Bangkok): Samnakphim Rŭamdūai Chūaikan.

———. 2007 [Buddhist year 2550]. *Khōrapchan rabōp Thaksin*. Krung Thēp (Bangkok): Samnakphim Rŭamdūai Chūaikan.

Santoro, Emilio. 1999. *Autonomia individuale, libertà e diritti: Una critica dell'antropologia liberale*. Pisa: ETS.

Sartre, Jean-Paul. 1976. *Critique of Dialectical Reason*. Translated by Alan Sheridan-Smith. London: New Left Books.

Schein, Arthur A., et al. 2001. *Global Financial Services Integration System and Process*. Google Patents, www.google.com/patents/US6226623.

Schumpeter, Joseph Alois. 1934. *The Theory of Economic Development: An Inquiry into Profits, Capital, Credit, Interest, and the Business Cycle*. Vol. 55. Cambridge, MA: Harvard University Press.

———. 1947. "The Creative Response in Economic History." *Journal of Economic History* 7 (2): 149–59.

Scott, James C. 1972a. "The Erosion of Patron-Client Bonds and Social Change in Rural Southeast Asia." *Journal of Asian Studies* 32 (1): 5–37.

———. 1972b. "Patron-Client Politics and Political Change in Southeast Asia." *American Political Science Review* 66 (1): 91–113.

———. 1985. *Weapons of the Weak: Everyday Forms of Peasant Resistance*. New Haven, CT: Yale University Press.

———. 1990. *Domination and the Arts of Resistance: Hidden Transcripts*. New Haven, CT: Yale University Press.

———. 1998. *Seeing Like a State: How Certain Schemes to Improve the Human Condition Have Failed*. New Haven, CT: Yale University Press.

———. 2009. *The Art of Not Being Governed: An Anarchist History of Upland Southeast Asia*. New Haven, CT: Yale University Press.

Shortell, Timothy, and Evrick Brown. 2016. *Walking in the European City: Quotidian Mobility and Urban Ethnography*. London: Routledge.

Siamwalla, Ammar. 2000. "Anatomy of the Thai Economic Crisis." In *Thailand Beyond the Crisis*, edited by Peter Warr, 66-105. New York: RoutledgeCurzon.

Siffin, William J. 1966. *The Thai Bureaucracy: Institutional Change and Development*. Honolulu: East-West Center Press.

Simone, AbdouMaliq. 2004. "People as Infrastructure: Intersecting Fragments in Johannesburg." *Public Culture* 16 (3): 407–29.

———. 2005. "Urban Circulation and the Everyday Politics of African Urban Youth: The Case of Douala, Cameroon." *International Journal of Urban and Regional Research* 29 (3): 516–32.

———. 2010. *City Life from Jakarta to Dakar: Movements at the Crossroads*. New York: Routledge.

Sirindhorn, Maha Chakri. 1981. *Thotsabarami nai Phutasatnatherawat.* Master's thesis, Chulalongkorn University.

Siriporn, Siripanyawat, Sawangngoenyuang Wanvimol, and Thungkasemvathana Pimporn. 2009. "Household Indebtedness and Its Implications for Financial Stability in Thailand." In *Household Indebtedness and Its Implications for Financial Stability,* edited by Nakornthab Don, 149–200. Kuala Lumpur, Malaysia: SEACEN.

Skinner, G. William. 1957. *Chinese Society in Thailand: An Analytical History.* Ithaca, NY: Cornell University Press.

Smith, Gavin. 2004. "Hegemony: Critical Interpretations in Anthropology and Beyond." *Focaal: European Journal of Anthropology* 43: 99–112.

———. 2011. "Selective Hegemony and Beyond: Populations with 'No Productive Function': A Framework for Enquiry." *Identities* 18 (1): 2–38.

———. 2013. "Intellectuals' Contributions to Popular Mobilization and Strategic Action under Different Conditions Of Possibility." Paper presented at Left Forum, New York. Available at Focaal Blog, www.focaalblog.com/2014/07/17/intellectuals-contributions-to-popular-mobilization-and-strategic-action-under-different-conditions-of-possibility-by-gavin-smith (accessed July 27, 2017).

Smith, Neil. 1992. "Contours of a Spatialized Politics: Homeless Vehicles and the Production of Geographical Scale." *Social Text* (33): 55–81.

Somchai, Phatharathananunth. 2006. *Civil Society and Democratization: Social Movements in Northeast Thailand.* Copenhagen: NIAS Press.

———. 2014. "Civil Society against Democracy." Hot Spots, Cultural Anthropology website, September 23, https://culanth.org/fieldsights/575-civil-society-against-democracy (accessed July 27, 2017).

Sopranzetti, Claudio. 2012a. "Burning Red Desires: Isan Migrants and the Politics of Desire in Contemporary Thailand." *Journal of Southeast Asia Research* 20 (3): 361–79.

———. 2012b. *Red Journeys: Inside the Thai Red-Shirt Movement.* Chiang Mai, Thailand: Silkworm Books.

———. 2014a. "The Owners of the Map: Mobility and Mobilization among Motorcycle Taxi Drivers in Bangkok." *City and Society* 26 (1): 120–46.

———. 2014b. "Political Legitimacy in Thailand." Hot Spots, *Cultural Anthropology* website, September 23, https://culanth.org/fieldsights/578-political-legitimacy-in-thailand (accessed July 27, 2017).

———. 2016. "Thailand's Relapse: The Implications of the May 2014 Coup." *Journal of Asian Studies* 75 (2): 299–316.

———. 2018, forthcoming. "Mobilizing and Immobilizing the City." In *Routledge Handbook of Anthropology and the City,* edited by Setha M Low. New York: Routledge.

———. Forthcoming-a. "Balancing Powers: Barami and Amnat in Thai Society." In *Coup, King, Crisis,* edited by Chachavalpongpun Pavin. Stanford, CA: Stanford University Press.

————. Forthcoming-b. "A Return to Regulated Neoliberalism: The Emergence of Schumpeterian Welfare State in Contemporary Thailand." In author's possession, seeking publication.

Soto, Hernando de. 2000. *The Mystery of Capital: Why Captitalism Triumphs in the West and Fails Everywhere Else.* New York: Basic Books.

Standing, Guy. 2011. *The Precariat: The New Dangerous Class.* London: Bloomsbury Academic.

Stent, James. 2010. "Thoughts on Thailand's Turmoil." In *Bangkok, May 2010,* edited by Michael J. Montesano, Chachavalpongpun Pavin, and Chongvilaivan Aekapol, 15–42. Singapore: ISEAS.

Sternstein, Larry. 1971. *Greater Bangkok Metropolitan Area Population Growth and Movement, 1956–1960.* Bangkok: Institute of Population Studies, Chulalongkorn University.

————. 1982. *Portrait of Bangkok.* Bangkok: Bangkok Metropolitan Administration.

Steward, Ian. 2012. "The Mathematical Equation That Caused the Banks to Crash." *The Guardian,* July 12.

Stiglitz, Joseph E. 2002. *Globalization and Its Discontents.* New York: W. W. Norton.

Stiglitz, Joseph E., and Shahid Yusuf. 2001. *Rethinking the East Asia Miracle.* New York: World Bank.

Stoller, Paul. 2002. *Money Has No Smell: The Africanization of New York City.* Chicago: University of Chicago Press.

Streckfuss, David. 1996. *Modern Thai Monarchy and Cultural Politics: The Acquittal of Sulak Sivaraksa on the Charge of Lèse-majesté in Siam; 1995 and Its Consequences.* Bangkok: Santi Pracha Dhamma Institute.

————. 2011. *Truth on Trial in Thailand: Defamation, Treason, and Lèse-majesté.* New York: Routledge.

Suehiro, Akira. 1989. *Capital Accumulation in Thailand, 1855–1985.* Tokyo: Centre for East Asian Cultural Studies.

————. 2014. "Technocracy and Thaksinocracy in Thailand: Reforms of the Public Sector and the Budget System under the Thaksin Government." *Southeast Asian Studies* 3 (2): 299–344.

Sulak, Sivaraksa. 1999. *Global Healing: Essays and Interviews on Structural Violence, Social Development, and Spiritual Transformation.* Bangkok: Thai Inter-Religious Commission for Development.

Sulak, Sivaraksa, and Donald K. Swearer. 2005. *Conflict, Culture, Change: Engaged Buddhism in a Globalizing World.* 1st ed. Boston: Wisdom Publications.

Sulak, Sivaraksa, and Christopher Titmuss. 1988. *The Religion of Consumerism.* Bangkok: Santi Pracha Dhamma Institute.

Sunate, Suwanlaong. 2006. "Historical Development of Consumerism in Thai Society." Ph.D. diss., Department of Philosophy, Westfälischen Wilhelms University.

Surin, Maisrikrod. 2007. "Learning from the 19 September Coup: Advancing Thai-style Democracy?" In *Southeast Asian Affairs,* edited by Singh Daljit and Carlos Salazar Lorraine, 340–59. Singapore: ISEAS.

Tamada, Yoshifumi. 1991. "Itthiphon and Amnat: An Informal Aspect of Thai Politics." *Southeast Asian Studies* 28 (4): 455–66.

Tambiah, Stanley J. 1973. "Classification of Animals in Thailand." In *Rules and Meanings: The Anthropology of Everyday Knowledge,* edited by Mary Douglas, 165–94. London: Routledge.

———. 1976. *World Conqueror and World Renouncer: A Study of Buddhism and Polity in Thailand against a Historical Cackground.* Cambridge: Cambridge University Press.

———. 1984. *The Buddhist Saints of the Forest and the Cult of Amulets : A Study in Charisma, Hagiography, Sectarianism, and Millennial Buddhism.* Cambridge: Cambridge University Press.

Tannenbaum, Nicola Beth. 1995. *Who Can Compete against the World? Power-Protection and Buddhism in Shan Worldview.* Ann Harbor: Association of Asian Studies.

Tausig, Benjamin. 2013. *Bangkok is Ringing.* PhD dissertation, Department of Ethnomusicology, New York University.

———. 2014. "Neoliberalism's Moral Overtones: Music, Money, and Morality at Thailand's Red Shirt Protests." *Culture, Theory, and Critique* 55 (2): 257–71.

Taylor, Frederick Winslow. 1914. *The Principles of Scientific Management.* New York: Harper.

Taylor, Jim. 2011. "Larger Than Life: 'Central World' and Its Demise and Rebirth; Red Shirts and the Creation of the *Urban Cultural Myth* in Thailand." *Asia Research Institute Working Paper Series* (150): 1–13.

———. 2012. "Remembrance and Tragedy: Understanding Thailand's 'Red Shirt' Social Movement." *Sojourn: Journal of Social Issues in Southeast Asia* 27 (1): 120–52.

Teasdale, Simon, and Chris Mason. 2012. "Up for Grabs: A Critical Discourse Analysis of Social Entrepreneurship Discourse in the United Kingdom." *Social Enterprise Journal* 8 (2): 123–40.

Terwiel, B. J. 1994. *Monks and Magic: An Analysis of Religious Ceremonies in Central Thailand.* Bangkok: White Lotus Press.

Textor, Robert B. 1961. *From Peasant to Pedicab Drivers.* New Haven, CT: Yale University Press.

Thak, Chaloemtiarana. 2007. *Thailand: The Politics of Despotic Paternalism.* Ithaca, NY: Cornell University Press.

Thanet, Aphornsuvan. 1998. "Slavery and Modernity: Freedom in the Making of Modern Siam." In *Asian Freedoms: The Idea of Freedom in East and Southeast Asia,* edited by David Kelly and Anthony Reid, 161–86. Cambridge: Cambridge University Press.

Thitinan, Pongsudhirak. 2006. "Thaksin's Political Zenith and Nadir." *Southeast Asian Affairs* 1: 285–302.

Thompson, E. P. 1978. "Eighteenth-Century English Society: Class Struggle without Class?" *Social History* 3 (2): 133–65.

Thompson, Hunter S. 1971. *Fear and Loathing in Las Vegas.* New York: Random House.

Thompson, Mark R. 2007. "The Dialectic of 'Good Governance' and Democracy in Southeast Asia: Globalized Discourses and Local Responses." *Globality Studies Journal* (10): 1–21.

Thongchai, Winichakul. 1994. *Siam Mapped: A History of the Geo-body of a Nation.* Honolulu: University of Hawaii Press.

———. 2000. "The 'Quest' for 'Siwilai': A Geographical Discourse of Civilizational Thinking in the Late 19th and Early 20th Century Siam." *Journal of Asian Studies* 59 (3): 517–35.

———. 2008a. "Nationalism and the Radical Intelligentsia in Thailand." *Third World Quarterly* 29 (3): 575–91.

———. 2008b. "Toppling Democracy." *Journal of Comtemporary Asia* 38 (1): 11–37.

———. 2010. "The 'Germs': The Reds' Infection of the Thai Political Body." New Mandala, May 15, http://asiapacific.anu.edu.au/newmandala/2010/05/03/thongchai-winichakul-on-the-red-germs (accessed May 12, 2017).

———. 2014. "The Monarchy and Anti-Monarchy: Two Elephants in the Room of Thai Politics and the State of Denial." In *Good Coup Gone Bad: Thailand's Political Developments since Thaksin's Downfall,* edited by Chachavalpongpun Pavin, 79–108. Singapore: ISEAS.

———. 2015a. "The Hazing Scandals in Thailand Reflect Deeper Problem in Social Relations." *ISEAS Perspective* 56: 1–9.

———. 2015b. "Thailand's Royalist Democracy in Crisis." *Newsletter: Center for Southeast Asian Studies, Kyoto University* 72: 4.

Tilly, Charles. 1978. *From Mobilization to Revolution.* Reading, MA: Addison-Wesley.

———. 1990. *Coercion, Capital, and European States,* a.d. *990–1990.* Cambridge: Blackwell.

Tilly, Charles, and Lesley J. Wood. 2009. *Social Movements, 1768–2008.* 2nd ed. Boulder, CO: Paradigm Publishers.

Tinnaluck, Yuwanuch. 2005. "Knowledge Creation and Sustainable Development: A Collaborative Process between Thai Local Wisdom and Modern Sciences." Ph.D. diss., Department of Science of Information and Communication, Université de Poitiers.

Toporowski, Jan. 2002. *The End of Finance: Capital Market Inflation, Financial Derivatives, and Pension Fund Capitalism.* London: Routledge.

Touraine, Alain. 1981. *The Voice and the Eye: An Analysis of Social Movements.* Cambridge: Cambridge University Press.

Truitt, Allison. 2008. "On the Back of a Motorbike: Middle-Class Mobility in Ho Chi Minh City, Vietnam." *American Ethnologist* 35 (1): 3–19.

Tsing, Anna Lowenhaupt. 2005. *Friction: An Ethnography of Global Connection.* Princeton, NJ: Princeton University Press.

Tye, Larry. 1998. *The Father of Spin: Edward L. Bernays and the Birth of Public Relations.* New York: Crown Publishers.

Ünaldi, Serhat. 2014a. "Bangkok's Ratchaprasong before CentralWorld: The Disappearance of Phetchabun Palace." *Asian Studies Review* 38 (3): 480–502.

———. 2014b. "Politics and the City: Protest, Memory, and Contested Space in Bangkok." In *Contemporary Socio-Cultural and Political Perspectives in Thailand*, edited by Pranee Liamputtong, 209–22. London: Springer.

———. 2014c. "Working towards the Monarchy and Its Discontents: Anti-Royal Graffiti in Downtown Bangkok." *Journal of Contemporary Asia* 44 (3): 377–403.

Urry, John. 2000. *Sociology beyond Societies: Mobilities for the Twenty-first Century*. London: Routledge.

———. 2007. *Mobilities*. Cambridge: Polity.

Vajiravudh. 1914. "The Jews of the Orient." *Siam Observer*, July 23.

Vandergeest, Peter. 1993. "Constructing Thailand: Regulation, Everyday Resistance, and Citizenship." *Comparative Studies in Society and History* 35 (1): 133–58.

Vaneigem, Raoul, and Donald Nicholson-Smith. 1983. *The Revolution of Everyday Life*. Seattle: Left Bank Books.

Veal, Clare. 2013. "The Charismatic Index: Photographic Representations of Power and Status in the Thai Social Order." *Trans-Asia Photography Review* 3 (2): 1–33.

Veer, Peter van der. 2001. *Imperial Encounters: Religion and Modernity in India and Britain*. Princeton, NJ: Princeton University Press.

Verney, Susannah, and Anna Bosco. 2013. "Living Parallel Lives: Italy and Greece in an Age of Austerity." *South European Society and Politics* 18 (4): 397–426.

Viswanathan, Gauri. 1998. *Outside the Fold: Conversion, Modernity, and Belief*. Princeton, NJ: Princeton University Press.

Voranai, Vanijaka 2011. "Ammat and Phrai: The Facebook War." *Bangkok Post*, May 15.

Wade, Robert. 1996. "Japan, the World Bank, and the Art of Paradigm Maintenance: The East Asian Miracle in Political Perspective." *New Left Review* 217:114–136.

Wah, Francis L. K., and Joakim Öjendal, eds. 2004. *Southeast Asian Responses to Globalization: Restructuring Governance, Deepening Democracy*. Singapore: NIAS Press.

Walker, Andrew. 2010. "Royal Sufficiency and Elite Misrepresentation of Rural Livelihoods." In *Saying the Unsayable: Monarchy and Democracy in Thailand*, edited by Soren Ivarsson and Lotte Isager, 241–65. Copenhagen: NIAS Press.

———. 2012. *Thailand's Political Peasants: Power in the Modern Rural Economy*. Madison: University of Wisconsin Press.

Warr, Peter G. 2005. *Thailand beyond the Crisis*. London: RoutledgeCurzon.

Wassayos, Ngarmkham. 2005. "Army Hiring Bikers and Informers." *Bangkok Post*, February 8.

Wassayos, Ngarmkham, and Thip-osod Manop. 2003. "Motorcycle Taxi Jackets Symbol of Mafia Control." *Bangkok Post*, May 26.

White, Lawrence H. 2012. *The Clash of Economic Ideas: The Great Policy Debates and Experiments of the Last Hundred Years*. New York: Cambridge University Press.

Williams, Eric. 1944. *Capitalism and Slavery*. Chapel Hill: University of Norht Carolina Press Books.

Williams, Raymond. 1975. *The Country and the City.* Vol. 423. Oxford: Oxford University Press.

Wilson, Constance M. 1997. "The Holy Man in the History of Thailand and Laos." *Journal of Southeast Asian Studies* 28 (2): 345–64.

Wilson, David A. 1962. *Politics in Thailand.* Ithaca, NY: Cornell University Press.

Wisalo, Phra Phaisan. 1999. "Spiritual Materialism and the Sacraments of Consumerism: A View from Thailand." *Seeds of Peace* 14 (3): 24–25.

Wisit, Sasanatieng, dir. 2004. *Maa Nakorn (Citizen Dog).* Produced by Aphiradee Iamphungporn. Bangkok: Five Star Production.

Wittgenstein, Ludwig. 1953. *Philosophical Investigations.* Translated by G. E. M. Anscombe. New York: Macmillan.

———. 1969. *On Certainty.* Translated and edited by G. E. M. Anscombe. Oxford: Blackwell.

Woodruff, Christopher, and Hernando de Soto. 2001. "Review of de Soto's *The Mystery of Capital.*" *Journal of Economic Literature* 39 (4): 1215–23.

Yot, Santasombat. 1990 [2533 Buddhist year]. *Amnat, Bukkhalikkaphap, lae Phunam Kanmuang Thai.* Bangkok: Thammasat University Press.

Žižek, Slavoj. 1989. *The Sublime Object of Ideology.* London: Verso.

love, 92–93, 104, 112–13, 147–48, 197–98, 233, 264–65
Luang Wichit, 51–54

marxism, 10–11, 77, 149n21, 184–85, 272–78
Marx, Karl, 96, 129–30, 149–50, 171–72, 183–85, 270–80
masculinity, 14, 27, 112–13, 220
mediation, 12–14, 69–75, 83–87, 91–100, 181–84, 278–80
messiness, 14, 36–38, 47–48, 59–61, 272–74. *See also* fragility
methodology, 8–10, 37n11, 272–80
migrants: adaptation to the city: 3–4, 17–20, 50–56, 74–76, 110–14, 119–21
  challenges of, 88–109, 147–48, 158–59
  dismissal of, 7–9, 130–31, 175–79, 193–95
  studies of, 11–12
  working as motorcycle taxi drivers, 8–10, 34–38, 61–62
military: coup, 13, 54, 56, 92, 140, 162–66, 170–80, 257–58
  dictatorship, 15–18, 55–56, 258–67
  dispersal, 1–2, 22–25, 191, 203–7, 212–24, 229–30
  expansion, 40–44
  influence, 140–50, 186–89, 236–43, 247–53
  struggle with Thaksin, 137–38, 154–62
Mitchell, Timothy, 137, 154–55
mobility, 1–14, 58–61, 70–71, 79n26, 182–83, 225–28
  blockage, 191, 196–98, 266–80
  conversion of 81–87, 249
  urban-rural, 90–108, 131. *See also* circulation
mobilization, 1, 10–13, 148–52, 155–61, 196–228, 230–35, 269–80
  agents of, 26–29, 244–56, 263–65
  labor, 47–51
  role of desires in, 183–95. *See also* social movements
modernity, 90–97, 117, 131n49. *See also* development
molotov, 204, 217–21
monarchy: abolition absolute, 51–56, 258

political role of, 161–63, 175–80, 229–35, 247, 253–54, 259, 264
  role in urban development, 46–47. *See also* king
moral: depiction of the village, 90–101
  hierarchy, 42
  leadership, 132, 156–84, 244–55. See also *barami*

narrative, 7–9, 12–15, 254
  of civilization, 40–42
  of development 90–108
  of neoliberalism, 123–25
  of sufficiency, 175–80. *See also* imaginaries
National Economic and Social Development Board (NESDB), 57–58, 176–78
nationalism, 50–56, 69, 123–24
Nattawut, Saikua, 190–91
neoliberalism, 117n13, 120–25, 132, 137–38, 168, 176, 272. *See also* post-fordism
network: of drivers, 105, 148–52, 159–61, 170–71, 186–95
  infrastructure, 7–73, 278
  road, 40–48, 60–61
newspaper, 18, 19, 62, 66–70, 80n29, 139, 145–46
NGOs, 157–58, 158n35, 161, 164
Nidhi, Eoseewong, 171
Nit, 139–50, 155, 160–63
Nok, 104–8
Nuamthong, Praiwal, 186

Oboto, 26–28, 151–52, 196–202, 209–16, 237, 243
oppression, 81–82, 113–29, 174, 193–95
Orange Shirts, 211, 243
order: attempts to impose, 13–15, 36–38, 41–48, 56–62, 138, 198, 226–27, 266–74
  moral, 175–81, 244–56
  not following, 117–19. *See also* control

palimpsest, 36–38, 46–47, 60–62
paradoxes, 13, 74–75, 90–91, 129–33, 164–65, 270. *See also* contradictions
participation: in capitalism, 126–33, 170–85
  in protest, 24, 27, 148–52, 164–66, 209, 239–42

theory of, 14–15, 194–95, 198
soi: Ngam Duphli, 33–35, 138–44
   social life, 80–85, 105–6, 241–43
   system 36, 60–64, 72–73
   use in protest, 205, 213–14, 219–21
Somchai, Wongsawat, 186–87
Sondhi, Limthongkul, 159
speed, 20–22, 85–86, 102–4, 199–200
Spinoza, 184
state: and markets, 121–26, 137–39
   challenges to, 197–202, 216–28, 230–35
   fight over, 151–66, 175–81, 186–88, 251–
     56, 259–68
   forces 1, 12–14, 28, 34–36, 140–48,
     236–42
   formation, 42–45, 54–61, 69–70
status, 85–86, 96–100, 113, 119, 173–74,
strategy: elite's, 175–80 , 236–43
   mediation, 91, 243–50
   protest, 27–29, 148–52, 198–224, 278–80
   Thaksin's, 122–26
   unified, 14, 36, 197–98. *See also* tactics
strike, 48–52, 57, 143–44
structural adjustment, 114–22
struggle: conceptual, 9–10, 251–56
   to control, 12–13, 36–38, 138–48, 152–66,
     175–80
   of migration 98–108, 170–71
   political, 27, 49–51, 76, 148–52 , 183–85,
     188–93, 212–28, 265–80
subject, 44–45, 118–19, 130–31, 173–74,
   216–17, 225–28, 266–76
sufficiency economy, 158n35, 175–86
Surayud, Chulanont, 176, 181
surplus, 274–79
surveillance, 238–40

tactics, 36n8, 191–98, 216–19, 227–28,
   234–35, 257–58, 269–71. *See also*
   strategy
tā sawāng, 228–36, 264
Taylorism, 76–77
temporality, 90–100, 207. *See also*
   development
Thaksinomics, 123–33, 171–74, 253–54
Thaksin Shinawatra: formalization of
   motorcycle taxis, 18, 24, 26, 140–56,
   238–43

personal history, 108, 122–24, 132–33
policies, 92–93, 125–28, 137–38, 156–59,
   167–77
removal from office, 13, 96, 159–81,
   229–30, 252–55, 257–59
significance for Red Shirts, 181–92, 197,
   211–12, 244–46
speech, 25–26
Thongchai Winichakul, 42–43, 52n43,
   164n43, 192–93
Tong, 250–56
traces, 36–37, 60, 267–68. *See also*
   palimpsest
traffic, 3–4, 17–22, 35–38, 61–62,
   68–70, 76–80, 199–200, 213–15,
   249, 279
transportation: blockage of, 115–16, 187–88,
   192–93, 199–216
   experience of, 1–6
   infrastructure of, 24–26, 64–75
   new modes of, 33–35, 40–48, 53–54,
     58–62

United Front for Democracy against
   Dictatorship (UDD), 25, 66, 96, 186–
   96, 209
unintended consequences: 12–13, 36, 138–
   39, 148–52, 162–66, 164–66, 170–71,
   243, 267–72
unmaking, 12–13, 231–35, 266–67
unraveling, 196–228, 278–79
unresolved tensions, 11, 14–15, 37n11,
   91–100, 112–16, 255–56, 266–80

Veera, Musikhapong, 205
vests: distribution of, 24, 140–42, 145–52,
   242–43, 263–65
   history of, 18–19, 33–37
   political use of, 28, 191, 200n7, 209,
     213–14, 216–17
village, 12–13, 18–19, 75, 108, 109–18,
   267–69
   construction of the, 42, 44, 89–100, 168,
     174–80, 184–85
   extraction from the, 54–58
   in the middle of the city, 205–10
visibility: of infrastructure 12–71–76
   in protest 13, 197–98, 215–17, 224–25